Revelation Made Simple

Greg Axe

LIVING
FAITH
BOOKS

Living Faith Books
3953 Walnut St
Kansas City, MO 64111

Director: Brandon Briscoe
Cover Design: Joel Springer
Editor: Melissa Wharton

ISBN: 978-1-950004-06-5
Printed in the United States of America

Table of Contents

Preface

The title of this commentary is by design. There is more wild speculation over this book of the Bible than all the other 65 combined, and as a result, more confusion. So I will "K.I.S.S." in this commentary, and by now most everyone is familiar with that acronym. If you are looking for some hidden gem of insight and detail that no one has ever seen before in the book of Revelation, I hate to disappoint you, but you have come to the wrong place. I trust you will learn a few things in this commentary, but my main goal is to make the book more understandable for us common ordinary folks. Revelation is the most challenging book in the Bible by far. I will dive quite deep in this commentary, but I would really desire more to make this simplified. I want to bring the level of weirdness from the commentators and prophecy gurus down to a more normal level. There are enough bizarre and strange things in the book of Revelation on its own. What most people need is not more strangeness added to it, but a way in which to tackle the incredibly difficult things in this book in a way that makes as much sense as possible given the nature and contents of the book. Thus, the title: *Revelation Made Simple.*

I will have lots of speculation and opinion in this book. When I do, I will be right up front and honest that it is opinion only. Speculation in the Bible is fine as long as you hold to some basic principles. First, we never change the words of the Bible to make it line up with what we want to believe or teach. This study will be based exclusively on the text of the King James Bible, with no apologies for its authority. I will allow the plain words of the English Authorized Bible to stand on their own and do my best to comment on them, but I will never alter those words. Another principle of Bible speculation is to recognize the role of opinions in teaching the Bible. God allows for some room in his Bible to apply it to our own personal and individual lives. This is one of the most fascinating aspects of the word of God. I have the same copy in print that you do, but God will use it in my life to guide me one way while he might use the same words to guide you in a different way. No one will ever master the Bible until heaven, and we continue to learn more about it daily individually and collectively as the body of Christ. So, I might see something in the Bible differently than others, and we might both be right to a point and wrong to a point at the same time. That is where our opinions come into play. I have said it hundreds of times, and my people know this well and will finish the quote themselves. Opinions are like armpits. Everyone has them, and they usually stink. I will give you many of my opinions in this commentary. You are free to have your own; this is what makes America great. Everyone is entitled to their own opinions, but no one is entitled to the wrong facts. So, when I give my many opinions and speculations in this study, I will leave the "trap door" open. If I am shown to be wrong from the clear words of the Bible, which is always likely with any opinion, I will change my opinion or speculation and readily admit it.

Another principle of Bible study is to never violate clear truths of the word of God when trying to grasp the details of an obscure passage. There are TONS of obscure and vague things in the Bible, and the book of Revelation is at the head of the class in this area. The Bible is complex in its simplicity and simple in its complexity at the same time. But the intense desire of Bible scholars and prophecy teachers to "be as gods, knowing" (Genesis 3:5) leads far too many of them astray in this book. In their efforts to impress everyone with their secret and deep insight, they take a sledgehammer to the simple things in the Bible. I will be very careful not to do that in this commentary. We will walk through this most fascinating book of the Bible verse by verse in an effort to understand what we can, reach further to what is just beyond our grasp, and trust God to show us the rest as we continue to grow in Christ.

I pray you will be grounded in your faith by a study of this most fascinating capstone of the word of God. Any glory is for our Lord and not for me or you.

Introduction to Revelation

The book of Revelation is the simplest book in the Bible.

Yeah, right!

No really, it is. Revelation is the simplest book in the Bible to <u>outline</u>. It is simple and clear in its basic <u>structure</u>. The first chapter of Revelation sets down a template for the entire book unlike any other book in the Bible. Once you understand that template, the entire book fits very neatly into a general framework that is easy to see and keeps you from wandering off into all the wild speculations that mark most studies of Revelation. This introduction will give you the structure. THEN we start filling in the details. It is in the details where the book of Revelation gets <u>very</u> challenging. Revelation is like a jigsaw puzzle. The border is usually pretty easy to put together, but then the insides can get quite complicated. One of the main reasons is that the events described in Revelation are yet future. It is easier to grasp the stories in the Bible that have already happened because there is historical confirmation. But to fill in exact details of prophetic events is more difficult.

Let me give you one brief example. Prophecy teachers for generations have said that the ten toes of Daniel chapter 2 and the ten kings of Revelation chapter 17 are the same, and I agree. They also have said that this is the "revived Roman Empire" manifest in the European Union of nations. When the EU was founded, everyone began hyperventilating about the imminent rapture. "As soon as we get to 10 nations in the EU, Jesus will return!" The European Union today has at last count 27 nations, others are applying, and Brexit is throwing another monkey wrench into the works. Now we look like we do not know what we are talking about because we tried to jam a specific piece of the puzzle into the spot we <u>thought</u> it fit. I can be sure of the framework of Revelation. The exact form of the details is yet another story. I will give you my opinion of the ten toes and ten kings when we get to Revelation chapter 17.

Another reason why Revelation is so challenging in its details is because we have no frame of reference for what will happen. Jesus said the Tribulation will be unlike any time in the history of man before or after (Matthew 24:21). Again, we can see the basic structure easily, but to confirm the exact details of a time where there is no historical template is next to impossible. During the Tribulation, every devil in existence will be kicked out of heaven or released from hell and confined to earth. There has always been unclean spiritual activity, but that has never happened before. More than once in Revelation, there is a massive "purging" of the human race due to famines, diseases and wars. Occurrences like these have always happened, but they are nothing compared to the Tribulation. Estimates are that 22 million people died in World War II over the space of about 6 years. <u>Billions</u> will die in the Tribulation in half that time.

As we make our way through this most fascinating book of the Bible, I will give you what I have, but if anyone thinks they have this book mastered they are a false prophet, and you can feel free to quote me on that. A study of the book of Revelation draws a crowd unlike other Bible studies. It also brings out a lot of the loonies. The wild speculations on this book are LEGION. The desire to "know" something that others do not know is inbred in humanity from the Garden (Genesis 3:5), and it is part of the curse of sin on our race. I will get quite deep in this commentary and I hope you get some solid Biblical doctrine and knowledge about the future events coming soon upon this world. But more than that, I pray you will be heart-fed also. Paul said, "Knowledge puffeth up, but charity edifieth" (I Corinthians 8:1). Knowledge of the book of Revelation is important for a believer in Christ. Your personal walk with the Lord is far more vital. The lost world needs the simple gospel of grace available by faith in the sacrifice of Jesus on the cross. They can get that without knowing a single thing about Revelation. So dive in deep with me, but never lose sight of the more necessary parts of a personal relationship with the Son of God.

Before we get into the verse-by-verse exposition, we need to spend time laying out the basic structure of Revelation. So let's tackle the "simple" part of the book of Revelation: Chapter 1. This chapter is where God gives us the outline of the book. Once we get the basics in place from chapter 1, it becomes much easier to clarify the rest of the book. We will walk through each verse of chapter 1 a little later, but for now, we need to stay focused on the key elements of the outline of Revelation.

In Revelation 1:10, John was "in the Spirit on the Lord's day." We usually call Sunday "the Lord's day", but every day is "the day the Lord hath made" (Psalm 118:24). The "Day of the Lord" is the Second Coming of the Lord Jesus Christ. That phrase and variations of it appears hundreds of times in the Bible, and it is always linked to the return of Jesus Christ to reign in his kingdom. So this verse tells us that John wrote Revelation from a distinctly unique dual perspective. Historically, John wrote in 100 AD. Prophetically, John writes Revelation from beyond the year 2000 AD. So Revelation was written from two different time periods at the same time. A first century man was transported ahead in time spiritually and observed the events of the 21st century and wrote about them as he saw them happen. This is another example of how Revelation is simple and mind boggling at the same time. What I just said is easily understood, but it tests the limits of our beliefs. How could John essentially experience "time travel"?

God knows no time, and knows the future before it happens. He gave John a vision into the events of the Tribulation and Second Coming and told him to write about them. Much of the language in Revelation is in somewhat cryptic terms because John was trying to describe 21st century events with a first century understanding. We will visit this phenomenon more than once as we make our way through the book. But to illustrate it, let's look at another example of this in one of the Old Testament minor prophets. Nahum writes a prophecy of the destruction of Nineveh, which is a picture of the Second Coming. Nahum 2:4 says, "The chariots shall rage in the streets, they shall justle one against another in the broad ways: they shall seem like torches, they shall run like the lightnings." You just read a clear description of automobile traffic on a typical urban freeway. Nahum called them chariots because he had never seen a car. He said they "justle in the broad ways". That would be an accident on a wide road. How many cities in the United States have a "Broadway" street? They "seem like torches" because Nahum would not have been familiar with the term "headlights". They "run like the lightnings" because at 70 mph, a car with headlights on a freeway goes a lot faster than anything he would have ever seen. Top speed of a camel might be about 10 mph. So, the first point of simplicity in Revelation is to understand the nature of the dual time frame of its writing. John writes as if he is living in the year 2020 and beyond while using the only terminology he knew in the year 100 AD.

Then Revelation 1:19 says, "Write the things which thou hast seen, and the things which are, and the things which shall be hereafter." The book of Revelation is written in three sections. It is divided into past, present and future from the vantage point of the Second Coming. The "past tense" portion is chapters 2-3 as a survey of church history from Calvary to the rapture of the church. The "present tense" portion is chapters 4-19 as a description of the Tribulation leading to the Second Advent. The "future tense" portion is chapters 20-22 describing the Millennial reign of Jesus Christ and eternity future. As we look at the chart or diagram shortly, we will see this again.

There are two places in Revelation when heaven opens. Those two "markers" frame the three divisions. In Revelation 4:1, heaven opens and John is transported UP as a picture of the rapture of the church. The word "church" or "churches" appears 19 times in chapters 1-3, then is conspicuously absent from the book until chapter 22. Then in Revelation 19:11, heaven opens again, and this time Jesus comes DOWN with his armies at the battle of Armageddon. What "thou hast seen" is chapters 2-3, "the things which are" from the viewpoint of the end times is chapters 4-19, and "the things which shall be hereafter" from that same time perspective take place after Jesus returns to the earth. That is simple!

There is another very important aspect of the outline of Revelation that is missed by many of the teachers and commentators on this book. Revelation has been commented on more than any book in the Bible by far. But for some reason, most authors cannot or will not see this, and yet it is very simple. The main section of Revelation is chapters 4-19 on the Tribulation and Second Coming. There are FOUR separate passes through these events in these chapters. In like fashion, the four gospels of Matthew, Mark, Luke and John report four separate accounts of the life of Jesus Christ at his first coming. They are not chronological from Matthew 1 through John 21; they are viewed on top of each other as four different layers reporting the same events from four different perspectives. God is consistent. He did the same thing in Revelation to report four different accounts of the Second Coming. This is very easy to see in the four gospels because there are four different human authors. In Revelation, it is the same author and in the same book, so it is more difficult to see. But it is very plain once you understand a couple of keys in the passage. The "markers" to identify the four sections are the reports of the Second Advent. The literal coming of the Lord Jesus Christ to the earth on "the Lord's day" is recorded four times:

Revelation 6:12-17 – "The great day of his wrath is come." (verse 17)
Revelation 11:15-19 – "The kingdoms of this world are become the kingdoms of our Lord." (verse 15)
Revelation 14:14-20 – The Son of man comes to tread the winepress of the wrath of God.
Revelation 19:11-21 – The Lord comes on his white horse to rule with a rod of iron.

Those four passages frame for us the four accounts of the Tribulation and Second Advent in Revelation. There is a slightly different perspective with each account, yet there is no question that they all describe the same event. So these four passages must be tied together. They are not sequential, they overlay each other to form the full picture of the Second Coming of Jesus Christ. With this understanding in place, the four accounts of the Tribulation and Second Coming in the book of Revelation are given to us as follows:

Revelation chapters 4-6 – The Seals   Revelation chapters 7-11 – The Trumpets
Revelation chapters 12-14 – The Personages   Revelation chapters 15-19 – The Vials

The best illustration of this is the "four color process" in printing. A typical color poster will have four separate overlays as it passes through the press. The press lays down red, blue, yellow and black in various amounts and tones on a white background to form the picture. If there is purple in the picture, the press will lay down red and blue and purposely omit yellow and black. Red and blue do not contradict each other, they form purple. God did this for us with the accounts of the first coming of the Lord Jesus Christ in the four gospels. He did it again with four accounts of the Second Coming in Revelation.

Continuing the printing illustration, in order to keep the various colors in the correct place on the page, the four overlays will have what are called "registration marks" on them. Those are something like a small cross in a circle in the corners that is outside the main print so it does not appear on the picture. Those marks have to be perfectly lined up or the picture is out of focus and fuzzy. The "registration marks" in Revelation 4 through 19 are the four passages I just referred to on the Second Advent. In order to see the picture correctly, these passages must be kept together. I will do that in this study so that when we make our way through the various details of the accounts, the different "colors" will yield a clearer picture of the events of the Tribulation and the Second Coming. A second minor "registration mark" is an earthquake described in Revelation 6:12, 11:13, and 16:18. That is not three different earthquakes, it is the same one just prior to and connected with the return of the Lord Jesus Christ to the earth. Notice that there are only three accounts of this earthquake and not four. The earthquake is not mentioned in the third pass through the Tribulation. This is the account of the "Personages", or for lack of a better term, the "cast of characters" of the Tribulation. The other three accounts focus on events, while this account details the persons and groups involved. The earthquake is an event, so it is omitted in pass number three by design. Keep this in mind as we walk through my chart in a few moments and as we take a closer look at the structure of the book of Revelation in a visual layout.

One of the things leading to the confusion is how Revelation 7:1 is worded. After reporting on the Second Advent at the close of chapter 6, John said, "And after these things I saw…" Since we tend to view things in sequence, we see this as a "time-line" continuation of the chronology of Revelation. But consider it this way. You read the book of Matthew and get a report of the events of the life of Jesus Christ. Then "after these things", you open the book of Mark and read them again. Mark does not pick up the story of Jesus Christ AFTER all the events of Matthew, he goes BACK to the beginning and brings you through them again from a different perspective. Then "after these things", you read them again in Luke. Then "after these things", you go back to the beginning again and read for the fourth time a record of the same events. God did the same thing for us in the book of Revelation.

Each gospel begins at a different point but ends at essentially the same place. They overlap each other with some differences. Matthew reports on Jesus as the King of the Jews, so he begins with Abraham as he traces the line of the King. Mark focuses on Jesus as a servant, so he begins with John the Baptist and does not trace a genealogy because the genealogy of a servant is inconsequential. Luke begins with the birth of Jesus because his focus is on Jesus as the human man. Then John presents Jesus Christ as the Son of God in his deity, so his record begins with, "In the beginning was the Word." Matthew begins in about 2000 BC. Mark begins in roughly 30 AD. Luke begins roughly at year 0 (maybe about 4 BC according to most historians), and John begins before Genesis 1:1. But all four accounts "register" at Calvary. As you read the four accounts, there are some events discussed in all four of them, some in only two or three, and others in only one account. This is God painting the picture of the life of the Lord Jesus Christ when he was here 2,000 years ago. Again, Revelation chapters 4-19 do the same thing for his return.

Clarence Larkin was one of the best Bible teachers in history, especially on prophetic matters. His book titled *Dispensational Truth* is the best Bible study manual ever written in the history of humanity. If you do not have it, get it! He views Revelation 4 through 19 as chronological. He sees chapters 4 through 11 as the first half of the Tribulation and chapters 12-19 as the last half of Daniel's 70th Week. As we look at the details of these chapters, there are PLENTY of "fuzzy" pictures as I have mentioned earlier because these are future events. But viewing these chapters as Larkin does increases the fuzziness dramatically.

So, as we begin our journey through this most fascinating and exciting book of the Bible, we must begin with the basic structure in place. It will keep us between the white lines. There are so many speculative issues with the book of Revelation that it is very easy to wander off the trail into la-la-land. This book is written about and taught and covered more than any other in the Bible. There is enough information on the book of Revelation available to you to keep you busy the rest of your life. That is actually part of the problem. With so many different teachers from so many different viewpoints trying to tell us the "truth, the whole truth, and nothing but the truth" about Revelation, it can get really confusing. By the time you make it through just a few books and websites, your head is in the clouds and you are pulled in so many different directions that you have vertigo. Hopefully I can orient you clearly with this study.

Let's keep the main structure in mind as we navigate the details:

John wrote Revelation in 100 AD but from the vantage point of the Second Coming.

The book is written in three sections from the time period of the Second Coming:
Past tense (Church age) – Chapters 2-3
Present tense (Tribulation and Second Coming) – Chapters 4-19
Future tense (Millennium and Eternity) – Chapters 20-22

The main section (Chapters 4-19) has four separate passes through the Tribulation:
Chapters 4-6 – The Seals   Chapters 7-11 – The Trumpets
Chapters 12-14 – The Personages   Chapters 15-19 – The Vials

Authorship – Who, When and Why

As with any book of the Bible, the issue of authorship is important. But it is even more so with the book of Revelation. One of the persistent attacks on this book is based on the issue of authorship, primarily the date. When it comes to the Bible, there is no limit to the attempts to twist and pervert the clear message of God. The book of Revelation is at the head of that class. This is the most attacked and despised book of the Bible because it paints mankind in a very negative light. Revelation records the complete collapse of civilization as we know it. Everything man has tried to build for 6,000 years will be utterly destroyed in "one hour" if Revelation 18 is taken literally, and knowing our Lord, he won't even need 59 of those minutes. Lost man does not like that truth. Therefore, he will try to do everything he can to obscure it and rewrite it to fit his own agenda. Scholars and skeptics are in company in this effort against the Bible and especially the book of Revelation. So there will be just as much twisting by the Christian academia as the atheists, and perhaps even more. Atheists walk away and leave the Bible alone for the most part, while scholars spend their lives trying to discredit it because they think they can outsmart its author.

The who of authorship is the apostle John. That is obvious from the clear statements in the first chapter. John is more accurately the "scribe" of the book than its actual human author. This is the Revelation of Jesus Christ given to John by his angel (1:1, 22:16). The literary style is different than other prophecies. Isaiah and Ezekiel "spake as they were moved by the Holy Ghost" (II Peter 1:21). They preached while a scribe recorded their sermons. John recorded visions revealed to him by the Spirit. The same style is used by Daniel. His book is "The Revelation of the Old Testament" and is the handmaid of this book. Daniel and Revelation are studied "hand in glove" together because they cover a lot of the same ground.

The biggest issue of the authorship is when the book of Revelation was written. Historically, Revelation was written between 95-100 AD when John was in exile on the island of Patmos off the coast of Greece (Revelation 1:9). The common objection tries to back-date the authorship to sometime before 70 AD. The reason is obvious. Rome is the target of the wrath of God in Revelation. Back-dating the time of the writing of Revelation allows them to apply the judgments to fit the destruction of Jerusalem in 70 AD. It also makes any negative prophecy of Rome apply to pagan Rome under the Caesars instead of Papal Rome under the Popes. The exile of John is confirmed by Josephus, a secular Jewish historian who had no "skin in the game" either way. Eusebius reports John's exile at the end of the reign of the Roman Emperor Domitian, who reigned from 81-96 AD. Philip Schaff also confirms the exile of John at the same time from multiple sources. Both Eusebius and Schaff would have reason to want Revelation back-dated since they were both very pro-Catholic. So we safely "book" the authorship at 95-100 AD.

The why of the book of Revelation is to seal up the canon of the written scriptures. I call Revelation the "Grand Central Station" of the Bible. All lines eventually lead here, and all loose ends are neatly tied up in the book of Revelation. The word "apocalypse" is another term for Revelation, and it literally means "to uncover". The veil is pulled back in Revelation and the seals are opened. The book of Revelation "seals up" prophecy by unsealing it for our study. The Lamb of God will open the seals for us so we can have the completed information in the form of a book in our hands that we can read and believe and live. Obviously, no man will ever come anywhere close to unlocking all of the Bible. But with this book, we have all the words God wants us to have. That is why he closes the book with a warning not to add more to it (Revelation 22:18-19). The predominance of sevens in the book confirms it as the final prophecy of the Bible. Revelation contains seven churches, spirits, candlesticks, stars, lamps, seals, horns, angels, trumpets, thunders, heads, crowns, plagues, vials, mountains, and kings. There is no new revelation after 100 AD, only more light on existing revelation. Those who claim new revelation are false prophets, and yet the false prophets circling this book looking for new revelation are legion. This is "The Revelation of Jesus Christ" (1:1), not the revelation of the latest prophecy guru making millions of dollars off the backs of gullible Athenian Christians looking for something "new" (Acts 17:21). So if you look for Jesus in this book more than for nuggets of fascinating prophecy, it will serve you best.

The Diagram of Revelation

At the back of this book is a visual layout of the major components of the book of Revelation. This is my best effort to take the most important aspects of the book and put them in one place so we can see them as God has organized them. Before we start walking through the details of a verse-by-verse exposition of the book of Revelation, we should become familiar with this layout. I will refer to it as we make our way through the commentary. The best way to read it is from the top down first, and left to right second. The reason is the "four-color process" I alluded to earlier. The only way to see the picture correctly is to lay the accounts on top of each other rather than side by side. So if you would, put a finger in this page, and open the chart at the back also and flip back and forth as we read "top to bottom" on the diagram.

The title of the book is first, followed by the three tenses or sections of its primary structure. As we move down the page, the next line is titled "Daniel's 70th Week". This is one of the main titles describing the Tribulation period. I will detail this further when we go through the prophecy of Daniel chapter 9 later in the commentary. On either side of "Daniel's 70th Week" are two phrases divided by a dotted line that descends from the middle of "Daniel's 70th Week". This is because the Tribulation is divided into two parts. The "False Kingdom of Antichrist" covers the first 3½ years and the "Great Tribulation" is the last half of the Week. The next line down on the chart describes the three phases of God's harvesting of the earth, which we commonly refer to as the rapture. I will cover this in detail when we get to Revelation chapter 4. The "Firstfruits" is the gathering of the Old Testament saints just after the resurrection of Jesus Christ. The "Main Harvest" is the rapture of the church, and the "Gleanings" would be the rapture of the Tribulation saints at the end of Daniel's 70th Week.

Then we should make note of the two long vertical lines. These are the dividing lines to mark off the three sections of the book. The left line has an arrow on top signifying the rapture of the church and the beginning of the Tribulation. It is framed when heaven opens in Revelation 4:1. The right-hand line has an arrow at the bottom noting the Second Advent of Jesus Christ when heaven opens in Revelation 19:11. By way of clarification, the term "Second Advent" is more focused and precise than "Second Coming". We use the term Second Coming to include the entire end times from the rapture of the church to the day Jesus physically returns to earth to reign in his kingdom. The "Second Advent" is that day when Jesus literally and physically returns to this ball of dirt to reign. Advent means "appearing". So when you see that term throughout this commentary, remember that it is specific to the day of his physical return.

Moving through the chart, at the left of the rapture arrow is a breakdown of the seven ages of the church. We will cover this in our brief comments on Revelation chapters 2-3.

Now we want to take note of the section between the arrows. This is Revelation chapters 4-19 and the four passes through the Tribulation. It begins with the Judgment Seat of Christ for the church just after our rapture. That takes place in heaven separate from the events unfolding on earth. Then we have the Seals, Trumpets, Personages, and Vials laid one on top of each other. Note that virtually all of this is seen to the right of the vertical dotted line. There is very little information in the Bible about the first half of the Tribulation. Most of the discussion centers on the "hell on earth" of the Great Tribulation spanning the last 3½ years. The Seals, Trumpets and Vials are placed in various positions based generally on when they will be opened during the Tribulation period. To the right of that section, just prior to the vertical line with the "down arrow" marking the Second Advent, you will find the "registration marks". The four passages noting the Second Advent, and the three times the earthquake is mentioned are listed.

Next we should take note of the third pass through the Tribulation period called the "Personages". This is probably the most important of the four accounts, although every word of God is pure (Proverbs 30:5) and every detail of this book is crucial. But the "cast of characters" gives us information and insight into the events that cannot be seen by simply talking about bombs and famines. The list of the seven main characters or people groups is given. I listed them at the beginning of the "Week" simply because they obviously play a role throughout the entire seven-year period. But take note of the first character called the "Beast". This is the Antichrist, and he is the "star of the show" (obviously aside from Jesus Christ who is the star of every show). I will not spend time here with the details. But notice the "Beast out of the Sea" (1a) and the "Beast out of the Earth" (1b) with a line connecting them. Then that line runs through the box titled "The Revealing of the Wicked". There are six major events that occur all at the same mid-point of the Tribulation that form the basis of the unmasking of the Antichrist to Israel and "morph" him from the beast out of the sea to the beast out of the earth. This box is the most significant thing on this diagram. We will cover all these details as we make our way through the commentary, and especially when we get to the "Revealing of the Wicked" in Revelation chapter 13.

Moving to the right of the down arrow, we see the Millennial Reign and Eternity Future. These are the subjects of Revelation chapters 20-22 and the "things which shall be hereafter". From top to bottom, we begin with the Marriage Supper of the Lamb, which is essentially the celebration or "wedding reception dinner" at the beginning of the Millennial kingdom. In case you were wondering, the main course will be STEAK (see Matthew 22:4). After the thousand-year reign of Jesus Christ, we move to the right again. Before we get to Eternity Future, there will be a final rebellion of Satan followed by the final judgment known as the "Great White Throne Judgment". Then Revelation chapters 21-22 take us into Eternity as we reign with Jesus and enjoy the blessings of heaven forever.

Again, reading top to bottom, there is still a little more to note on the chart. The next lines down mention the kingdom of God and the kingdom of heaven. I cannot go through an exhaustive study of this topic here in this commentary because it is too lengthy and would take us too far off the beaten trail of the book of Revelation. But I must give you the basics. The vast majority of Christians and even Bible teachers and pastors do not see any difference between these terms. Since there are several times that the Bible uses them interchangeably, most people think the kingdom of God and the kingdom of heaven are the same in every detail and at every time. That is NOT true! "In the beginning, God created the heaven and the earth" (Genesis 1:1). God is a Spirit (John 4:24). He created a physical heaven. God is not heaven and heaven is not God. The kingdoms that bear those titles are not the same either. The kingdom of God is spiritual. It is populated by spirit beings and ruled over by the Son of God, the Lord Jesus Christ. The kingdom of heaven is physical. It is populated by physical beings and ruled over by the Son of man, the Lord Jesus Christ. So yes, the King is the same, but Jesus is God and man both, and although you can never fully wrap your head around that, his two natures are "the same thing only different".

As we move through the Bible and history, including eternity in both directions, BOTH the kingdom of God and the kingdom of heaven are always there. God created a physical Universe that is governed by spiritual laws. One cannot exist without the other, yet they are not the same in every single detail and at every single moment in time. Here is a basic truth. In order to have a kingdom, you must have two essential things: a king and subjects. If there are subjects but no king, it is mob rule and anarchy. Every man does that which is right in his own eyes (Judges 21:25). Likewise, a king with no subjects is not a kingdom. It is just some dude sitting in his mommy's basement in his jammies playing video games claiming he is "king of the world". There are times in the flow of history when BOTH kingdoms are present on earth because both the king and the subjects are here. There are times when one or both of them are absent from earth because either the king is not here or the subjects are not here. For example, Jesus as the Son of man is the King over the physical kingdom of heaven manifest in the Nation of Israel. The subjects are here in their land, but the King is NOT here physically. However, during this time, the kingdom of God IS here on earth. The King (Jesus) is here spiritually, and his subjects are born again into the kingdom of God (John 3:3). Both kingdoms still exist at all times, but they weave their way in and out of the Bible and human history because of the location of the King and subjects. On the diagram, toward the bottom, I have noted the absence or presence of these kingdoms in each major section.

Finally, at the bottom of the chart you see "Means of Salvation" for each section except Eternity. There is no need for salvation in Eternity because the issue of sin and judgment will have already been fully dealt with. The lost of the ages will be in hell forever, and no one will need to get saved. But until then, each dispensation has certain aspects of salvation that vary slightly from one to the next.

Now, please understand. Before anyone writes me hate mail or tosses this book in the fireplace, please stay with me as I explain this. The Bible has dispensations. In fact, that is a Bible word that appears four times in Paul's epistles (I Corinthians 9:17, Ephesians 1:10, 3:2, Colossians 1:25). A dispensation is defined as a "time period of God's dealings with man". Surely you realize that God dealt with Adam in the Garden differently than he did with Abraham before the law, which was different than David after the law of Israel was given, which is different than today. We do not bring animals to church to drain their blood at our altars for our sins. You MUST acknowledge that there are differences between the law and grace. Some things were forbidden for Jews to eat, and we can eat them now in the church age. Jews were not allowed to wear garments of mixed fibers. Their day of worship was Saturday and ours is on Sunday. There are <u>hundreds</u> of things like this between the Old and New Testaments. If Jesus took the law out of the way and nailed it to his cross (Colossians 2:14), then there has to be at least SOME things that are no longer required of us that were required of the Jews under the Old Testament law. Another definition of dispensation is seen by using the word to define itself, which I know we are not supposed to do, but you will surely understand this. A dispensation is a method of God <u>dispensing</u> his truth to man. I can go to the store and get a two-liter of Pepsi. Or I can buy a case of 12 ounce cans. Or I can stop at the convenience store and fill a 32 ounce cup out of the fountain. Or I can find a vending machine and get a 20 ounce bottle. The <u>product</u> is identical: Pepsi. The method it is <u>dispensed</u> to me varies.

The "product" of God's salvation is grace through faith (Ephesians 2:8-9). God's grace and our faith are the essential elements of salvation in any age and any dispensation. But sometimes they are "dispensed" differently. "Noah found <u>grace</u> in the eyes of the Lord" (Genesis 6:8). Without the grace of God, no one could ever get saved. Because God's grace was made available to Noah, God gave him instruction as to what to do about it. "By <u>faith</u> Noah, being warned of God of things not seen as yet, moved with fear, prepared an ark to the saving of his house; by the which he condemned the world, and became heir of the righteousness which is by faith" (Hebrews 11:7). Noah exercised his faith and built a boat. He and his family were saved as a result of the action he took by faith. Noah did NOT "trust Jesus as his personal Saviour". The cross was over 2,000 years into the future. God's grace was dispensed to Noah through his faith which was demonstrated by building the ark.

God's grace was dispensed to Abel through his faith when he brought the right sacrifice of a lamb. God tried to dispense his grace to Cain but his lack of faith prevented it. God's grace is dispensed to people today through their faith in the sacrifice of Jesus Christ for their sins. Every one of those examples contains SOMETHING that the person must DO to receive the grace of God for salvation. Again, stay with me. I had to do something to get saved. I had to quit trying to do something and receive Jesus as my Saviour. "But to him that worketh not, but believeth on him that justifieth the ungodly, his faith is counted for righteousness" (Romans 4:5). My faith had to be exercised. People are not saved today simply because it is the age of grace and "the Lamb of God taketh away the sin of the world" (John 1:29). They have to step out by faith and <u>ASK</u> for it. God's grace for salvation does not just magically descend upon every human being like pixie dust from heaven. That would be universal salvation. "Whosoever shall <u>call</u> upon the name of the Lord shall be saved" (Romans 10:13). No call, no salvation.

So there is a "work" of salvation, though not in the way one might assume. That work today is to "cease from our own works" (Hebrews 4:10, Romans 4:1-8). Jesus alluded to it in John chapter 6. He was asked what we had to do to "work the works of God". He said in verse 29, "This is the work of God, that ye believe on him whom he hath sent." In other dispensations, the work of salvation will have different elements. As we travel through the book of Revelation, we will see the dispensations change, and the work of salvation changes also. I trust I have been clear about this and not confused those who might think I am promoting works-based salvation. Absolutely to the contrary. I have tried to repeat this in many different ways to get the point across. Man is saved by "grace through faith" and not of works regardless of the dispensation. Adam and Eve got "saved" when God covered their sins with the coats of animal skins. Knowing the consistency of God, it had to be a lamb. Adam and Eve did nothing to get their salvation. Their efforts with the fig leaves proved useless. Genesis 3:21 says God made the coats of skins, not Adam and Eve. But they had to accept the coats and put them on. An innocent animal shed its blood so Adam and Eve could have their nakedness covered. God performed the work to produce the skins. But had Adam and Eve refused the skins, they would have died in their sins and gone to hell. They did something, but they did nothing. The same is true of salvation in any age. People must respond by faith and do what God said to do in their dispensation. Right now, it is faith in the sacrifice of Jesus Christ. The instructions given in those other dispensations will change.

Let me expand further with this by using the example of perhaps the most famous prophecy series in history: the *"Left Behind"* books and movies. There is a lot of good information in those books and they present a fascinating journey through the Tribulation. There is obviously much embellishment because those books take up far more shelf space than even the entire Bible, let alone just Revelation. Millions of people have read at least one of the books in this series, and many have read all of them. This series of books contains a salvation heresy that has caused more harm than good. The authors present people in the Tribulation receiving Jesus Christ as their Saviour by faith in the same way we get saved now. They completely misunderstand the dispensational view of salvation. In the process, they damn more souls than are saved by reading the books. Yes, there have been plenty of people get saved by reading a *"Left Behind"* book, and for that I praise the Lord (Philippians 1:18). But they have one of the main characters who is "left behind" realize what has happened and get on his knees to trust Jesus as Saviour. Then he has that remnant group preaching the same gospel of grace from the church age. Here is what that does for those reading the books. They can say (and multitudes have done so), "Well, this is all interesting stuff. I am not too sure of it, but I will keep an eye out. If this rapture thing is real, then when I see it, I will go ahead and get saved." They have just eliminated the essential element of faith from the salvation "product". Faith and sight are mutually exclusive (II Corinthians 5:7). If a person is waiting for visual evidence of the truth of God's word, they will never get it.

In the context of a discussion of the end times, Paul says: "…with all deceivableness of unrighteousness in them that perish; because they received not the love of the truth, that they might be saved. And for this cause God shall send them strong delusion, that they should believe a lie: That they all might be damned who believed not the truth, but had pleasure in unrighteousness" (II Thessalonians 2:10-12). That passage says that those who "wait until they see it" can't get saved. Those who "receive not the love of the truth" now will believe a lie then. God himself will "help" them out in the same way he hardened the heart of Pharaoh. He will send them strong delusion. I know the objection. "How could a loving God of grace do such a thing?" A loving God of grace cannot. But the same God of love is also a holy God of justice, and he can and most certainly will send strong delusion to those who want to believe a lie. The God of judgment dispatched a "lying spirit" to deceive Ahab in I Kings chapter 21. Read it if you do not believe me. Anyone in this age of grace who has been presented with the clear gospel of Jesus Christ and rejects it will not get a "second chance" in the next dispensation. By confusing salvation in other dispensations, the *"Left Behind"* series seals the doom of many who believe they can wait.

I have said all of that to draw this conclusion. The means of salvation is different in each dispensation. Now in the church age it is grace through faith in the finished work of the sacrifice of Christ on the cross; plus nothing and minus nothing. But when this dispensation closes with the rapture of the church and a new dispensation opens called the Tribulation, the "product" is received in a different manner. Basically, there are three ways a person can get saved in the Tribulation. God's grace is available to people in the Tribulation if they will by faith do one of these three things:

1) Endure to the end (Matthew 24:13, 10:22) – We will spend time later on the "preppers" and how they think they will survive the Tribulation. In my opinion, God will not allow any of them to make it through because they will do nothing but brag about it during the entire Millennium. But some people will go into the Millennial reign alive. Matthew 24:22 says that God will "shorten the days for the elect's sake". The elect in this passage is the Nation of Israel. God promised them a kingdom, and they must have Gentiles as their subjects in that kingdom. If the disasters of the Tribulation are allowed to be played out to their full conclusion, it would result in the complete annihilation of the human race. So those who somehow manage to make it through will get to participate in the kingdom. This instruction is primarily given to the remnant of Israel. There are two verses that say it directly in Matthew that I listed above. Both verses were spoken by the Lord to the apostles, but prophetically to the 144,000 as we will see in Revelation 7. Though they will be the target of a world-wide manhunt the likes of which we have never seen, some of them will make it due to God's protection and their own skill. By grace, their faith in this instruction will gain them a place in the "kingdom prepared from the foundation of the world" (Matthew 25:34).

2) Refuse the mark of the beast and die by martyrdom (Revelation 20:4) – Again, these instructions are given primarily to the 144,000. But some Gentiles will refuse the mark also. Satan is good, but he cannot get everyone. The penalty for refusing the mark is beheading. Some of these witnesses will be captured in the world-wide manhunt. Jesus alluded to this in Matthew 16:25 where he said if "you lose your life you will save it". That is a reference to the Tribulation and the enforcement of the mark of the beast upon the world. By God's grace, those who exercise faith to refuse the mark will be granted their salvation.

3) Harbor one of the Jewish witnesses and care for them (Matthew 10:40-42, 25:31-46) – The first two means of salvation are generally directed to Israel, and this one is directed to the Gentiles. We will see this in more detail when we get to the instructions to the 144,000 in chapter 7. As the Jewish witnesses go throughout the world preaching the everlasting gospel of the kingdom, their audience is the Gentile nations. They will be inviting them to the "wedding" (Matthew 22:8-10). The guests in that passage are a few of the Gentiles who will respond to the invitation. By faith, they will do a work of providing for one of God's chosen people, and God's grace will be given to them as a result.

That brings us to the final line item on the chart, the "Means of Salvation" for the Millennium. During the Millennial reign of Christ, the world will be Jewish. The law and the sacrifices of the Old Testament will be back in force with some modifications. The Old Testament sacrifices pointed ahead to the cross; the Millennial sacrifices point back to the cross. Jesus will rule with "a rod of iron", which means he will enforce the law when it is disobeyed. Again, there is always grace and faith. The grace of our Lord Jesus Christ will be on full display as he sits upon the throne of his glory. Faith will be there, but not as much as at other times since the Lord will be here. "The earth shall be full of the knowledge of the LORD, as the waters cover the sea" (Isaiah 11:9, Habakkuk 2:14). Jesus will be on the throne in Jerusalem and the law will go forth out of Zion (Isaiah 2:1-5). God's grace will be given to any and all who obey it. If they don't obey the law, it will be enforced immediately and appropriately. Certain sacrifices will be back in effect, and the feasts of Israel will be observed to remind people of the ultimate sacrifice for sin. Anyone who chooses to rebel against the law will be dealt with swiftly. When we get to Revelation chapter 20, we will spend a major section detailing the nature and characteristics of the Millennial reign. We will see further at that time how people during the Millennium will be saved or judged.

Keep this chart handy as we make our way through the details of the book of Revelation. When we get to a challenging point, flip back to it and keep the basic structure in mind. This is the "simple" part of the book of Revelation. Now we begin navigating the more difficult part as we fill in the details. I pray your studies will bear fruit. One final thing before we move on. God tells us the future of humanity in the book of Revelation, which includes your future as well. God tells us our future so we can set our present on the right course. I trust you have received Jesus as your Saviour and are walking with him. By God's grace, your faith in the sacrifice of Jesus Christ will preserve you from the "hell on earth" about to come.

Revelation Chapter 1
The Outline and Introduction

We have already been through the most important points from Revelation chapter 1 as they relate to the outline of the entire book. But there is more in chapter 1 than just the basic outline.

VS 1-3 – This is the "Revelation of Jesus Christ". The events of the end times are revealed in this book, but that is not its main focus. The Antichrist will be revealed in the book of Revelation, but he is not the main character. This book is designed to reveal the Lord Jesus Christ in his person and in his kingdom more than any other subject contained therein. This is without a doubt the most fascinating book of the Bible, but if you are looking for "nuggets" of prophetic details more than you are looking to see Jesus, you are not looking at this book the right way.

> "Turn your eyes upon Jesus.
> Look full in his wonderful face.
> And the things of earth will grow strangely dim
> In the light of his glory and grace."

Verse 3 contains a blessing for those who read and hear the words of this prophecy. That statement does not appear in any other book of the Bible. Obviously, the Bible is a blessing on every page, even those which speak against us. But this book has a special blessing. Let me give you a personal testimony.

I got saved on September 4, 1978 when my brother Mark led me to Jesus Christ in his home in Sterling Heights, Michigan. I was living in St. Louis at the time and had visited him over Labor Day for a golfing weekend. I went home to St. Louis and did nothing with my newfound salvation for about a year and a half. In February of 1980, I moved to Cincinnati, Ohio. I had a good friend there who invited me to go to church with him the first Sunday night I was in Cincinnati. I had nothing else to do, so, hey, why not? I had been raised Catholic but rebelled against the church and against God. By this time, I was 27 years old and I had never owned a Bible or read more than a verse or two from it my entire life. That Sunday night at Landmark Baptist Temple in Cincinnati, there was a guest speaker: Dr. Peter S. Ruckman.

Sunday night services at the typical Baptist church in those days were usually a much deeper study. It was a large church, and there were about 1,000 people in the building, but I was the only one there. Many of you would identify with that statement. There has probably been a service where God spoke <u>directly</u> to you as if no one else was within a hundred miles. Dr. Ruckman spoke from the book of Revelation that night and laid out how the Pope is the Antichrist. Keep in mind who was the "only" person sitting in the room that night. I was a recently converted Catholic who knew not one blasted thing about the Bible. I would have had trouble holding it right side up. But the message got my attention. My friend David sat next to me with his Bible open, and every time Pete quoted a verse, I would look at David's Bible with my jaw on the floor. As the message was closing, Pastor John Rawlings gave an invitation. Dave looked at me and asked, "Do you want to get saved?" I said, "I think I might have done something like that about a year ago." I knew <u>nothing</u>. I said to David, "I guess I should get a Bible, huh? What kind should I get?" I really don't even know why I asked that second question because I didn't even know there were "kinds" at that point. Dave said, "Get a King James." I did not know a King James Bible from a King Edward cigar, but I went to the bookstore in the church after the service and bought my first Bible. Keep in mind this was Sunday <u>night</u>. The service was over about 8:30, then we hung out for a while as people always do after church, then I went to the bookstore, then I drove home to my apartment. I got home about 10:00 pm. I read the <u>ENTIRE</u> book of Revelation that night in one sitting. The very first words I ever read from my own Bible were the words of the book of Revelation. I understood virtually <u>nothing</u> of what I read. What little I did understand scared the living bejeebers out of me.

But I received a blessing that night from reading the book of Revelation. As of this writing, that was over 40 years ago. That night was a watershed moment in my life. It was the first step of a journey that has enriched and blessed my life beyond my wildest imaginations. I have had many failures along the way, and continue to have them daily, but God turned the course of my life that night with the reading of the book of Revelation. This is a very difficult book of the Bible even though it is simple. If not studied properly, it can cause great damage to a believer in Christ. But there is a unique blessing in reading and hearing its words. I hope in this commentary I can set your study of Revelation on a solid course so that you do not get drawn away into the multitudes of heresies that can come from this book. I only hope you get as much of a blessing from reading and hearing these words as I did.

VS 4-6 – This is the basic introduction to the book similar to what you find in Paul's epistles. A couple of things of note should be discussed. The "seven Spirits before the throne" (verse 4) will be covered in chapter 4. Those are not seven different Holy Spirits, but seven manifestations of the one Holy Spirit. In verse 5, Jesus is referred to as "the first begotten of the dead". Some have taken this to imply that Jesus is a lesser god begotten by the Father in eternity past. The Jehovah's (False) Witnesses use this verse as one of their "proofs" to deny the deity of Jesus Christ. It simply refers to his resurrection. There were a few people raised from the dead before Jesus. Elijah and Elisha both raised a young boy from the dead. Jesus brought out Lazarus and a couple of others. But Jesus was the first one "begotten" of the dead who came out by his own power and did not go back into a grave. All those others died again.

VS 7 – This is a statement of the physical return of the Lord Jesus Christ to earth. This will be a major part of the study of this book. The personal and literal Second Coming of Jesus Christ is a hotly debated subject in Christian circles and denied by many. Some claim he only comes spiritually. In order to teach that, they have to deny or monkey with more prophetic passages of the Bible than not. He is coming with clouds. In Acts 1:9-11, Jesus ascended to heaven literally and physically in plain sight of his apostles. It says, "A cloud received him out of their sight." They were told, "This same Jesus, which is taken up from you into heaven, shall so come in like manner as ye have seen him go into heaven." In Revelation 1:7 it says, "Every eye shall see him." Those are physical eyes, not the "spiritual eyes of faith". The eyes that see him are in the heads of those who have been blinded by Satan (II Corinthians 4:4). They have no spiritual eyesight to see anything. Matthew 24:30 says people will mourn when they see the Son of man coming in the clouds of heaven, and this verse in Revelation says "all kindreds of the earth shall wail because of him." That cannot be "seeing him which is invisible" (Hebrews 11:27). The phrase, "They also which pierced him" has a dual application. His brethren the remnant of Israel will "look on him whom they have pierced" (Zechariah 12:10) in the middle of the Tribulation and be converted. But it was actually Roman soldiers who drove the nails in his hands and feet and stuck the spear in his side. I think maybe God might "lift up the eyes" from hell of those who actually carried out the crucifixion (both the Roman soldiers and the Jewish elders who were his murderers – Acts 7:52) and say, "Lookie here, boys. Here he comes. What do you think about him now?"

VS 8 – Jesus is Alpha and Omega, the first and last letters of the Greek alphabet. He covers all the bases on everything from A to Z. "In the beginning was the Word" (John 1:1) "and he shall reign for ever and ever" (Revelation 11:15). He is the "author and finisher of our faith" (Hebrews 12:2). He stands at the starting line with the pistol in his hand and holds the tape at the end of the race BOTH at the same time. "Being confident of this very thing, that he which hath begun a good work in you will perform it until the day of Jesus Christ" (Philippians 1:6). What Jesus starts he will finish. He is not just AT the beginning and the end of things, he IS the beginning point of everything and he IS the conclusion of all things. We all know one of God's titles or names as the "I AM" from Exodus 3:14. That is eternally existent in the present tense. Whatever the issue of life, Jesus "AM" the answer. (Don't report me to my High School English teacher, I know that is incorrect grammar. But it is correct Biblical truth.) Jesus claimed the "I AM" for himself many times (John 8:24, 28, 58, 13:19, 18:4-9 just to name a few). The verse also says Jesus "is, was, and is to come". That covers past, present and future. He was in the beginning and he was here 2,000 years ago in the flesh. He is because he rose from the dead and is still alive at the right hand of the Father and dwells in us by his Spirit. He is to come physically and bodily back to earth one day very soon. Those who deny his literal coming to earth must also deny the other two statements in this verse.

VS 9-11 – Most of this passage has already been covered in the introduction when I laid out the structure of the book. Some have asked about John being a "brother and companion in tribulation". If John is a type of the church, does that mean we have to go through the Tribulation? There is a difference between just plain "tribulation" (trouble in this life) and THE Tribulation (John 16:33, Acts 14:22, Romans 5:3). John was exiled to Patmos as a very old man and was the only one of the twelve to escape the violent martyr's death. This is another point that makes him a type of the church, especially the raptured church. This book is not seven "letters" to seven churches, but ONE book delivered to all. Even though there is a clear breakdown of the seven ages of the church which we will see in chapters 2-3, the instructions given in this book and its encouragements and admonitions are for all believers in any age.

VS 12-20 – These verses give a description of the Lord Jesus Christ in his glorified form. It is one of the "home base" passages to help us define other angelic "visions" in other places in the Bible. Sometimes angels appear to men and women in the Bible. They can be "the angel of the Lord", which is typically a pre-incarnate appearance of Jesus Christ. Other times it can be simply any angel dispatched by God for a particular purpose. In Genesis 18, three men appeared to Abraham (verse 2). At the end of the chapter, "the Lord went his way" (verse 33), and in the next verse (Genesis 19:1), two angels went to Sodom. No description is given of these two angels like Revelation chapter 1, and there are two of them who are said to be distinct from the Lord, so they must be just "regular" angels. An angel appears to Daniel in chapters 8 through 10. A description is given of him in Daniel 10:6 which is very similar to Revelation 1. But this angel is identified specifically as Gabriel (Daniel 8:16, 9:21). The descriptions can be similar because angels bear the image of the Lord. Then in Revelation 10, a "mighty angel" appears, and his description lines up so clearly with chapter 1 that it has to be the angel of the Lord, who is Jesus Christ. So when you see other angelic appearances in the Bible, match them with Revelation 1 and see if you can identify them as the Lord or as another angel. It is not always easy, but this passage is your benchmark. We know for sure this passage describes Jesus, because this appearance says he is "the first and the last" (verse 17), and we have already seen Jesus as the Alpha and Omega. Also, verse 18 tells us that he was dead and is now alive for evermore, and that can only be Jesus Christ.

Verse 18 says he has the keys of hell and death. Those who place their faith in the Lord Jesus Christ need not fear either one of those things. Death will get all of us unless we are lucky enough to make it to the rapture of the church. But Jesus has the key. Hebrews 2:14-15 says he defeated the "death angel" (Satan) and has delivered us from the fear of death. He did that – not by "cheating death" – but by defeating it by going through it and coming out the other side never to die again. He got the key to hell by busting out of it at the firstfruits rapture (hang on to that and I will explain further when we get to chapter 4).

The Lord in this passage has several things in his possession other than those keys. He stood in the midst of seven golden candlesticks (verse 13). In verse 16, he has seven stars in his right hand and a two-edged sword coming out of his mouth. Let's examine those items, but before we do, we need to detail a very crucial aspect of Bible "interpretation". One of the main complaints from skeptics and unbelievers is when they say, "Well, that is just your interpretation of that verse". Peter said, "Knowing this first, that no prophecy of the scripture is of any private interpretation" (II Peter 1:20). That means that no one is allowed to "interpret" anything in the Bible apart from the author of the Bible itself, who is the Holy Spirit of God as it says in the next verse. Let me illustrate. If you went to the local art gallery and saw some of the more "abstract" paintings, you might have an opinion as to what it represents. You could gather a whole crowd of people and have each one write down what the painting "means" to them. You would likely get as many "interpretations" as there are people, and each one of them would have the perfect right to "interpret" the painting for themselves and get something from it. Everyone is entitled to their own opinions, and I would never deny that right to anyone even though they will deny mine. It is what makes America great. We can all have varying opinions and we are free to express them (at least for now, sort of, in the face of politically correct thought police and social media censorship, and as long as you don't care if you lose your job or have rioters show up at your house). But no one is entitled to the wrong facts. So let's go back to the art gallery. As everyone is expressing their "interpretations", the artist walks into the room. He gives us all the title of the work and "interprets" exactly what he intended it to be when he put the brush to the canvas. The discussion ends. No one can say, "Well, that's just your interpretation". He is the author. He has the sole right to say what the piece of art means.

The Bible interprets itself. The overwhelming vast majority of the Bible is clear and plain and "means" exactly and literally what it says. But there are places where symbols are used. When symbols appear, they will be "interpreted" clearly in the Bible itself, and almost always in the same passage where the symbol appears. The parables in Matthew chapter 13 are a classic example. This chapter is another one. So let's "interpret" the three symbols used by simply READING the plain words on the page.

__Seven Golden Candlesticks__ – The seven candlesticks are the seven churches (verse 20). The author of the painting just stepped into the room. The discussion is over. I don't care what anyone on earth says or writes, the candlesticks are the seven churches addressed in the next two chapters.

__Seven Stars__ – The seven stars are the angels of the seven churches (verse 20). Once again, the author defines his work in the same chapter and context where the symbol is given. As with many symbols in the Bible, the definition transcends the whole counsel of the word of God and not just the immediate passage. Therefore, stars in the Bible are a type of angels. That is not my "interpretation"; it is simply what the Bible says. Sometimes stars in the Bible refer to the gaseous blobs of fire in outer space. Even when they do, there is generally a spiritual truth behind it in the passage showing us something about angelic beings. Stars live in the City of Angels. Isn't it odd how things like that happen in life and no one gives it a thought, yet they complain about the Bible being irrelevant?

__A Two-Edged Sword__ – For this one, we have to go outside the context, but never outside the Bible. A sharp two-edged sword goes out of Jesus' mouth here. The same thing is said in Revelation 19:15. In Hebrews 4:12 it says, "For the word of God is quick, and powerful, and sharper than any two-edged sword, piercing even to the dividing asunder of soul and spirit, and of the joints and marrow, and is a discerner of the thoughts and intents of the heart." Ephesians 6:17 says, "And take… the sword of the Spirit, which is the word of God." The sword out of the mouth of Jesus is the Bible. The words of the Bible are vital to our spiritual survival. The sword is our only offensive weapon in the armour of God in Ephesians chapter 6. If we take the words and bring the "s" around to the front, we have a "sword". Again, this type is consistent throughout the Bible. In most places, it will be talking about a literal piece of metal fashioned into a big "knife" like a machete. Even in those places, it is not difficult to see an application to the words of God.

So as we make our way through the rest of Revelation, let us "interpret" what we see in light of the clear words of God which define any symbols in this book. There are plenty of them, and probably more than in any other book of the Bible. Where it is clear, we can be clear. Where it is not so clear, I will be sure to point out when I am speculating and offering my opinions. There is a lot of that in Revelation. But what we never want to do is run off the rails and get outside the definitions given to us in the Bible. It will keep us safe as we navigate the bizarre and challenging passages in this all-important "capstone" book of the Bible. May God richly bless our studies.

Revelation Chapters 2-3
"The Things Which Thou Hast Seen"

Church History

I am not going to spend a lot of time on these two chapters. I wrote an entire book of over 500 pages on church history, so there is no need repeat it here. I will summarize the flow of church history in case you do not have my other book (aptly titled *Church History*). Knowing the basic outline of Revelation makes it easier to see this in chapters 2 and 3. The past tense "things which thou hast seen" from the vantage point of the Tribulation and the Second Coming must be church history. That is confirmed by the clear picture of the rapture of the church in Revelation 4:1, as well as the mention of the church in the book. The word "church" or "churches" appears 19 times in chapters 1-3. Then a door opens in heaven and John is called out with the phrase "come up hither", and the word "church" disappears from the text until chapter 22. Based on that, Revelation chapters 2 and 3 must be applied primarily to the church age.

As with many other things in the Bible, and especially in Revelation, God often groups things in sevens. The book is written to seven churches that were in operation historically in Asia Minor during the first century. But they also represent seven ages or time periods that span the 2,000 years of the church. John was told to write a book (singular) and send it (singular) to seven different churches. So each age of the church was to be read by all. There are churches on earth in any age and at any point in history that line up with each of the seven churches in Revelation 2-3, and each local church exemplifies aspects of all seven of them. But the primary characteristics of these seven churches follow a pattern that can be clearly identified over the last 2,000 years of history.

Each of these letters to the churches contains five things in each section. It begins with, "Unto the angel of the church in Ephesus (Smyrna, etc.)..." The angel of the church is the representative spirit or nature of the age. The names of the churches are significant, and I will note them as we briefly walk through each age. The next common statement begins, "These things saith he..." What follows is a brief aspect or characteristic of Jesus Christ that helps us be an overcomer during that age of the church. Next is the statement, "I know thy works..." This is the "spirit of the age" and describes what is happening during a time period of a few hundred years. For example, the age of Thyatira (Revelation 2:18-29) covers the first half of the Dark Ages (500-1000 AD). Obviously, MUCH occurs during these 500 years, but God takes just a few verses to summarize his perspective of that time period. So if you want to see history the right way, you have to look at it from God's prism. The fourth section says, "To him that overcometh..." This is a promise to those who rebel the right way – AGAINST the spirit of the world driving that age. We live in the age of Laodicea; the lukewarm church of individual rights. So if you want to get a reward for overcoming, tap into the character of the Lord Jesus Christ and go against that spirit. Don't be the typical lukewarm "namby-pamby" Christian of today who is so wrapped up with their "individual rights" that they think the world revolves around them, and that God exists for the sole purpose of blessing their gizzards with the dump truck of heaven filled with health, wealth and social status. It is about HIM, not you. Finally, each section closes with, "He that hath and ear, let him hear..." Will you?

There is another aspect of Revelation chapters 2 and 3 that does not get a lot of "press". I did not cover this in my church history book because that was not the focus. There is a clear Tribulation overtone in these chapters as well. Do not let that confuse you or cause you to think that the passage does not apply to the church. Many teachers have discounted the church history summary of Revelation chapters 2-3 because there are things in those chapters that cannot apply doctrinally to the church. So they write off the entire section rather than deal with the exceptions. There is a clear outline of the book of Revelation. It is written in three sections. It is written from the historical vantage point of 100 AD, and it is written at the same time from the prophetic vantage point of the Second Coming of Jesus Christ. The first section is past tense (church history), the second section is present tense (Tribulation) and the third section is future tense (Millennium and Eternity). Teachers who claim that Revelation chapters 2-3 have no relevance to the church age must ignore this basic structure. Without it, the book of Revelation makes no sense and will be misapplied. They nit-pick a few places in chapters 2-3 that have dual application, and in the process, mess up the entire book. God knows how to communicate to more than one group of people at the same time. He has precious few pages (only about 1500) to give mankind everything he needs to be saved and have a relationship with him. He often has to "double up" to fit it all in. The book of James clearly applies to the Tribulation doctrinally, yet it is used – rightfully so – as a tremendous standard of godly living principles for the church age. There is as much New Testament doctrine in Leviticus as there is in the book of Romans. So as we briefly walk through each of the seven major sections of Revelation chapters 2 and 3, I will point out a few prophetic aspects that apply to the Tribulation and not the church.

The Seven Ages of Church History

Revelation 2:1-7 – The Age of Ephesus (33-200 AD) – "Fully Purposed"

The age of Ephesus was a "fully purposed" church that got the job done for Jesus Christ early, fulfilling the Great Commission in the book of Acts. But they left their first love when church fathers wrote things that deviated slightly from the word of God. The full canon of scripture was not confirmed until about 150 AD. Until then, equal authority was given to the writings of church fathers and the Bible. Future generations of gnostic philosophers used the dual authorities to infiltrate the church and weaken it from the inside and developed a "Christianity" based on worldly philosophy and deeper learning.

Doctrinal and prophetic applications:

VS 5 – Those who do not repent are in danger of losing their "candlestick". First, remember that these passages are addressed to the angel of the church. That is the age itself and its spiritual representation before the throne. It is not directed to an individual in the church. God can remove the candlestick by shutting out the "angel" without actually affecting any person. But if this does apply to an individual, a person in the Tribulation can lose his salvation. Keep this in mind. This principle of losing salvation in the Tribulation will be seen in many verses in Revelation chapters 2-3 as well as later in the book.

VS 7 – Those who overcome are granted the right to "eat" of the tree of life. This is a very important doctrinal distinction. After Adam sinned, access to the tree of life was blocked. Genesis 3:22 says, "Lest he [Adam] put forth his hand, and take also of the tree of life, and eat, and live forever…" Had Adam and Eve eaten of the tree of life after they had sinned, they would still be alive today. God placed a guard on the tree of life to prevent that. So what happened to the tree of life? The Bible is silent on that, but it would be safe to speculate that the curse on the ground would have affected a plant or tree that pure, and at least by the time of the flood of Noah, if not much earlier, it would have disappeared. But just minutes after Adam's sin, it would still be there. The literal tree of life disappears from the Bible after Genesis 3 and does not appear again until Revelation. In between, the tree of life is spiritual. It shows up four times in the book of Proverbs (3:18, 11:30, 13:12, 15:4). In each case, it is referring to a spiritual principle, and no one is eating anything. The purpose of eating from the tree of life is to reverse the Adamic sin nature in mankind. We will see this in detail when we get to Revelation 22, where the tree of life shows up again for man to eat from. The church does not have to eat of the tree of life to cleanse the sin nature. That was taken care of spiritually at salvation. At the rapture of the church, Christians will be perfectly conformed to the image of Jesus Christ physically as well as spiritually. Our "tree of life" is the one Jesus died on (I Peter 2:24, Galatians 3:13). Our "eating" of the tree of life is in the same context as the bread of life discourse (John 6:32-65) where Jesus told us to "eat" his flesh and "drink" his blood spiritually. So Revelation 2:7 is a spiritual promise to overcomers. It will only become physical after the Millennial reign when the sin nature of mankind will be cleansed and the curse completely reversed and removed.

Revelation 2:8-11 – The Age of Smyrna (200-325 AD) – "Bitterness and Death"

The age of Smyrna was a severely persecuted church which suffered the brutal persecutions of pagan Rome. With the infiltration of the Gnostics weakening Christianity from inside, Satan launched an all-out offensive to try to destroy the church by brute force. But this persecution failed because adversity always makes genuine Christianity stronger.

Doctrinal and prophetic applications:

VS 9-10 – The word tribulation appears twice in these verses to show us that the Imperial persecutions of Rome against believers are a foreshadowing of things to come. The brutality against the Jewish remnant will make Nero and others like him look like Girl Scouts. The "crown of life" mentioned in verse 10 is an earned reward for believers at the Judgment Seat of Christ. It is also mentioned in James 1:12 as a reward for those who "die to self" to overcome temptation. But those in the Tribulation will receive a little extra special reward. According to Revelation 20:4, those who refuse the mark of the beast and lose their heads will be given a special place in the kingdom of Jesus Christ in the Millennium.

Revelation 2:12-17 – The Age of Pergamos (325-500 AD) – "Much Marriage"

The age of Pergamos was the church that married the world. Gnostic philosophy was established as the recognized doctrine of Christianity and consolidated by the greatest heretic of all human history, Origen. The Emperor Constantine then adopted this worldly and sophisticated perversion of "Christianity", and through his "Edict of Toleration", established it as the Roman State religion. This ushered in the age of Imperial domination of the Church and set the stage for the rise of Roman Catholicism and the period of history known as the Dark Ages.

Doctrinal and prophetic applications:

VS 13 – The phrase "those days" appears, which is always a key to the Tribulation. This term is found 75 times in the Bible in 73 verses, and in every case without exception, something about the Tribulation can be seen in the context. Here we have "Antipas" martyred in the place of Satan's seat where he dwells. Literally, this is Rome. But "Antipas" is a cryptic character. There is a "Herod Antipas" according to the historians who was the son of Herod the Great, but that term is not used for him in the Bible. There is no actual person named "Antipas" in the Bible. The word is a contraction of two words: "Anti" (against) and "Pater" (father). The martyrs of the Tribulation are those who have the audacity to go against the "Holy Father" who dwells in Satan's seat and counterfeits Jesus as the "Anti" Christ.

Revelation 2:18-29 – The Age of Thyatira (500-1000 AD) – "Odor of Affliction"

Thyatira is the age of superstition and judgment against the established church. After the church joined with the world in Pergamos, it set the stage for a complete takeover by the Roman Catholic Church-State. Old Testament Baal worship surfaced in the pagan beliefs and practices of Catholicism, which results in the Dark Ages and some of the severest judgments ever poured out by God on the world.

Doctrinal and prophetic applications:

VS 20 – Jezebel is mentioned. Her main "antagonist" was Elijah. He is one of the two Jewish witnesses of Revelation chapter 11 who leads the 144,000. Elijah was hunted by Jezebel just as the Jews will be in the Tribulation. He was fed miraculously at the brook Cherith (I Kings 17) just as the Jewish remnant will be fed in the Tribulation. When the provision ran out at the brook, Elijah was cared for by a woman of Zarephath. She was a Gentile who pictures those who provide for the 144,000 during the Tribulation.

VS 22 – Jezebel and her lovers will be cast into "great tribulation". This is the same term Jesus used for the last half of the Tribulation in Matthew 24:21. Jezebel's lovers are defined in Revelation 17 as the kings of the earth who are seduced into her false one world Roman / Babylonian religion.

VS 26-27 – The overcomers of Thyatira are promised "power over the nations" and a rule with Jesus Christ in his kingdom. This will apply to two groups: Israel and the church. In the Millennium, Israel will be the "head of the nations" (Deuteronomy 28:13). Jewish overcomers in the Tribulation will reign with Jesus over them. The church also reigns with Christ as we receive our inheritance (Colossians 3:24, II Timothy 2:12). In the kingdom, we will work for the government! You should vote and be as active and engaged in your community and nation as time and energy allows. But the problems of mankind will not be solved until Jesus comes, and the government is "on his shoulders" (Isaiah 9:6-7). I can assure you there will be no corrupt politicians then! One of the best parts of the Millennial reign of Jesus Christ is that there will be no CNN or Fox News, no arguing about "politics or religion", no ad campaigns from politicians telling us if we vote for their opponent they will eat our children, and no political phone calls or polls to gauge public opinion. Jesus will rule with a rod of iron and his servants will rule with him.

Revelation 3:1-6 – The Age of Sardis (1000-1500 AD) – "Red Ones"

The age of Sardis was a church of persecution and military conquest which "made a name for itself" by brute force, but was spiritually dead. The gross moral debauchery of the Popes, the Crusades, and the Roman and Spanish Inquisitions characterized a church state system completely out of control, and gives us a picture of the false kingdom of Satan in the Tribulation period to come.

Doctrinal and prophetic applications:

VS 3 – Jesus gives a warning in this verse to those who are not diligent. He will "comes as a thief" when it is least expected. Jesus used the same language in Matthew 24:42-44 referring to the Second Advent. Peter used it in II Peter 3:10 to speak of the Lord making a new heavens and new earth that will happen after the Millennial reign. Paul also used the "thief in the night" terminology in I Thessalonians 5:1-10. His point in that passage is to remind us that the Lord will come to others in that manner, but not to his church. But Revelation 3:3 is directed to the church if our outline and structure is correct. So which is it? Does the Lord come as a thief to the church, at the Advent before the kingdom, or at the end of the 1,000 year reign? Answer: YES! The method of his coming unannounced is consistent in each case.

VS 5 – In this verse, Jesus admonishes his church to hold fast and overcome so that he will confess us before the Father and not blot our names out of the book of life. This appears to teach that believers can lose their salvation. Jesus used the term in Matthew 10:32-33: "Whosoever therefore shall confess me before men, him will I confess also before my Father which is in heaven. But whosoever shall deny me before men, him will I also deny before my Father which is in heaven." Matthew 10 is the instructions to the apostles as he sent them forth to preach the kingdom. It is ALSO the instructions to the 144,000 as they will be commissioned to carry the "everlasting gospel" to the world in the Tribulation (Revelation 14:6-7). Any "loss" of salvation for denying the Lord applies to that group. I will deal with this subject in full when we get to the sealing of the 144,000 in Revelation chapter 7.

Revelation 3:7-13 – The Age of Philadelphia (1500-1900 AD) – "Brotherly Love"

Philadelphia was the "Golden Age" of man, missions, and the movement of God through his people. The church of the open door demonstrated what true brotherly love really is: carrying the gospel to the lost world. The church with the "key of David" produced the authoritative English Bible and took the word of God to the ends of the earth under English Imperialism and the world-wide missionary movements of Great Britain and the United States of America.

Doctrinal and prophetic applications:

VS 10 – God promised the church of Philadelphia: "I will keep thee from the hour of temptation". This is a reference to the Tribulation. It has led some to speculate that only true "Philadelphian" Christians will go out at the rapture and that "Laodicean" Christians will have to endure the Tribulation. This is part of the infamous "split rapture" heresy; that Jesus will only take part of his body home at the culmination of the church age. I will deal with this in detail when we discuss the rapture of the church and all of its related side teachings. All this verse tells us is that the age of Philadelphia ends before the Tribulation.

VS 12 – New Jerusalem is mentioned. This is the true "city of God" which does not come down from heaven until Revelation chapter 21 after the Millennium. Again, I will give more detail in chapter 21, but New Jerusalem is the "home" of the church in eternity. Israel gets the earth. Gentiles will be subject to Israel. Everyone will have access to New Jerusalem, but it is the base of operations for the church and the eventual population of the human race throughout the Universe in eternity future. I will cover that in full when we get to Revelation chapter 22.

Revelation 3:14-22 – The Age of Laodicea (1900 AD – Rapture) – "Rights of the People"

Laodicea is the church of individual rights wallowing in apostasy just as Israel did in the book of Judges. There is no king in Christianity in Laodicea because the preserved text of the King James Bible has been rejected and the final authority of the word of God has been replaced by personal preference and opinion, paving the way for the rapture of the church and the rise of the Antichrist.

Doctrinal and prophetic applications:

VS 16 – One of the regular questions I get about the book of Revelation is about God spewing us out of his mouth. It is used by many to gin up fear among believers that they have to "endure to the end" or they will lose it. Again, these passages are addressed to the angel of the church, not to individual believers. I mentioned this earlier that the angel is the spiritual representative presence before the throne. Individual believers are not spewed out of the mouth of the Lord. The passage essentially says that God is so sick of us in Laodicea that he does not want to even look. The age of Laodicea is like coffee. A nice piping hot cup in the morning on a cold day is awesome. An iced cappuccino is refreshing. But when you get a sip of a cup of coffee that has been sitting on the counter for 30 minutes, it will gag you. This is not loss of salvation for individual believers, it is God commenting on how his church in today's world makes him feel when we are "rich and increased with goods" and think we do not need him.

Revelation Chapters 4-19
"The Things Which Are"

Revelation Chapters 4-6 – The Seals
The First Pass Through the Tribulation

Our first pass through the Tribulation period is titled "The Seals" because seven Seals will be opened to reveal certain aspects of the time of Jacob's trouble. With each subsequent Seal, the disasters mount and culminate with the Second Advent of the Lord Jesus Christ in Revelation 6:12-17. Chapters 4-5 report on activity in heaven, and the Seals are actually opened in chapter 6.

Revelation Chapters 4-5 – The Harvest

Revelation 4:1-2 – The Rapture of the Church

So much has been written about the rapture that it would take a good sized warehouse to hold all the materials. There likely isn't another subject in the Bible that causes so much confusion and controversy. There are as many theories and opinions as there are authors. So let me cut through the fog. Remember, this is *Revelation Made Simple*. There are two primary issues that <u>must</u> be understood about the rapture.

1.) The word "rapture" is not in the Bible. The Bible term is "harvest".
2.) There are THREE "raptures" or three <u>phases</u> of God's harvest in the Bible.

Every single rapture heresy can be easily cleared up by rightly dividing the word of truth. Virtually every time the rapture is discussed, teachers refer to <u>the</u> rapture as if there is only one. As a result, the passages of scripture that conflict will be jammed together instead of applied to the proper group and the proper time. There are passages that clearly show a rapture at the end of the Tribulation. There are also passages that clearly teach a Pre-Tribulation rapture. The uninformed teacher who fails to rightly divide the word of truth is forced to choose where he places <u>THE</u> rapture. Many will teach a Post-Tribulation rapture of the church as a result. Others will ignore or do damage to many passages that show a rapture at the end of the Tribulation. There are THREE raptures in the Bible!

Since the Bible term is "harvest", the terminology becomes clear. Every harvest has three phases. If you have ever planted a vegetable garden, you know this. About 60 days in, you look out at your garden and see a couple of red spots. Those are the first tomatoes of the season. The Bible term is "firstfruits". A couple of weeks later, you are canning tomatoes, eating them at every meal, and trying to give them away because they are coming out of your ears. That is the "main harvest". Then in the fall, you look outside and see a few red spots again. The Bible term for that part of the harvest is "gleanings". Make note of these terms as we make our way through this subject.

Let me illustrate this with a personal family story. I am second oldest in a large family. I was six and my older brother was eight, and he wanted a bicycle for Christmas. He was so adamant about it that he drove my mom and dad nuts. He just HAD to have a bike. When the big day came, we ran out to the living room together, and there under the tree was a bike for my brother Mark and one for me. Mark was so excited he said, "WOW! I got TWO bikes!!!" Um, excuse me, Mark. You have a little brother, and he gets a bike also. When the prophecy teachers talk about <u>THE</u> rapture, they have the same problem. They see two "bikes under the tree" or two sets of passages that describe a rapture in different terms and they forget that the church has a group of "little brothers" called the Tribulation saints, and they get a rapture also. Conflicting passages about "pre" or "post" are <u>instantly</u> cleared up by rightly dividing the word of truth and applying them to the correct group at the correct time.

Certain words and phrases in the King James Bible are specifically chosen to communicate truth. The phrase "come up hither" appears only three times in the Bible, and that is by design. The three places are Proverbs 25:7 (in the Old Testament), Revelation 4:1 (John's "rapture" in type), and Revelation 11:12 which is the main passage describing the Post-Tribulation rapture of the Jewish remnant. Those are the three phases of God's harvest of the earth, and those three verses line up with them in the order they appear in the Bible and the order they occur. Now that we have established that there are three raptures, or three phases of God's harvest, let's walk through them and note the similarities and the differences. Watch how the confusion of variant passages is easily straightened out by the correct application of Bible truths and passages to the correct time and the correct group of people.

Christ and the "Firstfruits" – The Rapture of the OT Saints

This rapture is laid out in the Bible like the old *Mission: Impossible* television show. The movies were based on this program from a couple of generations ago. The writers of the *Mission: Impossible* TV show were brilliant. They knew how to keep the audience through the entire program. The show was an hour long. You would watch the first 55 minutes with your head cocked to one side and with a visible question mark over it. Nothing made any sense. Then in the last 5 minutes, a whole series of events took place that brought everything into clarity. You would sit there and slap your forehead and say, "OH! That is why they did that!" Everything came together at the end. But if you did not watch the first 55 minutes, none of the last 5 would make any sense either. In order to detail the firstfruits rapture, we will need to see several passages of scripture. On the surface at first glance, they will seem to have little to do with the subject. Your head will cock to one side a couple of times. But stay with it. It will all come together at the end to show you how God harvested the firstfruits of his earth at the resurrection of Jesus Christ.

Luke 16:19-31 – This is the story of the rich man and Lazarus. The story is jam packed with great truths and principles, but the only thing we need to see from it for this study is the structure of "hell". The rich man is in flames of torment (as we understand hell). He sees Lazarus in a place of comfort and rest. He asks for a little water, and he is told that there is no passing between his place of torment and the place of rest because there is a "great gulf" between them. So "hell" has three compartments: a place of fire, a place of comfort, and a gulf between them. Don't try to take that any further yet. We have only just begun the *"Mission: Impossible"* journey. I know you think of hell as only the place of fire and torment for the lost, and that is certainly its main characteristic. But Biblically, the term is used in a couple of places in a larger context.

Luke 23:39-43 – On the cross, one of the dying thieves trusted Jesus to save him. Jesus promised him paradise "today" (the first day of the three days Jesus was dead).

Acts 2:22-31 – Jesus descended to "hell" for three days. He did not go to the torment side, as some believe. He promised the dying thief paradise <u>with</u> <u>him</u> immediately. Jesus did not suffer the fire of hell for our sins. Hebrews 12:1-2 says he endured the <u>cross</u>, not the flame. When he cried out, "It is finished", it was <u>finished</u>! But this passage says he went to hell for three days. Again, do not go any further with that information yet. All we have established at this point in our study is that "hell" has three compartments, and that Jesus and the thief on the cross who got saved both went to the paradise side together immediately after their deaths.

Matthew 12:38-40 – Jesus spent three days in the "heart of the earth". Now we can see the location of hell. The <u>structure</u> is three compartments; the <u>location</u> is the center of the earth.

I Peter 3:18-20, 4:6 – Jesus preached to the "spirits in prison" during these three days. This is one of the more bizarre passages anywhere in the Bible. Very little information is given in the passage, and no other place that I know of mentions it. So we are on very speculative ground. We can only be sure of what is actually stated in the text. Jesus preached to the spirits in prison, so these would be spirit beings. They are identified as the ones who "were sometime disobedient in the days of Noah". So they would be the "angels which kept not their first estate" (Jude 6, II Peter 2:4) and married the daughters of men in Genesis chapter 6. I Peter 4:6 says the gospel was preached to the dead. This gives fodder to those who would say that there is a second chance for people to be saved after they are dead. But no one responded to this preaching, and they were not going to. Stephen preached one of the most powerful gospel messages in history. His audience "came forward at the invitation" with rocks in their hands. Jesus preached to the Pharisees in Matthew chapter 23 and they killed him. The text in I Peter says the gospel was preached to them so that they could be "judged according to men in the flesh, but live according to God in the spirit." That is strange and cryptic language. Remember we are talking about the fallen angels from Genesis chapter 6. They were created as angels. They chose to leave that "estate" and become confined to our "estate" as men. So how does God judge them, as men or as angels? Either way he might try, they would hide behind the other "estate". So here is my speculation, and please be fully cognizant of that word "speculation". There are too many times in the Bible and especially in Revelation when people have dogmatically taught something that is their own personal opinion. When I speculate, I will tell you. I believe Jesus preached the gospel of his death, burial and resurrection to those in Abraham's bosom and said, "I won the victory. Pack your bags, boys and girls; we are headed out of here in three days." He preached the gospel of his death, burial and resurrection to the spirits in prison and said, "Your doom is sealed. None of your relatives can pray you out of this 'purgatory' because it does not exist. You are still angels (spirit) because that is how I created you. But I will judge you as men because that is the 'estate' you chose. Either way, your goose is cooked – literally."

Ephesians 4:8-10 – Jesus "led captivity captive". He descended first into the lower parts of the earth which we have already seen as hell. Then he ascended far above all heavens, but he did not go alone. There were a bunch of souls in Abraham's bosom. Those who died in faith in the Old Testament did not go to "heaven" as we commonly know it. Hebrews 10:11 says, "And every priest standeth daily ministering and offering oftentimes the same sacrifices, which can never take away sins." The animal sacrifices of the law of Israel covered sins, but it did not take them away. That is why Jesus was the "Lamb of God which taketh away the sins of the world" (John 1:29). Exodus 34:7 says that God is merciful and forgiving, but it does not clear the guilty. Those guilty of sins in the Old Testament could get them covered by the blood of Levitical sacrifices and go to Abraham's bosom (paradise), but until the perfect sacrifice was offered on the cross, those sins were not "taken away". That is why I believe part of the preaching of Jesus to the dead was to tell them about his perfect sacrifice. After his resurrection, he brought those redeemed souls out with him and "led captivity captive" to heaven.

Matthew 27:50-53 – This passage details the death of Jesus, and "flashes ahead" briefly to an event that took place after his resurrection. It says many bodies of the saints arose. They even walked around Jerusalem for a brief time appearing to people. That would have been awesome, huh? God has a sense of humor. Imagine standing in line at the DMV and Moses is in front of you; or running into Ruth at the farmer's market. Those Old Testament saints were resurrected and taken to heaven.

II Corinthians 12:1-4 – Paul said he was "caught up" to the third heaven and paradise. But paradise was in the heart of the earth when Jesus promised it to the dying thief. The only way paradise could be UP in heaven was for its occupants to be moved UP to heaven. That was the first rapture and the first part of the harvest. God harvested the earth of the fruit of his law and dealings with Israel. Those are the Old Testament saints who were held in Abraham's bosom until the perfect sacrifice.

Since this part of the harvest happened 2,000 years ago, most people ignore it. I am not aware of a single prophecy teacher who details the firstfruits rapture. The next time someone tries to force a teaching on THE rapture, ask him, "Which one?" Be prepared for the deer-in-the-headlights look.

The Main Harvest – The Body of Christ

Most people who have studied this subject in the Bible are aware of the primary passages that deal with the rapture of the church. There are other places in the New Testament that refer to this, and there are types and prophetic references to it in the Old Testament, but I will quote the two main passages here so you can see them in their full context.

> But I would not have you to be ignorant, brethren, concerning them which are asleep, that ye sorrow not, even as others which have no hope. For if we believe that Jesus died and rose again, even so them also which sleep in Jesus will God bring with him. For this we say unto you by the word of the Lord, that we which are alive and remain unto the coming of the Lord shall not prevent them which are asleep. For the Lord himself shall descend from heaven with a shout, with the voice of the archangel, and with the trump of God: and the dead in Christ shall rise first: Then we which are alive and remain shall be caught up together with them in the clouds, to meet the Lord in the air: and so shall we ever be with the Lord. Wherefore comfort one another with these words. (I Thessalonians 4:13-18)

> Now this I say, brethren, that flesh and blood cannot inherit the kingdom of God; neither doth corruption inherit incorruption. Behold, I shew you a mystery; We shall not all sleep, but we shall all be changed, In a moment, in the twinkling of an eye, at the last trump: for the trumpet shall sound, and the dead shall be raised incorruptible, and we shall be changed. For this corruptible must put on incorruption, and this mortal must put on immortality. (I Corinthians 15:50-53)

There are a significant number of people and even many prophecy teachers who deny <u>any</u> rapture. How do they explain these passages of scripture? It is abundantly clear that there will be a group of people "caught up to meet the Lord in the air" who will not sleep (die) but be changed. Both of these passages were written by the apostle Paul to the church. This is clearly a group of believers who are "alive and remain" when God finally draws a line in the sand for the end of the church age. Before he makes the full shift into the next dispensation, he pulls his bride out. The main harvest is far and away the biggest, just like it is in the natural world of farming. The fruit of the sacrifice of the Son of God on the cross is far greater than any other fruit God produces. Isaiah 54:1 is a veiled reference to this: "More are the children of the desolate than the children of the married wife, saith the Lord." The "married wife" in the passage is the Nation of Israel (verse 5-6). The born again children of God during the age of the church exceeds the number of the children of Israel by a wide margin.

Enoch is the Old Testament type of the rapture of the church. There are other passages that allude to it in picture form as we will see in a few moments, but as an individual type, Enoch fills the bill. He was the seventh from Adam (Jude 14), the number of perfection. He was called out BEFORE the judgment of God fell on the world in the flood of Noah. Noah pictures the Nation of Israel during the Tribulation. He and his family survived the judgment of God while going through it. Enoch was "translated" to heaven (Hebrews 11:5) in advance of the judgment and "did not see death" just as the group of believers who are "alive and remain" will not "sleep" but be changed in a moment of time.

Jesus alluded to the rapture of the church a couple of times. The clearest example is in John 11:25-26. He mentions two groups of people. Verse 25 says, "He that believeth in me, though he were dead, yet shall he live." This is the group in I Thessalonians 4 referred to as "the dead in Christ" who rise first. Then Jesus said in John 11:26, "Whosoever liveth and believeth in me shall never die." These are the people who are "alive and remain" at the rapture of the church. Those who teach no rapture would have a dickens of a time explaining those verses out of the mouth of our Saviour. Jesus also said in John 14:3, "And if I go and prepare a place for you, I will come again, and receive you unto myself; that where I am, there ye may be also." That cannot be the indwelling Holy Spirit because it is an actual location where Jesus will take us to where he is. That verse also cannot apply only to the eleven apostles who were present to hear it. They died one by one over the space of many years and went to heaven, but Jesus did not come for them one by one to take them there. The address in John 13-17 was given to the eleven apostles at the Last Supper, but by extension it applies to the entire church. In John 17:20-23, Jesus applied his words to all of us. The promise of John 14:3 is that Jesus will come literally and take us to a place he has prepared for us to be with him. How can that not be the rapture of his body?

In the writings of Paul, the term "day of Christ" or "day of Jesus Christ" is reserved to signify the rapture of the church. It is different than the "day of the Lord". The day of Christ is his big day; the day he gets his bride. The references are: Philippians 1:6, 1:10, 2:16, and II Thessalonians 2:2. The day of the Lord is the day he returns as Lord to reign on the earth. Those events are separated by seven years.

As far as an individual in the New Testament who pictures the rapture of the church better than anyone, it would have to be the apostle John. The text in Revelation 4:1 is certainly clear. John heard the voice of a trumpet (as in I Thessalonians 4:16) and immediately (in the twinkling of an eye – I Corinthians 15:52) he was at the throne of God in the Spirit. John is a type of the church. He is referred to as "the disciple whom Jesus loved" throughout the gospels. Did Jesus not love all of them? Of course he did. But John, whose name means "beloved" is the picture of "my beloved" spouse or bride of Christ. John was the disciple who leaned on the breast of Jesus at the Last Supper (John 13:23). He was at his side, near his heart, in the same position as Eve who came from Adam's side. Adam's "deep sleep" brought forth Eve from his rib just as the "sleep" of death brought forth the church from Jesus.

In Matthew 16:28, Jesus promised that there were some standing there who would not die until they had seen him coming in his kingdom. Then six days later, he showed them at the Mount of Transfiguration. John took part in that vision. Then in John 21:20-23, Jesus implied that it would at least be possible for John to be alive at his coming. Obviously, John is no longer with us and Jesus has not yet returned. So literally, this did not happen, and the text is clear that Jesus only said, "what if". In verse 23, the theory was bandied about that John would not die. But notice that Jesus dodged the question as well as any politician has ever side-stepped an issue. So I have a speculation, and again, take this with as many grains of salt as is necessary and know that this is only my opinion. John is the only apostle to escape a violent martyr's death. All of the other apostles have their deaths recorded in Foxe's Book of Martyrs. We know for sure that John was spiritually translated to the "Lord's day" and was at the throne of God to witness and record this Revelation. It is very possible that he just stayed when he was done writing it, and the document was left behind for someone to copy and distribute. If that is the case, John is not just a type of the rapture, he experienced it himself personally.

The Gleanings – The Rapture of the Tribulation Saints

One of the biggest errors in Bible study is projecting every truth of the Bible upon yourself personally. This is the number one reason why many people and Bible teachers believe the church will go through the Tribulation. There is definitely a rapture at the end of the Tribulation; that cannot be denied. But there are more people to be harvested than just us. One of the main reasons there must be this final part of the harvest is to finish the work. The Old Testament saints were harvested at the resurrection of Christ. The church will be harvested soon. But the rest of the people of God have to be harvested as well before the Lord returns to establish his kingdom. That is the purpose of the Post-Tribulation gleanings. Once this group is brought in, there are no more harvests necessary because Jesus will be here in his kingdom.

The main passage dealing with the gleanings rapture is Revelation 11:11-12: "And after three days and an half the Spirit of life from God entered into them, and they stood upon their feet; and great fear fell upon them which saw them. And they heard a great voice from heaven saying unto them, Come up hither. And they ascended up to heaven in a cloud; and their enemies beheld them."

Please pay close attention to the differences between this rapture and the rapture of the church. This is the problem with most of the prophecy teachers who conflate these two raptures, and why so many of them just cannot put them in the right time frame. All rapture references have to be combined according to them. But the premier verse in the Bible telling us how to study it says to "rightly divide the word of truth" (II Timothy 2:15). Things that are different must be noted. These are the two witnesses of the Tribulation period, Moses and Elijah. We will see that in more detail when we get to chapter 11. They are the leaders of the 144,000, so by extension, when they are raptured out, so will the entire group who still remains on earth just prior to the Second Advent. Moses and Elijah will have been dead for three days before this rapture. They will be supernaturally resurrected in plain view of their enemies. That does not happen with our rapture. As these saints are taken out, they ascend gradually in a cloud just like the Lord did in Acts chapter 1. Their enemies watch them as they go up. We are raptured in a moment, in the twinkling of an eye. No one will see our rapture happen. The Post-Tribulation rapture is followed immediately by the physical return of Jesus Christ to earth in Revelation 11:15. The church is raptured out seven years earlier. An earthquake takes place at this rapture, which as we have seen earlier is one of the "registration marks" of the four passes through the Tribulation, and this earthquake appears also in chapters 6 and 16 connected with and just prior to the Second Advent. These two raptures are NOT the same, and other passages that refer to a rapture must be analyzed correctly and applied to the right group.

One of the other primary passages on the Post-Tribulation rapture is seen in Matthew chapters 24 and 25. Consider this passage in Matthew 24:29-31:

> "Immediately after the tribulation of those days shall the sun be darkened, and the moon shall not give her light, and the stars shall fall from heaven, and the powers of the heavens shall be shaken: And then shall appear the sign of the Son of man in heaven: and then shall all the tribes of the earth mourn, and they shall see the Son of man coming in the clouds of heaven with power and great glory. And he shall send his angels with a great sound of a trumpet, and they shall gather together his elect from the four winds, from one end of heaven to the other."

Some of the more prominent on-line rapture / prophecy gurus have jumped on this passage as proof of the church going through the Tribulation. It clearly says, "AFTER the Tribulation" God will gather his elect from the four winds. See there, the rapture must happen after the Tribulation! It amazes me how such intelligent men cannot grasp basic simple common sense concepts. They are just like my 8 year old brother at Christmas. EVERY bike was his. The "elect" can only be ME. The context of Matthew chapter 24 is the Second Advent of the Lord Jesus Christ. It has nothing to do with the church. The Jewish apostles asked their Jewish Messiah when he would return. This particular phase of the rapture / harvest is for his Jewish remnant just prior to his return. The "elect" in this passage are the Tribulation Jews. He said in verse 30 that all the tribes of the earth shall mourn when they SEE the Son of man coming in his kingdom. The rapture of the church happens unannounced in a moment, in the twinkling of an eye. No one will see anything. But at the Post-Tribulation rapture, the enemies of God will watch Moses and Elijah and their followers (what is left of the 144,000 at that point) be raptured out. They will see it with their eyeballs. Matthew 24 is about the Son of man. Jesus had two titles like this; the other one being the Son of God. The Son of man is the title reserved for his relationship with Israel as their earthly Messiah. If you can show me ONE time in all of Paul's 14 letters when he used the term "Son of man" for Jesus, then I will acknowledge that this rapture applies to the church and that we will go through the Tribulation. Go ahead. I am waiting. I am STILL waiting... HELLO??? ANYONE THERE???

Matthew 25 follows the same discourse as Matthew 24. The two chapters are back to back without a pause from the Lord, so the context and subject is the same. This is the parable of the wise and foolish virgins. There is a "calling out" when the bridegroom comes in verse 10. But again, pay attention to the simple words of the King James Bible and rightly divide and you will always be in good position to stay safe from doctrinal error. The virgins in the Bible are the 144,000. That is defined in Revelation 14:1-4.

These virgins go out to MEET the bridegroom, not to MARRY him as the church does. They are some of the "attendants" at the wedding according to Psalm 45. AGAIN, he refers to the Son of man coming in verse 13. This is the Post-Tribulation rapture of the Jewish remnant, not the church.

There are other places in the Bible which speak of the gleanings portion of God's harvest at the end of the Tribulation. Isaiah 17:4-8 mentions a harvestman gathering a few "gleaning grapes". Jeremiah 6:9 talks about gleaning the remnant of Israel as a vine. Both of these passages are Old Testament and are directly linked to the Nation of Israel, who is the recipient of the Post-Tribulation rapture. Hosea 6:11 says, "Also O Judah, he hath set an harvest for thee, when I returned the captivity of my people." How could anyone try to apply this part of the harvest to the church? It clearly says it is for Judah.

Other passages in the Bible allude to a rapture. In some of them, it is simply a general principle of God harvesting his earth and taking people out of his field. For example, Isaiah 26:20-21 says: "Come, my people, enter thou into thy chambers, and shut thy doors about thee: hide thyself as it were for a little moment, until the indignation be overpast. For, behold, the LORD cometh out of his place to punish the inhabitants of the earth for their iniquity: the earth also shall disclose her blood, and shall no more cover her slain." This would be first applied to the Post-Tribulation gleanings because it is followed by the Lord coming out of his place to judge the world, which would be Armageddon. But it also applies to our rapture because it is just a general principle that God will "hide" his people from his wrath. Another verse is Psalm 18:16: "He sent from above, he took me, he drew me out of many waters." That verse can be applied to both raptures yet to come. It is simply a general truth that either group will be drawn out of the "sea of humanity" by God from above.

So now with that understanding in place, let's walk through some of the major rapture heresies you will find from the prophecy gurus. These are the main ones. If you find some other off the wall "spin" on this subject, it will only be a variation of these, and again, you can cut right through the fog in a nano-second with this information and the knowledge that there are three raptures.

NO Rapture – Some have seen the truth that the word "rapture" is not in the Bible, and they have swung too far to the extreme of eliminating it altogether from their teaching. I grant them the truth that the word is not in the Bible. I have been clear that the Bible term is harvest. But there is an event described in the Bible. I Thessalonians 4:13-18 says there is a group of people who will be "caught up" to meet the Lord while they are still "alive and remain". I Corinthians 15:50-54 says we will not all sleep (die), and that mortal people will put on immortality in a twinkling of an eye. I don't care what you call the event. But I want to hear the "no rapture" crowd explain those passages. There will be a supernatural transformation into another dimension by some group of people at some point in time. It is seen many times in the Bible. Enoch was translated (Hebrews 11:5). John was immediately in the spirit in Revelation 4:1-2. Elijah went to heaven in a whirlwind in II Kings 2. Call it what you will, but the event is described in the Bible.

Split Rapture – This is the teaching that only those who are actually "looking" for the rapture will go in the first wave, and then there will be a second rapture of the rest of the church later. These teachers see two distinct raptures, but they will not apply them to two different dispensational groups. They think the only rapture is for the church, so if there are two of them, the church has to be raptured out in two groups. There is very little Biblical basis for this heresy, but the main passage they use is Matthew 25 and the foolish and wise virgins. Those who are "ready" go to meet the bridegroom in that parable, and those who are not "ready" get left behind. There are so many holes in their theory that it would be easier to "carry the water" in an upside down bucket. First, Matthew 25 does not apply to the church, but to the Jewish remnant in the Tribulation. They go out to MEET the bridegroom. The church as the bride gets to MARRY him. Second, those foolish virgins are never raptured out. So you cannot have a split rapture of two parts of the body if the second part never gets raptured. The idea that Jesus would leave behind part of his body is absurd. When you went on your honeymoon, did you lop off your new wife's arm and leave it home? But the biggest problem with the split rapture teaching is that no one has ever been able to identify what it means to be "looking" for the return of the Lord. Do I have to keep my eyes upward? What if he comes while I am asleep and my eyes are closed? They say, "You have to be ready!" Define that. It is totally nebulous. The old hide-and-seek game says, "Ready or not, here I come." The rapture and the Second Coming are like that. These are the people who are obsessed with trying to date-set the rapture of the church. They spend all their time studying obscure passages of the Bible and the events of the Middle East trying to find the date so they can be "ready". But they can never explain what being "ready" actually means. I am ready for the rapture any day. I have been ready for it for 40 years. If it happens in my lifetime (hopefully!) it will not interrupt a single thing I have planned. But I go about my life's business as if I have a full three score and ten and more to serve the Lord. Jesus told us to "occupy till I come" (Luke 19:13). He did not give us the date. I believe the date of the rapture is in the Bible. But I do not believe that any man will ever find it until it happens. We will spend the first several hours after the rapture slapping our foreheads saying, "Why didn't I see that?!" God knows us. If he told us the date of the rapture we would not live our lives according to his principles. It is the same mind-set as the lost who are "just not ready yet". They want to live life to its sinful fullest first, then try to sneak in just before the deadline. All this date-setting does is keep the body of Christ from our mission to share the gospel. Those who are obsessed with date-setting are totally useless in the ministry.

Mid-Tribulation Rapture – This heresy comes from those who see two different rapture passages, but they do not have the courage to pick one. So they split the difference and have the church go through the first half of the Tribulation and get raptured out at the mid-point. There is no need to try to explain this heresy in detail since there is nothing in the Bible that directly supports it. This is simply a compromise that "straddles the fence" for those who cannot make up their mind. Men, you are all painfully aware of what happens when you straddle a fence. A "double minded man is unstable in all his ways" (James 1:8)!

Pre-Wrath Rapture – This teaching has become very popular lately. It is basically the same thing as the Mid-Tribulation heresy with a twist. The "Pre-Wrath" heresy has spawned from our answer to the Mid-Tribulation and Post-Tribulation heresies. We point out that the Bible very clearly says that we are "not appointed unto wrath" (I Thessalonians 5:9). The Tribulation is the time of God's wrath on this earth for the rejection of his Son. The church might be a mess at times, especially Laodicea, but no one in the actual church (as God sees it, not as the denominations or membership rolls report it) has rejected the Son. A person cannot be in the church unless he has received Jesus as his Saviour. So the church cannot be here for the time of God's wrath.

Then here comes the "twist" and it is definitely a "lemon". These teachers say that only the second half of the Tribulation really counts as the time of God's wrath. So they bring the church through the first half, but take her out just before "all hell breaks loose" on the earth. Let me put this into practical terms for you in a way that any parent will clearly understand. Your children would at times pester the devil out of you about something. You would say no to them a dozen times, yet they would continue to ask. In order to end the conflict, perhaps you would use a little reverse psychology and say, "OK, go ahead..." Did you really want them to do it? When you folded your arms and let him have his way, were you just as ticked off as if you had brought out the belt? Maybe more so? The first half of the Tribulation is similar to that. God withdraws from mankind and lets him have his own way. That is what man has wanted since Adam hid from God in the Garden. I will refer you ahead to Revelation 7:1 and my comments there for a full explanation. I can assure you that God's wrath is in full living color and all of its glory in the first half of the Tribulation.

Mid-Tribulation and Pre-Wrath heresies keep the body of Christ in the bondage of fear and turmoil of taking the mark of the beast. Again, it accomplishes essentially the same purpose as the date-setters. We become so worried about protecting ourselves from the Antichrist and prepping for the end that we lose sight of the mission. Guess who is behind the effort to keep God's people off focus?

Post-Tribulation Rapture – This is one of the more popular false teachings among the "prepper" community. We all know people like this, or at least we know OF them. They are convinced that they need to store up seven years of rice and beans with a bunch of ammo in a remote bunker so that they can survive the "zombie apocalypse". Many of these people are just "good old boys" who really are not born again, but they see what is coming and think they have the chutzpah to make it through. But there is an element of genuine Christianity that is falling for this teaching. They are scared to death of the coming Tribulation and they know just enough Bible to be dangerous (mostly to themselves). This is the teaching that the church has to go through the entire Tribulation. As we have seen, there IS a rapture at the end of the Tribulation, but it is not for the church. It is for the Jewish remnant. The church is the bride of Christ. Do you really think Jesus would send his bride through that? What kind of husband would he be?

In all the instructions Jesus gave in Matthew 24 about the Tribulation, show me where he told anyone to stockpile ammunition or hoard food supplies. Quite the opposite. He tells them to take off and NOT "prep" for anything. They don't need to hoard food because the Lord will miraculously feed them like he did with the manna in the Exodus. I get a kick out of these folks, but it is not funny. So Johnny Rambo has his bunker with his rice and beans and ammo. He claims to be a Christian, and let's assume he is. He is well into the Tribulation when his neighbor who is starving approaches him hoping to get a little help. Is he going to shoot his neighbor? That is the "Christian" thing to do, now isn't it? I wonder how the Good Samaritan would handle that scenario. His ammo is there to protect him from attack. I proudly and firmly support the second amendment and the right to protect yourself from criminals and from tyrannical government. But how is one dude holed up in a cellar going to ward off the combined military power of the United Nations "peace keeping force"? This is the David Koresh mentality without the Messiah complex heresy he had. Again, a lot of these preppers are not truly born again, they are just "macho men" who think they will outlast the apocalypse. I just don't see how God would let any of them make it through. Maybe a few will. But knowing God as I do, I can't see it. They would brag about it through the entire Millennial reign. I can imagine those saved preppers (there are many) being caught up at the PRE-Tribulation rapture. There they stand together with the assembled church of the ages before the Lord. A grand celebration is underway, but there is a strained look on their faces. "But Lord, I had all those supplies prepared for the Tribulation!" "I can send you back if you would like…"

An OT Picture of the Three Raptures: Deuteronomy 16:16

I will quote the full verse so you can see it here: "Three times in a year shall all thy males appear before the LORD thy God in the place which he shall choose; in the feast of unleavened bread, and in the feast of weeks, and in the feast of tabernacles: and they shall not appear before the LORD empty."

God told the Nation of Israel that they were to present themselves before him three times in the year, and he identified them as three specific feasts. So it will be necessary to lay out the seven feasts of Israel to see this picture. Leviticus chapter 23 has the information. Israel had seven annual religious celebrations, and all seven of them were significant and important. But in three of them, God required all the men to appear before him in Jerusalem. That is more than just a passing regulation on a whim. It pictures the three times in history in which the people of God will "present themselves" at one of his three raptures.

The Seven Feasts of Israel – Leviticus Chapter 23

We will not do a detailed study of these feasts because it is beyond the point of this book. But a couple of things must be covered first. The seven feasts of Israel were fixed annual celebrations. The calendar of Israel is different than ours. They operate by a lunar calendar on a cycle of 28 days instead of 30-31. Every few years, they add an extra month to sync up with the year, just like we add an extra day every four years in February. Their first month of the year is our March. The last four months of our year show us how our calendars are "off". September is our 9th month, but "Septem" is Latin for seven. An octave is eight, and October is our 10th month. "Novem" is Latin for nine. When you move something a decimal point, you move it ten, not twelve. Instead of nine through twelve, the last four months of our year are "Seven-ber", "Eight-ber", "Nine-ber", and "Ten-ber". Our calendars are different or "off" by <u>two</u>. So as we walk through the seven feasts of Israel, we will "sync" them to our calendar.

1.) <u>Passover</u> – Leviticus 23:5
Fourteenth day of the first month – Mid-to-late March

2.) <u>Unleavened Bread</u> – Leviticus 23:6-8
Fifteenth day of the first month for seven days immediately following Passover

3.) <u>Firstfruits</u> – Leviticus 23:10-14
On the "morrow after the sabbath" (VS 11) of unleavened bread, nine days after Passover; late March and even into early April

The first three feasts were lumped together spanning a period of nine full days. Connected to it was a celebration of the early spring harvest. Leviticus 23:10 mentions the "firstfruits of your harvest". That is not a coincidence. At the time of the "<u>firstfruits</u>", Israel was to present themselves en masse before the Lord. This was NOT at the Passover, but the feast of unleavened bread which immediately followed the Passover. Jesus died on the Passover. Three days later, in the middle of the feast of unleavened bread, he rose from the dead. As we have seen, there was a "firstfruits rapture" after Jesus rose from the dead.

4.) <u>Feast of Weeks (Pentecost)</u> – Leviticus 23:15-21
Fifty days after firstfruits – Roughly late May to early June

There is a gap of time between the first three feasts and Pentecost. The second presentation of Israel en masse before the Lord occurred at this feast. God is consistent. This was the time of the year of the birth of the church in Acts chapter 2. It would be consistent for God to end the church age at the same time of the year he began it, which would make for a clean break of exactly 2,000 years for the church age to the very day. God is precise about certain days of the year. The pattern of selecting a specific day and hitting it on the exact date many years later is not uncommon in the Bible. The classic example is the prophecy of Daniel regarding Messiah the Prince. Daniel prophesied of an exact period of time in Daniel 9:24-27 between the decree of Artaxerxes in Nehemiah chapter 2 and the crowning of Messiah the Prince of 69 weeks, or 483 Jewish years based on their lunar calendar. Sir Robert Anderson in his commentary on the book of Daniel chronicled an exact time of 173,880 days (483 X 360) between the decree and the day that Jesus rode into Jerusalem on a donkey to be proclaimed the son of David. Jesus wept over the city on that day and said, "If thou hadst known in <u>this</u> <u>thy</u> <u>day</u>..." (Luke 19:42). He fulfilled the prophecy of Daniel to the exact day.

So it is not uncommon or unbiblical to think that God would select a specific day to begin the church and then hit the same day to end it. The picture from Deuteronomy 16 shows us that the men of Israel were to present themselves as a group before the Lord on Pentecost. It was the second time in the year, and the rapture of the church which was born on Pentecost is the second rapture of the three. If I am a betting man, I will put my money on the month of June for the rapture of the church. My odds are one in twelve of being right, and I would have no idea what year.

Now hold on to this, please. It appears that I am "date-setting" which would make me just like all the other false prophets who have tried it in the last 30-plus years. I am NOT date setting. But there are certain patterns in the Bible that cannot be ignored. We do not know the day or the hour, but we can and should know the "times and the seasons". God likens his coming to a woman giving birth. She gets a due date early into her pregnancy, but seldom hits it to the day. But there is no question about the "times and the seasons". It is not difficult to know that a young lady is due "any day now", and it should not be difficult for the church of Jesus Christ to know that we are living in the "ninth month". I will revisit this issue of date-setting a little later, but for now we need to stay on point to lay out the picture of the three raptures from the feasts of Israel and the presentation of the men before the Lord.

> **5.) <u>Feast of Trumpets</u>** – Leviticus 23:22-25
> First day of the seventh month – September

> **6.) <u>Day of Atonement</u>** – Leviticus 23:26-32
> Tenth day of the seventh month – Roughly mid September

> **7.) <u>Feast of Tabernacles</u>** – Leviticus 23:33-44
> Fifteenth day of the seventh month for eight days – Roughly late September into early October

There is another gap of time in the Jewish feasts from Pentecost in June to these last three in September. There is a gap of time from the first rapture to the second of 2,000 years. There is a gap of time from the second rapture to the third of 7 years. The gaps of time between the feasts and the presentation of the men picture those gaps of time between the three raptures. This final presentation was to happen at the feast of tabernacles, the last one of the year.

These last three feasts again are closely linked like the first three. They are held in the fall of the year. Leviticus 23:22 mentions the fall harvest and the term "gleanings" is used. The words of the Bible are chosen specifically to communicate truth. The men of Israel were to present themselves en masse before the Lord during the gleanings harvest time, just as the remnant of Israel will be presented before the Lord when they are raptured out in the third part of God's harvest called the gleanings.

The feast of trumpets signifies the calling of the camp of Israel in their wilderness journey. Israel in the Tribulation will be called to the wilderness of Sela-Petra as they flee the Antichrist (Matthew 24:15-21). The Day of Atonement was a national cleansing of sin for Israel. In the middle of the Tribulation, Israel will be purged from their sin when the remnant recognizes Jesus as the Messiah. The feast of tabernacles commemorates the coming of the Lord. It is the one feast that must be observed by all during the reign of Christ in the Millennium (Zechariah 14:16-19). So the feast of tabernacles observes the coming of the Lord, and again, God is consistent. He appeared <u>physically</u> on earth the first time in September around the feast of tabernacles and he will likely tabernacle among men at the same time in his Second Coming.

What?!? I though Jesus was born on Christmas! Au contraire! The Easter Bunny does not visit us in the spring with chocolate eggs either. We do not know the exact date of the birth of Jesus, but September 25 is FAR more likely than December 25. There is ample evidence of this in the Bible, but it will take some digging to find it. Let's walk through the history of his birth as recorded in the word of God.

We begin with John the Baptist, the older second cousin of Jesus. John's father was a priest from the line of Aaron named Zacharias. Luke 1:5-9 says he was performing his duties in his office "in the order of his course" (verse 8). Verse 5 tells us he was "of the course of Abia". We read right past those things in the Bible, but God sticks details like that right under our noses to reveal truth to the honest student. David had arranged the priest's courses toward the end of his reign. By this time, the sons of Aaron had grown in number significantly, and they had the privilege and honor of serving as priests in the tabernacle, and later in the temple. So David divided them into 24 groups so that everyone could have their opportunity every year to serve in the temple. 24 groups would give them roughly half a month each throughout the year. The courses were set and named in I Chronicles 24:1-19. In verse 10, the <u>eighth</u> course was given to Abijah (Abia in Luke 1:5). I have just shown how the Jewish calendar and the Gentile calendar are "off" by two months.

So if March is the first month, then the first two courses would be in March. April would be courses 3 and 4, May would be 5 and 6, and June would be 7 and 8. So Zacharias the father of John the Baptist was serving in his priest's office during the last half of June. As we read the story in Luke chapter 1, Zacharias received a vision from the angel Gabriel announcing that he and Elizabeth his barren wife would have a son who would be the forerunner of the Messiah. Luke 1:23 says Zacharias completed his ministry and went home, and verse 24 says his wife Elizabeth conceived afterward. So John the Baptist was conceived at the end of June. Verse 24 goes on to say that Elizabeth "hid herself" for five months, and Luke 1:26 says in the sixth month that Gabriel was dispatched again with a message to Mary about giving birth to the Messiah. That makes John the Baptist six months older than Jesus, and if John was conceived at the end of June, Jesus was conceived at the end of December. In case you may have forgotten, human gestation is nine months. That places the birth of Jesus at the end of September, right at the time of the feast of tabernacles.

"In the mouth of two or three witnesses shall every word be established" (II Corinthians 13:1). We need at least one more Bible proof of this, so let's come at it from the death of Jesus backwards. We know that Jesus was crucified at the Passover (mid-to-late March). The public ministry of Jesus Christ begins with his baptism. Luke 3:21-23 says that this occurred when Jesus "<u>BEGAN</u> to be about thirty years of age". In other words, Jesus was baptized close to his 30th birthday. The water in the River Jordan in September would be conducive for this, but it would be a bit of a challenge in late December, would it not? Jesus ministered for exactly 3½ years. That is a well known fact, and confirmed by the predominance of that amount of time in the book of Revelation for the false king and the false kingdom to be foisted upon the world. God is consistent, and Satan counterfeits everything God does, so there should be no argument that the earthly ministry of Jesus Christ lasted 3½ years. If he died in March, and his 30th year <u>began</u> with his baptism, that would place his birth in September.

Those are two direct Bible passages that place the birth of Jesus in September. So let's take one more just from circumstantial common sense. Jesus was born outdoors in a manger. Do you really think that God the Father would plan to have that happen in December? We all know that Luke chapter 2 tells us there were shepherds out tending their flocks that night. Again, in December? I know this is just a song and not in the Bible, but we sing "The First Noel" with the line, "Keeping his sheep on a cold winter's night that was so deep…" Really??? Deep with <u>WHAT</u>? That would be <u>snow</u>, in case you were wondering. So what moron takes his sheep out to graze in late December with a foot of snow on the ground?

This has been a long way around the main point, but it was necessary. At issue is the picture of the three raptures from the three feasts of Israel where the men were to present themselves en masse before the Lord. The first time was just after Passover at the feast of unleavened bread picturing the firstfruits of the Old Testament saints just after the resurrection of Christ. The second time is at Pentecost in early June at the same time the church was born picturing the main harvest of the church. The third time was at the feast of tabernacles in the fall which parallels the literal coming of Jesus to earth; first as a baby and later as the conquering King. He will harvest his gleanings at that time just prior to his return.

The Picture of the Bride in Song of Solomon Chapter 2

The book of Song of Solomon contains perhaps the most mystical or cryptic language in the entire Bible. Without dealing with the details of the book, let me "back up" and give the overview. All scripture has three basic applications. Historically, Song of Solomon is a series of "love letters" between Solomon and his favorite bride among the thousand he had. (And I thought Solomon was the <u>wisest</u> man in history!) Practically or inspirationally, the book is a marriage manual. Doctrinally, King Solomon on the throne is a type of the Millennial reign of Jesus Christ, who has a bride called the church. With that picture in mind, watch how the rapture of the bride / church unfolds.

"The voice of my beloved! behold, he cometh leaping upon the mountains, skipping upon the hills. My beloved is like a roe or a young hart: behold, he standeth behind our wall, he looketh forth at the windows shewing himself through the lattice. My beloved spake, and said unto me, Rise up, my love, my fair one, and come away. For, lo, the winter is past, the rain is over and gone; The flowers appear on the earth; the time of the singing of birds is come, and the voice of the turtle is heard in our land; The fig tree putteth forth her green figs, and the vines with the tender grape give a good smell. Arise, my love, my fair one, and come away." (Song of Solomon 2:8-13)

The voice of the Lord will speak some day soon to his bride and bid her to "rise up and come away". Now look at the chronology. It will happen after the "winter is past". The last month of winter is March. Then the "rain" will be over and gone. (April showers…) The flowers will appear on the earth. (…bring May flowers). Then the next event is a June wedding, which traditionally is the preferred month. Earlier I made the case for the rapture of the church around the time of Pentecost, which is in June. Again, I have a one in twelve chance of being right, but my money is on June.

The Picture of Boaz and Ruth

This is another story that portrays the Lord and his church. Boaz is a type of Christ. He was a man of wealth and nobility and godly character from Bethlehem. Is that town familiar? There was a famine in the land (the Tribulation is really a famine), and after the famine, Boaz married a Gentile bride named Ruth, who was a widow. Romans 7:1-4 tells us that once we recognize that our first "husband" of the law is dead, we are free to be married to Christ to bring forth fruit. A widow in the Bible is a picture of a believer in Christ. A Jewish redeemer (Boaz) married a Gentile widow (Ruth) in the time of barley harvest, which is in the spring. Again, this points to a wedding in heaven after the rapture of the church and lands on roughly the same time of the year as the other pictures in the Bible. When that many passages all line up the same way, there has to be something there!

With all of those pictures in the Bible, the time of the rapture of the church has at least some safe clues to its speculation. But please understand that this is only speculation. I have said it many times that I have a one in twelve chance of hitting this, and I am only speculating on the month, not the year. So do not take this information and run with it into heresy. I believe fully that the date of the rapture of the church is in the Bible. I also believe that no one will find it until after it happens. The incessant attempt by prophecy gurus to pin down the exact date of the rapture is not only pointless, but counter-productive to the mission of the gospel. Every time another wacked out fruitcake sets the date and doesn't hit it, the more we look like complete morons to a lost world. It has been relentless for a couple of generations and more. The JW's set a date in 1914. World War I kicked off the same year. They have had dozens of prophecies since then, and every one has proven them to be more of a false cult. We all remember the famous book *"88 Reasons Why the Lord is Coming in 1988"*. It didn't happen. Does that mean there are zero reasons why he would come in 2000? Oh, wait, Y2K was so hyped as the "end of the world" that people were selling everything to live in a cave. Harold Camping set several dates and kept adjusting it every time he was proven yet again to be a false prophet. He finally "retired" from prophecy to keep from making a further fool of himself and rode off into the sunset with a cool $20 million from gullible suckers. We have seen recently the "blood moon" prophets try to set a date. Then the solar eclipse in August of 2017 was surely the day. Then we had Saturn and Mercury passing through Virgo to fulfill Revelation 12 (NOT!). All that does is turn a lost world into skeptics and further harden them against God and the truth of the Bible. I saw a lost newspaper columnist write an article many years ago titled, "Let's Hear It For the Rapture! Earth's IQ Doubles!" That is what they think of all this nonsense. We know Jesus is coming again very soon for his bride. Just shut up about the date and tell others about his sacrifice on the cross so the bride can be ready. Jesus said, "Occupy till I come" (Luke 19:13). He did not say, "Sit around and try to guess when I am coming while the world goes to hell around you." Lost people are not won by debates about the rapture. They are saved by the gospel of grace and the blood of Jesus Christ.

So much of what we read from the date-setters is nothing more than a "SWAG". If you do not know what that acronym stands for, write me and I will tell you. It is simply people who are too full of themselves and want to prove to the rest of the world that they are smarter than everyone. I have said it many times. If someone tells you they found something in the Bible that no one else has seen, RUN, Forrest, RUN!

There is a very good reason why God will not let anyone pin down the date of the rapture even though the information is undoubtedly in the Bible. He knows us. If we knew the date of the rapture, lost people would live in sin until the day before. If you knew that Jesus was coming three months from now, would you pay your mortgage? "Oh, of course I would, pastor!" Why? The bank could not evict you that fast. Then the super-spiritual among us say, "If I knew Jesus was coming, I would tell everyone and be more faithful." Why don't you do it now? If knowing the date of the coming of Jesus would change anything in your life today, then you are not living right today. The Bible describes the coming of the Lord "as a thief in the night" (I Thessalonians 5:1-4, II Peter 3:10, Revelation 16:15). This applies to the rapture and the Second Advent. Jesus is not a thief, but he will show up unexpectedly just like a thief does. So now we have all the prophecy gurus setting dates as if Jesus would reveal it to them. Does a burglar send you a text message telling you what time he will show up at your house? Does a bank robber notify the Police ahead of his heist? Then why would anyone think Jesus would announce the date of the rapture?

I believe the rapture of the church will happen exactly 2,000 years to the day after some Bible event, as God counts. I said earlier that I also believe that information is contained in the Bible, but it is hidden from us. The prophecy teachers have always used the year 2000 AD as sort of a benchmark. But now that it has come and passed, we are re-thinking some things. The church age did not begin with the birth of Jesus, it began with his death. Notice how I worded my statement. After some Bible event is nebulous and unknown. It could be his death. Maybe it was his resurrection. What about the ascension forty days later? Pentecost is a good target also as I have clearly laid out. Acts chapter 7 and the stoning of Stephen slammed the door on the nation of Israel for the time being. That could be another starting point. The destruction of the temple in 70 AD is another possible option, although in my mind less likely.

Add to this the fact that our calendar is likely off. Most historians date the birth of Jesus actually in 4 BC rather than the year zero. There is not enough clear concrete historical information available to establish the exact dates. Then I also said, "as God counts". God often counts differently than we do, and when he does, it is always accurate. God can hit the "pause button" as he sees fit. The classic example of that is in a so-called "contradiction" in the Bible that is not a contradiction. I Kings 6:1 says Solomon began to build the temple in the 480th year after the Exodus from Egypt. Paul identifies a time period of 573 years for the same events in Acts 13:16-22. The count is "off" by 93 years. In the book of Judges, there were five separate times when Israel was under foreign oppression and rule: Judges 3:8 (8 years), Judges 3:14 (18 years), Judges 4:3 (20 years), Judges 6:1 (7 years), and Judges 13:1 (40 years). That totals 93. The actual elapsed calendar time is reported accurately by Paul in Acts 13. But God was counting differently. God was not counting the time that Israel was serving another king, and no one even knew that God had stopped counting until I Kings was written. Who knows if God has counted the full 2,000 plus years of this age the same way we have counted it, and we are not sure we have counted it correctly. There have been many times during the church age when his bride was out serving other kings. God made the sun stand still in Joshua chapter 10 for about a whole day. When Hezekiah was sick, he made the clock go backwards 40 minutes in Isaiah 37:8. Matthew 24:21 says he can "shorten the days". This does not mean the days will be less than 24 hours (although he can do that if he wishes), but that the period of time in question will be cut short for his purposes. So 2,000 years after some event, as God counts, is quite fluid. Our counting is so messed up there is no way we can be sure of even our own calendar. So those who are trying to calculate the date of the rapture Biblically are wasting their time and working against the gospel.

I have one last question for our brethren who cannot let date-setting alone. Jesus said he purposely chose not to know the date of his own coming (Mark 13:32). Are you better than him?

Now that we have a clear understanding of the harvest of God (raptures), the text moves to a description of the sights and events immediately following the rapture of the church. Chapters 4 and 5 of Revelation are parenthetical. The focus is at the throne of God, while the events on earth are put on hold until the first Seal is opened in chapter 6. Again, nothing in Revelation chapters 4-19 applies to a believer in Jesus Christ <u>on</u> <u>earth</u>. None of this happens until we are caught out, and chapters 4-5 happen in heaven.

VS 3 – The first thing we will see is the Lord on his throne. The description is beyond beautiful with precious stones. The jasper is greenish along with the emerald, and the "sardine" (aka sardius) is reddish like a ruby. All three stones are in the breastplate of Aaron (Exodus 28:15-21), the covering of Lucifer (Ezekiel 28:13), and the walls of New Jerusalem (Revelation 21:19-20). We will hold the full study of the lists of these precious stones until we get to Revelation 21.

VS 4 – The twenty four elders are introduced. There is no information in the Bible to identify them. Many have speculated, and their guesses hold as much water as an upside-down bucket. The only thing we can say about them definitively is that they are some group of men from the church age. The number 24 does not give us any added clues to their identity. But since they are a body of elders, they would be representative of the full body of believers in the church age. These elders appear also in Revelation 4:10, 5:8, 5:14, 11:16, and 19:4. In each case, they fall down before the throne and are connected to worship. This verse gives a few added details. They are seated on thrones, so they have some position of authority in God's kingdom. They have white raiment, which is defined as the "righteousness of the saints" in Revelation 19:7. They also have crowns of gold. As representatives of the church age saints, this would be a description of those who have come through the Judgment Seat of Christ. Ephesians 5:27 says Jesus will present the church to himself as a glorious bride "without spot or wrinkle". All of our expressions come from the Bible. So once we "get the problems ironed out", the Lord will grant crowns to his faithful servants. These are the earned rewards of the Judgment Seat of Christ. These crowns are described in the New Testament as follows:

> The Incorruptible Crown – I Corinthians 9:24-27
> > The athlete's crown for those who "train" their bodies to serve the Lord
> The Crown of Rejoicing – I Thessalonians 2:19-20, Philippians 4:1
> > The soul winner's crown that causes rejoicing in heaven (Luke 15:7)
> The Crown of Righteousness – II Timothy 4:8
> > The servant's crown for those who finish the course in anticipation of the Lord's return
> The Crown of Glory – I Peter 5:1-4
> > The shepherd's crown for those who faithfully lead the flock of God
> The Crown of Life – James 1:12, Revelation 2:10
> > The martyr's crown for those who give their lives and / or die to self to deny the flesh

VS 5 – The lightning, thunder and voices are not described. The seven Spirits of God have caused some minor confusion among some. There is only one Holy Spirit of God, yet he manifests himself in many ways. Ephesians 4:4 says there is "<u>one</u> Spirit". This is addressed to the church, describing the indwelling Holy Spirit in the born again believer. After the rapture of the church, this indwelling Spirit leaves. The Holy Spirit does not "leave" the earth after the rapture of the church as some have taught, but the way in which he operates changes. A possible list of the manifestations of the Holy Spirit during the Tribulation is seen in Isaiah 11:2. Proverbs 9:1 says that wisdom has "seven pillars", which could also describe this function. The seven Spirits appear again in Revelation 5:6, again with limited information. Suffice it to say that after the rapture of the church, the Holy Spirit of God will still be omni-present as always, and very much alive and well on planet earth throughout the entire Tribulation. But his indwelling role in born again church age believers will no longer be at work.

VS 6(a) – A crystal sea of glass is mentioned. It is the frozen body of water at the top of the Universe. It will be the place where the redeemed body of Christ first stands after the rapture of the church. This is a little "deep" (pun intended). The Bible begins with a reference to the "deep" in Genesis 1:2. Before the six days of creation, "The spirit of God moved upon the face of the waters" because there was a problem with the "deep", which is a body of water separating God's throne in the third heaven from his creation. When the Bible refers to the deep as a body of water, it can be one of two things. Sometimes it refers to an ocean or large body of water like the Mediterranean Sea. Other times it refers to a large body of water at the top of the Universe. Sometimes it might even refer to both. A body of water on this earth can be a type or picture of the great "deep" in the heavens. Some of those references include these passages.

Psalm 148 – This Psalm describes three heavens in descending order. Verses 1-2 mention the angels, which would be in the "third heaven" (II Corinthians 12:2) known as the throne of God. Verses 3-6 mention the sun, moon and stars, which would be the second heaven (outer space). Then verses 7-14 describe hail, snow and stormy wind which occur in the first heaven of the atmosphere of earth. But take note in verse 4 that there is a body of water "above the heavens". This would be the sea of glass that John stood upon, and upon which we will stand after the rapture of the church.

Job 38:30 – "The face of the deep is frozen". John stands on it in Revelation chapter 4.

Job 41:31-32 – Satan (Leviathan) has his domain in this "deep".

Psalm 104:5-6 – There is a "deep" that is a covering over God's creation.

Proverbs 8 – This chapter describes wisdom, which is personified in Jesus Christ (I Corinthians 1:30, Colossians 2:3). Proverbs 8:23-29 describes creation and mentions the "deep".

Matthew 8:28-34, Mark 5:1-20, and Luke 8:26-39 – The story of the "maniac of Gadara" is told in three synoptic gospels. The account in Luke says the devils asked Jesus not to send them out into the deep (verse 31). Yet they entered a herd of swine and drove them into the lake. So, this could not be a body of water on earth. It was the "deep" of Genesis 1:2.

Isaiah 51:9-11 – "Awake, awake, put on strength, O arm of the LORD; awake, as in the ancient days, in the generations of old. Art thou not it that hath cut Rahab, and wounded the dragon? Art thou not it which hath dried the sea, the waters of the great deep; that hath made the depths of the sea a way for the ransomed to pass over? Therefore the redeemed of the LORD shall return, and come with singing unto Zion; and everlasting joy shall be upon their head: they shall obtain gladness and joy; and sorrow and mourning shall flee away." This describes the Exodus of Israel from Egypt through the Red Sea. Israel passed through a "deep" while being chased by a "dragon" (Pharaoh) and eventually came to Zion under Joshua. The stories of the Bible also have a prophetic application. The picture is of our deliverance at the rapture of the church. The ransomed church (verse 10) will pass over a great deep while being pursued by a dragon (Satan), and will stand upon the mount Zion (Hebrews 12:22). Instead of the temporary joy Israel had in the Exodus, we will have "everlasting joy" (verse 11).

This "sea of glass" will be eliminated in Revelation 21:1. More detail will be covered then.

VS 6(b)-8 – Here we have a description of four beasts at the throne of God. This is another very strange passage that is difficult to grasp fully. All I can give you is my best speculation based on other passages of scripture that describe a similar scene. It says these beasts have six wings each, are full of eyes, and continually praise the thrice Holy God. The four beasts here are a lion, calf, man, and eagle. Four similar beasts are described in Ezekiel chapters 1 and 10, and when we compare the beasts of Revelation 4 with the beasts of Ezekiel, it yields this picture.

Revelation 4:7	Lion	Calf	Man	Eagle
Ezekiel 1:10	Lion	Ox	Man	Eagle
Ezekiel 10:14	Lion	Cherub	Man	Eagle

There is an obvious correlation between the calf, the ox and the cherub. Satan's original position was the anointed cherub that covereth (Ezekiel 28:14), and the context of that passage has him at the throne of God in that position. It appears as if there is currently a vacancy since there are only four beasts "round about the throne" in Revelation 4:6, and none <u>covering</u> the throne. If these beasts are cherubs that picture or represent an aspect of God's creation, then Lucifer would be the "fifth cherub", or more accurately the <u>first</u> cherub, being the anointed one. Another item of note is the connection to the ox or the calf. Most depictions of the gods are bestial in nature. There also seems to be a special place given to the bovine in false worship. Hindus worship cows and India has strict laws regarding them to the point of giving cows more rights than humans in some cases. Baal worship in the Old Testament was <u>bull</u> worship. Aaron made a golden <u>calf</u> in the wilderness. Jeroboam set up calves in Samaria to draw the northern kingdom of Israel away from Jehovah God. Pagan ritual sacrifices of <u>oxen</u> are seen in Acts 14:8-13. When we think something is false, we say it is a "bunch of bulls---". I don't know what to make of all that other than the fall of Lucifer from his position over the throne left a void, and the bull is somehow related.

VS 9-11 – The 24 elders appear again with an added function. Not only do they fall down and worship as in the other places they appear, this time they cast their crowns before the throne. This would be related to the Judgment Seat of Christ. The elders represent the church age saints who have just come through this event and have been granted their crowns based on rewards for service to the Lord in this life. But we don't rightfully get to keep those crowns for ourselves. Anything we "earn" in service to the Lord is actually done by the power of the Spirit of God in us. Our job is to yield ourselves to his control. When we do, JESUS does the work through us. So he should ultimately get the crowns. That does not mean our service is of no benefit to us. I suspect we will get ample praise with a hearty "well done, thou good and faithful servant". Luke 19 says we will get cities to reign over, and Revelation 22:5 says we will be kings and priests with him forever. So there must be some reward for our labour, and there are dozens of verses and passages that say so clearly. But we do not glory in what WE have done, rather we glory in what God does through us as we allow his life to be made manifest in us. Besides, after all that Jesus did for you, how embarrassed would you be to have nothing to offer back to him at this time?

Revelation 5:1-7 – The Worthiness of the Lamb (The Book Unsealed)

Revelation chapter 5 continues in the same context as chapter 4. This is the view at the throne of God immediately after the rapture of the church. The main issue is the opening of the seven-sealed book and the worship that ensues as a result.

VS 1 – We see a book with seven seals that is "in the right hand" of the Father on the throne. So, what is this book? Some believe it is just the book of Revelation since the seals are opened in it. Some believe it would be the book of Daniel, since we are told it was sealed also (Daniel 12:4, 9). I believe it the entire Bible. Isaiah 29:9-12 also mentions a sealed book and says it is the "vision of <u>all</u>". In Isaiah, the book is delivered to the learned (scholars) who cannot read it because it is sealed. This speaks of the gnostics and the religious leaders who claim some form of deeper knowledge that is "sealed" to the rest of us. The Roman Catholic Church for centuries forbade its people to read the Bible under penalty of death for this reason. They say we can't understand it because it is sealed. But their leaders never read it either. They simply concocted a system of rules and rituals that have nothing to do with the Bible and passed it off as genuine. Then in Isaiah 29:12, the book is delivered to the unlearned (common man) who says he cannot open it because he is not learned. He has been lied to and intimidated into believing that the Bible is only for the scholars and that they will tell us what it means when they have no clue themselves.

The book is <u>IN</u> the right hand of God. Jesus is seated at the right hand of the Father, and he is the living Word (John 1:1, 14, I John 1:1-3). His name is the Word of God (Revelation 19:13). The only times in the Bible that the "Word" is capitalized is in reference to Jesus as the living Word incarnate. So this book is the entire mind of Christ and the written form of the living manifestation of the Godhead. Some accuse us of being "Bibliolaters" or worshipping a book. I understand the difference between ink and paper and the living Word of God. I do not have a shrine in my basement to a book. I write in my Bible. But you cannot separate Jesus from his mind, and he left us his full revealed thoughts in the form of ink and paper. That is why I believe this book refers to the entire Bible and not just one or two prophetic books.

The book is sealed with seven seals, the number of perfection. Even those who can crack it open and read it cannot completely unseal what is on the inside. Man has tried for centuries to master the Bible and has failed miserably. I will give you everything I have in this commentary, but the best thing I will give you is that I cannot give you jack diddly. If you bought this book hoping to find all the juicy nuggets of truth that no one else has, you bought it for the wrong reason, and you will be sorely disappointed. Those who claim "secret knowledge" that no one else has are cult leaders. Only God's Spirit can open the Bible to man (I Corinthians 2:9-14, Psalm 119:18, Ephesians 1:18). That is the theme of Revelation chapter 5.

At the same time, it is absolutely necessary to get some balance. The spiritual gift of teaching is in the Bible. That obviously comes from God, but it is given to men (and women, but not in the pastorate). God uses men to teach his word, but no one can teach the word without the empowerment of the Holy Spirit and no one can understand the word without the enlightenment of the Holy Spirit. That explains a very misunderstood verse in the Bible. I John 2:27 says, "But the anointing which ye have received of him abideth in you, and ye need not that any man teach you." This leads many people to abandon the local church and the ministry of the word. They can just get it on their own. They don't need church because "there are too many hypocrites in the church". But as someone has so aptly pointed out, if a hypocrite stands between you and God, it only means he is CLOSER to God than you are.

God always confirms his word through multiple witnesses (II Corinthians 13:1), and God uses not only his Holy Spirit, but gifted people who are empowered by his Spirit to open it to others by teaching. The Bible is for the common man, and anyone can understand it if they will just honestly approach it. But the Bible also must be taught. The entire movement of the new versions has been advertised to the church as the effort to make the Bible "understandable" in the modern vernacular to anyone. I Corinthians 2:14 says the natural man cannot understand the Bible; he has to get it from spiritual discernment. If you have a "Bible" that can be fully grasped by natural intellect, it is NOT God's word.

<u>VS 2-4</u> – The answer to the question of "who is worthy" begins by understanding first who is <u>not</u> worthy. No man in heaven, nor in earth, neither under the earth is worthy. This ties in to Philippians 2:9-11 which tells us that every knee shall bow and every tongue confess that Jesus Christ is Lord. All three classes of people are listed in that passage as well.

No man in heaven – The church has been raptured by this time, so the full body of Christ is in heaven, yet none of us even together can unlock the full revelation of God. If you cannot unlock it then, what makes you think you can do it now?

No man on earth – The Jewish remnant is still on earth at this point for the Tribulation. Daniel 12:4, 9 says the words of the book will be sealed "until the time of the end". There are some things about the book of Daniel that will not be known until the Tribulation, but they will be revealed then. That is another reason why I believe the sealed book of Revelation 5 is the entire Bible.

No man under the earth – Obviously those in hell will never "get it". Luke 16:19-31 describes a man in hell, and Abraham has to explain basic truths to him, yet he never understands.

VS 5-6 – Only Jesus is worthy to open the book. Several characteristics of Jesus are given.

The Lion of the tribe of Juda – The vast majority of the references in the Bible to a lion speak of the "roaring lion seeking whom he may devour" (I Peter 5:8) who is clearly Satan. He is the counterfeit lion. This verse is a reference to Genesis 49:8-12 and the prophecy of the Messiah from Judah.

The Root of David – Revelation 22:16 says Jesus is the "root and offspring of David". Jesus used this same concept to turn the Pharisees inside out in Matthew 22:41-46. How could Jesus be the son of David, and yet David call him Lord? Easy. Jesus is the root because he is God from everlasting and he is the offspring because he was born of the virgin from the line of David.

The Lamb as it had been slain – The speculation is that the nail prints and the side wound will remain in the Lord Jesus Christ for eternity as the only reminder of sin. Doubting Thomas saw those marks in the glorified body of the Lord after he was risen from the dead (John 20:24-29). If those marks were seen then, there is no reason to believe that any change happened to cover them up.

VS 7 – Jesus takes the book out of the hand of the Father on the throne. That is quite a bold move, and I would like to find the individual who thinks he is man enough to try it.

Revelation 5:8-14 – The Worship of the Lamb

VS 8-9 – They sing a new song. A new song in the Bible is NEVER about the style of music but the content of the heart (Psalm 33:3, 96:1, 98:1, 144:9, 149:1, Isaiah 42:10, Revelation 14:3). A "new song" is seen as much as it is heard (Psalm 40:1-3). The content of this new song is given in verses 9-10, and it is about blood and redemption. I will jump on the soap box for a brief rant, then move on with the study of the book of Revelation. Music style has become a battleground in the church today. Some people think that when the Bible mentions a "new song", it must be with drums and electric guitars. Most of the new songs today leave the blood out, just like the new Bibles remove it from Colossians 1:14 and many other verses. If God's new song is about the blood, why is the blood missing from new songs today? A new song is born from the heart. It has nothing to do with style and is never dependent on talent. I can sing a new song because I have been redeemed, but you probably do not want to hear it. That's OK. God hears it, and he likes it even though it is so far out of tune it makes the dogs in the neighborhood howl. Psalm 137:1-4 says we cannot sing the Lord's songs in a strange land. A person out of fellowship with God cannot sing a new song even if he is a Grammy winner.

In verse 8, the four beasts and twenty four elders worship (as always), yet there is an added detail. They have vials of odors which are the prayers of saints. These odors are defined as incense in Revelation 8:3. The incense of the Old Testament is a picture of prayer and the intercessory office of Jesus Christ. When the wise men brought their gifts to Jesus, they understood this. The gold was for his deity as a king. The myrrh (embalming spice) was for his death and sacrifice. The frankincense was for his priestly office.

VS 9 – There will be representatives from every kindred, tongue, people and nation at the throne. Many skeptics ask the age old question, "What about the heathen?" Without going into a long discussion of theology, the quickest and best answer is in this verse. Anyone who wants the truth will be able to get it, and no people group in history will be excluded. If there are no souls from a particular group, it would be an admission by God that he made a mistake in creating them and failed to "seek and to save" any from that group. "Yeah, but what about those who don't speak English? You say the King James is the word of God and the final authority. How can they know God without it?" Every tongue will be represented before the throne. God has chosen at this time in history to preserve his word in the "universal language" of English, but God is not bound by language. Yet the scholars tell us that the only way we can really know God is through Greek and Hebrew. Every tongue will sing a new song at the throne!

40

VS 10 – We shall reign <u>on</u> <u>the</u> <u>earth</u>. That is a direct reference to the Millennial reign of Jesus Christ and our position in it. Those who would spiritualize away the kingdom cannot explain verses such as this. It is future tense and it is after the rapture of the church. Jeremiah 23:5 says there will be a King who will reign in justice on the earth. His church will reign with him. The parable of the talents in Matthew 25 has a parallel in Luke 19 where the reward for his servants is to reign over cities. In the Millennial kingdom, we will work for the government and be kings (lower case) with our King Jesus. We will expand on this in chapter 20 when we detail the Millennial reign of Jesus Christ.

VS 11-12 – The number of angels around the throne is given. Before we get to the number, let's discuss briefly who these angels are. In the original creation, God had an entire angelic host all in subjection to him and singing his praises (Job 38:4-7). The number is not given. We know from Revelation 12 that one third of this angelic host was led astray in a rebellion of Lucifer. Again, we do not know the exact number, but we do know that two thirds remained true to God. These fallen angels became devils (the Bible term) or as we call them, demons. God makes things perfect. His creatures mess it up. Then God restores what was lost. That is the basic "storyline" of the Bible. Without going into a long dissertation that would take us off focus into angelology, those one third of fallen angels must be replaced. In the Old Testament, the term "sons of God" is reserved for angels. In the New Testament, Christians are born again into the kingdom of God as sons of God. So the church replaces the fallen angels. Jesus said that "in the resurrection, they …are as the angels of God in heaven" (Matthew 22:30). In Revelation 5, we are viewing the throne of God immediately after the rapture of the church. So it is likely that this huge group of angels praising God is the restored body of the original angelic host plus the redeemed of the church age. So now the number. It is ten thousand times ten thousand, which is 100 million. Oh, wait. There are also "thousands of thousands". That is an unknown quantity. A thousand thousand is a million and the plural form makes it impossible to know how many more millions there are. Suffice it to say that by this time, there will be oodles of us. And yet God knows each one of us individually as if we are the only one. It is said that the average person can only really have about 100 friends at most. After that, he may have a lot of acquaintances, but time and logistics and sheer human limitations prevent us from having more than about 100 people with whom we can have any meaningful personal relationship. Some of us have a few thousand Facebook friends. But we have no real relationship with most of them. Others may have tens of thousands of Twitter followers, but they don't even know the vast majority of them. Our Lord has <u>billions</u> of Facebook friends and Twitter followers, and he has a closer relationship with each one of them than a husband and wife have. Pretty amazing God we have, huh?

VS 13-14 – God opens the mouth of all creation to praise him. Every creature in heaven (the angels), on the earth (man and animals), under the earth (bugs and chipmunks) and in the sea (fish and amphibian life) together will praise our Lord. John "heard them say…" They will open their mouths or whatever other means they have of communicating and all creation will speak out in a discernable language the praises of our Lord and Saviour Jesus Christ! The last verse of Psalms says, "Let everything that hath breath praise the Lord" (Psalm 150:6). The breath of life is in all creation. Even fish "breathe" water through their gills. Luke 19:40 says the stones will cry out. Isaiah 55:12 says the trees of the field will clap their hands and the mountains and hills will break forth into singing. God will turn loose his entire physical creation to proclaim his glory. Oh what a day, glorious day, that will be!

Revelation Chapter 6 – The Seals

In chapter 6, the focus shifts back to the earth. This is the first of the four accounts of the Tribulation. There is an important point that must be made before we begin looking at this time period. Whenever the prophecy teachers talk about the Tribulation, they always speak of the "hell on earth" and the wars and famines and disasters. That is obviously the most important and interesting part of the Tribulation, but the peaceful first half is usually just glossed over. What little comments are made are just in passing with no details given. Revelation chapter 6 is the only pass that has a reference to the first half when the first Seal is opened. There are seven Seals, Trumpets and Vials (for a total of 21), and 20 of the 21 essentially ignore the first 3½ years of the Tribulation. But this time is crucial. For the Antichrist to get his full grip on the world, he must have a time of peace and prosperity to deceive the world into his false kingdom.

The utopian world-wide false kingdom begins with a peace plan described in Daniel chapter 9. We need to spend some significant time on this passage to tie it in to the Tribulation correctly. Daniel chapter 9 is one of the most vital prophecies of the Bible. All of the Bible is true, and "every word of God is pure" (Proverbs 30:5), but some of the Bible stands head and shoulders above the rest if you can grasp that. The Bible is like a mountain range. All of them are mountains, but Pike's Peak rises above the others. Daniel 9:24-27 is the "Mount Everest" of Old Testament prophecy. The other mountains around Mount Everest are pretty tall in their own right, but Everest sticks out. So does Daniel 9. I will quote the full passage:

> "Seventy weeks are determined upon thy people and upon thy holy city, to finish the transgression, and to make an end of sins, and to make reconciliation for iniquity, and to bring in everlasting righteousness, and to seal up the vision and prophecy, and to anoint the most Holy. Know therefore and understand, that from the going forth of the commandment to restore and to build Jerusalem unto the Messiah the Prince shall be seven weeks, and threescore and two weeks: the street shall be built again, and the wall, even in troublous times. And after threescore and two weeks shall Messiah be cut off, but not for himself: and the people of the prince that shall come shall destroy the city and the sanctuary; and the end thereof shall be with a flood, and unto the end of the war desolations are determined. And he shall confirm the covenant with many for one week: and in the midst of the week he shall cause the sacrifice and the oblation to cease, and for the overspreading of abominations he shall make it desolate, even until the consummation, and that determined shall be poured upon the desolate." (Daniel 9:24-27)

Let's "unpack" the essential elements. This will take some time, so bear with me.

The "seventy weeks" are a total of 490 years. When we see a week, we think seven days because that is the only way we use that term today. But the Bible uses the word "week" the same way we use the word dozen. A dozen is twelve of something, but by itself, the word dozen has no meaning until it is attached to an item. A week in the Bible is a unit of seven usually referring to seven days (Matthew 28:1, Daniel 10:2, 13). But in Genesis 29:27-28 a week is seven years. The weeks in Daniel 9 are years also, which is clearly established by the context of the passage.

This vision was for thy people (Daniel's Jewish brethren) and for the holy city (Jerusalem). Seven things are to be fulfilled during these 490 years. Some people count it as only six. I do not have an argument with that, but however you count them, here is what the Lord was to accomplish with Israel.

1) Finish the transgression – This would be Israel's rejection and "transgression" against God. When they looked the Son of God straight in the eye and said to him, "You work by the power of the devil" (Matthew 12:24), and then later cried out, "Away with him, crucify him!", they brought their rejection to the full. Then Jesus slammed the door on them when he said, "Behold, your house is left unto you desolate" (Matthew 23:38). Their transgression was finished at this point.

2) Make an end of sins – Obviously, there is still sin going on in this world, and even exponentially more than at any time in history. But when Jesus cried out on the cross, "It is finished!", he made an end of sins. He is the Lamb of God which <u>taketh</u> <u>away</u> the sin of the world (John 1:29), and he did that at Calvary.

3) Make reconciliation for iniquity – Jesus reconciled sinners to God through the blood of his cross (Colossians 1:20). The final step of that transaction occurred when he offered his blood on the mercy seat at the throne of God in heaven. It would take too long to detail all the passages in the Bible that tie in to this, but briefly, Hebrews 9:11-12 tells us that Jesus entered the "true" tabernacle of heaven with his own blood to secure our redemption from sin. The rest of Hebrews 9 establishes that the New Testament was sealed and confirmed by the offering of the blood of Jesus Christ "in heaven itself in the presence of God" (Hebrews 9:24). Reconciliation for iniquity was secured then and there.

Those first three items were accomplished at the first coming of the Lord Jesus Christ. Then there is a "break in the action". The last four (or three) items will not be completed until the Second Coming. The break is clearly seen when God only counts 69 of the 70 weeks and leaves the last one hanging.

4) Bring in everlasting righteousness – That cannot happen until Jesus Christ comes to rule and reign in righteousness. Surely you do not believe we have it now, do you? Do you watch the news?

5) Seal up the vision – Daniel has more "visions" to come yet in his life, and the greatest "vision" in the Bible is the book of Revelation. The actual writing of the book completed God's "vision" in print. But these visions are for the future. God even told Daniel to "seal it up until the time of the end" in Daniel chapter 12. We have the full <u>written</u> word of God in our hands, but we certainly do not have the full <u>understanding</u> of it. We will get it when Jesus returns and we get his mind internally.

6) Seal up the prophecy – Many teachers combine the vision and prophecy as one item, and again, I see their point and have no issue with it. But God's perfect number is seven, and you can make a case for the slight difference between vision and prophecy. Vision is what we SEE, and prophecy is what we WRITE. In either case, these items will be sealed up when Jesus is here for his kingdom.

7) Anoint the most Holy – Most commentators will give us one of two different takes on this, and it is quite likely that BOTH are correct. Most say it is the "most Holy <u>place</u>". That would be the cleansing of the Millennial temple at the beginning of the reign of Jesus Christ. That temple will be grossly defiled by the Antichrist in his reign of terror. Others say it is the anointing of Jesus himself as King as the "Holy One of Israel". Again, both are probably true, and actually, one cannot happen without the other. In either case, this will not happen until after the Second Coming of Jesus Christ.

There is a gap of time of about 2,000 years between those two sets of events. As the Jews looked at their prophecies, they could not see the gap. Clarence Larkin did a fantastic illustration of this called "The Mountain Peaks of Prophecy" in his *Dispensational Truth* book. As you approach a mountain range from a distance, you see the peaks, but you cannot see the valley between the peaks until you get past the first peak. The "valley" is the church age. In the middle of one verse in Daniel, there is a 2,000 year "pause button". The only thing that might give you a clue is the break in the time frames outlined in the text. Israel saw their Messiah from the "other side" of Calvary as a conquering King who would rid them of foreign control and establish them as the head of the nations. They did not see his sacrifice for sin until it happened, and they had such a hard time with it that they rejected the Lord as a result. But this "break" in the text in Daniel 9 gives us the concept of "Daniel's 70th Week".

Moving ahead in Daniel 9, verse 25 gives us the time frames. There is a period of seven "weeks" (49 years) and then an additional 62 "weeks" (434 years) to take us to "Messiah the Prince". That totals 69 weeks, but it is broken into two segments. The beginning point is established as the "commandment to restore Jerusalem". This would be the decree of king Artaxerxes of Persia which is recorded in Nehemiah chapter 2. Historians have identified the date of this decree as March 14, 445 BC. Moving ahead to the first period of "seven weeks" would take you just past 400 BC. This is the date of the writing of the last book of the Old Testament, Malachi. Moving forward through the 62 weeks takes us to "Messiah the Prince". This is a reference to "Palm Sunday" or the triumphal entry of Jesus into Jerusalem on the donkey. Sir Robert Anderson, a British scholar from a few generations ago, wrote a commentary on the book of Daniel titled *"The Coming Prince"*. In it, he chronicled a time period from the date of the decree of Artaxerxes in Nehemiah 2 to the triumphal entry. Based on a Jewish calendar of 360 days, these two dates are exactly to the very day 483 years apart. In Luke 19:42, as Jesus wept over the city of Jerusalem, he said, "If thou hadst known… in this thy day…" Skeptics complain about all the "errors" in the Bible (there are none), but how do they answer things like that? Try predicting something that will happen 483 years from now and hit it on the exact day. Go ahead. I double dog dare you.

Daniel 9:26 says after the 62 weeks that "Messiah shall be cut off, but not for himself." That is a direct reference to Calvary where Jesus was "cut off" for my sins, not for his own. Then the next phrase says, "…and the people of the prince that shall come…" That is a different prince, one who wants to mimic the true Prince and take his place. It is the Antichrist who will "destroy the city and the sanctuary". In order to be able to destroy the sanctuary (temple), it must be there, which means it has to be rebuilt before the mid-point of the Tribulation. I will get there in just a minute, but let's briefly touch on the rest of verse 26 before we do. Daniel mentions a flood and a war. The war is the famous battle of Armageddon, and the flood is referenced in Revelation 12:15-16, which I will detail in full when we get to that chapter.

Daniel 9:27 says, "And he shall confirm the covenant with many for one week." The Antichrist who is the false prince will orchestrate a peace plan that will allow the temple to be rebuilt. It will be a seven year treaty between Israel and the Arab nations around her. That will be an amazing feat. The Nation of Israel is the "hot spot" of the world and has been for generations. The "best and brightest" have tried everything they can to solve that problem and have failed miserably. It would take far too long to delve into all the nuances of the Israeli-Arab conflict, and besides, no one knows even a tiny fraction of the issues. It has been going on for 4,000 years and is so convoluted that it will never be solved until Jesus returns. But there will be a world ruler who will temporarily "solve" it with this peace plan. Let's look at just a couple of items of note about that issue before we move on.

Israel was "reborn" as a Nation on May 14, 1948. It has been a thorn in the side of the world and Satan since then. In 1967, Egypt launched an attack against Israel hoping to wipe them off the map. It took Israel six days to rout them so decisively that Egypt cried "uncle" and gave up. It is called the "Six Day War" for the obvious reason. In that war, Israel claimed victory and control of the city of Jerusalem, and specifically the Temple Mount. But the Prime Minister of Israel at that time, Moshe Dayan, agreed to a concession. Although Israel actually owns the temple site, all religious activity is controlled by an Arab council based in Jordan. So even though Israel technically could rebuild the temple because they own the dirt, they cannot because the Arab council owns the right to say what happens on that dirt. Many people look at the concession that Moshe Dayan made as a political blunder, and it probably was, but it sets the stage for the peace plan of the Antichrist. Again, world leaders for 70 years have tried to solve this problem, and every time they think they get somewhere, they only make it worse. Eventually, someone will come on the scene with the political and religious "street cred" to pull off a treaty that allows Israel to rebuild their temple. If it were tried today, how do you suppose the Arab nations would react?

For years, one of the main sticking points has been the "Dome of the Rock" Islamic mosque that sits on the temple mount site. Jerusalem is the third holiest site in Islam (after Mecca and Medina), and this mosque was originally built in 691 AD. We here in the United States have no concept of that type of time frame. If our kitchen is "dated" because it was remodeled a whole 10 years ago, we feel inclined to drop about $50 large to make it modern. This site has been under Arab / Islamic control for over 1300 years (aside from a few brief years during the Crusades). Jews and Bible believers claim that Palestine belongs to Israel, and rightfully so. But the Arabs have been there for 13 centuries! If you have lived in your house for 30 years and have paid it off, you own the property outright (sort of, aside from paying your property taxes or eminent domain). If a "Native American" came up to your front door and demanded that you leave claiming it was his land, you would probably take issue. Multiply those 30 years by a factor of about 45 and you have a small glimpse of the scope of this problem. Then add all the religious issues behind the conflict. So Israel wants to rebuild their temple. An Islamic mosque has been sitting on the site for 1300 years. Israel will not concede to just build it elsewhere; it has to be on the exact site of the original Holy of Holies, which is not their third holiest site, it is their ONLY one. This exact location is only 15 feet square (10 cubits), and it must be identified precisely to rebuild the temple. Jews today will not walk on the area out of fear of inadvertently stepping on the spot. Until recently the only solution was to tear down the mosque. Good luck getting 13 centuries of Arabs to agree to that. Add to that the intense hatred these groups have for each other, and you can see how impossible this problem is.

Recent information has come to light that suggests that the Dome of the Rock is not exactly on the site of the original Holy of Holies. It is now believed that the original temple site is about 300 yards to the north of the mosque, and that area right now is a vacant concrete slab. If that is true, then the temple can be rebuilt without touching the mosque. But once again, try getting the Arab council to agree to that. All this has been greatly summarized, but I trust you have the basic picture in mind. If you want to explore this further, there are many good sources to read about the plans to rebuild the temple in Jerusalem. One of the best is a book titled *"The New Temple and the Second Coming"* by Grant Jeffrey. I do not have time here to detail this much further, and I am only a neophyte on the topic. Mr. Jeffrey does it far better than I ever could, so I would encourage you to get his book. It is a fascinating read.

Drawing a bead on this to get back to our study of Revelation; there will be a world ruler rise on the scene of human history who will be used of Satan and gain enough of his wisdom to orchestrate a peace treaty between Israel and the Arab nations to rebuild the temple. He will be hailed as the "Messiah" of Israel, the "Christ" of Christianity, and the "Twelfth Imam" of Islam. But it will be a ruse and a ploy to draw Israel into his lair. He will "rope-a-dope" them into accepting him as their "Christ" (anointed Messiah) so he can turn on them and "sit upon the mount of the congregation in the sides of the north" (Isaiah 14:13) in the temple in Jerusalem, "shewing himself that he is God" (II Thessalonians 2:4).

In Daniel 9:27, this false prince will break the covenant "in the midst of the week". Halfway through, at the 3½ year mark, the Antichrist will "cause the sacrifices to cease". Here is where a little logic must be employed. If the sacrifices are stopped, they have to be taking place, and if the sacrifices are taking place, the temple must be there. The entire purpose of the peace plan is to get the temple in place so that the Antichrist can achieve his goal of claiming to be God. He will demand that Israel sacrifice to HIM now. I will leave this discussion here for now, but keep this all in mind, and be ready to refer back to it. When we get to the "Revealing of the Wicked" in Revelation chapter 13, more of this will come into focus.

Back to Revelation 6:1, this peace plan is the heart and soul of the first half of the Tribulation and the world-wide apostasy that is the first Seal. The vast majority of the Bible references to the Tribulation deal with the last half, and virtually all of the prophetic studies available today likewise. But the peaceful first half must also be understood. It is the "roll out period" for the full implementation of the world-wide lock down under the mark of the beast. The rapture of the church will occur, and it will obviously be a significant event. CNN and Fox News will cover it. The world religions will explain it away somehow as the judgment of God on the "anti-humanitarian" Bible thumpers. It will be explained as a positive step forward for mankind. Some of the prophecy teaching and productions have people screaming and crying about "missing the rapture". No one will do that. The world will be glad that we are gone, and by the way, the feeling will be mutual!

Revelation 6:1-2 – The First Seal – The White Horse

The first Seal announces a white horse rider. This is the first of the "Four Horses of the Apocalypse". This rider is NOT Jesus Christ. Many of the commentators believe this is Jesus going into all the world to "conquer it" peaceably through the church. This is the position of both post-millennial and a-millennial teaching. Those who teach post-millennialism say that Jesus will subdue the world through the church, and once we have made the world "Christian" and suitable for the Lord, then he will return and reign over it. The Catholic Church tried that for 1,000 years. It is called the Dark Ages for a reason. That is an evolutionary view of mankind, claiming that we are getting better and better until we finally figure it all out. Those who want to "conquer" the world through religion will always have jails, torture chambers, and death campaigns against their dissenters. A-millennialists believe Jesus will never reign on earth. So they also think he is the white horse rider in chapter 6. Their approach is different, but the basic outcome is the same. Jesus rides his white horse until he conquers the world and everyone is a "Christian". Then we all go to heaven and sit on white clouds playing our harps in our white robes eating marshmallows for eternity. Just like the post-millennialists, this group also carries out their kingdom building by force.

The white horse rider of Revelation chapter 6 is Satan. He is the counterfeit Christ. The closer he can get to the real thing, the better his deception works. The confusion comes from comparing this passage with Revelation 19:11-15 and another white horse rider. That one IS Jesus. Some teachers try to make them the same, but compare the passages and what follows after them and note these differences.

Antichrist (Revelation 6)	Jesus Christ (Revelation 19)
A bow	A sword
A crown	Many crowns
Peace is taken from the earth (VS 4)	King of Kings reigns – Peace thru strength
Death and Hell follow (VS 8)	Armies in heaven follow (VS 14)

The first Seal is the "peaceful" takeover of the Antichrist by his world-wide deception. This is the falling away described in II Thessalonians 2:3. This rider has a bow, but he has no arrows. He does not need them (yet) because the kingdom is granted to him without the need for force. Daniel 11:21 alludes to this, "He shall come in peaceably, and obtain the kingdom by flatteries". Revelation 6:2 says a crown is given unto him. The world just cedes all control to this man because of his masterful art of diplomacy. It will be a bloodless conquering of minds. II Corinthians 4:3-4 says Satan is the god of this world who blinds the minds of unbelievers. II Thessalonians 2:11 says God will send "strong delusion" to those who have rejected his Son, and they will believe a lie. The deception of the news media and the oratory skill of the religious and political leaders will bring the entire world under the mind control of the Antichrist. The primary vehicle will be the peace plan described in Daniel chapter 9 which will allow the temple to be rebuilt. We will see more on this when we get to Revelation chapter 13 and the Revealing of the Wicked.

Revelation 6:3-4 – The Second Seal – The Red Horse

Seals 2 through 4 are opened virtually simultaneously 3½ years after the first one. They announce the coming disasters commonly associated with the Tribulation. This second Seal introduces the red horse of the Apocalypse, the color of blood. This horse is given power to take peace from the earth. Peace must be in place in order for it to be taken from the earth! This is another reference to the peaceful first Seal spanning the first half of the Tribulation period. The rider of this horse has a sword, but it is not like the one coming out of the mouth of the Lord Jesus Christ in chapter 19. This sword "paints the town red" with bloodshed. This is man's base nature coming into full manifestation. Jesus alluded to this in John 8:44 when he said that Satan was a "murderer from the beginning". The Antichrist's "one world religion" of the Tribulation is designed to get humanity under the control of his agenda and then launch bloodshed to get as many of them in hell as fast as possible before anyone can get the truth to them.

Revelation 6:5-6 – The Third Seal – The Black Horse

The third Seal introduces the black horse which represents famine and economic collapse. The rider of this horse has a pair of balances in his hand for "weights and measures". Proverbs 11:1 says, "A false balance is abomination to the LORD: but a just weight is his delight." We often use this verse to teach that we need balance in our lives, and it is certainly applicable. But it is more appropriately related to the "scales of equality" in business matters. The context in Revelation points that out by describing the value of commodities during the Tribulation. A measure of wheat and three measures of barley will go for a penny. Those are the basic food supplies for bread. We see a "penny" and think that is dirt cheap, but the Bible says otherwise. The parable of the vineyard in Matthew 20:1-16 shows us that a penny is a day's wage. In today's economy in the average American family, that would be about $200. Imagine an economy where $200 will buy just enough bread for one person for one meal. How would an average family survive such an economy? This is not a book on investment strategies, so don't get carried away. But a lot of the financial gurus today are urging us to buy gold as a "hedge against inflation". That might be fine advice for now. I won't say one way or another; you work that out in your own life. But during the Tribulation, the most precious commodity will be food. When this market crash comes, a gold coin won't do anyone any good. It doesn't taste good and has no nutritional value. Daily survival will be about finding something to eat, as much of the world lives even today.

Then there is a cryptic statement at the end of verse 6: "See thou hurt not the oil and the wine." I have seen various opinions on this, but nothing definitive, and I don't have anything clear either. It could be that no one has any money to buy these items. It could also be a reference to the "elites" and their role in this world-wide economic depression. James chapter 5 makes it clear that anyone with money during the Tribulation is wicked. That is not the case today, and was certainly not the case in the Old Testament. It is the LOVE of money that is the root of all evil, and people today can have plenty of it yet still be right with God. Not in the Tribulation. For anyone to have anything, they have to sign up with the mark of the beast. All money is controlled through that system. So the oil and wine are not hurt because the elites have their money and have set up the world system and economy to protect themselves.

Revelation 6:7-8 – The Fourth Seal – The Pale Horse

The fourth Seal has a horse with all the color drained out of it. The horse is "lifeless". That is why its rider is named Death (capitalized). Capitalization in the Bible generally means personification, so this rider is the "Death Angel". The power of Satan to cause death will be unleashed (Hebrews 2:14-15). Hell (personified) follows this rider. Those who succumb to this carnage have the lake of fire waiting for them. One fourth of the earth's population will be affected by the Death Angel in a very short time. Four methods of death are mentioned: the sword (crime and warfare), hunger (famine), death (pestilence and disease), and beasts of the field. God will turn the animal creation loose against people who reject him.

Let's run a couple of numbers. There are currently over 7 billion souls on this planet. Only God knows how many are truly born again believers, but let's just say that a billion of us go out at the rapture, just to make the numbers round off. That would leave 6 billion. If one fourth of them die in the space of a very short period of time, that would be 1.5 <u>billion</u> people! I live in Kansas City. The population of metro Kansas City is roughly 2.5 million. Again rounding off, if 2 million are still here at the mid point of the Tribulation, it would mean that half a million people in my city would die in one event. Who would bury them? How would commerce continue? If you had your gold coin to buy some food at the local grocery store, who would be working there to stock the shelves?

I began working on this commentary just before the outbreak of the "COVID-19" pandemic that gripped the entire world during most of 2020. We often say, "I have seen it all", but that was something none of us had ever experienced before. Essentially, the entire world was "shut down" for several months as we dealt with this "pestilence". The real numbers are subject to debate and will likely never be known until glory, but the estimated count was approximately 400,000 deaths during the span of the first 6 months. Compare that to 1.5 billion in much less time. During the Coronavirus pandemic, we saw shortages on supplies. Store shelves were bare for some of the supposed "essential" items (like toilet paper?!). People were on "lock down" to try to stop the spread of the pandemic. Governments used cell phone GPS surveillance to varying degrees to try to control the spread. You saw a brief snapshot of the Tribulation.

The Black Death plague hit Europe nearly 700 years earlier, and was most intense from about 1348-1350. The plague affected the people and animals both. Animals caught the plague while rooting through the clothing and corpses of dead humans. Once caught, life expectancy was about two days. An estimated one third of the population of Europe died in the span of about 18 months. About 57,000 people died in Marseilles, France in one month. England saw 2.5 million people die from the plague, which was half of the population. Some areas saw as many as nine out of ten dead. Ships at sea would just float along with everyone on them dead. Commerce was totally disrupted as the only thought was daily survival. This is the closest the world has ever seen to a complete collapse.

The pale horse will take those events and ramp them up beyond the wildest imaginations of even the most creative script writers and movie producers. If we had trouble finding supplies during COVID-19, just think what it will be like when many of the farmers who produce the food are dead, and one third of the truckers who deliver it are dead, and stores cannot stock it on shelves because they are all out of business. It will be dog-eat-dog, every man for himself, and total and complete anarchy and chaos.

Revelation 6:9-11 – The Fifth Seal

The fifth Seal takes us back to the throne of God for another brief view of activity in heaven. The martyrs will be crying out for justice. Specifically, these are the martyrs of the Tribulation period up to this point in time. The view into the throne actually spans the entire time of the Great Tribulation, so any of the 144,000 who are captured and beheaded will be in this group. They ask, "How long, O Lord?" That is the same cry found many times in the book of Psalms. In fact, the exact phrase "how long" appears 18 times in the book of Psalms (a 666 coincidence?). It is the cry of the Tribulation saints as they are going through the sufferings and the persecution of the Antichrist. In the next chapter, we will cover the sealing of the 144,000 and the instructions given to them by the Lord in the middle of the Tribulation. Most of what he will tell them relates to the persecution they will face at the hands of the Antichrist. The message of the 144,000 is very harsh and unpopular. Many will be betrayed and turned over to the authorities for having the audacity to go against the system (Matthew 24:9-10). This passage says they will be slain for their testimony. When they cry out for justice, they will be given white robes and told to wait until some of the others in their group are also "killed as they were" in the same manner of beheading. Notice these souls are not "asleep". They are aware and conscious of their surroundings and they are also aware of what has happened to them, and what is happening on earth at the same time. The "robes" cover a bodily shape. A soul is the "spiritual body" of man (I Corinthians 15:44) with all of the same characteristics of our physical bodies. A human being is a three-part creation of God. God formed man of the dust of the ground (body), breathed into his nostrils the breath of life (spirit) and man became a living soul as it says in Genesis 2:7. Man is a soul. He has a body wrapped around the outside and a spirit inside to animate it. I Thessalonians 5:23 lists all three parts. The story of the rich man and Lazarus in Luke 16:19-31 shows this. Lazarus had fingers. The rich man had eyes and a tongue. He remembered his life on earth. They were aware and conscious of their surroundings. The rich man was suffering the torments of the flame. Lazarus, though he did not speak, was being comforted, so he was aware. Abraham carried on a dialogue with the rich man. The rich man knew that he had five brothers still on earth who needed to hear the news. Funny how "evangelistic" some folks get after it is too late.

This group is called the "souls under the altar". I want to take off into an area of speculation that may leave many of you in shock. Again, when I give my opinion on things like this in Revelation, please understand it is my opinion, and is subject to disagreement and error. I throw these things out because I see them in the Bible, but these things are WAY down the list of doctrine or dogma. But it is important to examine the whole counsel of the word of God (Acts 20:27), especially in Revelation. The question has been posed, "Which altar are these souls under?" As John is viewing it, he sees souls in heaven, not bodies on earth, so the altar must be the one at the throne of God in heaven. These souls are "under" it in the sense that they have been covered by the blood of the sacrifice of Christ, allowing them to be there. But remember that the temple has been rebuilt in Jerusalem, and there is another altar there as well. I believe the first application of this is the altar of heaven as I have just established. But as with everything in the Bible, there are always many layers of revelation and information. Things on earth picture things in heaven, and the Bible is filled to the brim with types. These souls "under the altar" could also be said to have been located at one time under the altar in Jerusalem while they were still attached to the body they inhabited. Stay with me as I dive headfirst off a huge cliff into the deep end of the pool with this.

The Antichrist will move to Jerusalem half way through the Tribulation just after his assassination and the false resurrection described in Revelation 13. He will proclaim himself to be God (II Thessalonians 2:4) and enter the "holy place" reserved for God alone (Matthew 24:15). At this point, he will break his treaty with Israel and cause their sacrifices to cease (Daniel 9:27). But instead of making all sacrifices stop, he will re-direct them. Since he wants to be God, he could easily claim that all sacrifices are now to be done to HIM. This is one of the main contributors to unmasking him as the Antichrist. We will cover that in detail in the Revealing of the Wicked in chapter 13. If so, he will want sacrifices. Israel will flee into the wilderness and the animal sacrifices will cease. So, guess who? When one of the Jewish witnesses is captured and refuses the mark, he could be brought to Jerusalem and be "put on trial" before the "god of this world" who is now enthroned in Jerusalem. He could be given the opportunity to recant. The Roman Emperors and the Roman Catholic Church carried out this scenario millions of times throughout church history. Many believers in Jesus Christ recanted out of abject fear and in a moment of weakness. Don't criticize. We would hope our faith is strong enough to endure such a trial, but you have no idea what you would do until you would actually be in that position. Most if not all of the Jewish witnesses who are captured will refuse the mark and lose their head in the process. Satan counterfeits everything God does, so the animal sacrifices of the Old Testament could likely be repeated with these captured witnesses.

The animal sacrifices of Israel were brought to the altar of the tabernacle. The priest laid his hands on the head of the sacrifice as a picture of conferring judgment for sins upon the animal (Leviticus 1:4). The animal then had his blood drained at the altar and was cut into pieces for the burnt offering. After the sacrifice was burnt, the meat was taken home by the priests and consumed by him and his family. It is not out of the realm of possibility that this could also be replayed in the "sacrifices" of the 144,000 at the altar in Jerusalem. The Catholic Church for centuries has claimed that they are eating the actual literal flesh of Jesus and drinking his actual literal blood, taking John 6:48-58 literally instead of spiritually as it was intended (John 6:63). The Catholic Church is the Antichrist's religious system. They have been eating human flesh for centuries (so they say). Why not take their literal perversion even more literally when their vile Antichrist is actually on his throne? We thought man had "evolved" enough (not!) that we would move past the gruesome and barbaric practice of beheading. Then here comes modern day Islam to bring it back. Just because the idea of human cannibalism is so repulsive to a civilized mind does not mean it cannot or will not happen, especially given who we are talking about. There is an actual instance of this recorded in the Bible in II Kings chapter 6 when a woman ate her own son in a famine. Consider Psalm 14:4, "Have all the workers of iniquity no knowledge? who eat up my people as they eat bread, and call not upon the Lord." Catholics eat bread that is flesh that is bread every time they go to Mass. The world will be so duped and enthralled with the man of sin that it will not take any effort at all to get them to make the transition from bread-flesh to real flesh.

Zechariah 11:15-17 is a direct prophecy of the Antichrist. Verse 16 has him eating the "flesh of the fat", and the verse talks about people, not animals. In the same context, verse 9 says it clearer, "…let the rest eat every one the flesh of another." Psalm 16:4 says, "Their sorrows shall be multiplied that hasten after another god: their drink offerings of blood will I not offer, nor take up their names into my lips." Drink offerings of blood have been part of Satanic ritual practices for ever. God confirms his word with multiple witnesses, so consider these verses also: Psalm 27:2, Jeremiah 19:9, Ezekiel 5:10, and Micah 3:3.

I gave the disclaimer up front that this would be shocking and revolting. To think of cannibalizing other human beings is just about as gross and heinous a sin as I can imagine. But you know it happens. Why would it be so unreasonable to think that the most disgusting and vile person to ever walk this earth (the Antichrist) would stoop to such filth?

Revelation 6:12-17 – The Sixth Seal

Here we have the first account in Revelation of the return of Jesus Christ to earth. Verse 17 could not be clearer: "The great day of his wrath is come". Let's deal first with the physical phenomena described in verses 12-14. I take the Bible literally until it is not possible, so most of what we find in these verses will be actual literal physical occurrences connected to the Second Advent of the Lord Jesus Christ.

There was a great earthquake (VS 12) – I mentioned this earthquake briefly in the introduction as one of the "registration marks" to keep the four accounts together. This earthquake is mentioned again in Revelation 11:13-19 and 16:18-20. More details are given in the other accounts. Chapter 16 says it will be the largest in the history of the world. The Richter scale will go full tilt. It will be so massive that Jerusalem will be divided into three parts. No more information is given as to how and what the purpose is, so we are left to speculate. This earthquake will cause mountains and islands to be moved out of their place (6:14, 16:20). There was a massive earthquake in Chile a few years ago that actually moved a significant chunk of land. It could be measured by satellite GPS technology. Scientists told us that it slightly altered the earth's rotation briefly. That is a powerful quake! It is nothing compared to this one. This time is prophesied in Isaiah 24:16-23. It says the earth will be "moved exceedingly" and "reel to and fro like a drunkard". Zechariah 14:4 says when Jesus returns, he will "put his foot down" on the Mount of Olives and it will split in two. It is likely the same event as this earthquake. Revelation 11:13 gives some more information. Jerusalem will be divided into three parts, and one tenth of the city will fall. Again, nothing more is said about the geological result of one tenth of the city being destroyed, but it also mentions that 7,000 people will die in this quake.

The sun will be black as sackcloth of hair and the moon as blood (VS 12) – The phenomenon of this sign in the heavens is covered many times in the Bible. The most notable is in Joel 2:28-32, which was quoted by Peter in his Pentecost message in Acts 2. Charismatics love to jump on this prophecy as the fulfillment of their speaking in tongues. But the heavenly phenomenon did NOT occur in Acts 2, and it certainly does not occur every time another messed up believer speaks in tongues. This will not happen until the return of Christ, and when it does, it will be seen by all as a literal event. This is also a picture of a spiritual truth. The <u>sun</u> is darkened because the world has rejected the <u>Son</u>, and the earth is like blood because we return with him to judge the Christ-rejecting world.

The stars of heaven will fall to the earth (VS 13) – Here is an example of something that cannot be taken literally as far as a physical event. Each star in the heavens is many hundreds of times larger than earth. If they "fell to earth", the earth would be incinerated and vaporized. If it is physical, it could simply be a massive "shooting star" light show. Stars are a type of angels (Revelation 1:20), so I take this to literally apply to fallen angels. Here also is another example of how the Bible is not always exactly linear or chronological. Satan and his angels will fall to the earth at the mid-point of the Tribulation (Revelation 12:7-9). This statement simply reinforces that truth.

The fig tree casts her untimely figs in a fierce wind (VS 13) – The fig tree is a type of Israel. Jesus told a parable about a fig tree in Luke 13:6-10. Israel is a self-righteous Nation trying to cover their sin with the fig leaves of works and the law. In that parable, it takes four years for this particular fig tree to bear fruit. Abraham was born in 1996 BC according to the standard Bible chronology, so it will take Israel 4,000 years to finally bear fruit for God in the Millennium.

The heavens will be rolled up like a scroll (VS 14) – When the Lord Jesus Christ returns, the physical world and the spiritual world will converge. Right now, we cannot see into the spirit world apart from the revelation of God in his word. In the kingdom, it will be visible to the human eye. The best example of this is during the 40 day ministry of Jesus after his resurrection. He was in his glorified form at that time, yet he appeared to the apostles (and others – I Corinthians 15:5-8). They saw him with their eyes and even ate with him (Luke 24:36-43). During the Millennial kingdom, Jesus will be on the throne and the glorified church will reign with him on earth and be visible to all.

Verses 15-17 describe the abject fear that grips the lost world as they see the Lord Jesus Christ "coming in the clouds of heaven with power and great glory" (Matthew 24:30). The people who are alive at this point will cry out, "Hide us from the wrath of the Lamb!" Lost man instinctively knows right from wrong and good from evil. He understands perfectly the wrath of God against sin. One of the common excuses is "I never knew", but that cuts ZERO ice with God. They want the rocks and the mountains to fall on them, meaning they try to hide in their fortified underground bunkers from the wrath of God. Saddam Hussein tried it. Didn't work. Osama Bin Laden, ditto. Every world leader has an escape route against attack from the enemy. Job 34:20-22 says, "In a moment shall they die, and the people shall be troubled at midnight, and pass away: and the mighty shall be taken away without hand. For his eyes are upon the ways of man, and he seeth all his goings. There is no darkness, nor shadow of death, where the workers of iniquity may hide themselves." Ready or <u>NOT</u>, here he comes! Are you ready?

But I want to point out a significant detail in verse 15. We will see this more as we move forward, but by the time of the Second Advent, the population of the earth will have been <u>significantly</u> reduced by a huge margin. There is at least one time when one fourth of the population will die in one single event, and another time when one third will die. Add the general famines and pestilences along with the world-wide nuclear war, and we could see the earth's population reduced by maybe even 90%. But notice who is left at the end of this. There are seven groups listed: (1) kings, (2) great men (3) rich men, (4) chief captains, (5) mighty men, (6) bond men, and (7) free men. Six of those seven groups are the "elites". Anyone who is "free" in the Tribulation is in the "club". The elites KNOW something is coming. They have no idea what it is and why and where it comes from, but they KNOW the course of this world is unsustainable on its current trajectory. They have the system set up to protect themselves, and "to hell with the rest of us". They will keep a few "bond men" around to be their servants, but the vast majority of the population will just be "collateral damage". When Jesus actually returns, he will get a shot at them directly.

We need to see one final thing from the Seals in Revelation chapter 6 before we move on to the Trumpets. It is astounding to see the parallels between the Seals and Matthew chapter 24. Watch how the exact order of the Seals is laid out as Jesus prepares his people to come through this "time of Jacob's trouble".

Matthew 24:4-5	*Deception*	*1st Seal – White horse*
Matthew 24:6-7a	*War*	*2nd Seal – Red horse*
Matthew 24:7b	*Famine*	*3rd Seal – Black horse*
Matthew 24:7b	*Death and Hell*	*4th Seal – Pale horse*
Matthew 24:9-28	*Trib martyrs*	*5th Seal – Souls under the altar*
Matthew 24:29-30	*Second Advent*	*6th Seal – Second Advent*

Whoever preached Matthew 24 knew something about Revelation 6 before it was written!

Revelation Chapters 7-11 – The Trumpets
The Second Pass Through the Tribulation

Revelation Chapter 7 – Seals or Trumpets?

There is a bit of a conundrum with Revelation chapter 7. If there are four passes through the Tribulation (no doubt in my mind), then this chapter poses a problem with its placement. It is set between the 6th and 7th Seal which would include it with the Seals and the first pass. However, it is <u>after</u> the Second Advent passage in Revelation chapter 6, which would place the chapter with the Trumpets and the second pass through the Tribulation. So where does it fit? Is the first pass chapters 4-6 or 4-7? I would not have a major issue either way. It doesn't matter as long as there are four separate passes through the Tribulation. Revelation chapter 7 could be taught as part of the Seals, but if so, it would have to be a "flashback". The subject of chapter 7 is the sealing of the 144,000 which happens at the mid-point of the Tribulation. The Bible is not always chronological, so it would not be an issue. So as I see it, the seventh Seal effectively opens the seven Trumpets, which we will see in Revelation 8:1.

But I place Revelation chapter 7 with the Trumpets for a couple of reasons. The main one is to keep the "registration marks" of the Second Advent together. The best way to see the four separate passes of chapters 4-19 is to identify clearly the four times the Second Advent is seen. Keeping them together puts the first division after chapter 6 and not 7. Another reason I divide it this way is because of the wording of Revelation 7:1. That statement is one of the keys to the "four color process" of chapters 4-19. When John said, "After these things I saw…" it resets the chronology. We have to go back to the beginning of the Tribulation and come through again. That makes chapter 7 fit into the section of the Trumpets. This chapter illustrates the overlap and connection between the four sections and how they relate to each other.

Revelation 7:1-8 – The Sealing of the 144,000

VS 1 – Here we have one of the so-called "scientific errors" that skeptics find in the Bible. It says four angels stood on the four <u>corners</u> of the earth. So the Bible cannot be scientifically accurate because the earth is round and does not have corners. Yes, Einstein, we know that. Isaiah 40:22 says the earth is a circle. Luke 17:28-37 describes the Second Coming, which happens at a set time instantly. The passage says it will be day for some and night for others. In other words, there is day and night at the same time on earth, and that happens because the world is round. By the way, science always has to catch up with the Bible. Those passages were written long before scientists figured out the earth was round.

The "four corners" are the four wind directions which are mentioned in the context. When you look at a two-dimensional map, it has four corners. The skeptic scientists always miss the point. While they are trying to find errors in the Bible so they can justify their rebellion against God, God puts a truth in the passage for the honest student that the scientists can never see. Wind in the Bible is a picture of the Holy Spirit (John 3:7-8). This verse says the wind will cease for a period of time over the entire earth. It is debatable whether this will be an actual physical phenomenon. It might be, and I tend to believe it is. If so, that will be quite the event. I am sure the weather channel will have some comment. Global warming will be blamed. But whether this wind event is physical or not is still not the main point. God is showing us one of the key aspects of the Tribulation. God will withdraw his Spirit from mankind. Genesis 6:3 says God's Spirit will not always strive with man. That verse historically deals with the time of Noah and the flood. But it also points ahead to the Tribulation. Noah's flood is a type of that time as Jesus said in Matthew 24:36-41. Man has wanted God to butt out of his affairs from the beginning of time. As soon as Adam sinned, he hid from God (Genesis 3:9-10). Job 21:14 says, "Therefore they say unto God, Depart from us; for we desire not the knowledge of thy ways." Jesus told us in John 3:19-21 that lost men run from the light. Man wants nothing to do with God, and in the Tribulation, he will grant them their desire. Be careful what you ask for, you might just get it. In this case, they will rue the day.

VS 2-3 – The command is given not to hurt the earth or sea until the servants of God are sealed. Implied in this is that <u>after</u> they are sealed, that they <u>can</u> hurt the earth and the sea. That is the nature of the Seals, Trumpets and Vials as the judgment of God is poured out on the earth. The 144,000 will be sealed at the mid-point of the Tribulation. Then all hell will break loose on earth including environmental disaster. Al Gore and his wackos are RIGHT (to a point). There will be an environmental apocalypse far beyond the wildest nightmares and doomsday predictions of even the most ardent extremists. But it is not caused by our S-U-V, it will be caused by man's S-I-N. We will see it in more detail in the Trumpets and the Vials.

VS 4-8 – The 144,000 are identified as 12,000 men from each of the twelve tribes of Israel. But there is a minor "tweak" in exactly which tribes are included. Israel had twelve sons who are the twelve tribes, but practically speaking, there are actually 13 tribes of Israel. Levi was singled out as the priest tribe in the Old Testament and did not receive a land inheritance. Joseph's sons were split into two tribes (Manasseh and Ephraim) to bring the number back to twelve. The list in Revelation 7 includes Levi but does not include the tribe of Dan. Both of the sons of Joseph are included, but they are listed as Manasseh (VS 6) and Joseph (VS 8) instead of Ephraim. There are five major places in the Bible where the tribes of Israel are listed. They are listed in a different order in all five places. So the question becomes, "Is there any significance to the differences in the order of the tribes in these passages?" The answer is "Yes". But I have no idea what the significance is. Everything in the Bible is by design for a specific purpose, but quite often, I have no clue what that might be. I will list the five places in birth order first since that is how they obviously first appear, then list the other four to line up with the birth order so we can see which tribe is "missing" and draw some lessons from that. I don't know why the order is jumbled up in the various passages, but I do have a fairly good idea why the lists have differences. Obviously with Levi, they were the priest tribe with no land inheritance, but a couple others are also to be noted.

Genesis Birth Order	Wilderness Tabernacle	Joshua Inheritance	Tribulation Revelation 7	Millennium Ezekiel 48
Reuben (Leah)	Reuben	Reuben	Reuben	Reuben
Simeon (Leah)	Simeon	Simeon	Simeon	Simeon
Levi (Leah)			Levi	
Judah (Leah)	Judah	Judah	Judah	Judah
Dan (Bilhah)	Dan	Dan		Dan
Naphtali (Bilhah)	Naphtali	Naphtali	Naphtali	Naphtali
Gad (Zilpah)	Gad	Gad	Gad	Gad
Asher (Zilpah)	Asher	Asher	Asher	Asher
Issachar (Leah)	Issachar	Issachar	Issachar	Issachar
Zebulun (Leah)	Zebulun	Zebulun	Zebulun	Zebulun
Joseph (Rachel)			Joseph	
	Ephraim	Ephraim		Ephraim
	Manasseh	Manasseh	Manasseh	Manasseh
Benjamin (Rachel)	Benjamin	Benjamin	Benjamin	Benjamin

The "omissions" in the list in Revelation 7 are Ephraim and Dan. Ephraim is actually still included, just under the name of Joseph. Ephraim went into apostasy as a tribe (Hosea 4:17, 11:12) and they could be missing for that reason. Possibly another reason for the name change might involve the Mormons. They claim to trace their ancestry through Ephraim; in fact, Ephraim is a very common Mormon name. God obviously knows the future, and perhaps he anticipated this and left out Ephraim by name to let us know that the Mormons are really not who they claim to be. Then there is Dan. The tribe of Dan has some unique characteristics among the twelve. Dan was the first son of the concubines. That was not his fault, but it still is of note. Jacob's prophecy of his sons in Genesis 49:17 says that Dan will be a serpent that nips at the heels to cause others to fall backwards. That is not a very flattering description. Samson was of the tribe of Dan (Judges 13:2). If there is one man in the Bible you do <u>NOT</u> want to pattern your life after, it is Samson. The tribe of Dan was the last to get their inheritance (Judges 18:1). The idol worship of Jeroboam and the northern tribes with the golden calves was established in Dan (I Kings 12:25-33). The last mention of Dan is in Hosea 8:14 which says that those who follow his example will fall and never rise up again. Dan went into apostasy and has never returned. Every time that tribe appears in the Bible, something bad happens. Most people believe that the Antichrist must have Jewish ancestry. I am not too sure about that. I see no clear indication in the Bible of that. But if so, he will come from Dan. Then we see the grace of God at work. Ezekiel chapter 48 describes the Millennial city of Jerusalem, and lo and behold, Dan is there. They are not represented in the sealed witnesses of the Tribulation, but by the time of the reign of Jesus Christ, they will be restored.

Another side note about the 144,000: they do NOT include the Jehovah's Witnesses! They claim this group applies to them. No need for a long examination of this heresy. But the next time one of these birds comes to your house, ask him what tribe he is from. We had a couple of JW ladies show up to our house a few years back and one of them claimed she was one of the 144,000. After getting a blank stare about which tribe she was from, I noticed a wedding ring on her finger and asked her about it. She told me about her children and I said, "Well, that is odd. Revelation 14 says the 144,000 are virgins, and they are not defiled with women. So strike one, you are not a Jew. Strike two you are not a man, and strike three you are not a virgin." She did not want to talk any further.

The sealing of the 144,000 occurs at the mid-point of the Tribulation with a personal visible appearance of the Lord Jesus Christ. This is another of the doctrines of the Bible that will take some time to establish from multiple passages. So stay with me. We will get back to Revelation in a while, but for now I need to take you through a Bible journey to set forth the Mid-Tribulation appearance of Jesus Christ.

In Matthew 24:15-21, Jesus described the "Abomination of Desolation" and the flight of the Jews into the wilderness. This is when the Antichrist takes over the Temple and breaks the covenant with Israel. I will take more time on this in Revelation chapter 13 with the assassination of the Antichrist and the Revealing of the Wicked. But as the Jews flee, they will be met by the Lord at Sela-Petra. Revelation 12:6 says Israel has a place prepared of God where he will take care of them for 1260 days. Psalm 46:1 says, "God is our refuge and strength, a very present help in <u>trouble</u>." The Tribulation is called the "time of Jacob's <u>trouble</u>" (Jeremiah 30:7). So when Israel flees the Antichrist after he turns on them, they will run to their only refuge: God himself (Jesus) who will meet them in their trouble.

The "cities of refuge" in the Old Testament are a beautiful doctrinal picture of this. Moses spoke of this concept several times (Exodus 21:13, Numbers 35:9-34, and Deuteronomy 19:1-10). Joshua was the one who established these six cities after Israel came into the Promised Land. Read Joshua chapter 20 to get the details. Basically, God set up six cities for a refuge for someone guilty of what we call manslaughter. If someone caused the death of another person by accident (not by murder), he could flee to one of these cities and if he got there before the family of the slain person caught him, he was safe. But he had to come before the judges to hear his case and prove it was not pre-meditated. Once they judged it as so, the man then had to stay in that city "until the death of the high priest that shall be in <u>those days</u>". Again, the simple words of the Bible mean things. The phrase "those days" signifies the Tribulation period, and whenever it appears in the Bible, something in the context will be linked to that time. We use the term even today. When we say, "It's been one of <u>those days</u>..." it is NEVER in a good context. The context of Joshua chapter 20 and the cities of refuge paint this picture of the Tribulation.

Israel was responsible for the death of their Messiah. Although it is evidently obvious that the leaders of the Nation conspired knowingly to crucify him, most of the common people were led into it "unwittingly" in many ways. Just a week earlier, they had hailed him as the Son of David. Jesus prayed on the cross, "Father, forgive them; for they know not what they do." (Luke 23:34) In Acts 3:17, Peter gave Israel a pass, saying they did it in ignorance. So Israel was guilty more of manslaughter than murder, and even those who were the "murderers" (the leaders – Acts 7:52) are no longer here. So the people of Israel who will flee to the "city of refuge" called Sela-Petra are not murderers. They were not there 2,000 years ago. They are guilty of manslaughter in crucifying their Messiah unwittingly. When they recognize their error and flee the Antichrist, they will run to their refuge and stand in judgment before him for their rejection. But when they appropriate to themselves the death of their "High Priest" (Jesus – Hebrews 3:1) and acknowledge him as Lord, he will forgive their sin and restore them to himself.

This is the doctrinal and prophetic application of II Corinthians 3:13-16. Israel has been blinded "in part" (Romans 11:25) and has "the wool pulled over their eyes" due to the rejection of Jesus Christ. Again we see another common expression come from the Bible. What animal produces wool? Yes, you know; the Lamb of God which taketh away the sin of the world. Israel is blinded because they do not recognize Jesus as their Lamb. II Corinthians 3:15 says the veil is upon their heart, not their head. Once Israel in the Tribulation acknowledges what they did to their Lamb, God will remove the veil. That is what verse 16 says, "Nevertheless when it (the heart of Israel) shall turn to the Lord, the veil shall be taken away." This will occur 3½ years into Daniel's 70th week when they meet the Lord as they flee the Antichrist.

There are several Old Testament prophecies that speak directly of this event:

Hosea 2:14-23 – God will "allure" his people into the wilderness to restore her unto himself. They will call him "Ishi" (my husband), and God will betroth them to himself as the restored wife of the Old Testament (Isaiah 54:1-10, Jeremiah 31:31-34) when they say, "Thou art my God" (verse 23).

Zechariah 12:10 – Israel will "look upon me whom they have pierced". They cannot do that unless he appears to them. Once they see him and mourn for him as a son, he will pour out the spirit of grace on them and restore his people.

Zechariah 13:6-9 – This prophecy contains both first and second coming details. "Smite the shepherd and the sheep shall be scattered" was clearly fulfilled in Gethsemane, and even quoted as such. But then they will see the wounds in his hands which were obtained in "the house of my friends". Verses 8-9 speak of the trials of the Tribulation that they must endure. But when they "call on my name" and say, "The Lord is my God" he will hear them and restore them (verse 9).

Isaiah 66:5-8 – Israel was born as a Nation when God delivered them from Pharaoh and Egypt. God told Pharaoh in Exodus 4:22 that Israel was his "firstborn son". But as Israel continued their rejection of God, he ultimately dispersed them in the church age, and the Nation "died" for 1900 years. They were "born again" politically and secularly on May 14, 1948, and will be "born again" spiritually in one day, at once (verse 8) in her travail (Tribulation) when "he (Jesus) shall appear" (verse 5).

Not only are there prophecies, there are also pictures in the Bible of Israel's Mid-Tribulation restoration.

Deuteronomy chapter 4 – Israel as a Nation was assembled before Moses (a type of Christ) and was reminded how they "stood before the Lord in Horeb" to receive the law (verse 10). This is the same general location where they will stand before the "Prophet like unto Moses" in the Tribulation. They are reminded in verses 20-22 that they have been taken out of Egypt (the world) to be God's people of inheritance "this day". Moses (as the type of Christ) then tells them that he must die. "The Lord was angry with me for your sakes…" (verse 21). That speaks of the death of Christ when God's anger was poured out on his Son for our sakes. Verses 30-31 urge them to turn to the Lord "when thou art in tribulation" which is exactly what they will do at this meeting 3½ years into the real Tribulation. Then in verses 41-43, Moses chooses cities of refuge, which we have already seen as a picture of the refuge of Jesus Christ for his people in the Tribulation.

The picture of Joseph – Joseph is perhaps the greatest type of Christ in the Old Testament in the sheer volume of details that picture the Lord. In chapters 37-40 he was rejected by his brothers just as Jesus was at his first coming. Joseph was sold into slavery and spent two years in prison, picturing the 2,000 years of the church age. At the end of this time, Joseph received a Gentile bride (type of the church). Pharaoh had a dream about seven years of plenty followed by seven years of famine. The "seven" lines up with Daniel's 70th week, and the two halves of Pharaoh's dream picture the two halves of the Tribulation; a time of plenty (false kingdom) followed by a time of famine (the "Great Tribulation"). During this famine, Joseph revealed himself to his brethren in a private meeting. In the famine of the Tribulation, Jesus will reveal himself to his brethren in a private meeting.

Matthew 17:1-9 – The Mount of Transfiguration is probably the best picture in the Bible of the Mid-Tribulation appearance of the Lord Jesus Christ. In the verse just prior to this story, Jesus promised that some would see him coming in his kingdom (Matthew 16:28). This was fulfilled by Peter, James and John in chapter 17. It was also fulfilled later by John when he saw the kingdom as he wrote the book of Revelation. It will be fulfilled again in the Tribulation by the remnant of Israel who endure to the end. In the vision in Matthew 17, Jesus appeared with Moses and Elijah who are the two witnesses of Revelation chapter 11. We will detail them when we get to that chapter. Jesus was in his glorified form, just as he will appear when he returns. After Peter shot off his mouth, Moses and Elijah went back to heaven and only Jesus remained. In the Mid-Tribulation appearance, this will be reversed. Jesus will return to heaven after his instructions to the 144,000, and Moses and Elijah will remain as their leaders during the final 42 months of the Great Tribulation.

The sealing of the 144,000 is different than the seal of the Holy Spirit that we enjoy in the church age. When a person gets saved in this age, God performs an operation called spiritual circumcision where he cuts his soul loose from his body. Then the Holy Spirit enters and takes up permanent residency inside the believer, and the new man on the inside is sealed with a seal that cannot be broken. The book of Ephesians mentions this seal twice, with a slightly different wording. Ephesians 1:13-14 says we are sealed "until the redemption of the purchased possession". Ephesians 4:30 says we are sealed "unto the day of redemption". The variation in the wording gives us a dual application of our seal. We are sealed until; meaning a time period. The seal cannot be broken until that time is fulfilled and our redemption is ultimately realized. We are also sealed unto; meaning for a purpose. God's purpose for his church is to present it to himself a glorious bride, and when God purposes something, he will do it. So our seal cannot possibly be broken or lost because God has sealed us for a specific purpose and a specific time.

However, the seal of the 144,000 can be lost because it is for a different purpose. There is no "until" or "unto" mentioned in Revelation chapter 7. The 144,000 are sealed for a mission. Their purpose is to preach the "everlasting gospel" (Revelation 14:6). Their seal remains as long as they preach that gospel. But if they quit or deny the Lord, they forfeit the seal. The Jewish witnesses in the Tribulation do not have the same salvation that we have in the church age. Neither did the Old Testament saints. David committed the sins of adultery and murder, for which there were no provisions or sacrifices under the law for his forgiveness. He was guilty of death. Numbers 35:31 says, "Moreover ye shall take no satisfaction for the life of a murderer, which is guilty of death: but he shall be surely put to death." David was spared the death penalty by the grace of God, the only man in the Old Testament to receive such a pardon as a picture of the eternal security of the believer in the church age. His prayer of repentance is Psalm 51. He acknowledged that there was no sacrifice that could cover this sin (verse 16). He knew he was guilty of death, which under the law included the second death of separation from God as well. He prayed, "Take not thy holy spirit from me" in verse 11, because he knew he could lose it.

The church age believer can not lose his salvation, but the Old Testament saints could, and the Tribulation saints can because their seal is not the same as ours. There is an element of "keeping" their salvation that we do not have. Many of the verses in Revelation that refer to this group speak of it. Revelation 12:11

says, "And they overcame him by the blood of the Lamb, and by the word of their testimony; and they loved not their lives unto the death." This group will overcome by the blood AND their testimony AND as long as they give their life if captured. I John 5:4 says we overcome by faith, period. Revelation 12:17 says these men, "keep the commandments of God, and have the testimony of Jesus Christ." We do not have to keep the law to be saved because Jesus did it for us. Revelation 14:12 says the same thing; that this group has to keep the commandments of God. If they do not, they can lose their seal.

The 144,000 are sealed for a mission. Their mission is to proclaim the "everlasting gospel" to the Gentile world for the 3½ years of the Great Tribulation. The text of the message is found in Revelation 14:6-7:

> "And I saw another angel fly in the midst of heaven, having the everlasting gospel to preach unto them that dwell on the earth, and to every nation, and kindred, and tongue, and people, Saying with a loud voice, Fear God, and give glory to him; for the hour of his judgment is come: and worship him that made heaven, and earth, and the sea, and the fountains of waters."

There is nothing in that gospel message about the blood of Jesus Christ or faith in his death, burial and resurrection. It is basically, "My Messiah is coming and you better fear him and give him glory or else." The scope of the message (or where and to whom the message is preached) is found in Matthew 24:14: "And this gospel of the kingdom shall be preached in all the world for a witness unto all nations; and then shall the end come." Many prophecy gurus teach that Matthew 24 applies to the church, but it does not. The Jewish apostles have asked their Jewish Messiah when and how he is coming to establish his Jewish kingdom (verse 3). Did I mention Jewish? The gospel of the kingdom is the "good news" (gospel) that a kingdom is forthcoming and to fear the coming King. This message is proclaimed to "all the world" and "all nations". The Jewish witnesses will preach to Gentiles in every corner of the globe. Oh, wait, I can't use that term because it is "unscientific". So if I can't, then neither can anyone else. So the next time you hear anyone say that, call them on it. You won't because everyone knows what we mean when we say that something goes into "every corner of the earth".

Many missions agencies today use Matthew 24:14 as their strategy and motivation to take the gospel to the unreached. Please understand what I am about to say. This missions strategy is awesome and vital. God is all about taking the gospel to the uttermost. Any effort to carry the truth of God to those who have not heard is blessed. I am 1000% in favor of it and we support missionaries who do so. Missions studies tell us that 90% or more of the resources of the gospel (people and money) are devoted to areas where the name of Jesus is well known, meaning that only a tiny portion of our efforts are in places with the greatest need. There is something fundamentally wrong with that. Please do NOT take what I am about to say out of that context. But some of the strategy says that until we get the gospel into "all the world for a witness unto all nations" that the end cannot come. They think that the rapture of the church cannot happen until the unreached have the gospel. First, that makes Matthew 24 apply to the church, which I have said a hundred times that it does not. The "end" in prophetic passages in the Bible always refers to the Second Advent, which is the actual "end of the world" as we know it. That is seven years after the rapture of the church. Second, it makes the rapture of the church depend on us. Jesus is not sitting in heaven waiting until the church gets the gospel into all the world. Good luck getting Laodicea to accomplish that.

So we have seen the text of the message and its reach or world-wide scope. Next, we need to see the purpose of the "everlasting gospel of the kingdom" that will be preached by the 144,000. The best place for that is in a parable of Jesus in Matthew 22:1-10. Rather than take the space to quote the full passage here, just look it up in your Bible and follow along as I walk you through it. Jesus told parables for the expressed purpose of communicating clear truth through the use of a story. This story is about the "kingdom of heaven" which is the Jewish Messianic reign of Jesus Christ (verse 2). A king makes a marriage for his son. Any guess who that Son might be? If you did not guess Jesus, you are really not paying much attention, are you? So the king would be God and the bride would be the church. The king sent out servants to call them who were bidden to the wedding (verse 3). These would be the people who had received direct invitations. When you put together your list for your wedding invitations, you begin with your closest family and friends. That would be Israel in the Old Testament.

There are three sets of servants in this parable. The first ones in verse 3 are the Old Testament prophets. Their invitation was rejected, so the king sent out another set of servants (verse 4), which would be the apostles, along with Stephen and Paul and the others in the early church who begged Israel to respond to their Messiah. But this group of messengers was also rejected and persecuted (verses 5-6). So the king got angry (verse 7) and sent his armies "and destroyed those murderers and burned up their city". When Stephen preached to the Sanhedrin in Acts 7, he called the leaders of Israel "murderers and betrayers", using the same terminology that Jesus used in this parable. In 70 AD, God sent a Roman army against Jerusalem and destroyed it in fulfillment of Matthew 24:2 as well as verse 7 in this story. Then verse 8 says he sent forth a third set of servants. This would be the 144,000. Jesus jumped right over the church age and did not mention it, because this parable is about the Jewish kingdom. But in Matthew 22:8-10, the target audience of the message changes. Those who were bidden (Israel) were not worthy, so others will be called. That would have to be Gentiles. Ultimately, some of them will respond, and the "wedding was furnished with guests". These guests do not marry the bridegroom, and neither do the servants who are the messengers to call them to the wedding. The third set of servants is the 144,000, and the guests are the Gentiles who respond to their invitation. So the text of the message is, "Fear God and give him glory", the scope of the message is the Gentile world, and the purpose of the message is to draw a few of them to a relationship with God for the kingdom.

Let's go back to Matthew 22:4 and pick up perhaps the most important detail in the story. God sent the second set of servants and said, "all things are ready". That means just what it says. At the first coming of Jesus Christ, "all things were ready" for the kingdom. "All things" in the Greek means ALL THINGS. When Jesus presented himself to his people, he "bid them to the wedding" with, "Repent, for the kingdom of heaven is at hand" (Matthew 4:17). He offered himself as their King, and if they had accepted his offer, his kingdom would have been established at that time. We know now that they rejected him and the offer was postponed 2,000 years, but that is easy to see with the perspective of 20-20 hindsight.

Jesus made an offer to his people. God's offers are valid. He does not dangle a carrot and pull back his offer if the person wants it. He knew they would reject him, but he made the offer anyway. Everything was set up. Rome was in power. Judas the Antichrist was there. The church age was a mystery in the Old Testament. Imagine Jesus offering his kingdom and having his people accept it. He would not have said, "Oh, snap! You guys were supposed to say no. Now what am I going to do?" The offer was valid, and history turned on the response of his people. It could have gone either way. Had Israel received Jesus as Messiah, Rome would have carried out the execution and the prophetic events of the Antichrist and establishment of the kingdom would have been fulfilled 2,000 years ago. I know that is incredibly difficult to wrap our heads around. To me, it is without doubt the hardest thing to understand about the Bible. But it has to be, or Jesus was lying to his people when he presented himself as their King.

With that essential understanding, we can find the instructions to the 144,000 in the Bible. There is nothing in the book of Revelation about this, so we have to find it elsewhere. The basic instructions to the apostles contain ALSO the instructions to the 144,000. If "all things" were ready when he was here the first time, then he had to prepare his followers for the Tribulation. Jesus spoke of that time in several places in the gospels, most notably in Matthew chapter 10 and chapters 24-25. Some of the instructions in those chapters were fulfilled by the apostles. Some of them could not possibly have been accomplished by them. So we must walk through those two places in the Bible and make note of the things that apply only to the first century, then the things that apply to both, and the things that could only be fulfilled by a later group. Many things in Matthew 10, 24, and 25 could not possibly apply to any other group than the 144,000 because they have not yet happened. So the instructions to the apostles in Matthew have a dual application. They are for the audience at hand (the apostles) as they stood before him. But there are also many things that cannot be applied to the generation of the apostles. They WOULD HAVE if Israel had accepted Jesus as their Messiah. But since he was rejected, many of the instructions to the apostles were pushed back 2,000 years. So this is one of those odd passages of the Bible where Jesus is speaking TO the apostles and THROUGH them to the 144,000 at the same time.

Again, for the sake of space, I would encourage you to open your Bible to Matthew 10 and follow along with me, then to chapters 24 and 25 after that. We will be here for quite some time before we are able to get back to our study of the book of Revelation, but a grasp of these chapters in Matthew is critical.

Matthew 10:1-4 – The twelve apostles are named.

Matthew 10:5-8 – The apostles are sent forth with a basic charge to heal and to preach the kingdom of heaven "at hand". They are told to go only to Israel and not to the Gentiles. This applies only to the first century group. Jesus intended to call his people first to have them participate with him in carrying the message to the world. Paul said in Romans 1:16 that the gospel went to the "Jew first".

Matthew 10:9-10 – Instructions are given to provide no resources for their mission. This was done by the apostles, and it also points ahead to the 144,000. With the mark of the beast in full operation, they will have no ability to buy or sell or have any means of support. God will miraculously provide for them as it says in Revelation 12:6, and they will also receive occasional help from the Gentiles as they take their message to the world. We will see this a little later.

Matthew 10:11-15 – The messengers will encounter opposition, but they will also have some positive reception. This applies to both groups, but the apostles got far more "good vibes" than the 144,000 will receive. They are told to abide in a "worthy" house, which means finding lodging with those who would receive the message. It happened somewhat with the apostles, but in the Tribulation, this will be in much greater detail. It will be *"The Diary of Anne Frank"* and *"The Hiding Place"* on steroids. The 144,000 will be hunted with a far greater tenacity than in World War II, and with modern technology. Verse 15 refers to the "day of judgment", which follows right after the ministry of the 144,000.

Matthew 10:16-20 – Jesus warned them of the opposition. Verses 17-18 speak of Jewish persecution; that they will be scourged in synagogues and be publicly harassed as a testimony against them (Jews) and Gentiles. This is the opposition that the apostles received from the Jewish leaders in the early part of the book of Acts, as well as the extreme harassment Paul received from the Jews in the book of Acts. By the time of the Tribulation, the Jewish Nation will be the target of world-wide persecution, and the heart of Israel will have turned to their Messiah. So this opposition was fulfilled by the first century group. But verses 19-20 apply to both groups. In their trials, God will speak through them.

Matthew 10:21 – Family rifts and squabbles have been going on ever since Cain and Abel. But this verse speaks of family members turning on each other and delivering them to the authorities to be put to death. Some of this may have happened in the first century, but there is little if any information about it in the Bible. This verse speaks of the "dog-eat-dog, every man for himself" mentality of the Tribulation. It is hard for us to imagine such a thing, but Jesus did say it would be unlike any time the world has ever seen.

Matthew 10:22-23 – Yes, both groups were hated for the cause of Jesus Christ. "But he that endureth to the end shall be saved." The end is always the end, remember? None of the apostles made it past 100 AD, let alone the Second Coming. He even makes reference to his return in verse 23. Why would Jesus say, "until the Son of man be come" when he is standing right in front of them? Jesus is clearly speaking through the apostles, and to the 144,000 here.

Matthew 10:24-31 – Jesus gives encouragement to his messengers. Even though they will be hated of all men and persecuted like he was, he has their back. But of note is verse 28: "Fear not them which kill the body." Yes, the apostles all suffered martyrdom except John. But this is a direct reference to the torture and murder of the 144,000 in the Tribulation. He even mentioned their <u>head</u> in verse 30.

Matthew 10:32-33 – Here we see a clear statement about the possibility of losing the seal for the 144,000. These verses apply to both groups. It does NOT apply to you as a New Testament believer. You should be willing to testify of Jesus at all times, but if you clam up a few times, don't fear losing your salvation. The 144,000 are sealed for a mission. If they fail in that mission and deny the Lord when captured, he will deny them before the Father in heaven. Jesus would not give this warning if it were not possible.

Matthew 10:34-39 – These instructions apply to both groups. Jesus came to cause division, and every time he shows up in the gospels, people are divided over his claims. It is purposeful and intentional to draw out a decision. No one can stay "neutral" about Jesus. You cannot be like Switzerland and hope it works out for you. Just remember, their cheese is full of holes. We have already seen the "family issues" of verses 35-37 and how they are played out in the extreme in the Tribulation. But also note verse 39. Those who will save their life will lose it. Again, this is a reference to those who deny the Lord in the Tribulation. Those who lose their life will find it. Anyone who remains faithful to the Lord and to the mission even if it costs them their head will be rewarded (Revelation 20:4).

Matthew 10:40-42 – Here is more evidence that this passage applies to the Tribulation. I find no place in the Bible where a first century disciple got a cup of cold water from someone. In the Tribulation, the water supply will be poisoned. We will see it in detail in the third Trumpet in Revelation 8:10-11. Most of the stores will be closed due to a large percentage of the population dying. Economic collapse and military disasters will disrupt the society. It will be every man for himself. If "one of these little ones" (the 144,000) could find a store to sell him bottled water, he would be out of luck because he would not have the mark. A cup of cold water to us right now is nothing. We get it for "free" out of our tap. In the Tribulation, it will be a precious commodity. As the 144,000 spread out throughout the Gentile world with their message of the coming of the Lord, a few brave and rare souls will respond. When faced with the message of the coming judgment of God, they might say to one of these little ones, "What should I do?" The answer will be, "Man, I have not had a meal in a week. Can you just give me something to eat?" Just a simple act of humanitarian good will like a cup of cold water will be rewarded. Even if one of the apostles did get one, it was not under circumstances even close to what the 144,000 will face.

Now let's move on to Matthew 24 and see more indication of the instructions that will be given to the 144,000. We will see even more possibility of the loss of their "seal" based on the need for them to stay true to the call and mission to carry the message to the world. Before we get to the chapter, it is essential to reinforce the understanding that Matthew 24 does NOT apply directly to the church. All scripture is profitable for doctrine <u>first</u> (II Timothy 3:16). We can learn from any passage of scripture, and there are practical lessons from Matthew 24 for believers in the church age. But most prophecy teachers misapply the chapter doctrinally. It leads to Christians fearing the loss of salvation by not "enduring to the end" (Matthew 24:13). It causes prophecy gurus to look for "signs of the rapture" when the signs are for the Jews (I Corinthians 1:22). Still others use Matthew 24 to try to identify the Antichrist so they can buy property in the country and stock up on rice and beans and ammo. I will deal with this obsession and heresy in much more detail in Revelation chapter 13 when we get into the "Revealing of the Wicked".

The most important verse in Matthew chapter 24 is verse 3: "And as he sat upon the mount of Olives, the disciples came unto him privately, saying, Tell us, when shall these things be? and what shall be the sign of thy coming, and of the end of the world?" This was a direct and honest question from the apostles. Whenever Jesus was asked a question like this, he gave a direct answer. He would occasionally dance around a dishonest question from a Pharisee, but never one like this. Jesus did not have the attention span of a two year old. Direct questions were answered clearly. These are Jewish apostles who as yet know nothing about a church age. There are no Christians present. The death, burial and resurrection has not yet occurred. They are asking him about a <u>sign</u> (Jewish) of his <u>coming</u> (not rapture) and of the end of the world (Advent). The current "world system" will end when the King of the Jews returns physically to earth to establish his kingdom on the throne of David in Jerusalem. Jesus is explaining the time period leading to that event and the nature of the Tribulation. Remember also that this kingdom could have been set up at this time had Israel received him as their Messiah. So the answer and the instructions given in Matthew chapters 24 and 25 are specific. They are given to the apostles as if they could be the ones to fulfil ALL of them. But not all of them were fulfilled by the apostles due to the rejection of Christ and postponement of the kingdom as a result. So again, like Matthew chapter 10, we will walk through the major points of these two chapters and make note of which group applies (apostles, 144,000, or both).

Matthew 24:4-8 – These verses speak of the worldwide deception and false kingdom of the Antichrist in the first half of the Tribulation. Not much is happening yet. It is only the beginning of sorrows.

Matthew 24:9-13 – This is very similar to Matthew 10. Again they are told of a worldwide hatred and persecution. Some of this took place in the first century, and all but one of the apostles was killed for his faith. But the "hated of all nations" part was only just slightly touched on with the apostles. Paul traveled the Gentile world, but most of the hatred against Paul came from the Jews and not the Gentile nations, and most of the twelve hung around Palestine most of their lives. Again we see the warning that they had to "endure to the end" in verse 13. The end <u>still</u> has not come!

Matthew 24:14 – We have already dealt with this verse and its connection to Revelation 14:6-7. This is the message of the 144,000 called the everlasting gospel. Even Paul did not make it to "<u>all</u> nations".

Matthew 24:15-22 – There is no way possible for this passage to apply to the apostles. This is a very misunderstood and misapplied passage. The "Abomination of Desolation" causes much controversy among prophecy teachers. Many of them believe this was fulfilled by Antiochus Epiphanes in 165 BC when he sacrificed a pig on the altar in Jerusalem. Of course, this defilement of the altar is a historical fact confirmed by many, most notably Josephus who is the standard of Jewish historians. I hate to name names, but sometimes it is necessary. Hank Hanegraaff touts himself as the "Bible Answer Man". When it comes to issues of salvation by grace through faith in the sacrifice of Jesus Christ, he gives decent answers. When it comes to the actual <u>Bible</u>, however, he is out in left field. When it comes to prophetic matters, he is not just in left field, he is two miles from the stadium wandering around looking for the beer vendor. Hank is A-millennial. That means he rejects the literal physical coming of the Lord and his Jewish reign in Jerusalem. That messes up about two-thirds of the Old Testament. Any passage that deals with Jesus coming to reign must be spiritualized away and applied to the "church" (Catholic). Hank is Eastern Orthodox, which is "Catholic Lite"; it is essentially the same thing but without a Pope.

Hank is adamant that the Abomination of Desolation is Epiphanes. My question for the "Bible Answer Man" is, "If the Abomination of Desolation happened in 165 BC, why did Jesus in 33 AD refer to it as a <u>future</u> event?" Imagine the insanity of Jesus telling his apostles to be on the lookout for something that happened 200 years earlier and giving them instructions on what to do when they see it. But now apply this to what I have clearly established about the nature of the offer of the kingdom to Israel at the first coming of Christ. Jesus could easily tell his apostles to watch for this event if it <u>could have</u> happened in their lifetimes. Since it did not due to the rejection of Israel, he also could easily <u>speak</u> into the future to another group of people who would see it in the Tribulation. These instructions in Matthew 24 are more for the 144,000 than for the apostles. Either of those possibilities (or both) are sensible. But to speak of a 200-year-old event as future has Jesus wandering around in a field of Colorado Cabbage.

Let's get some more information from this section of Matthew 24. The Abomination of Desolation in verse 15 is followed by the warning to flee immediately. It is so urgent that they are told not to take anything with them, but to just run. There are a couple of reasons for that. One is the time issue. The Jews need to get out of town immediately, and any delay puts them in serous danger. This is the 21st century. Technology to keep tabs on people is extremely sophisticated now, and the implementation of the mark of the beast and all of the related tools for that system will be 3½ years in the making. The system will be worked up behind the scenes during the first half of the Tribulation and will be in full force at this point in time. Big Brother will be able to find a Jew in Jerusalem easily. Another reason to flee with nothing is to keep from being hindered. That is why Jesus said to pray that the flight is not in the winter (travel issues) or with small children. But note also that he said to pray that this does not happen on a sabbath day. The law will be back in effect, and there is only so far a person is allowed to travel on the sabbath without breaking the law. The Abomination of Desolation is when the Antichrist moves to Jerusalem and enters the temple to proclaim himself God. We will deal with that subject in detail in chapter 13 when we get to the pivotal part of this study on the Revealing of the Wicked.

Verse 21 says this "Great Tribulation" will be unlike any time the world has ever seen or ever will see. That is one of the main themes of the book of Revelation. The descriptions of this time in this book are so bizarre because we have no reference for this in history. As we make our way through all the disasters of the Seals, Trumpets and Vials, this will become increasingly evident.

Verse 22 is sort of cryptic. It says, "Those days shall be shortened". It leads some to speculate that God will do something about the 24-hour cycle and that the physical disasters will be so profound as to alter nature. God has demonstrated that he is capable of doing something like that. Joshua chapter 10 describes a battle where the sun actually "stood still" for about a whole day. When Hezekiah was sick, God gave him a sign where the sundial (clock) actually went backwards 40 minutes (see Isaiah 38). But I do not believe that Matthew 24:22 is describing anything like that. Instead, it refers to the great fear that man has had ever since we developed nuclear weapons. The doomsday cults have feared that mankind will wipe himself out. That is the point of Matthew 24:22. If God does not interrupt the process, this would happen. Man is so completely corrupt and depraved (especially without God in his life) that left to himself with no restraining force, we would all kill each other off. At the end, the last man standing would be "Bad Bad Leroy Brown" and he would kill himself out of utter loneliness. Nuclear weapons treaties have the concept of "MAD" built into them, which is a very appropriate acronym. Mankind is stark raving MAD. It stands for "Mutual Assured Destruction". If one side launched, the other side could also launch, and it would be assured that both sides would be mutually obliterated. The Tribulation will be so bad that God must "shorten the days" before it gets to this point. The reason is stated in the verse: "for the elect's sake". God promised a world rule to the Nation of Israel, and if he let us play it out to the ultimate conclusion without stepping in, he could not fulfil that promise.

Matthew 24:23-28 – Jesus revisits the deception of the Antichrist in the first half of the Tribulation again in these verses. He was warning his apostles about this, but it really did not happen in their lifetimes. Sure, there have been "false Christs" by the trainloads in every generation including the first century, and even more so today. But it is nothing like the Tribulation. As we will see in Revelation chapter 9, the bottomless pit will be opened and every devil in hell will be let loose on earth. Then in chapter 12, Satan and all the rest of the foul spirits will be kicked out of heaven to be confined to earth as well. The work of Satan and his minions to deceive will be magnified a million times beyond what it has ever been in history. Verse 27 mentions the "coming of the Son of man" again. So, this section must be primarily applied to the Jews of the Tribulation since he is still not here yet.

Matthew 24:29-31 – We spent some time on these verses when we were discussing the raptures and the various heresies about when the rapture of the church would take place. You can flip back to that section from the comments in Revelation chapter 4 for a refresher. All of this clearly applies to the literal return of Jesus Christ to the earth "after the tribulation of those days". The prophecy of the sun and moon being darkened is found many places in the Old Testament (Isaiah 13:10, Joel 2:10, 3:15, Amos 8:9, and Habakkuk 3:11 to name a few). I take this to be a literal phenomenon. I see no reason to think otherwise. There is clearly a visible appearance of Jesus Christ as he comes in power and glory to reign. No one who is on earth will be happy about that (verse 30), but we will return with him on our white horses (see chapter 19). The "elect" who are gathered from around the world are the Jewish remnant who "endured to the end" and are rewarded by being raptured out before he comes.

Matthew 24:32-35 – This is another of the parables of Jesus; this one about the fig tree. The Nation of Israel is likened to two different trees in the Bible, the fig tree and the olive tree. The fig tree is used to signify the national and secular life of Israel, and the olive tree speaks of their spiritual life. The fig tree was the one Adam and Eve used in the Garden to try to cover the nakedness of sin. It pictures the self-righteousness of works, which is a hallmark of Israel under the law and the Pharisees. Jesus said when you see the fig tree bring forth <u>leaves</u>, realize the coming of the Lord is close. Leaves appear before the fruit does. Israel is not bearing any fruit for the Lord right now because they do not have their "vine" Jesus (John 15:1-5). But Israel's "leaves" budded on May 14, 1948 when they became a Nation again. The time of his coming is near.

Jesus said, "This generation shall not pass until all these things be fulfilled". But as we have clearly seen, not ALL of the things in these chapters have been fulfilled. Some of them are yet to be fulfilled in the Tribulation, and the generation who stood before him in Matthew 24 has been dead a long time. So we have to apply this verse correctly. Remember that Jesus was talking to <u>two</u> groups at the same time: his apostles AND the 144,000. Also, he was talking to the apostles AS IF they would be the generation to fulfil everything in these chapters. But the rejection of Jesus by Israel pushed some of these instructions back 2,000 years. <u>ALL</u> things that were fulfilled at the first coming of Jesus Christ happened within that generation. The most notable prophecy of Matthew 24 that has already been fulfilled is the destruction of the temple (verses 1-2). That happened in 70 AD. If Jesus spoke these words in 29 AD (the date most historians give), then there were 41 years between the prophecy and the fulfillment. Likewise, <u>ALL</u> things in Matthew 24-25 that will be fulfilled prior to the Second Coming will also happen within a generation. This truth has led many to base their date-setting predictions on the restoration of Israel in 1948. That is a valid point, except for the date-setting part as I have talked about many times in this commentary. If we use the exact time of the first century fulfillment, then 1948 plus 41 is 1989. I write these words in 2020. We are 31 years late. But Jesus did not say it would happen in 41 years, he said the generation would not pass without fulfillment of his prophecies. That is open-ended. It gives ample room while at the same time revealing his plan clearly.

Again, this is not date-setting. But it is yet another of the scores of indications both in scripture and in the state of world events that demonstrate clearly that we are in the generation that will see the Second Coming of the Lord Jesus Christ. To understand this, we need to define a generation Biblically. This passage gives us 41 years. Psalm 90:10 says we get 70 years on average and maybe 80 if we are strong enough to make it that far. Many people these days go well past 80. In Matthew chapter 1, the genealogy of Jesus from Abraham is traced, and God broke it into three sections of 14 generations each. The first section is Abraham to David. Abraham was born in 1996 BC, and David in roughly 1100 BC. That would be 896 years, or 64 years per generation. David to the captivity (606 BC) was 494 years, or 35 years per generation. The captivity to Jesus (4 BC according to most historians) would be 602 years, or 43 years per generation. In Genesis 15:13-16, God told Abraham that his children would be afflicted in Egypt for 400 years and come out in the fourth generation. That would make 100 years per generation. That gives us six different calculations for a Biblical generation ranging from 35 years to 100. If we traced the generations of the kings of Israel and Judah it would yield a different result. I give you all this to illustrate once again the impossibility of pinning down an exact time. But there is no doubt that we are in the "times and the seasons".

I take it this way. The generation that was alive at the time Israel was planted as a Nation will not be completely gone before Jesus returns. At least ONE person who was born on May 14, 1948 will still be alive at the rapture of the church. Please note that this is only my best speculative guess, and I have told you many times that I can speculate with the best of them. But whenever I do, I always leave the "trap door" open. My opinions are just that – opinions. They are quite subject to error. Many people live past 100 these days, so I have TONS of wiggle room here. Don't forget that God counts differently than we do. So I have even more room to play with. The main point is that we are right there. The clock is soon to strike midnight, and Cinderella is just about to get her glass slipper from her bridegroom.

Verse 35 is a tremendous promise. We take a side trip briefly from the study of the book of Revelation to discuss a simple point of the doctrine of Bible preservation. Scholarship tells us that ONLY the original manuscripts can truly be said to be completely inspired and without error. Since then, according to all the academic pointy-heads, man has been involved and has made mistakes in copying and in translating. Jesus said his words would not pass away. He said they would last longer than the physical creation. He said his WORDS would not pass away, not just his general message. The original manuscripts have all passed away. There is not a single atom or molecule in existence today from the first copies that are supposedly the only truly pure words of God. So, if the words of Jesus in the original manuscripts have passed away without being preserved for us, then Jesus lied. So where are those words, doctor?

Matthew 24:36 – This verse has a parallel in Mark 13:32 that says even Jesus himself does not know the day of his return. This leads many (like the JW's) to conclude that Jesus could not have been God. After all, the Father knows the day. If Jesus was God, he would know the day also. Again, quite often those who try to outsmart God end up being ensnared in their own devices. "He taketh the wise in their own craftiness" (Job 5:13). AS A MAN, Jesus chose not to know the day of his return. It is not that he did not know, he CHOSE not to know. As God, he knew. So here is a little exercise for our Bible perverting "friends". Try NOT knowing something that you know. Take a very important piece of information like your wife's name and without the issues of dementia or Alzheimer's, choose not to know it. I did not say forget it. We are some of the most forgetful folks around, especially the men. Our wife can ask us to take out the trash, and as we get up and walk toward the door, we can stand there in the middle of the living room with a blank stare on our face thinking, "Why am I standing here?" The date of the Second Coming of Christ is pretty important to him. It is the day he gets his bride. You may forget your anniversary, but no one forgets to show up for their wedding day. The "day of the Lord" is the theme of the Bible. It is the biggest day on God's calendar BY FAR. He knows it. He is counting down the days. Jesus knows it. But he deliberately chose to lay that knowledge aside and wipe it from his memory bank. If you can choose NOT to know something that important to you when you clearly know it, then you are God.

Matthew 24:37-51 – Jesus gives us the example of Noah as a picture of the Second Coming. Again, this is not the rapture, but the Advent. Enoch was taken out before the flood. He is the picture of the rapture of the church. Noah was protected in the ark during the judgment, a picture of Israel in the Tribulation. Verse 39 mentions the coming of the Son of man. That is the title for Jesus in his kingdom with Israel. In verses 40-41, those who are "taken and left" are different than the rapture of the church. At our main harvest, we are taken to heaven and the lost are "left behind". This passage deals with the end of the Tribulation and the roles are flipped. Those who are taken are judged and condemned, and those who are left go into the kingdom alive as the subjects of the Millennial reign of Christ.

Then verses 42-51 give a general warning to stay diligent in service to the Lord. The principle applies to any believer in any age, even those who lived long before the current time as we rapidly approach the end times. We need to stay diligent because we have no idea when Jesus is coming for his bride. Others should stay diligent because they have no idea when their "number is up". But this passage applies specifically to the remnant at the end of the Tribulation. Notice in verse 51 that these people can lose their salvation, which is true of the Tribulation, but not the church age.

Matthew 25:1-13 – The parable of the wise and foolish virgins has caused considerable confusion and bad teaching in many prophetic circles. We saw it earlier in the "split rapture" heresy, and there are other errors made from this passage. The basic problem (as with many bad doctrines) is the failure to rightly divide the word of truth (II Timothy 2:15). Of course, since that verse has been changed in most of the new Bibles, it is no wonder that many Bible teachers do not know how to rightly divide the book. They are not told to do so in their "Bible".

The context of Matthew 25 continues from chapter 24. Both chapters were spoken at the same time by the Lord to the same audience about the same subject: the Second Advent and the events leading up to it. There are no Christians present, and there are no Christians addressed. It is before Calvary. Jesus was speaking to the disciples privately (Matthew 24:3). He was giving them instructions for the Tribulation as if they would be the ones to fulfil all the prophetic matters in the address. But to repeat myself (because repetition is the price of learning), the elements of this prophetic discourse that were NOT fulfilled by the apostles are then shifted 2,000 years into the future to apply to the Jewish remnant in the Tribulation.

This is a prophetic story about the kingdom of heaven. That is the literal Jewish reign of the Messiah in Jerusalem. There are ten virgins in the story. Again, for at least the millionth time out of my mouth and from my keyboard, the words of the Bible mean things and each one is important to communicate truth. The virgins are the 144,000 (Revelation 14:4). That word is specifically reserved in the Bible in its plural form to designate this group when it is used in a prophetic sense. The church is a chaste virgin (singular) in II Corinthians 11:2, and the Jewish witnesses in the Tribulation are virgins (plural). There are ten of them (the number of the Gentiles) because that is who their ministry target is. They go to meet the bridegroom, but the church is the bride who marries him. They are called out in their Post-Tribulation rapture at midnight, which is the darkest part of the night. The Tribulation is a pretty dark time, and it lines up prophetically with all the passages which speak of the sun being darkened at the Second Advent.

Some of the virgins have oil, and some do not. Oil in the Bible is a type of the Holy Spirit. If you are a born again Christian, the oil of the Spirit is "hermetically sealed" in you until the day of redemption. Those without oil are told to go out and "buy" for themselves. The age of grace for Christians says we are saved by grace through faith and not of works, and that the wages of sin is death. We cannot "buy" our oil because it is given to us as a free gift (Ephesians 2:8-9, Romans 6:23). With all of that, can anyone please explain to me how so many people try to force this parable of the virgins on Christians? These are the 144,000 Jewish witnesses of the Tribulation who can lose their seal and run out of oil as we have clearly discussed with this group many times.

Yet herein lies one small conundrum. The 144,000 are sealed. As we have seen, it is not the same as our seal in that it can be forfeited. But it appears that the full group makes it through the Tribulation intact. Revelation 14:1 describes a scene in heaven with the full 144,000 standing with the Lord on the mount Sion, which would be heaven (Hebrews 12:22). However, half of the virgins in Matthew 25 are shut out. Jesus would not tell this story if it were not possible for it to happen. Other instructions given to this group include admonitions and warnings that they can lose it. Again, Jesus would not say those things unless it could happen. Then where is the passage that shows some of the 144,000 being left out of the group? I don't see it anywhere in the Bible. This is one of those places (and there are many) where I get to fall back on my three favorite words in the English language: "I don't know". My best guess (and it is only a guess) is that Jesus gives enough warnings and examples such as this that these witnesses take it seriously and none of them actually lose their seal. Just because it might be possible for it to happen does not mean it will. If so, that is some tremendous faith and courage!

Matthew 25:14-30 – This is the famous parable of the talents. It is a great practical lesson of "use it or lose it" that we can all apply to our lives. But there is a clear Tribulation application in this parable. Again, it is about the kingdom of heaven (verse 14). The Lord delivers his goods to his servants and leaves. Then he comes back. Yes, the Lord is coming back for his bride, but he will meet us in the air. This story is about a man who returns literally and physically, which would be the Second Advent of the Lord Jesus Christ. Those who are rewarded are made "ruler over many things", which is the promise of Millennial inheritance given to both the church and the Jewish remnant. The inheritance is not realized until the Lord returns in his kingdom. But the clincher is in verses 26-30 with the servant who hid his talent. He clearly loses his salvation as he is cast into the outer darkness of hell. This can not apply to the church, so this must be a Tribulation parable.

Matthew 25:31-46 – This passage describes what is known as the Judgment of the Nations. It cannot be much clearer about the time frame in verse 31. The Son of man (Jewish Messiah) will be seated upon the throne of his glory in the Millennial kingdom. Nations will be assembled before him, which will be the Gentile groups of the Tribulation. They will be judged based on how they treated the Jews during the Tribulation. I alluded to this earlier in the instructions in Matthew chapter 10. In Hitler's Germany in World War II, Jews were singled out for extermination. In the Tribulation, this will be played out again, only on a much larger world-wide scale and with far greater intensity.

Many people in Germany at that time sheltered Jews out of compassion for fellow human beings, some even with Biblical motivation. This will be repeated in the Tribulation. Sheltering or harboring a Jew in the Tribulation is one of the means of salvation and entrance into the kingdom of the Messiah. The "least of these my brethren" are the BRETHREN of Jesus Christ. See how hard the Bible is to understand? Jesus was Jewish. His brethren are Jewish. They have no means of survival under the mark of the beast (which they have refused). They will be the "least" during the reign of terror of the Antichrist who will be seeking to exterminate them from the earth once and for all. He has been trying it for 4,000 years and has failed miserably. He will get his chance at one last "final solution" after he turns on them in the Tribulation. Those who go along with his plan and do not help the brethren of Jesus will be judged. Those who care for them will be rewarded. It even implies that many will not even fully realize what they have done. Out of sheer humanitarian compassion and basic human decency they will take care of a Jewish witness. The promise to Abraham that God will "bless them which bless thee" (Genesis 12:3) will be played out in its full implementation.

If you will indulge me for just a moment, I need to jump on my soap box and vent. This is my book, so I can say what I want, and when you write one, so can you. I am absolutely fed up sick and tired of hearing politicians quote this passage of scripture as if they have the first idea what the H-E-double hockey sticks they are talking about. They claim we have to pass socialist legislation to "care for the least of these my brethren". They want all of us to give them trillions of dollars so that they can dole out a few of them to homeless crack addicts who will vote for them to keep them in power. I hate to be cynical, but that is precisely the motive, and if you do not think so, I have a bridge in New York I would like to talk to you about. Read John 12:4-6 if you would like God's take on this. Of course, when I say these things, immediately I am accused of being heartless and cruel and selfish, and that I do not care about the "less fortunate" among us. That is an insult. Pastors who do this job right devote their entire lives to helping those who are down and out. We just define help differently. We want to see the "least" come to know Jesus Christ as Saviour. That way, they will have a mansion waiting for them in heaven (John 14:2) and be a joint heir of the Universe with Jesus Christ (Romans 8:17) and be stinking filthy rich beyond their wildest dreams. Then we want to see them grow in the grace and knowledge of their Lord and Saviour and learn how to manage life within the pages of his blessed book. God takes care of his children. Those who live according to the truths of the word of God have a promise: "My God shall supply all your need according to his riches in glory by Christ Jesus" (Philippians 4:19). That person may not have two nickels to rub together his whole life, or he may be a multi-millionaire. But I can assure you he will never need a self-righteous power-mad greedy politician to "take care of him". David said, "I have been young, and now am old; yet have I not seen the righteous forsaken, nor his seed begging bread" (Psalm 37:25). That principle is just as true today as it was 3,000 years ago when it was first penned.

The irony is that those who run around quoting this passage while crying buckets of fake crocodile tears over the "least of these my brethren" will be the FIRST ONES at the head of the class to try to rid the world of the <u>actual</u> "least of these my brethren" in the Tribulation.

Sorry for the rant. Thanks for bearing with me. Do you know how you hate to throw up, but it always makes you feel better afterwards? I feel better now.

That was a rather lengthy section on the sealing of the 144,000 from Revelation chapter 7 and some other passages related to it. We now return to finish the rest of Revelation chapter 7.

Revelation 7:9-17 – The Great Multitude Around the Throne

Once again, the scene shifts to heaven and the throne of God. This section gives a brief description of two groups of people; the church age saints and the Tribulation saints. It is important to make this clear distinction or it will confuse the passage and make the church go through the Tribulation.

<u>VS 9-12</u> – This passage describes the church age saints. They are a great multitude, just as Isaiah 54:1 says the children of the desolate (Gentiles) are more than the children of the married wife (Israel). They are from every nation, kindred, people and tongue, exactly like Revelation 5:9. This is not Israel, but a Gentile body redeemed from every people group. The elders and the four beasts appear in verse 11, which we have already detailed as representative of the church age. They are clothed in white robes (verse 9), which is the righteousness of the saints (Revelation 19:8). This group is described nearly identically to the church in heaven just after the rapture in Revelation chapter 5.

<u>VS 13-17</u> – This passage describes the Tribulation saints. Some of the details differ. In order to see this clearly, we have to get the sense of verse 13. One of the elders (from the church) asked a question about those arrayed in white robes. Naturally, we would think he is asking about the group just described that is in white robes. But if so, then we have a problem. Verse 14 says they came out of "great tribulation". People in the church age can certainly experience great tribulation and trials. Many of them suffered for their faith greatly, even unto torture and martyrdom. But we are raptured out and delivered before THE "Great Tribulation" (Matthew 24:21). So the question asked in verse 13 is of this nature. "Yes, here is the great multitude of church age saints redeemed by the Lamb, but who are THESE (pointing to another group) and where did THEY come from? This distinction must be made because the description of these groups varies. Otherwise, the church comes out of the Tribulation, which means we have to go through at least a part of it, if not all of it.

The passage makes several inferences to the Jewish nation in the Millennial kingdom. Verse 15 says they will serve him "day and night in his temple". Since there is no night in heaven (Revelation 21:25), this has to be the temple on earth in the Millennium. The verse continues, "He that sitteth on the throne shall dwell among them"; again, when he returns to earth for his kingdom. Verse 16 says they will not hunger or thirst any more, like they did in the Tribulation when they could not buy even the basic essentials of life. Then verse 17 says that God will wipe away all tears from their eyes. This happens twice in the book of Revelation. This is the first time, and is connected to Israel as they are restored for the kingdom. Psalm 126 speaks of this. It begins with the Lord turning the captivity of Zion at the Second Advent and the establishment of Israel as "head of the nations" (Deuteronomy 28:13). Notice in verses 5-6 how their tears are turned into joy. Jesus said the same thing in John 16:20, that sorrow will be turned into joy. We can apply this to anyone in any age who trusts the Lord, but doctrinally, Jesus is speaking to his Jewish apostles, and by extension his people in the Tribulation. He even used the analogy of a woman giving birth in John 16:21, which is one of the key terms in the Bible speaking of the Tribulation. The second time tears are wiped away is in Revelation 21:4, which we will cover when we get there.

Revelation Chapter 8 – The Trumpets Begin – Trumpets 1-4

Revelation 8:1-6 – The Seventh Seal is Opened and the Seven Trumpets Begin

VS 1 – There was silence in heaven about the space of half an hour. I have not heard a valid explanation of this verse. I have heard a few jokes about it. Men like to say it means there are no women in heaven. They don't say that around their wives, however. I have also heard it said that there are no preachers in heaven either. It is nearly impossible to keep them quiet for half an hour. I joke that it refers to dinner time. If you set a plate of food in front of most guys, they will be so busy shoveling groceries in their pie hole that you won't hear a peep. The only thing I can possibly think of is that as the Trumpets of God's judgment are about to be opened, the carnage and severity is so extreme it causes heaven to collectively gasp and hold their breath. But that is pure speculation.

VS 2-6 – This passage is basically an introduction to the Trumpets as seen from the throne. The prayers of the saints have ascended to the throne of God like incense, and God is now ready to move against those who have rejected him. The silence is broken and the prayer of Revelation 6:10 will be answered: "How long?" You see this prayer many times in the Psalms also. This verse tells us that the incense in the Old Testament and in the Tabernacle pictures prayer.

Trumpets were sounded in the Old Testament for several purposes, and all of them have some connection to the Tribulation. Moses prepared two trumpets in Numbers 10:1-2 "for the calling of the assembly, and for the journeying of the camps". When the first trumpet sounded, Israel was to gather before Moses at the door of the Tabernacle. This pictures the assembly of Israel presenting themselves before the Lord at his Mid-Tribulation appearance. Jesus is the door (John 10:9), and he will meet them as they begin their wilderness journey through the next 3½ years, which is the purpose of the second trumpet in Numbers 10. Another trumpet sounded in Exodus 19:16-20 as Moses went up to the top of Mount Sinai to get the law. Verse 17 says, "Moses brought forth the people out of the camp to meet with God". Moses will return in the Tribulation and Israel will meet with God to get their instructions for the Great Tribulation. In Joshua chapter 6, Israel conquered the cursed city Jericho by blowing trumpets. It was a call to battle without armaments. At the end of the Tribulation, Israel will win a battle against a cursed city, Babylon (Rome) without firing a shot. A trumpet is blown in Zion in Joel 2:1 and 2:15. Zephaniah 1:14-18 also sounds a trumpet of judgment. Both places are linked to the day of the Lord.

We need one more little side detour before we begin walking through the Trumpets of Revelation. The rapture of the church has a trumpet connected with it as well. Both of the main passages describing the rapture in the New Testament include a trumpet (I Corinthians 15:52, I Thessalonians 4:16). The verse in Corinthians calls it "the last trump". This has led some to teach that the church will not be raptured until the final trumpet of the Tribulation. We have already dealt with that previously in the three raptures. The "last trump" of Corinthians is the last one of the church age which draws that dispensation to a close.

Revelation 8:7 – The First Trumpet

Trumpets 1 through 4 are sounded essentially in unison just after the Mid-Tribulation point, just as Seals 2 through 4 were. The first Trumpet is environmental disaster. The plagues of Egypt in Exodus will be repeated in some fashion. This one mentions hail, but it is stated in much different terms. Remember that John is trying to describe 21st century events with first century knowledge and terms, and even under the inspiration of God, it would not be possible for him to use the term "nuclear war". But the description is fairly clear with hail falling from the sky mingled with fire and blood and scorching large sections of the ground. Burning up the vegetation interrupts the food chain. If cows and chickens cannot eat, man will not be able to eat either. In the plagues of Egypt, locusts came in just after the hail and stripped the land. In the third Seal of the black horse, an economic collapse corrupts the food supply. These are related.

Revelation 8:8-9 – The Second Trumpet

"A great mountain burning with fire was cast into the sea". The sea is likely the Mediterranean, as it usually is when referring to a literal body of water on the earth. A burning rock sounds like a meteor strike, although it could also be nuclear. The result is oceanic and maritime disaster. Waters will be turned to blood as they were in Egypt in the plagues. One third of the sea life will die. Burning up the grass disrupts the food supply, and killing that much sea life will throw the eco-system out of balance. Then one third of the ships will be destroyed which will massively disrupt commerce.

Revelation 8:10-11 – The Third Trumpet

This is the classic "Wormwood" passage. A burning star falling upon the rivers and fountains of waters could be another meteor strike or possibly even a comet or something similar. The previous Trumpet hit the sea corrupting the saltwater marine life. This one hits the fresh water supply. Wormwood is a bitter poisonous herb (Jeremiah 9:12-16, 23:14-15). It is translated "hemlock" in Amos 6:12. Once again one third of the water is affected, and many people will die from drinking it.

This brings a couple of passages of scripture into play. I have previously mentioned Matthew 10:42 and the "cold cup of water" for the Jewish witnesses. That doesn't sound like much now, but if the fresh water supply has been affected, it is fairly significant. Then there is Mark 16:17-18 and the signs that will follow these witnesses. The Charismatics have twisted these verses out of their doctrinal context for some of their more extreme and bizarre practices. One of them is snake handling. What they do NOT tell you is that they put the snakes in a refrigerator before they bring them out to play with them. Since they are cold-blooded, it slows down their metabolism and they won't bite. There was a recent "reality" show (not much <u>real</u> about most of them) about some snake handlers, and they had to cancel the show because the main character got bitten and died. The other "extreme" sign in this passage in Mark is about drinking any deadly thing. So why did Jesus throw this in? There is no record of this being fulfilled in the Bible or in history. The snake thing could be fulfilled by Paul in Acts 28:3-6. The deadly drink will be fulfilled in the Tribulation if one of the witnesses has to drink poisoned water to survive as a result of this third Trumpet that poisons the water supply.

Revelation 8:12 – The Fourth Trumpet

The sun, moon and stars will be "darkened" for one third of the day. This is the plague of darkness from Egypt revisited. The sun and moon being darkened is prophesied many times in the Bible (Isaiah 13:10, Joel 2:31, 3:15, Amos 8:9, Matthew 24:29 to name a few). Exactly <u>how</u> this happens is not discussed directly, and quite frankly does not matter. The God who brought light into existence and made the stars also can govern them as he sees fit. It also does not say how long this phenomenon will last; whether one day or the full 3½ years or some time in between. The issue is the object lesson. In all four of these first Trumpets, the ratio of one third is prominent. One third of the angels fell in the original rebellion under Lucifer (Revelation 12:4). He led a group of beings of light away from God, so God answers in kind. Jesus said there will be signs in the heavens (Luke 21:25) and the hypocrites can look at the sky but can not "discern the signs of the times" (Matthew 16:1-3). People in the Tribulation will look at the sign of the darkened sun and be clueless because of their blind rejection of the Son.

Revelation 8:13 – Woe, Woe, Woe

The Trumpets are divided into three "Woes". Revelation 9:12 says, "One woe is past; and, behold, there come two woes more hereafter." Then the next verse announces Trumpet number six. So the first five Trumpets are Woe number one, and Trumpet six is Woe number two. Then Revelation 11:14 marks the next division. Trumpet number seven is Woe number three culminating in the Second Advent.

Revelation Chapters 9 and 10 – Trumpets 5-6

Revelation 9:1-12 – The Fifth Trumpet

Revelation chapter 9 is one of the critical parts of the book of Revelation. It deals with the opening of the bottomless pit and the return of Judas Iscariot to attempt to "finish the job" of the betrayal of Jesus Christ. This will take us some time to get through. So buckle up, grab a Pepsi and some chips, and let us spend some quality Bible study time detailing this all important passage.

Before we get into the details of the fifth Trumpet, we must take a trip to the "underworld" (not literally, thankfully). I covered some of this when we discussed the three raptures. I showed how "hell" is located in the center of the earth and has three compartments. There is the place of fire and torment we are all familiar with as the common understanding of hell. Then there is the place of comfort called paradise or Abraham's bosom. Then there is a great gulf between them. That gulf is the bottomless pit of Revelation chapter 9. There are a few other terms in the Bible describing what we understand as "hell". There may be minor differences, but practically, no one who is in a place of fire and torment will notice or care.

Revelation 20 describes a "lake of fire" reserved for those who have rejected God. This is the eternal and final "non-resting" place for Satan and his followers. There will be an earthly manifestation of this during the Millennium described in Isaiah 66:23-24:

> "And it shall come to pass, that from one new moon to another, and from one sabbath to another, shall all flesh come to worship before me, saith the LORD. And they shall go forth, and look upon the carcases of the men that have transgressed against me: for their worm shall not die, neither shall their fire be quenched; and they shall be an abhorring unto all flesh."

During the Millennium, the nations of the world will be required to give regular attendance to the Lord on the throne at set times of the year. Before they go back home, they will take a side trip to the area south of the Dead Sea where Sodom and Gomorrah once were. There will be an open "crater" revealing the souls of those who have rejected the Lord. It is described in Isaiah 34:9-10, which mentions the regions of Idumea and Bozrah which are on either side of this area. It will be a vivid reminder of what awaits anyone who thinks they have a better idea than the King. The terminology of "their worm shall not die, neither shall their fire be quenched" was used by the Lord in Mark 9:44-48. Now, hell is the "holding place" for the lost until the Great White Throne Judgment. At that time, hell will "deliver up the dead" (Revelation 20:13) for judgment. Then the lost will go "out of the frying pan (hell) into the lake of fire".

There is also a "prison" where fallen angels are held in "chains of darkness" (I Peter 3:19, Jude 6). This is the holding place for certain unclean spirits who left their first estate. These would be the Genesis 6 boys and their copycats in later times. I alluded to this briefly in the "firstfruits rapture". This is probably the same as the bottomless pit, which will become evident as we see it get opened in Revelation chapter 9.

The bottomless pit is a strange description. How can something be tangible yet have no bottom? Well, if hell is in the center of the earth, and the great gulf (bottomless pit) is in the center of that, then its location is in the very core of the earth. It is like a volcano but at the center of the earth instead of on the surface. It is a continually rolling, boiling pot of fire. The next time you bring a pot of water to a "full rolling boil", watch how it is constantly moving. If you put a small item in the pot, it will never actually touch bottom. Gravity pulls items to the center. At the same time, the earth spins on its axis at a fairly decent clip of about 1,000 miles per hour at the equator at its surface. An object (soul) in this rolling, boiling pot of fire is being drawn to the outside by centrifugal force while being pulled to the inside by gravity. Have you ever had the dream where you are falling? Souls in hell will be "falling" and burning eternally at the same time and never hit bottom. Sure makes you glad the Lord saved you from that, doesn't it?

Many lost people claim that they don't mind going to hell because "all my friends will be there". The cartoons characterize people sitting around on ledges in the "underworld" with a few flickers of fire scattered around and Satan standing there in his red suit and pitchfork. Nothing could be further from the actual truth and reality. Hell is described as "outer darkness" in the Bible. No one will see their friends or anything else for that matter. They will be "boiling" in fire, constantly moving at a great speed and slamming into billions of other souls who are continually falling and never hitting bottom either. Satan will be chained in this pit for 1,000 years (Revelation 20:3). He desired the "sides of the north" yet ends up in the "sides of the pit" (Isaiah 14:12-15). If there are only sides in this pit, then it has no bottom.

Now that I have hopefully "scared the hell out of you", let's walk through Revelation chapter 9.

VS 1 – A "star" falls from heaven with the key of the bottomless pit. Some teach this is Jesus Christ, but I beg to differ. They reason that Jesus is the "angel" of Revelation 20:1 with the key to the pit to bind Satan, and this would be true. But God can give a key then take it back later. Have you ever loaned your keys to someone? In Revelation chapter 20, an angel uses the key to <u>close</u> the pit. In Revelation 9, an angel uses the key to <u>open</u> the pit. That is the same key, but for two different purposes at two different times. Others say that Jesus has the "keys of hell and of death" (Revelation 1:18), so this angel has to be him. But the key of hell and the key of death and the key of the bottomless pit can all be different keys. How many keys are on your keychain? The angel in Revelation 9:1 cannot be Jesus Christ for a number of reasons. First and foremost, the angel of Revelation 9:1 <u>falls</u> from heaven. Jesus <u>came down</u> from heaven (John 3:13). In his bread of life discourse in John 6:32-58, Jesus used the exact term seven times to communicate clearly that he did not fall from heaven, he came down from heaven. There is a huge difference. Looking ahead for a brief moment to Revelation 10:1, we see a mighty angel <u>come down</u> from heaven, and the description that follows can be none other than Jesus.

Lucifer is <u>fallen</u> from heaven (Isaiah 14:12). There are only five times in the Bible when someone or something is said to "fall from heaven". Isaiah 14 is the classic passage on the fall of Lucifer. Job 1:16 says "the fire of God is fallen from heaven." This was the report of the messengers to Job about the first round of disasters he faced at the hand of Satan. The messenger only <u>thought</u> it was the fire of God, but it was actually a counterfeit from Satan. Then Matthew 24:29 says "the stars shall fall from heaven" at the Second Coming of Christ. These are fallen angels. Luke 10:18 should seal the deal. Jesus said he beheld Satan <u>fall</u> as lightning from heaven. The fifth and final occurrence is in this text in Revelation 9:1. How could anyone think this angel who <u>fell</u> from heaven could be anyone other than Satan? This is the fifth angel announcing the fifth Trumpet. Five in the Bible is the number of death. This is the "Death Angel" who has been given the key to the bottomless pit so he can let his buddy Judas and all his demon friends out. Yes, God has the keys, but he gives this one to Satan to accomplish his purpose of judgment. It is a "jailbreak" allowed by God to fulfill his plan and allow mankind to reap as he has desired.

With this in mind, I want to point out perhaps the most glaring and blasphemous error of the new Bibles. In Job 38:7, God reports on creation, "When the morning stars sang together, and all the sons of God shouted for joy." This was before the fall of Lucifer. A race of beings were created that we know as angels, but have various terms given to them in the Bible. Without delving into a study of angelology, these beings carried the image of the Lord Jesus Christ, just as the sons of God in the New Testament (born again believers) do. They are called sons of God because they are just like THE Son of God. He also uses the term "morning stars" (plural) in the same sense. They carried the image of THE morning star, who is Jesus Christ (Revelation 22:16). The plural term appears only in Job 38:7. The singular term appears also in Revelation 2:28, and clearly refers to Jesus Christ. So we get to Isaiah 14:12 which says in the King James, "How art thou fallen from heaven, O Lucifer, <u>son</u> of the morning…" The new Bibles remove the title Lucifer from this verse. This is his only mention by that name in the Bible, so they have helped the master of disguise "cover his tracks" by removing him completely from their "Bibles". Then some of the new Bibles go on to say, "How are you fallen, O morning star…" They have <u>Jesus</u> falling from heaven instead of Lucifer. Nice job, guys! Other versions will use the term "Day Star" which again makes Jesus fall from heaven because that is another of his titles in II Peter 1:19. Even the "New" King James gets in on the act. They leave the text stand as it is in the real King James with the name Lucifer, but slip in the margin note, "literally Day Star". No, doctor, Lucifer is not "literally" Jesus! There are hundreds of passages in the new Bibles that make one suspect of its credibility, but none more egregious than this. The perversion of Isaiah 14:12 and transferring Lucifer's rebellion and fall to my Lord and Saviour Jesus Christ should be all you need to throw the new Bibles in the dumpster where they belong.

VS 2-3 – This is a description of demonic "locusts". It alludes to the plague in Egypt, but these are not the same type of locusts. This is a demonic horde released from the chains of darkness in the bottomless pit to wreak havoc on the earth. These locusts come out of the smoke (verse 3), but natural locusts are repelled by smoke. Literal locusts "have no king" (Proverbs 30:27), they act independently of each other and just swarm. But these in Revelation 9 have a king over them (verse 11). Physical locusts are plant eaters, but the locusts in Revelation 9 attack men, not vegetation. These locusts are given power over men as scorpions (verse 3, 5). Other than just being "bugs", scorpions and locusts are not related.

VS 4-6 – The activity of these "demon-locusts" makes it clear further that you won't find them in your friendly neighborhood entomologist's lab. Verse 4 says they will not hurt any green thing (which is what locusts eat), but only people who have not been sealed (the 144,000). They will torment men and women physically and spiritually so much that they will seek to die, but will not be able to. We have an epidemic of suicide all over the world today. It stems from physical, emotional, mental, and spiritual torment that is so bad it causes people to take their own life. Just think how bad it will be when people get to that stage and cannot complete the act. But even if they could, it would only exchange their temporary minor problem with an eternal major problem. That torment will last for five months, the number of death. Also, the wording of verse 4 establishes the time frame of the opening of the bottomless pit. The locust-scorpions are commanded to "not hurt the grass" (vegetation). The same term is used in Revelation 7:3 where the "hurt" to be inflicted is held off until the 144,000 are sealed. Since this occurs at the mid-point of the Tribulation, the bottomless pit will have to be opened at this point. This will be important as we continue on to the Revealing of the Wicked in chapter 13.

VS 7-10 – The description of these demon-locusts again excludes the insects that devastated Egypt. They are like horses with a crown of gold on their head, faces of a man, hair like a woman, teeth like a lion, with iron breastplates, wings, and tails like a scorpion. Someone with a vivid imagination and the skill of an artist could draw those creatures and it would shock most people. Yet our children watch these types of creatures every Saturday morning on Cartoon Network, and we buy them action figures to go along with it. Then we watch movies and play video games that depict these things and think nothing of it. The iron breastplates connect them to the race of "giants" in the Bible which are demonic. Goliath had an iron spear (I Samuel 17:7). Daniel's image of the ten toes of the Antichrist is from a kingdom of iron and clay. Og king of Bashan was of the remnant of the giants and slept on an iron bedstead over 13 feet long (Deuteronomy 3:11). Sisera, a type of the Antichrist, oppressed Israel with 900 chariots of iron (Judges 4:3). Those are only a few of the references in the Bible about iron. Almost every time it appears, it is linked to demonic beings or their offspring. Lost scientists have been desperately attempting to make contact with life in outer space for generations. Some day soon, they will do so, then wish they hadn't. When this bottomless pit is opened, every devil held in chains right now will be unleashed upon earth, and the suffering and torment will be unspeakable. Yet man will persist in his stubborn rebellion.

VS 11 – These demons have a king over them who will lead them out of their chains. This king is named (Abaddon / Apollyon) which means "destroyer". He is an angel (fallen, of course). His identity can be very clearly discovered by comparing scripture with scripture and tying together various passages. Let me just jump right into the deep end of the pool and tell you that it is the soul of Judas Iscariot, then I will bring out all the passages of the Bible to support this teaching.

First, notice I said the <u>soul</u> of Judas. That is a deliberate statement to set up something I will cover when we get to chapter 13. When Judas hung himself, his human spirit "went back to God" (Ecclesiastes 12:7) and his body rotted in the ground like everyone else. When God created Adam, it says, "...man became a living soul" (Genesis 2:7). The term "man" in that verse is inclusive of all. A human being is a soul that will live forever in heaven or hell. That soul has a spirit inside to animate it and give it natural life on this dirt ball, and the soul has a body wrapped around the outside of it. So the soul of Judas is still very much "alive and well?", but not on planet earth. Just as Jesus will return the second time physically, and just as Moses and Elijah will return in the Tribulation, Judas will return to finish his work.

The "spirits in prison" in the bottomless pit have a king over them. Acts 1:25 says of Judas that when he died, "...he might go to his own place." It does not say that he went to hell, although we have already seen that hell and the bottomless pit are practically the same. The words of the Bible mean things and are specifically chosen for a purpose. If Judas has his <u>OWN</u> place, he "owns" it as its "king". The Antichrist is called "the son of perdition" in II Thessalonians 2:3. Jesus used that exact same term for Judas in his final prayer in John 17:12. Revelation 17:8 says, "The beast that thou sawest was, and is not; and shall ascend out of the bottomless pit, and go into perdition." Judas "was" and he "is not" at the time of John's writing in 100 AD. But he will ascend out of the bottomless pit and go into perdition. Revelation 17:11 says the Antichrist "goeth into perdition". Judas will come out of perdition as its "son" as a counterfeit of the Son of God and lead his demon hordes out as their king.

Revelation 9:11 also says he is an "angel". Most people think all angels are good, but they forget that one third of them were led away by Lucifer's rebellion. Jesus said of Judas, "Have not I chosen you twelve, and one of you is a devil? He spake of Judas Iscariot the son of Simon: for he it was that should betray him, being one of the twelve" (John 6:70-71). Jesus did <u>not</u> say that Judas was acting like a devil, or full of the devil. He said he <u>IS</u> a devil. There was something rather unique about Judas. He is the only man in the Bible to be personally indwelt by Satan himself (John 13:2, 27). Many have been possessed by unclean spirits, but Judas got the "honor?" of getting the chief one. As I mentioned earlier, Jesus used the exact same term for Judas that is reserved for the Antichrist. Also of note is the exact wording of Jesus' statement that Judas was the "*son* of Simon". If you will note carefully, the word "*son*" is in italics. That means the word does not appear directly in the original text, but it is implied. I do not have time to go through a long discussion of the italicized words in the King James Bible. They belong in the text just as much as the others, but they are added to make the context flow and be understandable in English. The phrase, "*the son of…*" is italicized several times in the Bible, but most of the time it is not. A son in the Bible is not always a first-generation biological male descendant. It can refer to a step-son, a son-in-law, a grandson, or a descendant of many generations. The omission of the word in the original text and the addition of the italics allows for the possibility of any of those. In the case of Judas, I believe there is a point God is trying to make. Satan counterfeits everything God does. Jesus was born of a virgin without the male seed being physically involved. Note this passage about the "*son*" of perdition:

"Set thou a wicked man over him: and let Satan stand at his right hand. When he shall be judged, let him be condemned: and let his prayer become sin. Let his days be few; and let another take his office. Let his children be fatherless, and his wife a widow. Let his children be continually vagabonds, and beg: let them seek their bread also out of their desolate places. Let the extortioner catch all that he hath; and let the strangers spoil his labour. Let there be none to extend mercy unto him: neither let there be any to favour his fatherless children. Let his posterity be cut off; and in the generation following let their name be blotted out. Let the iniquity of his fathers be remembered with the LORD; and let not the sin of his mother be blotted out." (Psalm 109:6-14)

These verses very clearly speak prophetically of Judas. Satan stood "at his right hand" when he indwelt Judas personally (verse 6). Judas' prayer became sin when he "repented" and tried to give the money back to the Pharisees (verse 7). Peter quoted verse 8 directly in Acts chapter 1 speaking of Judas when they chose Matthias to replace him in the apostolic office. The children of Judas were fatherless and his wife a widow after he hung himself (verse 9). The "extortioners" caught the thirty pieces of silver and bought a field with it (verse 11). His posterity was cut off, meaning not only his physical line, but his "legacy" as well, and their name is "blotted out". Does anyone in their right mind today name their son Judas? Then verse 14 is the bombshell. The "iniquity of his fathers" would be those who were "of their father the devil" (John 8:44). But what is the "sin of his mother"? God does not want it to be blotted out, meaning he wants us to be reminded of it. The sons of God (fallen angels) in Genesis chapter 6 saw the daughters of men and produced with them a race of giants. These are the angels who "kept not their first estate" (Jude 6) and came to this part of God's "real estate" to co-habit with women. Genesis 6:4 says this happened "also after that", meaning the events of Genesis 6 have occurred again since then. If Judas was a devil (Jesus' words), then he came by it through the sin of his mother. With the special role he had with the prince of the devils (Satan), he was used to infiltrate the twelve to overthrow the plan of God. He was so good at this charade that the rest of the apostles were fooled. He was "Anti-Christ" the first time he was here, and will come back again when the bottomless pit is opened to finish the job. But never fear. The Lord has him pegged, and he will not succeed. Hang on to all of this. When I get to Revelation chapter 13 and the Revealing of the Wicked, it will come into clearer focus.

VS 12 – God has divided the seven Trumpets into three "Woes". After the fifth Trumpet, the first Woe is past. Trumpet number six begins immediately in the next verse. Then in Revelation 11:14, the second Woe is past, and the third Woe begins in the very next verse with the introduction of the seventh Trumpet. So what does that mean, preacher? It means Trumpets 1 through 5 make up Woe number one, Trumpet six is Woe number two, and Trumpet seven is Woe number three. That is all I know because that is all it says, and I find nothing else in the Bible to expand on it. The danger with the book of Revelation is the speculation of trying to jam private interpretations into obscure passages. If God does not give any more light on it, just let it say what it says and leave it alone and move on.

Revelation 9:13-21 – The Sixth Trumpet

The description of Trumpet six is rather lengthy. The passage spans from Revelation 9:13 through 11:14. There is obviously a lot of information here, so don't get lost in the "forest" as we examine the "trees" and make our way through essentially two full chapters before we get to the seventh Trumpet. This first section in Revelation 9 describes a massive army coming against Israel from the east.

VS 13-14 – The sixth Trumpet opens with the loosing of four angels which are bound in the Euphrates River. This prepares the way for an army to cross the river from the east to come against Israel. This implies that there is a spiritual legion being restrained, and by extension, a physical legion restrained as well. Daniel chapter 10 reveals information that cannot be found from any other source other than the Bible. There are spiritual representatives over nations. Daniel 10 mentions the prince of Grecia and the prince of Persia, and Daniel 12 says Michael is the "prince which standeth for the children of thy people" which is Israel. Certain locations on planet earth have spiritual significance. Rome is controlled by the Catholic Church. When I say Mecca, you immediately think Islam. In fact, if you are not Muslim, you cannot even enter the city of Mecca legally, which is fine with me. Salt Lake City, Utah is the home of the Mormon Church. A few years back, my wife and I went on vacation to southern Utah. Bryce Canyon and Zion National Park are beautiful. If you are looking for a vacation trip, I highly recommend it. On our way home we took a day to tour the Mormon Temple area in downtown Salt Lake City. Because of what I do, I am hyper sensitive to things like this, but I actually physically FELT the spiritual oppression in that location. Satan has assigned some of his minions to certain areas on earth. The angels who are "on hold" at the Euphrates are probably demonic spirits controlling that area. God will kick them loose at his set time to continue his judgments upon a Christ-rejecting world.

VS 15-17 – These verses describe the time when these spirits are set loose, and the number and nature of the army which will be called to the battle. Verse 15 says this will last for "an hour, and a day, and a month, and a year." This could be poetic imagery much the same way we use terms like this. We might ask someone, "Do you have a minute?" What follows rarely lasts exactly 60 seconds. Time frames like these are quite often used in the Bible differently than what we understand as exact elapsed time. God's calendar and clock are always exactly precise, but they do not always match ours. One day with the Lord is as a thousand years (II Peter 3:8). Daniel's weeks are seven years long, not seven days. When Jesus said, "My <u>hour</u> is not yet come", he referred to the events of his sacrifice beginning with the triumphal entry into Jerusalem through the resurrection. All that took much longer than 60 minutes. But it is highly possible that this time period is precise on our calendar as well as God's. We are making our second pass through the Tribulation, and we know it to be 3½ years. So if this army from the east is unleashed a little over a year ahead of the Second Coming, then it is the beginning of what Saddam Hussein called "the mother of all battles" or Armageddon.

Verse 16 gives the size of the army as 200 million. Many commentators say this has to be a spiritual army of demonic creatures, and they could be right. The description that follows in the passage is similar to what we saw earlier in the chapter of the demonic horde that comes up out of the bottomless pit with Judas. Horses with heads of lions and breastplates of fire are hard to imagine as the equine creatures we know today. But again remember that John is describing 21st century warfare using first century terms, so he could be seeing modern military technology. Many of the commentators say an army of 200 million is not feasible naturally speaking. But some of them were writing long before China could boast an army that size, and if you consider the <u>entire</u> Far East together, 200 million soldiers could easily be gathered. Revelation 16:12 is a parallel passage. An angel dries up the Euphrates to prepare the way of the kings of the east to come against Israel. These are kin<u>gs</u> (plural), so it is likely all of the "Far East" including Japan, Korea, Southeast Asia, and even India. The population of that part of the world today is well over 3 billion. Amassing an army of 200 million from those nations would not be unreasonable. If this is an actual human army, which I tend to think, then it lines up with the fulfillment of prophecies where God will be drawing the nations to Palestine and the valley of Megiddo for judgment (Joel 3:1-2, Joel 3:9-14, Zephaniah 3:8). We will cover this in more detail in Revelation chapter 14.

VS 18-19 – The carnage and death will be unspeakable. The loosing of this army results in one third of humanity being killed in warfare. Keep in mind that we have already seen a couple of other times where huge portions of human life will be "purged". A general famine and pestilence wipe out one fourth in Revelation 6:8, and Wormwood takes out another large group in Revelation 8. Along with the general death and mayhem of this time, the human race will be significantly depleted in God's judgment. World War II took out 22 million, but that was only a "blip" compared to this. One fourth of humanity as it is on earth right now would be pushing close to 2 billion (with a B). Jesus said the Tribulation would be unlike any time in the history of man before or after (Matthew 24:21). Keep in mind that after all this death and destruction, we still have the final battle of Armageddon to consider. That is why God refers to a <u>remnant</u> being left at his coming. The population of the earth at the beginning of the Millennial kingdom will be <u>significantly</u> less than it is today. See Isaiah 24:1-12 for a description.

VS 20-21 – The blind stubborn hardened heart of mankind is beyond belief. These verses describe men and women who have firmly set their hearts against God. Despite the disaster and judgment, they simply refuse to repent. It is absolute proof of the depravity of the human heart apart from our Creator. Every rejection only serves to harden hearts further. Pharaoh is the classic example. He hardened his own heart against God so completely that God stepped in and "helped" him along. God can save anyone at any time as long as they are still inhaling and exhaling his air. But people get in this condition because they "paint themselves into a corner" and refuse to allow God to save them. Seven sins are listed: (1) The works of their hands (2) Worship of devils (3) Worship of idols (4) Murders, (5) Sorceries (Greek: pharmakia is drug abuse) (6) Fornication (7) Thefts. It describes mankind in full and complete rebellion against God.

Revelation Chapter 10 – The Sixth Trumpet and Second Woe Continued

Revelation 10:1-7 – The Vision of the Mighty Angel

VS 1 – It is clear that this angel is the "angel of the Lord", Jesus Christ. This angel stands alone among the other angels in this book in his description. It is very similar to Revelation 1:12-16, which is also Jesus. Just walk through the verses and note these points. He is a mighty angel (Almighty God) who comes down from heaven (he does not fall from heaven), clothed with a cloud (as Jesus ascended in Acts 1), with a rainbow upon his head (there is a rainbow around the throne – Revelation 4:3), his face is as the sun (the Sun of Righteousness – Malachi 4:2), and his feet as pillars of fire (like in Revelation 1:15 and like the pillar of fire that led Israel in the wilderness). All of that is just in verse 1. He has a little book in his hand picturing the word of God. In verse 3, he has a voice like a lion (of the tribe of Juda), and his voice utters seven thunders, which is a picture of the voice of God (John 12:28-29, Psalm 29:3). In verse 6 this angel swears by the God of creation (the God of creation swears only by himself – Hebrews 6:13), and this angel has the power to control time and also "times". If you cannot see how all of that points to the Lord Jesus Christ, I would wonder what book you were reading.

VS 2-3 – The little book in the hand of this angel is open. Jesus has been found worthy to open the book (Revelation 5:5). He then sets his foot on "land and sea" as an act of ownership. Psalm 24:1-2 says, "The earth is the LORD'S, and the fulness thereof; the world, and they that dwell therein. For he hath founded it upon the seas, and established it upon the floods." I just commented on verse 3 as a picture of Jesus.

VS 4 – John is told to seal the voices of the seven thunders. Whatever they said will not be known until the Lord returns, if even then. It may never be known. It may just be "unspeakable words, which it is not lawful for a man to utter" (II Corinthians 12:4). I believe things like this are dropped into the Bible (and especially in Revelation) by a specific design of God. Why would God waste precious space in his book to tell us something, then say, "Oh, never mind. Move along, nothing to see here." Passages like this pique our curiosity and lead self-proclaimed prophets to try to dig out the details; which serves the attentive Bible student well. If any prophecy guru tries to tell you these thunderous words have been revealed to him, you can safely count him as a false prophet. God put this in here so we can keep an eye peeled and smoke them out. That is the fascination with the book of Revelation. The desire to "know" what others do not know is a curse inbred from the Garden.

VS 5-7 – I made reference to this earlier when I said this angel can control time. Yes, God can control the clock, and moves it ahead or back at his will. He did so in Joshua chapter 10, and again when Hezekiah was sick (Isaiah 38:8). But when Jesus swears by himself (and his Father) that "there should be time no longer", it is not necessarily referring to the clock. We are in the middle of the sixth Trumpet. The next verse announces the seventh Trumpet which is the Second Advent of Christ. This statement means that the "time is at hand", or that "time is up, ready or not, here I come." The prayer of "How long, Lord?" is finally answered. The culmination of history revealed to the prophets of the Old Testament is at hand. The theme of the Bible is the kingdom of Jesus Christ, and by the time we get to the last Trumpet, or last Seal, or last Vial, Jesus is ready to come. God is not willing that any should perish (II Peter 3:9), and his grace and mercy and longsuffering with man is perfect and will never run out. But there comes a time when he puts it on hold to manifest his righteous judgment and justice, and that time is here.

Revelation 10:8-11 – The Little Book

VS 8-10 – This little book is clearly the word of God. John is instructed to "eat it up". When he does, it turns his belly bitter while at the same time being sweet in his mouth. David wrote, "How sweet are thy words unto my taste! yea, sweeter than honey to my mouth!" (Psalm 119:103). Ezekiel had this same vision. In Ezekiel 3:1-3, he eats a roll of a book that is sweet to the taste, but has some bitter things in it.

The context of Ezekiel chapter 2 has him going to the house of Israel to speak God's words to them. God said they would not hear because they are a rebellious people, and that the words he wants Ezekiel to speak contain "lamentations, and mourning, and woe". But the Bible is sweet even when it has some bitter parts. Proverbs 27:7 says, "The full soul loatheth an honeycomb; but to the hungry soul every bitter thing is sweet." If you are really hungry for God's truth, every verse of the Bible will be sweet to your taste even when it goes against your grain and nature. People often say when they are convicted, "That just rubs me the wrong way!" The Bible will do that to anyone, no matter how long you have been into it and no matter how much you love it. When something in the Bible "rubs you the wrong way", just turn around. It will quit rubbing you the wrong way!

VS 11 – The reason the Bible is "bitter" is because of the message we are called to deliver from it. John and Ezekiel both are told to eat it with the "belly". In other words, we cannot just give a little taste to the Bible and expect it to change our lives. In needs to go down into the innermost parts of our being, and when the word of God is completely "digested", it is sweet and bitter both. Clarence Larkin says the word is bitter because of the announcement of the pending judgment of God which is coming in the book of Revelation. Yes, and John is told he has to be the one to give the announcement. The Bible will "ruin" you in the right way. Those who reject it will face the wrath of its judgment, and those who "eat it up" will have their lives changed forever. Jonah can testify to the bitterness of the message he was called to deliver. Paul was called to testify before Gentiles, kings and Israel, and suffered great persecution from all of them as a result (Acts 9:15-16). Jeremiah was told not to marry and preached through the captivity of Babylon with no recorded converts. Noah preached for 120 years and only got his family. If you make the ministry of the word of God the passion of your life, you can count on at least some of the same.

Revelation Chapter 11 – The Sixth and Seventh Trumpets

Revelation 11:1-2 – The Times of the Gentiles

The temple and the altar are measured in this passage. In order to measure the temple, it has to be there! The most significant part of the peace plan that is the cornerstone of the first half of the Tribulation is the rebuilding of the temple and the reinstatement of the sacrifices on the altar. The exact measurements are not given, other than "with a reed like a rod". One "reed" is an old unit of measurement of 6 cubits, or about 9 feet. But it does not tell us how many. There is a measurement given in Ezekiel 40-48, but that section of the Bible deals with the Millennial city. Another measurement is of the people who worship in the temple. That would be Israel, and one of the main purposes of the Tribulation is for God to "measure" his people as he judges them and purges them for his kingdom. Habakkuk 3:3-6 describes the return of the "Holy One" (Jesus) to reign. Verse 6 says, "He stood, and measured the earth: he beheld, and drove asunder the nations; and the everlasting mountains were scattered, the perpetual hills did bow: his ways are everlasting." God measures people and finds them "wanting" (Daniel 5:25-28).

The one part that is not measured is the court that is outside the temple. This area is given to the Gentiles for the final forty two months of the Tribulation. This probably refers to the Islamic Dome of the Rock Mosque that currently sits on the site. The peace plan allows the temple to be rebuilt, but it has always been believed that the Mosque sits on the original site of the temple, and the only way to rebuild it would be to tear down the Mosque. Fat chance the Arabs would allow that. But recent studies have led many to believe that the original location of the Holy of Holies is about 300 yards to the north of the Mosque. That area today is a concrete slab. The temple could be rebuilt without affecting the Mosque. But once again, fat chance the Muslim world would allow that. This has been covered before when I laid out the Middle East peace plan from Daniel chapter 9 that sets off the Antichrist's false kingdom in the first half of the Tribulation. But I needed to mention it again here because of the text of Revelation 11:1-2.

Gentiles are given control of the temple site for the entire Tribulation. This frames what Jesus called "the times of the Gentiles" in Luke 21:24. This is the time period that Gentile political powers control Israel and Jerusalem. It began when Nebuchadnezzar took Israel into captivity in 606 BC. Since that time, Israel has never had full control of Jerusalem and its entire land. The Times of the Gentiles continues through the entire Tribulation. Some teach that the Times of the Gentiles ended in 1948 when Israel became a Nation again, or in 1967 when they won the Six Day War and recaptured Jerusalem (at least somewhat as we saw earlier). But the Gentiles will "tread the holy city" for the 42 months of the Great Tribulation. You cannot have the "Times of the Jews" until the King of the Jews returns.

From 606 BC through to the present day and to the end of the Tribulation, the land of Israel has been under foreign control. In one of the many arguments with the religious leaders of his day, Jesus said that if they would accept the Son, that the "truth would make them free" (John 8:32). They responded in the next verse with one of the most ridiculous statements in history: "We be Abraham's seed, and were never in bondage to any man." Abraham's seed spent 400 years afflicted in Egypt (Genesis 15:13). Five separate times in the book of Judges they were held captive by foreign nations. Nebuchadnezzar conquered Abraham's seed in 606 BC. They were returned to their land 70 years later, but remained under foreign rule. At the time these self-righteous wackos made their claim, Rome was in full domination of Abraham's seed. Rolling it out to the future from there, they were dispersed through the entire world in 70 AD and have been in bondage to the nations ever since. At present, although they are back in their land, Israel does not have full autonomy. They do what the United States tells them, because we are the only ones in their corner. Once we pull our support (which will happen at some point), it will be the world against Israel, which is the "world alliance" of the "game of Risk" called the Tribulation. We have been in the Times of the Gentiles for 2600 years, and it will continue until the King of the Jews puts and end to it as only he can.

Verse 2 refers to Jerusalem as the "holy city". That term is used also in Nehemiah 11:1 and Isaiah 52:1 for Jerusalem. Then in verse 8, it is referred to as "Sodom and Egypt" spiritually. Based on the rejection of Christ, God tagged the city like that. Imagine how offensive that must be to a Jew to name his "holy" city after a filthy cesspool of sin that resulted in the fire of God, and then the nation that represents the world and was their greatest enemy for centuries. Jerusalem is NOT holy today and it cannot be until the Holy One of Israel returns. I know it is called the "Holy Land" today, but that is only a name we give it and does not describe its actual state with God. Yet God still calls it "the holy city". God calls those things which be as though they were not (Romans 4:17) and he looks through the current mess of sin and worldliness that characterizes his people and his city and calls it holy. It is a look forward to the time when his Son will reign over the earth in that city when it will truly BE holy!

Revelation 11:3-6 – The Two Witnesses – Moses and Elijah

Much has been written and speculated about the identity of these two witnesses. The three candidates would be Moses, Elijah and Enoch. Further, the two possible pairs are either Enoch and Elijah or Moses and Elijah. I have not seen any others put forth as the two witnesses, so if you find another suggestion, you can safely dispense with it as a far-out wild speculation with no basis in the Bible or in fact. The only proof text used for Enoch is Hebrews 9:27 which says, "It is appointed unto men once to die, but after this the judgment". The claim is that since Enoch and Elijah are the only two men in the Old Testament who did not die that they must be the witnesses to fulfil that scripture. One of the rules of Bible study is to not build a doctrine on one verse or passage, and this is the only proof text for Enoch. So let me give you several other Bible reasons why Enoch can not be one of the witnesses of Revelation chapter 11.

First, Hebrews 9:27 is not proof of the "once to die" teaching. Those who quote the verse for that purpose have misquoted it. They leave out the first two words of the verse. Read it again. It says, "And as it is appointed unto men once to die…" The fact that we die once is an illustration of a larger issue in the text. Look very closely at Hebrews 9:27-28: "And as it is appointed unto men once to die, but after this the judgment: So Christ was once offered to bear the sins of many; and unto them that look for him shall he appear the second time without sin unto salvation." There is no period at the end of verse 27, meaning the context and the sentence continues. You cannot take part of a sentence out of context to prove a doctrine. So let me briefly paraphrase what these two verses actually SAY. Before you try to find out what a verse means, you have to know what it says.

Hebrews 9:27-28 says that just as surely as death is followed by judgment, the Second Coming of Jesus Christ follows his first coming. Denying the literal physical coming of the Lord Jesus Christ to reign on earth in the future is as wacked out and looney-tune crazy as trying to deny that no one will be judged or that man will "reincarnate" several hundred times before he finally gets it. "Once to die" is a general truth applying to 99.99% of humanity. But there are exceptions. Lazarus died twice. So did every other person in the Bible who was brought back from the dead. There is a group of people at the end of the church age who will never die. I Thessalonians 4 says the dead in Christ shall rise first at the rapture of the church, then we which are alive and remain shall be caught up together with them. Jesus himself confirmed this truth in John 11:25-26. He spoke of two groups of believers; one who dies and yet will live again, and another group who will never die. That is a direct reference to the rapture of the church described in I Thessalonians 4:16-17. I Corinthians 15:50 says we shall not all sleep (die). Enoch is the type of this group. He did not see death (Hebrews 11:5) because he was caught out before the judgment of God fell on lost man in the days of Noah. Another cardinal rule of Bible study: any New Testament doctrine must have a corresponding type in the Old Testament. If Enoch is one of the witnesses because he must fulfil "once to die", then there is no type of the rapture in the Old Testament. Another primary reason Enoch cannot be one of the Jewish witnesses is that he was not a Jew! As we make our way through the rest of Revelation chapter 11, it will become abundantly clear that Moses and Elijah are the only two possible explanations. So rather than do a lengthy study up front, just watch it unfold.

VS 3 – These witnesses prophesy. All three of our candidates did so, therefore they are all three still in the running for the position. Their ministry spans the entire 1260 days of the Great Tribulation.

VS 4 – The two witnesses are "olive trees and candlesticks". The olive tree in the Bible is always linked to Israel (Romans 11:13-27), so they must be Jewish. The candlestick was the source of light for the Jewish tabernacle in the wilderness. There is a direct reference in Zechariah 11:11-14 to the two "olive trees" standing before the Lord of the whole earth. This prophecy was fulfilled when Jesus appeared on the Mount of Transfiguration in Matthew 17:1-9. Standing before the Lord of the whole earth (Jesus) were Moses and Elijah. We touched on this in Revelation chapter 7 with the Mid-Tribulation appearance of the Lord Jesus Christ to the 144,000.

VS 5 – God sets a seal of protection on these two men until they finish their testimony (verse 7). No one will be able to hurt them in any manner until God's purpose for them is finished. If anyone tries, these two witnesses will have fire proceed out of their mouths. This is probably <u>not</u> an actual flame thrower in their physical mouths, but more of a reference to their words and the ability to call down fire from heaven against their enemies. James and John thought they could do that (Luke 9:54), but Jesus stopped them. But Elijah DID call down fire from heaven in II Kings 1:9-12. In that passage, the king of Israel (type of the Antichrist) sent a delegation of fifty men to Elijah to apprehend him to bring him to the king. Twice, Elijah called down fire from heaven to consume his enemies. That is a clear picture of the attempt of the Antichrist to capture the two witnesses. Moses also called down fire from heaven in Numbers 16:28-35. He did so to judge Korah and his gang of rebels. There is no record in the Bible of Enoch doing so.

In a practical sense, we have the same promise as believers. As long as we are in the center of God's will, we are bullet-proof. That does NOT mean nothing "bad" will ever happen to you or that no one could ever hurt you. The protection for Moses and Elijah is unique. So don't get all full of yourself and start running around like a moron inviting danger. Don't try calling fire down from heaven. It won't happen.

VS 6 – Power is given to these two witnesses to turn off the rain from heaven. They can do so "in the days of their prophecy", which we have already seen is 1260 days. Elijah shut off the rain from heaven for 3½ years (James 5:17, I Kings 17:1). They are also given power to turn water into blood and bring plagues. Who did that in the Old Testament, Moses or Enoch?

There are more passages of scripture that point directly to Moses and Elijah as the two witnesses. Moses led Israel in the wilderness, and the Tribulation repeats many of the events of that time. Elijah prophesied during the reign of Ahab and Jezebel. Ahab is a type of the Antichrist, and Jezebel is clearly the best type in the Bible of the "Mother of Harlots" of Revelation 17 who commits fornication with the kings of the earth. Elijah was persecuted by Jezebel and run out of town. He was fed miraculously (I Kings 17:1-7) just as Israel will be fed in the Tribulation. During his exile, he ministered to a Gentile woman. The ministry of the 144,000 will be to call the Gentiles to faith in Jesus Christ.

In Matthew 20:20-23, James and John got their mother to ask Jesus if they could sit on his right and left hand in the kingdom. Jesus concluded his answer by saying those positions were already spoken for. The prophecy of Zechariah 4 says the two olive trees will be on the right and left side. Moses and Elijah will occupy those positions during the kingdom.

Jesus was asked once what the greatest commandment in the Bible was. He gave two, then said that on these commandments "hang all the law and the prophets". The term "law and prophets" is used several times to speak of the Old Testament, specifically under the Nation of Israel and their rule (Luke 16:16, Matthew 5:17, John 1:45, Romans 3:21). Moses gave the law. Elijah is considered the greatest of the Old Testament prophets of Israel. Enoch is nowhere to be found.

The last two men mentioned in the Old Testament are Moses and Elijah (Malachi 4:4-6). Israel is told to remember the law of Moses and to look for Elijah to return before the "day of the Lord". These are the two men who will lead the remnant in the Tribulation.

I made the point a minute ago that Enoch is the Old Testament type of the rapture of the church. But all three of these men have a prophetic application to groups of people in the end times. Those who teach Enoch is one of the two witnesses use the "once to die" principle, but Moses will die twice. His first death is recorded in Deuteronomy 34:5-6: "So Moses the servant of the LORD died there in the land of Moab, according to the word of the LORD. And he buried him in a valley in the land of Moab, over against Bethpeor: but no man knoweth of his sepulchre unto this day." Moses was alone with God at his death. It says, HE (God) buried him, and no one knows where. Then there is a cryptic statement in Jude 9 that sheds a little light on why. It says that Michael contended with Satan in a dispute about the body of Moses. If the body just rots in the ground, and God buried Moses in an unknown place, why would there be any dispute over his body? Could it be that God is not finished with Moses yet? Moses will come back in the Tribulation to lead the 144,000 and at the end will be killed by the Antichrist. Moses will die twice. He pictures those in the Tribulation who refuse the mark and suffer martyrdom, and then are raised to go into the kingdom where they will die again.

Elijah only dies once. He pictures those in the Tribulation who "endure to the end" and go alive into the kingdom, only to die later. Methuselah was the oldest man in the Bible at 969. God told Adam, "In the day that thou eatest thereof, thou shalt surely die" (Genesis 2:17). Adam died spiritually on the very 24 hour day he ate the forbidden fruit. He died physically 930 years later, and none of his children made it to 1,000. One day with the Lord is as a thousand years. Those who go into the kingdom alive in natural human bodies will die before the 1,000 years are finished. Moses and Elijah will lead the 144,000 in the Tribulation. Some of them will die once, pictured by Elijah, and some of them will die twice, pictured by Moses. Enoch never dies because he pictures the raptured church.

So the Enoch crowd has part of a verse taken out of context with clear proven exceptions. I have all these passages that can only be linked to Moses and Elijah. What thinkest thou?

Revelation 11:7-10 – The Death of the Two Witnesses

VS 7 – God will allow the beast to have a temporary victory over the two witnesses, just as Satan thought he had Jesus at Calvary. We have already seen that the beast "that ascendeth out of the bottomless pit" is Judas, and again we will see more of him when we get to chapter 13. He is allowed to make war against Moses and Elijah, and by extension the Nation of Israel. This will be a direct military campaign which we know as Armageddon. We generally think of that as simply the final battle when Jesus returns, but it is actually a 3½ year war against Israel that culminates with the Second Advent.

VS 8-9 – When Moses and Elijah are killed, their bodies will be brought to Jerusalem (if they are not killed there) and be put on display for the entire world to see. We might think this is rather barbarous, and it is, but we have precedent in our recent history. The Iran hostage crisis in 1979-1980 ended with the release of the prisoners, but we attempted a military rescue half way through the ordeal. The mission was aborted when we had an equipment failure and nine of our soldiers died. The Iranians brought the bodies to the capital, Teheran, and laid them in the streets for all to see and party over. In the Tribulation, this will be done in Jerusalem. The city is called spiritually Sodom and Egypt. The same description is given of Jerusalem in Isaiah 1:10 and Jeremiah 23:14. It is the "city where our Lord was crucified" in case you were confused. It says people all over the world will see this spectacle. We think nothing of that now that we have cell phones and television. Imagine how unthinkable that idea was before those inventions. To get even more gross, the verses say three times that their dead bodies will lie in the street. Knowing the manner of capital punishment in the Tribulation of beheading paints a very gruesome image.

VS 10 – For three and a half days this party will go on. The depravity of lost mankind knows no depths. Imagine sending gifts to each other and "making merry" (probably drinking themselves into a stupor) because some headless corpses are rotting in the sun. There is something else about this event that "flies under our radar" as Gentile Americans. According to Jewish law and culture, burial within 24 hours is required (Deuteronomy 21:22-23). Leaving these bodies in the street for three days is a gross insult and dishonor. The world is rejoicing over them and mocking their deaths with a celebration with the vilest hatred of God in full living color. Mankind is so deluded that they will think the death of these two men will "free" them to continue their "progress". How much progress has been made for the last 42 months as the world has been utterly destroyed by the judgment of God? It says these two witnesses "tormented them that dwelt on the earth". All they have are words! Mankind is so depraved that the "torment" of someone speaking the truth of God's word is far greater than the torments of the lake of fire. "Be not deceived; God is not mocked" (Galatians 6:7). "The triumphing of the wicked is short, and the joy of the hypocrite but for a moment" (Job 20:5). God _will_ deal with this rebellion!

Revelation 11:11-14 – The Post-Tribulation Rapture

I covered this passage when we studied the three raptures earlier. This is the base text for the doctrine of the Post-Tribulation rapture. Let's walk through the scene.

VS 11 – After 3½ days, the dead bodies of Moses and Elijah will rise from the dead and stand upon their feet. Obviously, their heads will pop back on to those bodies. Yeah, I know that sounds like sci-fi weird nonsense, but that is what the passage says. "And great fear fell upon them which saw them." I guess so! Remember that people all over the world will be watching this on TV and cell phones. Jews believe that a man's spirit stays with his dead body for three days. That is why Jesus waited until the 4th day to raise Lazarus. After three days and a half, the miracle of resurrection of these two men confirms that they were actually dead (according to Jewish belief) so they can't deny it.

VS 12 – Again, this verse was thoroughly commented on in the section on the three raptures. Moses and Elijah will be taken up while everyone watching on TV and cell phones sees them. Along with the two witnesses, their followers will be taken out also in preparation for the Second Advent. This group will go up and then come right back down with Jesus on their white horses.

VS 13 – This is the second mention of an earthquake just prior to the Second Advent. This verse along with Revelation 6:12 and 16:18 are the same event. Refer back to Revelation 6:12 and the comments we saw there to get the whole picture of this earthquake.

VS 14 – This verse finally closes the sixth Trumpet and the second Woe. Remember that the Trumpets are divided into three Woes: Woe 1 – Trumpets 1-5, Woe 2 – Trumpet 6, and Woe 3 – Trumpet 7.

Revelation 11:15-19 – The Seventh Trumpet

This is the second account in Revelation of the Advent of Jesus Christ. He takes the kingdom at this point to reign for ever and ever. His eternal reign is kicked off by a thousand years on earth in the Millennium, but it does not end there. For ever and ever is a long time. It says, "The kingdoms (plural) of this world are become the kingdoms of our Lord." That has dual application as much of the Bible does. First, it is the political kingdoms and empires of earth that man has tried to govern for 6,000 years. Since man has so utterly and miserably failed to rule "in the fear of God" (II Samuel 23:3), Jesus has to show up and demonstrate how it is supposed to be done. That is one of the main purposes of the Millennium, as we will see when we get to chapter 20. We will spend a major section in that chapter detailing the purpose and nature of the Millennial kingdom of the Lord Jesus Christ.

The second manifestation of the "kingdoms" applies to the two parts of God's rule: the kingdom of God and the kingdom of heaven. I do not have time here to detail those kingdoms and how they make their way through the Bible. I touched on them briefly in the introduction when I went through my diagram on the book of Revelation and pointed out the statements related to those kingdoms. Most Bible teachers conflate them. There are a few times in the Bible where the terms are used interchangeably, but those two kingdoms are not the same. The kingdom of God is spiritual. The kingdom of heaven is physical. When Jesus returns, he gets them BOTH. As the Son of God, he is the King over the kingdom of God. As the Son of man (and Son of David), he is King over the kingdom of heaven. But the kingdoms are not identical. The kingdom of heaven will be manifest through the Nation of Israel as they become the head of the nations on earth for one thousand years. The kingdom of God will be manifest through the body of Christ in glorified bodies as they reign with him in his earthly kingdom. I will also point you ahead once again to Revelation 20 and the description of the Millennium for more information.

Every nation on earth will become subject to Jesus Christ and he will rule over them. Israel will be the only "superpower" and control the world as was promised to Abraham 4,000 years ago. The kingdoms were prophesied and promised to Jesus in Daniel chapter 2. Satan tried to jump the gun and offered them to Jesus in Luke chapter 4 in exchange for worship. That was shot down immediately with "It is written". Pilate asked Jesus if he was a King, and he essentially answered, "Yes, but not yet". Part of the answer of Jesus is in John 18:36: "My kingdom is not of this world: if my kingdom were of this world, then would my servants fight, that I should not be delivered to the Jews: but now is my kingdom not from hence." One of the key words in that verse is a simple three-letter word: "<u>NOW</u>". Jesus is King over a spiritual kingdom that is not of this world <u>now</u>. But it will be LATER. There is coming a time very rapidly when the Son of God will return to earth and take control of the physical kingdoms of this world, and when he does, his servants WILL fight with him! I will point you ahead to the fourth account of his return in Revelation 19:11-15 where the armies in heaven will come with him. I will describe those armies in detail when we get there. Of course, the word "now" is missing from most of the new Bibles. That plays right into the hand of the A-millennialists who deny that Jesus will ever come back. He is just a spiritual King who will eventually "conquer" the world spiritually, then we will all go to heaven. Be careful of people who believe that. Ultimately they will have to kill and imprison people "in the name of Jesus" in order to bring the world under their subjection.

The greatest benefit of the Second Coming will be to see Jesus get what he rightfully deserves. His name has been used as a cuss word for 2,000 years. His truth has been trampled under foot for a longer time. His people have been tortured and murdered for no reason for two millennia. His book has been hunted and burned for generations, and even his own people have rejected it in favor of "scholarship". He has put up with that and infinitely more for 6,000 years. We think of the rapture of the church as a wonderful deliverance from the world, and rightfully so. The Bible ends with, "Even so, come, Lord Jesus". It should be the overriding prayer request of every believer for Jesus to come <u>now</u>. We want that to happen primarily for selfish reasons. No more aches and pains and we won't have to die. There will be no more bills to pay, no cranky bosses, no more screaming children, and no more crazy neighbors to put up with. All of that is for ME. I want to see Jesus get the praise he deserves. Psalm 24:1 says, "The earth is the Lord's and the fulness thereof". He will finally take it when the kingdoms become his. I will know the King of the earth personally. It will be enough for me to see his glory finally realized.

<u>VS 16-18</u> – Again we see the 24 elders involved in worship before the throne, as they are every time they appear in Revelation. This passage speaks of the reign of the Lord in the past tense, which leads us to one of two possibilities, both of which are probably true. First, the Bible is very often "out of sequence" in its chronology. If these verses are speaking of the time <u>after</u> Jesus reigns then it is a "flash forward" to the time the dead are judged both small and great. That is a reference to the Great White Throne Judgment at the end of the Millennium which is described in Revelation chapter 20.

But it could also simply be God talking about future events as if they are past tense. That also happens quite frequently in the Bible. The mind of God knows no time. He calls things that are not as though they are (Romans 4:17). He saw us in Christ before it happened. In God's mind, Jesus has already won the battle and Satan is already a defeated foe even though the calendar has not caught up to it yet.

VS 19 – The temple of God is opened for John to see a vision into the throne. He sees and hears thunder, lightning and hail with voices and an earthquake. These are things that generally take place on earth, so it could be a reference to that, or even some similar phenomenon taking place in heaven. Nothing is said of this, so it is anyone's guess. He also mentions the ark. There is much speculation about the location of the original Ark of the Covenant. The only time it was ever in enemy hands was in I Samuel chapters 5-6 when the Philistines took it. That is the funniest place in the Bible. God gave the Philistines hemorrhoids for taking the ark. I Samuel 5:9 says they had "emerods in their secret parts", and Psalm 78:66 speaking of the same events says God smote his enemies in the "hinder parts". Other than that time, the ark was always in either the tabernacle or the temple. The priests were so cautious about it that when they would disassemble the tabernacle to move it, they would stand at the inner veil backwards and take the veil off the place where it hung and walk backwards to cover the ark without looking at it. Once the temple was built as a permanent home for the ark, it was not moved again. Only the High Priest went into the Holy of Holies once a year on the Day of Atonement, so no one ever messed with it.

However, in 606 BC, Nebuchadnezzar of Babylon came to Jerusalem and conquered it and carried some of the children of Israel captive, including Daniel and his friends. Then 20 years later in 586 BC, he came back and destroyed the city and carried off all the vessels and instruments of the temple. But nothing is said of the ark. It had been clearly placed in the temple by Solomon in I Kings 8:1-11. There are several theories about what happened to the ark. If Nebuchadnezzar had gotten it in 586 BC, he would have said something. So what happened to the ark? Here are some of the theories I have heard, and there are likely more. Any of these things could possibly be true, or at least partly true.

A group of Ethiopian Jews claim that they have the original ark. They say that Solomon gave it to one of his sons born to the Queen of Sheba and that he carried it to Ethiopia. There is a "vault" there today that is guarded 24 / 7 supposedly housing the ark. But many people say that Solomon would have never taken the original ark out of the temple. I tend to agree. I Kings 8:8 says the ark stayed in the Holy of Holies and was not moved. If there is an ark in Ethiopia, it could be a duplicate of the original and not the real thing. The Ethiopians would disagree and claim that they have the real thing, but I seriously doubt that. Then that still begs the question of the location of the original ark.

Some speculate that as the armies of Babylon were descending on Jerusalem in 586 BC, the priests took the ark out of the temple and hid it in an underground vault. Then when the temple was rebuilt under Ezra and Nehemiah, it was put back. But the ark is not mentioned in either Ezra or Nehemiah. When this temple was rebuilt, it could be possible that another ark was made for it, or it could be that there was no ark in the restored temple. This once again leads us to ask what happened to the original one.

Another theory says that essentially the same thing happened in 70 AD when the Romans destroyed Jerusalem and the temple. Some think the ark was hidden again at this time just as it was supposedly done when Nebuchadnezzar came in 586 BC. There are even some who claim that the ark has been recently located in one of the underground vaults near the temple. If this is true, the Ethiopians would say that this would be the duplicate and theirs would be the original. No one can prove for sure where it is or if there is a duplicate and which one would be the duplicate. It is all speculation at this point. It seems a bit of a stretch to me that something of this importance and significance could be hidden for over 1900 years, but it is certainly possible.

But of course, we know that Indiana Jones found it and put it in a huge warehouse somewhere. We actually have "video" of that, so it must be true, right? By the way, that movie was based on fact even though there was plenty of "embellishment" in it. Adolf Hitler was undoubtedly the most demonically controlled human being who ever lived outside of Judas Iscariot. He was DEEP into the occult. There is evidence that he really did try to find the ark thinking it had some form of magic power. It is odd to think that Hitler would have given any credence to anything Jewish seeing his hatred of the race. But if you are trying to make sense out of the activity of Satan and his minions, we need to talk.

With all of that, here is my theory. I believe the original ark is in heaven as we speak. Revelation 11:19 says John saw it there. WHEN it got there is not known for sure, but I believe it would have been before Nebuchadnezzar destroyed Solomon's temple in 586 BC. Any subsequent arks would be duplicates, including the one in the temple of Ezra and Nehemiah or the one in Ethiopia if it exists. HOW the ark got to heaven is also not known for sure, but it is not hard to guess. The ark represented the presence of God for the Nation of Israel. It was just a physical object, but it was more than that in its symbolism. Just ask the Philistines who thought it would be a good idea to take it back in the days of Samuel. They could not sit down for months without a vivid reminder of the significance of that object. When Babylon conquered Israel, it put an end to their physical kingdom. God's presence was withdrawn from his people due to their rejection. So he physically "withdrew" the symbol of his presence. If God can rapture out millions of human beings in an instant, he certainly can do the same with the ark.

So I believe God physically took the ark to heaven just as Nebuchadnezzar was approaching Jerusalem in 586 BC, and that it has been there ever since. When Israel rebuilds the temple during the first half of the Tribulation, they will place another ark in the Holy of Holies. It might be the one in Ethiopia, which is not likely since they probably would be reluctant to give it up. It could be an ark found under the temple in a vault, or a new one constructed for the purpose. But it will not be the original ark. Being symbolic of the presence of God, the original ark cannot be in the temple of the secular Jewish Nation that will be overtaken by the presence of the Abomination of Desolation during the Tribulation. Jesus is the "express image" of the Godhead (Hebrews 1:3). God's presence will not be manifest on this earth until he returns to establish his kingdom. So his ark is in heaven until he returns. What will happen to it at that time is anyone's guess. He may bring it back and put it in the restored temple in the Millennium. But then again, with the TRUE presence of God here in person, it may not be necessary or appropriate. But I believe Revelation 11:19 tells us where the original ark is located today. Again, that is my theory. You can add it to the mounting list of speculations in this commentary that could likely be proven wrong someday. If so, you cannot say, "I told you so" because I have been clear about my ignorance.

Revelation Chapters 12-14 – The Personages
The Third Pass Through the Tribulation

This time through the Tribulation is unique from the other three. The Seals, Trumpets and Vials deal with the <u>events</u> of the Tribulation while this one deals primarily with the main <u>characters</u> of the story. It is like the movie credits at the end that tell you who the actors were and what role they played. The reason I call this section the "Personages" rather than just the persons is because of how it is framed in the text. There is the dragon and the man child and the woman, etc. Yes, these are persons (Satan, Jesus, Israel), but they are given in descriptive terms as well. There are some things in this pass through the Tribulation that will be a little different than what we have seen so far. This is essentially God showing us who the primary players are and what some of their characteristics are. There are seven main characters. I will introduce them here then as we walk through the passage we will see them in more detail.

Revelation Chapter 12 – The Personages Introduced

The Seven Personages – The Main Cast of Characters of the Tribulation (The Stars of the Show)
> The beast out of the sea – Pope / Antichrist; The beast out of the earth – Judas / Antichrist
> The woman – Israel
> The man child – Jesus as a human
> The serpent / dragon – Satan
> The archangel warrior – Michael
> The virgins / remnant – The 144,000
> The Lamb – Jesus as God / King

Revelation 12:1-6 – The Woman and the Dragon Introduced

<u>VS 1-2</u> – The woman is the Nation of Israel. I have to deal with a couple of wrong teachings first to get them out of the way before we proceed. A few prophecy teachers have tried to say this is the church. But we have established clearly many times that the church is taken out at the main harvest rapture and not here in the Tribulation. The church did not bring forth the man child (Messiah), Jesus brought forth the church at Calvary. The church is called a wife, a bride, and a virgin, but never a woman.

However, the greatest perversion of this woman is from the Roman Catholic Church. They teach it is Mary. Their purpose is to exalt her as the "Queen of Heaven". Much of the Catholic art depicts Mary as standing upon the earth with a crown of stars around her head as this image is described. Mary did indeed bring forth Jesus, but that speaks only of his physical birth. The Nation of Israel also brought him forth as a people group (Isaiah 9:6-7, Matthew 1:1, Hebrews 2:16). The woman of Revelation 12 flees to the wilderness to be fed by God for 3½ years. Mary never did that. She died almost 2,000 years ago. What role could Mary possibly have in the Tribulation?

The imagery of the sun, moon and stars is defined by the dream of Joseph in Genesis 37:9-10. The sun, moon and stars are Jacob (Israel) and Rachel and the twelve sons of Israel. Israel as a Nation is referred to as a woman many times in the Bible. She is a "comely and delicate woman" in Jeremiah 6:2. She is a wife and a woman "forsaken and grieved in spirit" in Isaiah 54:1-10. She is an adulterous woman in the book of Hosea and in Ezekiel 23:44. Israel is referred to as a "woman in travail" in MANY places in the Old Testament (Isaiah 26:17, Jeremiah 4:31, and Micah 4:10 just to name a few) which is the terminology used in this passage in Revelation chapter 12.

The vision also has Millennial overtones. Israel is "clothed with the sun" in their kingdom as they finally show forth the light of their Lord (Daniel 12:3, Matthew 13:43). The woman has the moon under her feet. The moon is a picture of the church; with no light of its own and simply reflecting the light of the "Son" (sun). In the kingdom, Israel will be the head of the nations (Deuteronomy 28:13), and the natural Jewish branches of the olive tree will be grafted back in (Romans 11:23-27). The bride of Christ will be "under the feet" of the Jewish King on the throne. Israel will be crowned with twelve stars as the twelve apostles sit upon twelve thrones judging the twelve tribes of Israel (Matthew 19:28).

VS 3-4 – The next Personage is the great red dragon, Satan. Should there be any question, verse 9 defines it clearly. The seven heads, ten horns and seven crowns will come into play in the next chapter as Satan becomes incarnate in the beast (Antichrist). The first half of verse 4 deals with the rebellion of Lucifer in eternity past. Stars are a type of angels (Revelation 1:20, Job 38:7). That is why all the "stars" live in the "City of Angels". The time frame of this rebellion is between Genesis 1:1 and 1:2 in what we know as the "gap". This is not a book on that subject, so I will be brief.

"In the beginning God created the heaven and the earth." PERIOD. "And the earth was without form, and void; and darkness was upon the face of the deep." God does not make a "rough draft" then clean up his mess afterward. Something happened between those verses for the condition of darkness and void to be in place. "God is light, and in him is no darkness at all" (I John 1:5). God did not do something as spectacular as speak the universe into existence only to have it reflect darkness. The prince of darkness was responsible for that. Job 38:7 says the morning stars and sons of God shouted for joy and sang at creation. Did they sing over a formless dark blob? Many have said that Bible teachers came up with the gap to try to refute Darwin and evolution. The gap was taught centuries before Darwin's grandmother was born. I don't give a flying hoot what Charlie dreamed up. The gap could have been five minutes long. Isaiah 14:12-15 and Ezekiel 28:11-19 describe the fall of Lucifer, and those verses have to be placed somewhere in history. He did not just show up one day in the Garden out of nowhere. In Satan's rebellion, he took one third of the angels with him. That is one of the reasons why we keep seeing "the third part" of things destroyed in God's judgment in Revelation.

The "one third" principle is seen elsewhere in scripture. There are only three angels named in the Bible: Michael, Gabriel, and Lucifer. All three have seven letters in their name (the number of perfection). Lucifer was "perfect in thy ways from the day that thou wast created" (Ezekiel 28:15). That is how God makes things. Then his creatures step in with their free will and mess it up. From that point forward, one of the three named angels in the Bible becomes Satan, Devil, Beast (five letters; the number of death). He was a "murderer from the beginning" (John 8:44). The first murder in history took out one third of the human race. The only men were Adam, Cain and Abel, and the seed of reproduction comes through the man. The constellation called Draco the Dragon has a "tail" wrapped around the North Star. It pictures the attempt of the great red dragon of Revelation to ascend to the throne of God and take it over.

The last part of verse 4 says the dragon was ready to devour the "man child" (Jesus) as soon as he was born. Satan moved a lost pagan Caesar to issue a "taxing" for the whole world in Luke chapter 2. Caesar was blitheringly ignorant of a young lady in Nazareth who was great with child at the time, but the spirit behind him was not. So he loaded that young woman on the back of a donkey and had her ride 20 plus miles over rugged terrain trying to get her to miscarry. All that did was serve to get her to the city of his prophesied birth (Bethlehem). When that plan did not work, he moved in the heart of Herod to inquire of the wise men so he could come and "worship", intending to kill the man child. But all it did was drive Joseph and his young family to Egypt so the scripture could be fulfilled (Matthew 2:15). Satan always overlooks the obvious, and every time he tries to frustrate God's plan, he ends up playing right into his hand. The attempt to get rid of Jesus did not stop there. All through the four gospels he tried everything he could to eliminate the man child, but until "his hour was come", he could do nothing.

The dragon's attempt to get rid of the man child goes back much further than the birth of Christ. Sin had just been introduced to the human race when God promised the seed who would pay for it (Genesis 3:15). He said there would be enmity between Satan and that seed, and it began immediately. Cain killed Abel, and behind that was the attempt to wipe out the line. If your grandfather died before he had any children, you would not be here. But the seed came through Seth and not Abel. Then Satan tried to pervert the seed of humanity in Genesis chapter 6 by dispatching a bunch of his fallen comrades in an attempt to build the "pure race" that would eliminate God's line. Hitler was not original; he got his plan from his father the devil. But Noah found grace in the eyes of the Lord. The human race was saved before it was completely perverted so the line of the "seed" could continue.

God raised up Abraham and promised a seed that would fulfil Genesis 3:15. So Satan jumped in with Hagar attempting to short-circuit the plan. So God brought the seed through the second born of Abraham (Isaac) to picture the need for man to be born again. After the Ishmael plot was foiled, the dragon had Sarah taken into a foreign harem, not once but twice, to try to pervert the promised seed. God stepped in and protected her both times. The enemy tried to prompt Esau to kill his brother Jacob to cut off the line, but God put up the stop sign on that one also. Then the children of Israel found themselves in Egypt under the bondage of Yul Brynner. Satan prompted 'Ol Pharaoh to kill all the male children of Israel. The loser on the throne of Egypt had no idea what was really happening, but the spirit behind him was at work in a much greater way than just killing some baby boys. So God gave the women of Israel courage and strength, and "the more they afflicted them, the more they multiplied and grew" (Exodus 1:12).

Abimelech killed 69 of the 70 royal children of Israel in Judges chapter 9, but he missed one of them named Jotham. In II Chronicles 22:10-12, Athaliah tried the same thing and got all but one, Joash. Then Israel went into captivity and Nebuchadnezzar tried to turn all the "seed royal" into eunuchs. Later in the captivity, Haman devised his devilish plot to eliminate the Jewish race from the earth. How many times did the enemy send his hottest babes into the camp of Israel to draw away the young skulls full of mush full of hormones in an attempt to water down the line? Solomon ended up with a thousand wives who turned his heart away from God (I Kings 11:1-3). How was he supposed to keep track of the line of the Messiah with 999 "extras" to choose from?

The dragon stood before the woman to devour her child from the first moment he was promised in the Garden in Genesis chapter 3. His attack has been relentless since then, was intensified when he was here, and continues to this day. One of the hallmarks of the Tribulation is the plot to eliminate Israel. It is the political issue in the world today, and will remain so until the King of the Jews returns.

VS 5 – The man child is destined to rule all nations with a rod of iron. This will be seen in detail when we get to Revelation 19:11-15. Notice this is future tense. The Bible jumps around in its chronology. The verse goes on to say that her child was caught up to God and to his throne. That is the ascension of the Lord Jesus Christ at the end of his earthly ministry.

VS 6 – The woman fled into the wilderness. The passage jumps right over the church age and does not mention it. The church age is a mystery in the Old Testament. The flight is prophesied by Jesus himself in Matthew 24:15-21. We have already seen that God will draw his people into the wilderness to meet with them in the middle of the Tribulation. He has a place prepared for them called Sela-Petra, and they will be miraculously taken care of in their flight and subsequent persecution by the Antichrist. When Satan tempted Jesus to turn stones into bread (Matthew 4:3), he could have done it! In the Tribulation, if need be, he will feed his people with stones turned into bread. The miracle of the manna will be revisited as the events of the Exodus are repeated (Micah 7:14-15).

Revelation 12:7-12 – War in Heaven: Satan Cast Down Into the Earth

The next Personage is introduced: Michael the Archangel. Michael is mentioned five times in the Bible, and in each case it is connected with spiritual warfare and the end times. The first mention is in Daniel chapter 10 in a conflict in the spirit world. Gabriel was attempting to deliver a message to Daniel, but the prince of Persia (a spirit being) fought against him and detained him for three weeks. Michael was finally summoned to help, and Gabriel made it through. Michael next appears in Daniel 12:1 as the "great prince which standeth for the children of thy people" (which would be Israel). The third time Michael appears is as the "voice of the archangel" in I Thessalonians 4:16 announcing the rapture of the church. Michael is not mentioned by name in that passage, but there is no other archangel mentioned in the Bible. His fourth appearance is in Jude 9 as he was contending with Satan over the body of Moses. We saw this earlier with the two witnesses of Revelation 11. Michael's final mention is here in chapter 12 as the warrior for God in this heavenly battle.

VS 7-9 – This war in heaven results in the defeat of Satan and his banishment from heaven. The text clearly identifies exactly who the dragon is so that there is no misunderstanding. It is vitally important to understand the location and position of Satan. The common thought has him as king of the underworld and currently in hell with his red suit and pitchfork. That is cartoon imagery and as false as Santa Claus, the Easter Bunny or the Tooth Fairy. Let's walk through his timeline.

In eternity past he was the "anointed cherub that covereth" (Ezekiel 28:14) with an honored position at the throne of God. Due to his rebellion, he lost his position, but not his access to the throne. Isaiah 14 describes his fall, and verse 15 says, "Yet thou shalt be brought down to hell, to the sides of the pit." That is future tense. He has not been brought down to hell yet. Satan can still enter the throne room of God. Job 1:6 and 2:1 both describe a "board meeting" in heaven where Satan appeared with the sons of God before the Lord. The text we are studying says Satan accuses God's people before God day and night. Not only does Satan still stand before God at the throne; he has representatives and minions with him also. I Samuel 16:14 says "an evil spirit from the Lord" troubled Saul. Understand the exact wording: an evil spirit FROM the Lord, not OF the Lord. In other words, this is not God being evil but allowing an evil spirit to torment Saul. Don't miss the fact that he was dispatched from the Lord which means he had to be in his presence. In I Kings 22:19-23, we have an account of another "meeting" at the throne of God. A lying spirit was dispatched from God. God had enough of Ahab's nonsense, so he allowed an evil spirit to go out from his presence to accomplish his purpose.

Satan lost his position when he fell in eternity past. He will not lose his access until the middle of the Tribulation. When he does, he and all of his buddies will be kicked out of heaven and be confined to earth. We have already seen the bottomless pit open and every chained demon unleashed. These two things happen at the same time. The Great Tribulation will see every single foul evil spirit in existence confined to earth to indwell and torment humanity. I have a tabloid in my files from many years ago. YES, I know they are fiction! But the cover has a picture of a massive explosion and fire, and someone photo-shopped the billowing smoke to make it look like an evil face. The headline said, "Satan escapes from Hell!" Sorry, fake news. He is not there to escape. He will not be there until the Lord returns and tosses him in there in Revelation chapter 20.

Verse 9 also says that Satan "deceiveth the whole world". That is a doctrinal reference to the first half of the Tribulation and the false kingdom. II Thessalonians 2:3 refers to a "falling away" which some believe is the age of Laodicea, but the apostasy and deception of the Tribulation will make Laodicea look like the greatest revival in history. Practically, verse 9 identifies him as the serpent who is "more subtil than any beast of the field". He is so good at this deception that Jesus even said that if it were possible he could deceive the very elect (Matthew 24:24). He is the master of disguise and counterfeit.

VS 10 – Satan is "the accuser of the brethren". One of his main functions is as a "prosecuting attorney" against God's people, both Jews and Christians. At the "board meeting" in the book of Job, he accused Job of only loving God because he had a lot of stuff. Satan is constantly throwing spiritual barbs at the people of God. Doctrinally, Satan is the "horn" who will speak at the Great White Throne Judgment (Daniel 7:11). When we get to Revelation chapter 20, we will see this in more detail. In the practical sense, Satan is behind so much of the mental and emotional anguish in the world today. I don't want to get too deep into this because it would take us off focus in the book of Revelation. But there is a concept of the difference between conviction and guilt that we need to understand. All of us sin daily. God uses conviction to draw us to him to get it right. Conviction is the gentle leading of the Holy Spirit to move us toward God for the forgiveness and cleansing from our sin. Satan uses guilt to brow-beat God's people into depression. Guilt drives us away from God. The accuser of the brethren loves nothing more than to make God's people feel like worthless pond scum. The very Son of God left his throne in heaven to come to this earth and give his life to pay for your sins. He loved you that much and thought that much of you that he would do so. Do not let anyone or any being tell you that you are worthless.

VS 11 – Another character in the story is introduced: the Lamb. We will see his role in chapter 14. But this verse gives us another look at the "work of faith" necessary for salvation in the Tribulation and how it differs from ours in the church age. The "brethren" of the Tribulation overcome the devil by the blood of the Lamb, AND by the word of their testimony, AND they loved not their lives unto the death. All three of those things can and will factor into Tribulation salvation for the remnant of Israel. They will have met the Lord in the wilderness and acknowledged him as their Lord and Saviour. This event in the middle of the Tribulation will apply the blood of the sacrifice to them. THEN they also have to keep the word of their testimony. That is the message that is delivered to them to preach. Remember that the "seal" of the 144,000 is for a mission. They will be sealed to preach, but if they abandon that call, they can forfeit their seal. We covered that issue in detail with the sealing of the 144,000 in chapter 7. THEN it says, "They loved not their lives unto the death". This is a reference to what happens when one of them is captured. If they deny the Lord, they can lose their seal. Again, salvation is by grace through faith. These Jewish witnesses receive the grace of God when they receive Jesus Christ as their Messiah in the middle of the Tribulation. Then by faith, they are told to preach and to stay faithful to that call even if captured. Jesus said, "For whosoever will save his life shall lose it: and whosoever will lose his life for my sake shall find it" (Matthew 16:25). That has a practical application of faithfulness to the Lord for us, but its doctrine is for the remnant in the Tribulation. Jesus also said, "Whosoever therefore shall confess me before men, him will I confess also before my Father which is in heaven. But whosoever shall deny me before men, him will I also deny before my Father which is in heaven" (Matthew 10:32-33). Again, this is addressed to the witnesses of the Tribulation who can lose their salvation if they deny the Lord in their persecution.

VS 12 – When Satan is cast out of heaven to earth, he will be ticked off. It has a totally different effect on different groups. We will party when he is gone. But the inhabitants of earth are in for a rude awakening. Satan knows he is defeated and he knows the plan of God all the way to his own demise. But he is so stubborn and rebellious that he will not give up. When this happens, he knows the "jig is up". He will go berserk. Woe when it happens! 6,000 years of his plans have been frustrated at every turn. Every time he has tried to take Jesus out and sit on his throne it has failed. He is every "loser" in history rolled into one. The devil is the prosecutor in the old *"Perry Mason"* TV show. There were hundreds of episodes. He lost every time. Satan is "Bluto" on the old Popeye cartoons. The can of spinach did him in every time. The devil is Wylie Coyote in the Road Runner cartoons, perhaps the best cartoon series ever. He never caught the Road Runner and every one of his plans not only failed, they turned against him and blew up in his face. Satan is the Washington Generals, the opponents of the Harlem Globetrotters in their basketball exhibitions. They lost every game. At the mid-point of the Tribulation, Satan will be cast out of heaven and confined to earth, and all of his fallen angels (devils) with him, including the horde from the bottomless pit. It will literally be "hell on earth" when reality sets in.

Revelation 12:13-17 – The Dragon Persecutes the Woman

Another Personage is now introduced to the story: The Remnant (verse 17). This is another key word of the Bible to designate the 144,000. The word "remnant" appears about 90 times in the Bible, and in most cases it is linked to Israel. There are a few places where it is referring to a remnant of another nation, but whenever it refers to Israel, it points to the end times and the final group of Jewish believers who will be taken out at the Post-Tribulation rapture. Here are just a few examples of the usage of this term in the Bible: Isaiah 1:7-9, Isaiah 10:20-23, Jeremiah 31:1-7, and Ezekiel 6:8. As you are reading through the Bible, and especially in the prophets, make note of this term. More specifically, the remnant are the ones who are left at the end of the Tribulation. Some of this group will be caught and killed before the end.

VS 13-14 – This passage describes the flight of the Jews into the wilderness when the Antichrist takes over the temple as the "Abomination of Desolation". We saw this in chapter 7 with the sealing of the 144,000, and we will see it further with the Revealing of the Wicked in chapter 13. But here we want to focus on the persecution against Israel. Unless you have been under a rock for the last 4,000 years, you know that THE issue in the geo-political world is the Nation of Israel. There has been an absolute blind irrational hatred of the Jews for 40 centuries, and an all out effort to rid the world of that "cursed" race for just as long. It originates from Satan. He is the "god of this world" (II Corinthians 4:4) with control of the Gentile political kingdoms of earth (Luke 4:5-6). His all consuming rage is directed at Jesus Christ, and he is Jewish. His chief aim is to exalt his throne and take God's place (Isaiah 14:12-14). The Bible says in II Timothy 2:26 that lost people are "taken captive by him (Satan) at his will". He deceived our first parents and brought humanity under his control. He promised Eve, "Ye shall be as gods… Come, on Eve, go ahead. A little bit won't hurt. It won't kill you. If you take of that tree, you will be just like me. You can be on my team." When she and Adam fell to that temptation, he became their "god" in a sense. While they were still in the Garden, God promised a seed that would deliver mankind from that curse (Genesis 3:15). Of course, that is Jesus. The battle lines were drawn in Genesis 3 and it has been "game on" ever since. The seed is promised through the line of Abraham, Isaac and Jacob.

Satan wants the throne, and Israel will take it from him when their King returns. When he finds himself cast into the earth in the middle of the Tribulation, he will know he has a "short time", and he will pull out all the stops against the Jews. It has been bad for a long time. Hitler did a number on them in World War II. They have been chased around the world for 2,000 years, and even now in their homeland there is a relentless effort to get rid of the Jews. At this point of the Tribulation, it will become an all out kamikaze blitzkrieg. The Antichrist will be indwelt by Satan, and what he will do to Israel will make all the rest of their persecutions feel like a slice of heaven. The blind rage against God's people will go into warp drive.

The persecution and preservation of the Nation of Israel is one of the clearest proofs of the truth of the Bible and the existence of God. Maybe that does not make sense to you, but think about it. What other group of people could stand such an onslaught and survive? Current estimates say there are roughly 14 million Jews world-wide, with about half of them living in Israel now. That is roughly the same as the population of Zimbabwe. What if the combined forces of the world were assembled against Zimbabwe? They would not last as long as it took me to type this sentence.

Israel will flee to the wilderness at this point in the Tribulation. It clearly establishes the time frame as 1260 days in verse 6, and "time, times, and half a time" in verse 14. That wording is used in Daniel 7:25 and Daniel 12:7 to mean 3½. It says Israel will be given "two wings of a great eagle" to get there. Some have concluded that this refers to an airplane. Remember that John is describing modern means of travel using first century terminology, and he would not have been familiar with an airplane. I understand the concept, but I do not agree. First, they are told to get out of town immediately and not pack anything because it is urgent. The conditions of their fleeing into the wilderness are not to be encumbered with physical obstacles like suitcases, weather, the sabbath, or even young children. None of those things are much of an issue on an airplane, unless you happen to be seated next to the screaming baby. But they would be hindrances if traveling on foot. Also, there is no landing strip at Sela-Petra. Besides, good luck getting through TSA as a Jew at this point. Whenever things like this are mentioned in the Bible, the first place we should look is to the Bible itself for the definition. This speaks of the miraculous provision of God in their flight. Check these verses: Exodus 19:4, Deuteronomy 32:9-12, and Hosea 2:14-15.

The woman flees to "her place" which has been prepared of God (verse 6), which is commonly believed to be Sela-Petra. This location is mentioned only twice in the Bible. King Amaziah of Israel captured the city in II Kings 14:7 and renamed it Joktheel, but nothing more is said. Then it is mentioned in Isaiah 16:1 with an indication of its role in the Tribulation. Isaiah 16:4 says, "Let mine outcasts dwell with thee, Moab; be thou a covert to them from the face of the spoiler: for the extortioner is at an end, the spoiler ceaseth, the oppressors are consumed out of the land."

Sela-Petra is in the land of Moab south of the Dead Sea. The Hebrew word "Sela" means "rock" and appears about 60 times in the Old Testament. It is similar to the word "Selah" which is found quite often in the Psalms, in fact it is even spelled with the "h" on the end in II Kings. But none of the references in Psalms relate to this city. Selah in the Psalms (and three times in Habakkuk) is a musical term meaning "pause or rest". The "Petra" comes from the Greek for "rock". So Sela-Petra is literally "rock-rock" and Selah-Petra is literally "rest-rock". When Israel flees to this place, they will be fleeing to their rock (Jesus) to rest in him.

During the Tribulation, Israel will use this city as a base of operations. They won't all hole up there because many of them will be spread out through the world preaching the gospel of the kingdom. Also, the Jews who are hiding from the Antichrist will likely be spread out throughout that particular region of wilderness where there are lots of places to hide. If they were all in one place they would be too easy to find. The city of Sela-Petra is literally carved out of rock cliffs. The only way in to the city is through a winding narrow gorge that at some points is not wide enough for two horses side-by-side. It would be a good hideout because no army could get there. They would be picked off one by one as they tried to approach single-file. Some of the cliffs surrounding the entrance are as high as 1,000 feet. The city was an ancient capitol but abandoned centuries ago. It was rediscovered in the 1800's and has been the site of much speculation since. It was pictured in one of the *Indiana Jones* movies. Since its rediscovery there have been several expeditions and documentaries about the city which would be available to those who wish to delve deep into the study of Sela-Petra. For this commentary we will leave it there and realize that this is likely the location where the Jewish remnant will hide during the last half of the Tribulation.

VS 15-16 – These verses mention a flood as part of the attack of Satan against the Nation of Israel. Tying together various passages of scripture can give us a picture of this. Daniel 9:26 says, "… the end thereof shall be with a flood." This indicates an effort to drown Israel toward the end of the Tribulation. Then Job 40:23 adds a cryptic detail. Speaking of Satan (not an elephant or hippo), this verse says, "Behold, he drinketh up a river, and hasteth not: he trusteth that he can draw up Jordan into his mouth." The flood in Revelation 12 is "cast out of the mouth" of the serpent / dragon. By this time, some of the remnant of Israel will be holed up in Sela-Petra. Remember the description of the city and its one entrance down a narrow canyon. Sending a torrent of water down that canyon would do some serious damage. Jordan is mentioned in Job, so it could be a reference to an attempt to re-route the River Jordan to accomplish this. If so, God will re-route the re-route.

VS 17 – Of course, Satan is foiled again. So he doubles down and launches an all out war against "the remnant of her seed". That is the same wording as Genesis 3:15. But the woman does not have a "seed", the man does. This is a reference to the virgin birth of Jesus Christ as well as the descendants of Israel. Again we see the "work of faith" that includes keeping the law for the Tribulation saints.

Revelation Chapter 13 – The Beast

We have now reached undoubtedly the most "pivotal" chapter in the book of Revelation, and I used that term by design. The "pivot" of the Tribulation is the deadly head wound of the Antichrist and how he will be healed (raised). The events surrounding this chapter have been the subject of more controversy and speculation than any other place in Revelation, and by extension, probably more than any other place in the Bible. This is the chapter containing the famous 666 verse.

Before we get into the details of Revelation chapter 13, we must lay a significant amount of groundwork. I have alluded to this chapter several times already, and said, "Wait until we get to the Revealing of the Wicked". Well, we are here. So clear off a spot and let's get ready to rumble. It might be a good time right now to go visit the restroom, grab some chips and a Pepsi, and turn off the TV. We are diving in to the Mariana Trench of the Bible. That is the deepest part of the Pacific Ocean in case you did not know.

Let's begin with a passage of scripture that for generations has had scores of issues in interpretation, both in fundamental circles and in virtually every strain of prophetic teaching that I have been aware of. Let me quote the entire passage here, then we will walk through it and tear it apart and put it back together without leaving any spare parts laying on your driveway.

> Now we beseech you, brethren, by the coming of our Lord Jesus Christ, and by our gathering together unto him, That ye be not soon shaken in mind, or be troubled, neither by spirit, nor by word, nor by letter as from us, as that the day of Christ is at hand. Let no man deceive you by any means: for that day shall not come, except there come a falling away first, and that man of sin be revealed, the son of perdition; Who opposeth and exalteth himself above all that is called God, or that is worshipped; so that he as God sitteth in the temple of God, shewing himself that he is God. Remember ye not, that, when I was yet with you, I told you these things? And now ye know what withholdeth that he might be revealed in his time. For the mystery of iniquity doth already work: only he who now letteth will let, until he be taken out of the way. And then shall that Wicked be revealed, whom the Lord shall consume with the spirit of his mouth, and shall destroy with the brightness of his coming: Even him, whose coming is after the working of Satan with all power and signs and lying wonders, And with all deceivableness of unrighteousness in them that perish; because they received not the love of the truth, that they might be saved. And for this cause God shall send them strong delusion, that they should believe a lie: That they all might be damned who believed not the truth, but had pleasure in unrighteousness. (II Thessalonians 2:1-12)

The primary point of contention is in verse 7 where it says that "he who now letteth will let, until he be taken out of the way". Who is "he who letteth"? The word "let" in this context is used in the Old English sense of restraining or standing in the way of. When we see "let", we think "allow" as that is its main usage today. But the opposite definition is also valid and is still in use today. In a tennis match when a serve hits the net but the ball still travels over it to the other side, you will hear the line judge yell, "LET!" You <u>think</u> you hear "NET!" because the ball hit the net, but that is not the word. The net "<u>let</u>" (hindered) the serve from a free flow, so the "<u>let</u>" serve is invalid and must be done again. In our passage, something or someone hinders and must be taken out of the way. There are two major schools of thought on this, and before I detail them, let me put to rest the endless squabbling over these "conflicting" points of view because they DO NOT CONFLICT! Both teachings are true, and both of them can be supported by the text without doing any damage to the other. In fact, you cannot fully teach one without the other and vice versa. This is a common issue in the Bible. God has precious few pages to communicate his truth to us thick headed dolts, so he often combines multiple layers of teaching at the same time. I don't have time in this book to fully demonstrate this, but let me just give you one simple example, then I will get back to the text in Thessalonians so that I can get back to the text in Revelation.

In Genesis 22, Abraham and Isaac were walking up the mountain to the place of sacrifice. Isaac was still not in on the full scope of the plan yet, and he asked his father where the lamb was for a burnt offering. In verse 8, Abraham said, "My son, God will provide himself a lamb for a burnt offering." The wording is precise. In any language there are always implied words, and also, words in the same sentence can be rearranged in a different order while saying the exact same thing. In Abraham's response, TWO things are said. First, "God himself will provide a lamb." In other words, ONLY God can provide the lamb; and he will not leave it up to us. God will take care of that detail on his own without any help from mankind. Second, "God will provide himself [as] the lamb." That says not only will God do the providing, HE will be the provision himself personally. Of course, we know this lamb in Genesis 22 is the picture of the Lamb of God which taketh away the sin of the world (John 1:29). Only God can provide that Lamb, and only God can BE that Lamb. So which aspect of Genesis 22:8 is true? BOTH are, Einstein! In fact, if one of them is NOT true, neither is the other one! If God provides the Lamb for our sin but it is not the sinless Lamb of his own self, it is a flawed sacrifice and cannot take away our sins. That is why the Old Testament animal sacrifices covered sin, but did not take it away. ALSO, no human could ever provide a sinless Lamb, only God could do that. BOTH of those things are true, BOTH of them are communicated in the verse, and one of them cannot stand without the other.

Now let's go back to the two schools of thought from "he who now letteth" in II Thessalonians 2:7. One side says this is the Holy Spirit taken out at the rapture of the church. The other side says it has to be the assassination of the Antichrist in the middle of the Tribulation. BOTH are true, and I will show that here. The problem with "controversies" such as this is when one side bangs their drum to the exclusion of the other. This causes the other side to bang their drum even louder, which causes the other side to bang louder. Pretty soon the innocent bystanders who are watching the argument put their hands over their ears and run out the door into the arms of a cult.

So now allow me to detail the two basic truths a little further. To hone in on this, we need to quote just verse 7 and the first part of verse 8: "For the mystery of iniquity doth already work: only he who now letteth will let, until he be taken out of the way. And then shall that Wicked be revealed." The most prevalent and common teaching is that the church must be taken out of the way at the rapture before the work of the Antichrist can proceed. So the "he" is the indwelling Holy Spirit inside the Body of Christ. That is stated in the text. The mystery of iniquity (Antichrist) has been at work since the days of Cain and Abel and continues to this day. His work is currently being restrained. I have been more than abundantly clear in this book that the church cannot go through the Tribulation, so the full person and work of the Antichrist can only go so far until we are gone. That is supported by this passage as well as dozens of others we have already mentioned. The "minority report" (or the second application) does not deal with the work of the Antichrist, but the revealing of the Antichrist. This says the "he" is the Antichrist who is not revealed to Israel until he is assassinated and resurrected and moves in to the temple. Until then, he is "letting" the Jews from recognizing who he is and that they have trusted the wrong "Christ" (Messiah). The work of the Antichrist is only mentioned once in the text, and his revealing is mentioned three times.

The reason both of them have to be true is because they complement each other. One of the persistent issues with the prophecy gurus is their incessant attempt to try to identify the Antichrist. There have been as many guesses as there are authors, and none of them really hit it right for an obvious reason. The Antichrist is not revealed to the church; he is revealed as the "wrong Christ" to the Nation of Israel in the middle of the Tribulation. This is why BOTH applications of the verse must be true, and not only that, one cannot be true without the other. The full scope of the work of the Antichrist cannot unfold until the church is gone, and until the church is gone, the Antichrist cannot be assassinated to reveal him as the Antichrist to Israel. Hopefully we have laid to rest the argument. Whoever you are arguing with about this is right, and so are you. So now it is time to actually make our way inch by inch through the passage in II Thessalonians chapter 2 and see the FULL scope of what is in here. Whenever anyone locks out half the truth by arguing about it, they miss half of what God is trying to show them.

Go back now to I Thessalonians 2:1: "Now we beseech you, brethren, by the coming of our Lord Jesus Christ, and by our gathering together unto him." Paul gives us the "goal posts" of the passage here. He mentions two events that we are all familiar with in prophetic terms: the rapture of the church and the Second Advent of Jesus Christ. Whatever is discussed in the rest of the text has to fit within those two pillars. He goes on in verses 2-3 to say: "That ye be not soon shaken in mind, or be troubled, neither by spirit, nor by word, nor by letter as from us, as that the day of Christ is at hand. Let no man deceive you by any means: for that day shall not come, except there come a falling away first, and that man of sin be revealed, the son of perdition." We now expand the discussion of the two main pillars of the passage to include FOUR events listed. First, the day of Christ is at hand. This term is used exclusively in the Bible to describe the rapture of the church. Then Paul mentions "that day" which again is a specific Bible term that always refers to the Second Advent. Then he mentions a falling away, then the revealing of the man of sin. So, the four events are <u>listed</u> in this order:

1.) The day of Christ (rapture of the church)
2.) That day (Second Advent)
3.) A falling away or a great deception and apostasy
4.) The revealing of the man of sin

The Bible is not always linear. That means the events are not always listed in strict chronological order as we see them. So we have to slow down and read the text carefully to discern the correct order. It is given clearly in the text. The day of Christ is at hand, so that has to be first. But then Paul says "that day" shall not come until the other two happen. So it makes "that day" (Second Advent) number four on this list. So the other events must be 2 and 3, and the text tells you their order when it says there is a falling away <u>first</u>. Some teach that this falling away is the apostasy of Laodicea to close the church age. Granted, this age of the church is a mess, but the worldwide deception of the first half of the Tribulation will make this age look like the greatest revival in history. Revelation 12:9 says Satan will deceive the whole world. That is Seal number 1 in Revelation chapter 6; the peaceful takeover of the Antichrist to implement his agenda and false kingdom. This deception was the first thing Jesus warned the apostles about in Matthew chapter 24. So the correct <u>chronological</u> order of these four events is:

1.) The day of Christ (rapture of the church)
2.) A falling away (the worldwide deception of the first half of the Tribulation)
3.) The revealing of the man of sin
4.) That day (Second Advent)

This places the Revealing of the Wicked at the mid-point of the Tribulation. So it is rather futile to try to locate his identity now, even though I already know who he is! But the prophecy teachers obsess over finding some guy running around the Middle East who they can hang the tag on. I am still not really sure what the motive or the point is, other than trying to impress everyone with their secret knowledge. What are they going to do, walk up to him and stick out their hand and introduce themselves? "Hi! My name is John. You are the Antichrist, aren't you? Nice to meet you." Maybe they think he will respond with, "Yeah, you're right. You got me! You pulled the mask off the old Lone Ranger. But hey, do me a favor. Let this be our little secret and don't tell anyone. I have a 'rep' to protect, and I can't let this get out yet."

One of the main reasons the prophecy gurus are obsessed with finding the Antichrist is so they can "protect" themselves from him. First, that violates what we just spent significant time on; the DUAL teaching in II Thessalonians 2. There is no need to protect yourself from the Antichrist unless you are not saved. I have already accessed the only protection there is, the blood of Jesus Christ, and that is WAY better than seven years of rice and beans and ammo. The Antichrist cannot implement his full <u>work</u> until I am gone, and he will not be revealed until 3½ years later. Second, can you explain to me how, pray tell, that you intend to withstand the full assault of the most powerful being in existence outside the Godhead?

So if the passage only deals with the rapture of the church, the church will have to go through the first half of the Tribulation. We will "let" or restrain the Antichrist from being revealed until we are taken out of the way, but we will have to go through the "falling away" of the worldwide deception of the first half of the Tribulation before that happens. If "he who now letteth" is only the assassination of the Antichrist, then you can place the rapture of the church anywhere, which is what all of our friendly neighborhood prophecy gurus try to do. They end up confusing more people than they confirm with the truth.

The Antichrist will not be revealed as the false man of sin until mid way through the Tribulation. But the passage in Thessalonians does give us a clue as to his identity in the Bible: the son of perdition. We saw him in Revelation chapter 9 as Judas Iscariot in the opening of the bottomless pit. But there is way more to this than just "Judas is the Antichrist". Hopefully we can unwrap this further as we make our way through Revelation chapter 13. But there is still a little more "unpacking" we have to do before we can get back to Revelation.

The great "falling away" is the false kingdom of the Antichrist during the first half of the Tribulation. It is kicked off with a peace plan described in Daniel chapter 9. We spent a significant amount of time with this peace plan back in Revelation chapter 6 with the first Seal. If you need to refresh your mind on it, go back to that section of this commentary.

So we have the doctrinal chronology set. The rapture of the church (day of Christ) ends the church age and begins the Tribulation. The church is "taken out of the way" so that the work of the Antichrist can proceed full steam ahead. A false utopian kingdom deceives the whole world for 3½ years until the great world leader who came up with the peace plan is "taken out of the way" by an assassin to unmask the Antichrist. Then "all hell breaks loose" as God pours out his judgment on a world that rejects his Son, culminating in that Son returning to reign. Identifying the "something" that reveals the Antichrist brings us back to Revelation to examine a series of events that all occur at exactly the same point in time half way through the Tribulation. The thing to note about these events is WHEN they occur. I will show from the text in each one that they all take place at the "1260 days" point, so they must be connected. In fact, this series of events will occur over the space of roughly three days. It will involve the "healing" of the head wound of the Antichrist, which will be a "resurrection" of sorts. Since Satan counterfeits everything God does, it is more than likely that this "resurrection" will happen three days after the assassination.

Much of the confusion stems from the wording of a couple of verses in Revelation chapter 13. So let's deal with this briefly now, and then get more detail when we actually walk through the chapter. For now, we are simply trying to lay out the Revealing of the Wicked. Revelation 13:1 describes a "beast out of the sea". Revelation 13:11 mentions another beast. Are there two? This beast is said to come up "out of the earth". But the beast is the beast. There is only one Antichrist. There are scores of types in the Bible and in history, and oodles of others associated with the Antichrist, but there is only one beast. Then how can there be another one, and how does he come out of the sea and out of the earth? I am glad you asked.

When the Bible refers to the "sea", it can be essentially one of three things. Sometimes it refers to the "great deep" at the top of the Universe. When there is "no more sea" (Revelation 21:1), it is referring to that body of water. When the Bible mentions a sea as a body of water on the earth, it is usually talking about the Mediterranean unless there is a specific reference to the Sea of Galilee or another body of water in the text. The name Mediterranean means "middle earth" (Medio-Terra) and that sea is the center of the "known world" and the lands of the Bible. The third way the Bible uses the term "sea" is in reference to the "sea of humanity". Revelation 17:15 says "the waters are peoples". Since this passage has nothing to do with the "deep" of Genesis, the beast that rises out of the sea comes from the Mediterranean area and is just a man like the rest of us in the sea of humanity. His mother changed his diapers when he was a baby like anyone else. Just by way of a little FYI, what nation has its entire leg stuck into the "middle earth" sea? But then there is the beast "out of the earth" who is "another" beast, but not really. This "second" beast is, as we say, "the same thing only different". This is Judas Iscariot who comes out of the earth in Revelation chapter 9 with the opening of the bottomless pit. Go back to chapter 9 for the full details. But if there is only one beast, it means that something has to happen to transition from the beast out of the sea to the beast out of the earth. This is what we refer to as the "Revealing of the Wicked".

Here is the series of events that form the transition from the Pope to Judas. They all occur at the "1260" mid-point, and will unfold over the space of essentially about a week (seven days). We have all noticed how rapidly the world can change with things like 9-11, and it will not take very long for everything in the utopia of the first half of the Tribulation to fall completely apart. This is the detail of the "box" in the middle of the diagram we saw earlier. As I have mentioned, this box is the most significant thing on the diagram and the main event (or series of events) that flips the script from utopia to disaster.

1) The deadly head wound (Revelation 13:3) – This is where it all begins. There is no information given in the Bible about who does this or how. Revelation 13:3 says his wound will be healed, and verse 14 says he has a wound by a sword and "did live". It does not have to be a literal "sword"; it could be a gun or other weapon. Remember that John writes using the only terminology that a first century man knows, and he had never been introduced to a firearm. It will be a "wound unto death", so connecting all those dots requires us to conclude that this man will actually die and be raised from the dead. Zechariah 11:15-17 gives a little added detail. When this sword hits the "idol shepherd" (Antichrist), the result will be that his right arm will be paralyzed and his right eye will be blinded. So even though he comes back from the dead, there will be a visual reminder of the assassination. But there is more to it than just his new physical "handicap". Everything in the Bible means something. Jesus is "seated at the right hand of the Father". He is God's "right hand man". Satan counterfeits everything God does because his essential desire is to "be like the Most High" (Isaiah 14:14). So he also has a "right hand man".

Look at Psalm 109:6: "Set thou a wicked man over him: and let Satan stand at his right hand." This is a "wicked" man. Satan stands at his right hand. Read the context of Psalm 109 and you will clearly see Judas Iscariot. In fact, Peter quoted Psalm 109:8 in the upper room in Acts chapter 1 when they replaced Judas with Matthias as the 12th apostle. So when "that Wicked" is revealed, he will bear the marks of his assassination as a reminder of who it is he serves. His right arm will be "dried up" to remind us who stands at his right hand, and his right eye will be "utterly darkened" to remind us how he blinds the minds of them which believe not (II Corinthians 4:4). After three days, the "healing" (resurrection) will take place. There is nothing directly in the Bible about that time frame, but do you have a better guess? Since this man was heralded by the world as the "Messiah / Christ / Imam", he will likely lie in state for all the world to mourn his death. Cell phones will enable everyone the world over to see it. Imagine the celebration when he rises out of his casket and shows himself alive in imitation of the resurrection of Jesus Christ. Revelation 13:5 says power is given unto him to continue 42 months. In order for him to continue, he had to be in place before, so it is the same beast (only different). The 42 months places this assassination at the mid-point of the Tribulation.

2) War in heaven (Revelation 12:7-9) – This passage describes a spiritual battle in the heavens that results in the banishment of Satan from heaven. Before his fall, Lucifer had an honored position as the "anointed cherub that covereth" the throne (Ezekiel 28:11-19). When he fell, he lost that position but did not lose access to the throne of God. Revelation 12:10 says he is the "accuser of the brethren" at the throne of God until his banishment in this war. Job chapters 1 and 2 both show us that Satan still "presents himself before the Lord" at times. The cartoon image of Satan in hell with his red suit and his pitchfork is just that; a cartoon. He is not there yet. The war in heaven is dated at the mid-point of the Tribulation also. In the previous verse, the 1260 days is mentioned, and later in the chapter, when Satan finds himself confined to earth, he will persecute the woman (Israel) for a time, times, and half a time. One (time) plus two (times) plus a half is 3½.

3) The bottomless pit is opened (Revelation 9:1-11, 17:8) – Earlier we spent some time in Revelation 9:1 detailing the "star" who falls from heaven with the key to the bottomless pit. We saw that this was Satan. When he loses the war with Michael, he will "fall" from heaven and be allowed to let out his partner in crime Judas. We can identify this time period also mid-way through the Tribulation, though it takes just a little more effort. Look back at Revelation 9:4: "And it was commanded them that they should not hurt the grass of the earth, neither any green thing, neither any tree; but only those men which have not the seal of God in their foreheads." When Judas brings out his hordes, there are men who have been sealed (the 144,000), and the grass and the trees are still green. The 144,000 are sealed at the mid-point as we have already seen in chapter 7. As for the vegetation, Revelation 8:7 says the first angel opens the first Trumpet and all the green grass will be burnt up. Judas will come out of the bottomless pit while all the grass is green. The first Trumpet will be unleashed at the beginning of the last half of the Tribulation, or at the 3½ year mark to burn up all the grass. This is another example of how we must lay the accounts of the events of Revelation on top of each other rather than side by side. The same events are reported more than once in various places.

With these three events (assassination, Satan banished, Judas let out), we see the Antichrist "morph" from the beast out of the sea to the beast out of the earth. The beast "out of the earth" comes out of the heart of the earth to finish his work. When Judas was here the first time, he got 42 months with Jesus to try to undermine and subvert the Son of God. He will come back and get another 42 months to try to finish the job. I am not a gambler, but I will put my money on Jesus. Besides, it is not gambling if it is a sure thing.

While this man is lying in state after his assassination, nothing really takes place for probably three days as I have mentioned. Then these two things occur. So the body of a Pope will be lying in a casket at the Vatican, and a worldwide "viewing" will be taking place both in person and online. Satan will be kicked out of heaven, and as a spirit, he is disembodied and needs someone to inhabit. The soul of Judas will come out of the pit, and needs a body as well. What better one to grab than the world leader who got this whole kingdom thing going to start with? Satan indwelt Judas before (John 13:2, 27); the only man in history to have that "honor?". They will be reunited for their last chance kamikaze redo. So the "beast out of the earth" is the Antichrist after this assassination. He is a counterfeit false trinity of the body of a Pope, the soul of Judas, and spirit of Satan all rolled into one nasty ugly monster. Once this happens, the entire nature of the Tribulation "pivots".

4) The Abomination of Desolation (Matthew 24:15, Daniel 9:27, II Thessalonians 2:4) – At this point, the risen man of sin is still being proclaimed as the "Messiah / Christ / Imam", and possibly even more since he has now done something that only Jesus had done before. In fact, he begins to draw worship (Revelation 13:15). Great miracles and wonders are performed, and the whole world is deceived into believing that this man will solve every problem of mankind. Then he does something that causes the Jews to finally recognize that they have put their faith in the wrong man.

We need to spend some significant time with this for a number of reasons, one of them being the bad teaching in many circles about the Abomination of Desolation. I mentioned it earlier in the section on the flight of Israel and the sealing of the 144,000 in Revelation chapter 7. We saw there how some have tried to make the Abomination of Desolation apply to a Greek army general named Antiochus Epiphanes who sacrificed a pig on the altar of Jerusalem in 165 BC. But Jesus referred to this as a future event. It could not have happened before then. We have already seen that the first half of the Tribulation is the false kingdom and that the "beast out of the sea" will be received by the world as the "Christ". Israel falls into this trap as well. Jesus said in John 5:43: "I am come in my Father's name, and ye receive me not: if another shall come in his own name, him ye will receive." That is a direct reference to the Jews receiving the man of sin as the Antichrist. He has to fool them in order to pull it off, and he does so with the peace plan to rebuild the temple. He wants that temple! His great desire is to "sit upon the mount of the congregation in the sides of the north" and be like God (Isaiah 14).

Proverbs 25:19 says, "Confidence in an unfaithful man in time of trouble is like a broken tooth, and a foot out of joint." That is a cute little "ditty" that tells us not to trust the wrong people, but it is far more than that Biblically. The phrase "time of trouble" is a direct reference to the Tribulation. It is called the "time of Jacob's trouble" in Jeremiah 30:7. Israel will place their confidence in the wrong man in the time of their trouble. But then he will be unmasked half way through.

The Abomination of Desolation stands in the holy place (Matthew 24:15). The holy place for Israel is the Holy of Holies in the temple, the picture of the throne of God. This place is reserved for the High Priest of Israel only ONE day per year on the Day of Atonement (Leviticus chapter 16). The risen man of sin will enter this holy place and declare himself to be God. II Thessalonians 2:4 says, "Who opposeth and exalteth himself above all that is called God, or that is worshipped; so that he as God sitteth in the temple of God, shewing himself that he is God." When the Jews see that, they freak out to put it in modern living language. One of the reasons Israel rejected Jesus Christ is that they could not bring themselves to believe that God could be a man. Then here comes this man claiming to be God, and then he defiles their temple by entering the holy place. Then it gets worse. Daniel 9:27 says he will break the covenant at this mid-point and cause the sacrifices to cease. In reality, the sacrifices will not stop, they will be re-directed. Since this beast out of the earth will claim to be God, he will demand that the sacrifices now belong to him.

When Israel refuses, it will turn very ugly. Instead of the animal sacrifices of Judaism, the Jews will be the sacrifices. If any of them are caught, they will be brought to the temple in Jerusalem and be given the chance to renounce the Lord or suffer the fate of beheading. Then they will be sacrificed and cannibalized. We covered that disgusting, vile and gruesome aspect of the Tribulation earlier in Revelation chapter 6 with the fifth Seal. Satan has desired to take God's throne from the beginning. He has tried many times and has gotten close. Constantine presiding over the Council of Nicea was one such time. Pope Urban launched a Crusade hoping to get there himself, but he died before news of victory got back to him. When Pope Judas enters the holy place, he will have achieved his goal as close as he ever will, but only temporarily.

5) Israel flees into the wilderness (Revelation 12:14, Matthew 24:16-20) – Extensive comments were already made on this issue in both Revelation chapter 7, and especially chapter 12 with the discussion of Sela-Petra and the flight into the wilderness.

6) Jesus appears Mid-Tribulation and seals the 144,000 (Revelation 7:1-8, 14:1-7) – We also spent a lot of time on this subject in Revelation chapter 7. So there is no need to revisit these last two points in any major detail. But these are the final steps in the "pivot" that changes the Tribulation from the false peaceful kingdom to the hell on earth commonly associated with Revelation. All six of these events can be clearly identified as happening at the same 3½ year mid-point, so they must be related.

"And now you know what withholdeth that he might be revealed in his time" (II Thessalonians 2:6). His time is not the church age, it is the Tribulation. The church withholds any of this until it is taken out of the way at the rapture. But then the beast out of the sea, the Pope who orchestrates the peace plan of Daniel 9, must be taken out of the way before the Antichrist can be revealed to Israel as the wrong Christ.

That is a LOT of "intro" to Revelation chapter 13, but as I have said, this is probably the most significant chapter in the book and the most hotly debated. It was necessary to give that much background before we got into the chapter itself. So with all of the background from Jesus' words in Matthew 24, the peace plan from Daniel chapter 9, the Revealing of the Wicked from II Thessalonians chapter 2, and several other Bible passages, let us very deliberately and methodically move through Revelation chapter 13. Hopefully we can make some common sense out of the passage and provide a better understanding of this incredibly challenging section of prophetic truth.

Revelation 13:1-10 – The Beast Out of the Sea

VS 1 – John describes a beast rising out of the sea. It is a beast of blasphemy with seven heads and ten horns. In Biblical and prophetic language, heads represent authority (as in being "head" of something) and horns represent power. So this beast is "large and in charge", and he is quite willing to let it be known by his "name of blasphemy". Blasphemy means to speak evil of God and / or to exalt yourself above him. The first mention of blasphemy in the Bible is in Leviticus 24:11. Two guys were fighting in the camp and one of them "blasphemed the name of the LORD, and cursed." Pardon my language for a minute but let me put that into a term you have undoubtedly heard a million times and perhaps even used yourself a few of those million times. The man said, "God damn you." This is different than simply "taking the name of the Lord in vain". Look at the entire story behind this event in Leviticus 24. The man cursed using God's name, and the people brought him to Moses. They "put him in ward" to ask God what to do about it. Moses was not sure yet how to handle such an incident. But Israel already had the Ten Commandments at this time. They already had the warning to "not take the name of the Lord thy God in vain." Vanity in the Bible means "nothing" or "empty". Taking the name of the Lord in vain is much more than using it as a cuss word. If you are a <u>Christ</u>ian, you have taken the name of Christ upon you. If you do nothing with that name, you have taken it in vain even if you never utter a bad word out of your mouth your entire life. When this man called for the damnation of God to fall upon another human being, he placed himself on God's judgment throne. He spoke evil of God in calling for judgment simply because they were having a fight. God's judgment is serious business, and God's grace covers a lot of things like this. We do not know what these two were fighting about, but we do know that God issued NO judgment against the other party. The blasphemer exalted himself above God and ascribed evil to him. He swore an oath reserving for himself the right to determine who gets blessed and who gets cursed by God. Only God can "swear by himself" (Hebrews 6:13-17).

So when this beast rises out of the sea, he may be the most mild-mannered and soft spoken person on earth, and as "pure as the wind-driven snow" in his language. Most Popes are, at least publicly and even privately. But he will place himself in the shoes of God and confer evil on others in his name. That is blasphemy in its purest form, and will be ultimately manifest when he declares himself to be God in the middle of the Tribulation in the temple. The verse says this name of blasphemy is "upon his heads". For generations, the Pope wore a mitre with the following inscription on it: "VICARIVS FILII DEI". That is Latin for "The Faithful Vicar of God". Take the letters in that title that are also Roman numerals and add them up. There is a "D" (500), a "C" (100), an "L" (50), two of the "V" (5) and six of the "I" (1). That totals 666. You will not find that title on his head today because it is too obvious. Enough people pointed it out that he had to remove it to stay "underground".

As with all "symbolism" in the Bible, the heads and horns are defined in the word of God so that we do not have to guess or get out a big sledgehammer to make it fit the private interpretations of those who do not have a clue what the Bible says. I will refer you forward to Revelation 17:3 and my comments under that verse where the seven heads and ten horns are <u>clearly</u> defined by the Bible itself.

Now let's identify the "sea" referenced in Revelation 13:1 so we can pin down the location where this beast rises from. Whenever the Bible mentions a sea as a body of water on earth, it is usually referring to what we know as the "Middle Earth Sea" known to us as the Mediterranean ("Medio-Terra"). A world leader rises from this area to exercise power and authority over humanity. The sea in the Bible is also a picture of the great "sea of humanity". This world leader out of the sea rises from the sea of humanity; in other words, he is one of us and not an alien (yet). He is just a man, but rises above the rest of us to exalt himself as God. Do you know a world leader who is just a man, yet has risen to incredible power and sits upon a royal throne in the Mediterranean area and claims to be the true "Vicar" of Christ and the "Holy Father"? That is the Pope in case you didn't quite get that. The "beast out of the sea" is the Antichrist in the first half of the Tribulation. He is the world leader who will orchestrate the peace plan of Daniel chapter 9. We don't know exactly which Pope it will be, but that office will be used to craft this treaty. As of this writing, there have been 266 Popes in the history of the Catholic Church according to their records. I do not trust their records as far as I can throw a loaded 747, especially further back in history. They obviously have Peter as the first Pope, when he was nothing of the sort. The first actual Pope was appointed by Constantine in 314 AD, and every one of them since then has been "the Antichrist" without being the actual one. At some point, one of the men in that office will be used of Satan to "solve" the Middle East conflict and open the way for Israel to rebuild their temple. No other office on earth has as much "street cred" to pull it off.

Before we move on, let's get a little visual confirmation of this office being the seat of the Antichrist. In Daniel chapter 2, the dream of Nebuchadnezzar concludes with a stone (Jesus) hitting the image of man's kingdom on the TOES and destroying the entire system. Jutting out into the "Middle Earth Sea" is the land mass of a nation shaped just like a boot. Right off the end of the "toes" of the boot is a "stone". God gave humanity a vivid picture of the culmination of the image of Daniel chapter 2 with Italy and Sicily. People have seen that with their eyes for centuries yet still cannot see the truth of the Bible.

VS 2 – The beast is like a leopard. The leopard is an "integrated" animal; he has a yellow coat (Shem), brown spots (Ham) and a white belly (Japheth). He is from the same genus as the "roaring lion": a cat. If a person works too much, they call him a "workaholic" because he is completely devoted to his work. If a person drinks too much, he is an "alcoholic". Does that mean that a person completely devoted to the "cat" is a Cat-holic? Just wondering…

This beast has the feet of a bear and the mouth of a lion. The bear is a symbol of Russia and the lion is a symbol of England. Regardless of that possible literal connection, a bear and a lion are not compatible creatures. They would not get along in a cage together. Note that this beast has feet that will move him in one direction and a mouth that will speak in the other direction. In other words, he is "two-faced". Job 41:13 says Satan has a "double bridle". This beast will speak capitalistic and move communistic. He will be religious and political both at the same time. He will be squeaky clean morally on the outside and full of blasphemy inside. This beast out of the sea (the Pope) gets his power, seat and great authority from the dragon (Satan). The seat is the Papal throne and the power and authority that comes with it. The Pope claims universal authority over every human being on earth whether they are Catholic or not. He is supposedly "infallible" when he speaks "ex-cathedra", which literally means "out of the chair / seat".

VS 3-8 – These verses deal with the assassination of the Pope which has been thoroughly covered earlier. But there are a few things in the text worth noting. Verse 3 says "all the world wondered after the beast" when his head wound was healed (when he is raised). All the world cannot do this unless they have access to the information. Technology has made that possible. Worship will be ascribed to the beast and the dragon (Satan) which is his ultimate goal. The world will ask, "Who is like unto the beast"? although they probably won't use the term "beast". This is another of the places in the Bible where Satan steals the glory of God. Isaiah 46:9 says, "Remember the former things of old: for I am God, and there is none else; I am God, and there is none like me."

Verse 5 says power will be given to this beast after his assassination to "continue" 42 months. In order for him to continue, he has to be in place to start with. So the "two" beasts (out of the sea / out of the earth) have to be the same even in their differences. But there is another level of understanding with this. Judas got 42 months with the Lord when he was here the first time. In the Tribulation, he will continue the effort he made the first time to usurp his throne for the same amount of time. Verses 5-7 follow the same sequence as the Revealing of the Wicked. Verse 5 brings him back from the dead to "continue". Verse 6 takes him to the tabernacle (temple) to blaspheme God's name by taking it upon himself. Then verse 7 has him making war against the saints as he turns on them in the middle of the Tribulation.

Verse 8 mentions the Lamb's book of life. We will see it again in chapter 20 at the Great White Throne Judgment. But let's unpack some of it now. At the final judgment "the books will be opened." I believe that is the 66 books of the Bible, which is the "law book" of the courtroom. Then another book is opened called the "book of life". I believe that refers to this one in chapter 13 called "the Lamb's book of life". In order for someone to be saved, his name has to appear in the Lamb's book of life. My name does not appear in the Bible, but I "have a new name written down in glory" as the old hymn says. When Israel made the golden calf in the wilderness, Moses stepped in to intercede for the people. He said in Exodus 32:32, "Yet now, if thou wilt forgive their sin--; and if not, blot me, I pray thee, out of thy book which thou hast written." Moses became a type of Christ in this passage by accepting the judgment for the sin of God's people. But God responded in verse 33: "Whosoever hath sinned against me, him will I blot out of my book." In other words, even though Moses was a type of Christ, and even though this was a very godly and noble thing to do, God would not allow it. No mere mortal man with his own sins could take upon himself the judgment of God for the sins of others. This is the Lamb's book of life, not Moses' book of life. There is very little information given about the Lamb's book of life. It is possible that when a person trusts Jesus as his Saviour that his name gets recorded so that he will not be judged at the Great White Throne. But the account in Exodus infers that some could be blotted out of that book. We are not even sure that the book Moses referred to is the Lamb's book of life, but I tend to think so since the result is similar. We know a church age saint cannot be blotted out of the book because of our eternal security. But that is not available to Old Testament saints or those in the Tribulation.

There is also the famous line in verse 8: "The Lamb slain from the foundation of the world". John Calvin and his hyper buddies love verses like this in the Bible. "See, God chose the elect from the foundation of the world." It does not say that. It says Jesus is the Lamb slain from the foundation of the world. The plan for Jesus to die for sins was in place before Genesis 1:1. Those who find salvation in that Lamb do so in time. Titus 1:2 says, "In hope of eternal life, which God, that cannot lie, promised before the world began." I did not get saved before the world began, but God promised salvation before the world began to those who would receive the sacrifice of his Son.

VS 9-10 – This is a summary warning to pay attention to the book. "Ears to hear" is a common phrase in chapters 2 and 3, and Jesus used it himself quite often. Verse 10 gives us the principle of "reap as you sow". The warning is given to those who try to implement their agenda by force. God will answer in kind in the same fashion they give it out. Here is another of our expressions that comes from the Bible: "Live by the sword, die by the sword." Funny how many people reject the Bible and still quote it.

Revelation 13:11-18 – The Mark of the Beast

If there is one subject that has been beaten to a bloody pulp by prophecy gurus, it is the mark of the beast. The mark of the beast, the date of the rapture, and the identity of the Antichrist dominates prophetic studies. This is *Revelation Made Simple*. So let me cut right to the chase. There are more cell phones in the United States than there are people. That includes newborns. I got my first cell phone in 1994, and when I did, I was somebody! They were fairly common by then, but cell phone users were still in the minority in 1994. Now it seems they issue them at birth like they do a social security number. My first cell phone was a "flip phone" and it was ONLY a telephone. Calling a cell phone a phone today is sort of like calling your car a mobile radio. There is a radio in your car, but your car does a whole lot more than that. The technology for world-wide Orwellian control of every nano-detail of your life is already in place and has been for many years. It gets more sophisticated every day. That technology and our world can change exponentially in a very short time. COVID-19 brought out a nice "dry run" for this. We were told what we could buy or not buy based on what was "essential" according to the authorities. A bottle of whiskey was essential, but a can of paint was not. Why? Because I say so. No other reason was needed, and how dare you even ask. A new term was invented called "contact tracing". This is where they track everyone's movements to see who you have been in contact with so they can stop the spread of the virus.

I get it with the virus (to a point). It is a nasty disease that claimed far too many lives. But you can see the parallel very easily. We have to stop the spread of the virus of Jesus, so we need to know if you have been in contact with one of those infected Jewish preachers, and we can find out through your cell phone. Not only are some products essential and some not, people are in the same category. If you perform an abortion you are essential. If you minister the word of God, you are not. Those who are in a certain category are free to go out in public because they are either not "at risk" or have been deemed safe because they have been tested for the antibodies. If and when they finally get a vaccine, they can issue what some are even now calling an "immunity card". If you have the card you can come into our store, but if not you cannot buy here. Then there are those who are hyperventilating over the vaccine itself claiming they are going to include a "chip" in it that will register whether or not you have been "approved". Who knows about all of the details of those things? Again, with the virus, some of this might make some sense. Most of it does not and it has simply offered the opportunity for power-mad Orwellian leaders to practice total control of the populace at their whim. Probably most of the people involved in these things do not really understand the scope of what is happening and are simply along for the ride and trying to do what they think is beneficial for all of us. But the way is being paved and the system has been in place for a long time, and it can and will "turn on a dime" at a moment's notice.

I am not going to run down the roads of all the various conspiracy theories that are running around out there. I am sure you can go on line and fill your head with as many of them as your little heart would desire. You are NOT going to stop this. There are too many Christians who live in abject fear of "taking the mark". Let's go back to some of our basic principles. The mark of the beast is one of the essential elements of the work of the Antichrist. Remember that work cannot proceed until the indwelling Spirit of God is "taken out of the way" at the rapture of the church. So although the system is in place and ready to go, it is restrained until we are gone. If you have a cell phone, you have not taken the mark. If you get a vaccine, you will not take the mark even if they do somehow manage to "chip" you in the process. The first half of the Tribulation is the voluntary roll out period for the mark. It will not be fully implemented until the world is well into the reign of the false Christ, and it will not get to total "lockdown" until after the beast is revealed. The mark is not a thing as much as it is a system, and it is already with us.

So then, preacher, how can I protect myself from the mark of the beast? I am glad you asked. Jesus died on the cross to pay the penalty for your sins. Then he rose from the dead to prove who he was and got the victory over sin and death. He calls you to quit trusting in your own goodness or religion or even your own efforts to "prepare" for this time. Turn from your sins and come to the cross. Receive what Jesus did for you by faith. The best way you know how, just ask Jesus Christ to save you from your sins. If you will, he will "vaccinate" you and "protect" you by saving your soul and taking you out before this nonsense takes over the world. Tell others what Jesus did for you on your way out.

VS 11 – There is another beast??? This refers to the change in the Antichrist due to the Mid-Tribulation Revealing of the Wicked that we have already seen. This beast has two horns. Horns are the symbol of power, and it does not specify exactly what powers those horns represent, so we are left to speculate. This beast has both religious and political power. Satan and Judas now both indwell the resurrected body of a Pope. He is "like a lamb", so he is the counterfeit of the true Lamb of God. He speaks as a dragon, meaning the ultimate "boss" driving him is Satan. This is Satan manifest in the flesh as the counterfeit of the Lord Jesus Christ (I Timothy 3:16). This is the beast out of the earth. Chinese legend says Genghis Khan will come up out of the earth and take over the world with his army and his hordes will roll across Europe and conquer it. Apollo supposedly comes out of Hades in Greek mythology. College professors in comparative religion courses will claim all religions are the same and that the Bible copies mythology. Satan knew the basic plan from the "get-go" also. His false systems copy the Bible even before the Bible was written. God does not imitate Satan, it is the other way around, Einstein.

VS 12-15 – These verses give more insight into the relationship between the "first" beast and "another" beast, although for the umpteenth time, they are the same (only different). Verse 12 says he exercises the power of the <u>first</u> beast and causes people to worship the <u>first</u> beast, because as the world sees it, it looks like the same man. Great wonders and miracles will be performed. They will be visible phenomena that are designed to "prove" that this man is God. Paul spoke directly of this (before Revelation was written) in II Thessalonians 2:9: "Even him, whose coming is after the working of Satan with all power and signs and lying wonders."

An image will be constructed of this great world leader which will be eerily similar to another image that was constructed in the plain of Dura in Babylon in Daniel chapter 3. Anyone who refused to worship that image was targeted for death. Three Hebrew young men had the audacity to stick their bony fingers in the face of the "king of the world" and tell him to pound sand. They were cast into a fiery furnace and survived because the Son of God showed up to miraculously protect them. I am sure you are familiar with the story. It is a type of the 144,000 in the Tribulation. These young men were eunuchs (virgins). Remember that word? They defied the type of the Antichrist and were targeted due to their Jewish religion. The image was constructed in Babylon, picturing Mystery Babylon (Rome). By the way, what were their names? Don't say Shadrach, Meshach and Abednego. That was their Babylonian names, not the names God gave them. That is one of my pet peeves in the Bible. The world should NOT know you by how you conduct yourself according to the "course of this world".

The image in Revelation differs from the Babylonian image in that it will be given "life". I do not profess to understand all the details of this image, and I am one of the biggest "Luddites" on earth. That is a term to describe a technophobe. I use what technology I have to in order to function in this insane asylum we live in, but I hate it with a bloody purple passion. Hologram technology has been around for decades that can make items appear lifelike that are not even real. Many of you have a device in your home that you can speak to and it will act as if it is human and do things for you. The image in Revelation chapter 13 will speak. The technology is here. This will be the Wizard of Oz on steroids and not just a movie.

VS 16-18 – Here are the verses on the mark of the beast. Notice the 6-6-6 is in verse 18 (6+6+6) and in chapter 13 (the number of rebellion). Surely that is just a coincidence, right? The basic design of this system is to control commerce. People today have all sorts of investment strategies: stocks, bonds, gold, mattresses or coffee cans buried in the yard, or whatever. Those are fine. I have them as well because I have no idea when Jesus is coming for me and I might need a nest egg when I can no longer work. But the most precious commodity in the Tribulation will be food and water. Go ahead and invest in gold now if you think that is your best option. But try walking into a grocery store (if you can find one open) in the Tribulation with your quarterly statement from your financial planner showing the value of your gold fund and see how much food they let you take out of there. Even if you have a piece of gold, it won't do much good because no one can eat it. The mark will control the essential elements of physical survival as well as all other forms of commerce. If you control whether people can eat, you control everything.

Revelation Chapter 14 – The Lamb and the 144,000

Revelation 14:1-5 – The Virgins

The word "virgins" (plural) is reserved in the Bible specifically to speak of the 144,000. God chooses the simple words in the Bible to communicate truth, and often gives us much larger truths than just a simple Webster's definition of a word. There are three related words or phrases used in the King James Bible. Virgin (singular) designates the church when it is being used beyond just speaking of a single woman or one who has "not known man" (II Corinthians 11:2). But even in that, there are times when God speaks of a woman like that who is a type of the church. For example, Genesis 24:16 describes Rebekah as "a virgin, neither had any man known her". Well, duh, I thought that is what a virgin is. Why did God seem to repeat himself in this verse? He is communicating that Rebekah had not known man physically, and also that she pictured the church. She was the bride of Isaac, a type of Christ. Then there is the "virgin daughter" in the Bible. Even though this uses the word "virgin" in the singular, it is connected to another word to form the phrase. This is a designation for the Nation of Israel in the Tribulation. It speaks of the entire Jewish people and not just specifically the 144,000. Some of the references to show us this are: Isaiah 37:22, Jeremiah 14:17, and Lamentations 1:15 and 2:13. Then there are the virgins in the plural. When this term is used prophetically or to describe more than just a group of young single women, it is a reference to the Jewish witnesses in the Tribulation. We saw it earlier in Matthew 25 with the parable of the wise and foolish virgins. Solomon speaks of "virgins without number" in Song of Solomon 6:8, and David mentions virgins in Psalm 45:14. Both of those passages are linked to the "wedding party" for the marriage of the Lamb. Notice David said that the virgins follow the bride. Typically in our Western marriage processionals, the "virgins" (bridesmaids) come before the bride. But the virgins in the Bible (144,000) come after the bride because the Tribulation is after the church age.

So indulge me for a moment, please, as I discuss one of the major problems with the new Bibles. It is important to leave the words of the Bible alone. The new Bibles want to "update" the words for us so we can understand them better. What is so hard to understand about virgin or virgins? The NASV uses the word virgins in Matthew 25, but in Revelation 14:4 it says, "have kept themselves chaste". The NIV also uses virgins in Matthew, but says "have kept themselves pure" in Revelation. They want to simplify the Bible and make it easier to understand, so they replace one simple word everyone knows with four words. "Yes, but it says the same thing." This is the argument of what is called "dynamic equivalence". That is fancy speak for saying the same thing with different words. It is "equivalent" (says the same thing), but it is also "dynamic" in that it is updated to current vernacular. That excuse is used to change thousands of words in the King James Bible. In the process, it destroys cross references. Virgins in Matthew can be exactly and clearly tied to virgins in Revelation because it is the exact same word. Changing the wording in Revelation allows teachers to misapply Matthew 25 and teach the split rapture and other such nonsense because it is not clear to connect the passages. This issue is common in all the new Bibles. It is nearly impossible to "compare scripture with scripture" (I Corinthians 2:13) because words are changed that are designed by God to communicate more than just the word itself. So "dynamic equivalence" is just fine, huh? Let's do a little experiment, shall we? Tonight when you get home after work, say to your wife, "Honey, when I look into your eyes, the hands of time just stand still." She will melt in your arms. Then tomorrow night, say, "You have a face that could stop a clock." Did you SAY the same thing? Yes you did. Did you COMMUNICATE the same thing? Try it and let me know how it works out for you.

This passage ties in with the Mid-Tribulation appearance of Jesus to Israel, which was covered in detail back in chapter 7 with the sealing of the 144,000. However, when we get to this account in chapter 14, the scene shifts from the meeting in the wilderness to the gathering at the throne of God. The chapters are related to each other, but chapter 7 takes place 3½ years into Daniel's 70th Week, and chapter 14 occurs closer to the end of the Tribulation just prior to the Second Advent. There are some similarities between the two accounts, but there are far more differences.

The meeting here is not in Sela-Petra but "on the mount Sion". There is a mount Sion on earth which is a picture of the "heavenly Sion" described in Hebrews 12:22. Sion (or Zion) in the Old Testament is the physical location of the old city of Jerusalem containing the Temple Mount. The first time it appears in the Bible is in II Samuel 5:6-10 when David captured it from the Jebusites. It is called "the city of David" in that passage as well as in I Kings chapter 8 in the dedication of the temple. Throughout the rest of the Old Testament, Zion is connected to the Millennial reign of Christ. Psalm 2:6 says, "Yet have I set my king upon my holy hill of Zion." That is past tense because it is already a "done deal" in the mind of God and we are simply waiting for the reality of it once the calendar rolls far enough ahead.

This account in chapter 14 describes the group of Jewish witnesses just after the Post-Tribulation rapture and just prior to the Second Advent. If you recall from our "three raptures" study, the remnant of Israel led by Moses and Elijah will be taken out at the very end of Daniel's 70th Week. The 144,000 in chapter 7 are standing before the Lord in the wilderness to receive the instructions for the next 1260 days. The group in chapter 14 is standing at the throne of God (verse 3). They are singing a new song, which is unlikely while they are experiencing the persecution of the Antichrist in the Tribulation. They were (past tense) redeemed from the earth (verse 3). They are "without fault before the throne of God" (verse 5). All of this indicates that they have been taken out to be presented before the Lord. The Post-Tribulation rapture will be "up then immediately down" as Jesus comes back to earth. He will be leading two armies (Israel and the church) that will be detailed when we get to chapter 19. As we saw in chapter 11, the rapture of the remnant will be immediately followed by the Second Advent of the Lord Jesus Christ.

I mentioned this issue earlier in chapter 7 when we discussed the seal of the 144,000 and whether or not they could lose that seal. The Bible gives multiple warnings and examples of how they can. Yet we see the entire body of 144,000 in this passage on the mount Sion (heaven) just prior to the Second Advent that is to follow at the end of this chapter. If some can lose the seal, why are there a full 144,000 here? There are a couple of possibilities. Either the instructions are so fully heeded that no one forfeits their seal or there are more than 144,000 Jews who meet Jesus in Sela-Petra at his Mid-Tribulation appearing. I said earlier that I did not know this answer, and I still don't know seven chapters later.

Revelation 14:6-7 – The Everlasting Gospel

The scene shifts back to earth, and the chronology shifts back to the mid-point of the Tribulation to detail the message that the virgins will preach. Again, I spent some time on this earlier in chapter 7. This is also called the "gospel of the kingdom" in Matthew 24:14, which is a different gospel than the one Paul preached. Stay with me. The word "gospel" means "good news", and there is more than one thing in the Bible that can be considered good news. Jesus Christ dying for our sins is good news, despite the fact that it is treated worse than the plague by the lost world. This gospel preached by the 144,000 says, "Our King is coming and you better fear him or else". That would be the "updated version in living language". Again, that gospel will be viewed as "hate speech" by the world, but it sure is good news for Israel!

This message is preached to "every nation, and kindred, and tongue, and people" which would be the Gentiles. Its mission is to draw a few to faith in Jehovah God and his Son Yeshua in preparation for his return. Though an angel has the message, he delivers it to the remnant so they can deliver it to the Gentile world. So, we need to clarify an apparent problem with this message and the gospel Paul preached. Galatians 1:8-9 says, "But though we, or an angel from heaven, preach any other gospel unto you than that which we have preached unto you, let him be accursed. As we said before, so say I now again, If any man preach any other gospel unto you than that ye have received, let him be accursed." Notice an angel has this "other gospel" first, then a man preaches it. Yet the angel and the preachers of Revelation 14 who have "another gospel" are not cursed. The message in Revelation 14 does not mention the blood of Christ or his substitutionary sacrifice or his resurrection. It is a different dispensation. It is the same "product" of God's grace given to those who will receive it by faith, but some elements are different.

Revelation 14:8-11 – Judgment Pronounced

VS 8 – Babylon is called a "great city", and so is Jerusalem (Jeremiah 22:8, Revelation 11:8) as well as Nineveh in the book of Jonah. But the reference in this passage is to Rome, not the literal ancient city of Babylon. Some think that ancient Babylon must be rebuilt to fulfill prophecy, but that is not necessary. We will establish this clearly when we get to Revelation chapters 17-18. This Babylon "is fallen, is fallen". Did God stutter? Why repeat himself like this? Again, we will detail this in chapter 17, but "Babylon / Rome" falls twice because it does refer to both cities. Babylon historically fell as a world empire in 625 BC and Rome will fall at the end of the Tribulation. So the passage is historical as well as prophetic. Babylon / Rome will fall physically and spiritually. They will also fall politically as well as religiously. They are the same system.

VS 9-10 – Between verses 8 and 10 there are two cups of wine. In verse 8, <u>she</u> (the whore of Revelation chapter 17) seduces the nations to drink of the wine of the wrath of her fornication. This is not a pleasant woman. She is the bitter, angry, contentious and wicked woman of the book of Proverbs. Her end is "bitter as wormwood" (Proverbs 5:4), which is seen in Trumpet number three. "Her house is the way to hell" (Proverbs 7:27), which is described in this passage. We will see more of this woman in chapter 17. Those who drink of her "wine" will also drink of the wine of the wrath of God (verse 10). This refers to the cup of Gethsemane. Jesus prayed, "Let this cup pass from me." He was not referring to death, but to the judgment of God that he would endure on the cross. Jesus drank the cup of the wrath of God for me. Those who reject his offer of salvation will drink of that cup themselves. It is your choice.

VS 10-11 – Those who want to spiritualize hell have trouble with passages such as this. As someone so aptly said, "Be careful of those who are trying to air-condition hell. They are getting ready to move in and want to take you with them." Jesus told the parable of the tares of the field in Matthew 13:24-30. Then he explained it later in Matthew 13:36-43. He defined every element of the parable; the field is the world, the enemy is the devil, the reapers are the angels, etc. But he did not define the fire. Fire is fire. It needs no further clarification and it is as literal as anything in the Bible. The rich man in hell in Luke 16 was "tormented in this <u>flame</u>". This passage has torment, fire and brimstone, smoke, and no rest day nor night. "How could a loving God send anyone there?" A loving God sent his Son to drink the wine of his wrath against sin for every human being. Anyone who rejects that love then comes face to face with the God of wrath. They will stand "in his presence" and be judged for their rejection. The "holy angels" will be present also for that judgment. That is a reference to the Great White Throne Judgment in Revelation chapter 20. David said in Psalm 139:8 that if he made his bed in hell, that God would be there. God is not "there" in the sense of being in hell <u>with</u> the lost. But his presence is everywhere. Not only will the lost be tormented in the fire forever, they will also be tormented with the knowledge that they had every chance in this life to accept the love of God displayed at Calvary. God's "presence" to the lost in hell will remind them of that for all of eternity. If you have not trusted Jesus as your Saviour, why not now?

Revelation 14:12-13 – The Promise of Reward

VS 12 – We see another reference to the "faith / works" combination for the Tribulation saints. Again, do not take this too far. I am not teaching works-based salvation. Grace through faith is the formula. God's grace is available to the Tribulation saints when they exercise their faith, then prove their faith is genuine by doing what God tells them to do. In this case, it is faith in Jesus (as Messiah) <u>and</u> the commandments of God. Both are necessary to confirm that their faith is real because the law comes back into effect for the Jews in the Tribulation. When James says, "faith without works is dead", he refers to this group.

VS 13 – The Tribulation saints will "rest from their labours" after they are dead. The same is true of us. We are called to labour for the Lord in this life, and it will not be over until we are home. They say, "A woman's work is never done", and we are the bride of Christ. It does not mean a Christian cannot retire from his secular job. To the contrary, it would be nice if many of us could get to that financial point long before we are too old to do anything productive. But a believer should never "retire" from service to his King. Too many Christians do that. They go just fine for a while, then figure they have done enough and it is time to let others do the work. Stay with it. You are not done until God takes you home, and when God is done with you, he will take you home. "Their works (and ours) do follow them." God is keeping track. He will reward his faithful servants justly and fully (Hebrews 6:10, I Corinthians 3:11-15).

Revelation 14:14-20 – The Second Advent

This is the third time in Revelation the Second Advent of Jesus Christ is covered. There are some unique things covered in this passage that add details to the other three accounts.

VS 14-16 – A sickle is used to reap the earth. The one who reaps sits upon a white cloud and is "like unto the Son of man". Jesus went up in a cloud in Acts chapter 1, and it says that he will come again "in like manner". Clouds are connected to the Second Advent in many prophecies (Ezekiel 30:3, Revelation 1:7, Daniel 7:13, and Zephaniah 1:15) to name just a few. So this reaper is Jesus Christ. Verse 15 says, "The harvest of the earth is ripe." Notice the term "harvest". I am sure you remember that this is the term used for the "raptures" (plural) in the Bible. This is the final one. The harvest of the earth is ripe; it has come to full maturity for its final phase. This is the Post-Tribulation rapture of the Jewish remnant.

VS 17-20 – But there is a second sickle. This one does not harvest the earth; it gathers the "fruit of the vine" into a great winepress. Let's take a little time with this sickle to identify exactly what is happening here. An angel with "power over fire" announces this gathering. Fire in the Bible is connected to the judgment of God. This sickle gathers for the purpose of judgment. The "clusters of the vine of the earth" are gathered. Jesus said he was the true vine in John 15:1. These clusters are from a different vine. The false vine of the earth produces rotten fruit. Deuteronomy 32:32-33 tells us the source of this vine and its fruit: "For their vine is of the vine of Sodom, and of the fields of Gomorrah: their grapes are grapes of gall, their clusters are bitter: Their wine is the poison of dragons, and the cruel venom of asps." Ezekiel chapter 15 says the vine tree is useless for any work and its only benefit is to be burned for fuel. The angel with power over fire calls for this vine and its fruit to be gathered to be burned.

So let me "digress" for a brief moment (but not really). The only forbidden fruit in the Bible is from the vine (Numbers 6:3-4), not the apple. When Noah and his boys got off the ark, the first sin was a result of a vineyard that made him drunk, not an orchard. If a young man wants to seduce a young lady into sin, which is more likely to help him do so, a glass of wine or a glass of apple juice? Right before Jesus went to the cross, he made a direct connection between the fruit of the vine and his blood that would be shed to pay for sin. No apples were mentioned. The grape is always connected to sin in the Bible, and the apple is never connected to sin. There were four trees mentioned in the Garden of Eden in Genesis: the tree of life, the tree of the knowledge of good and evil, the fig tree (for the fig leaves) and "thorns and thistles" that were dormant until sin was introduced. Now read Judges 9:7-15. Jotham's speech mentions four trees: the olive, the fig, the vine and the bramble. No apples are mentioned. Match up the four trees:

Genesis	**Judges**
Tree of life	Olive
Tree of knowledge of good and evil	Vine
Fig tree	Fig
Thorns and thistles	Bramble

Note what Jesus said in Matthew 7:16: "Ye shall know them by their fruits. Do men gather grapes of thorns, or figs of thistles?" That is three of the four trees of Eden. Why did he mention a grape and not an apple? What do you suppose was the "forbidden fruit" of the Garden of Eden?

So this second sickle gathers clusters of a forbidden fruit to cast them into a winepress to be trodden by the wrath of God. The "winepress" is a picture of judgment in the Bible connected to the Second Advent of the Lord Jesus Christ (Revelation 19:13-15). This particular winepress is located outside the city of Jerusalem. When the "grapes" are stomped, the blood will flow for the space of 1600 furlongs. A furlong is a Bible unit of measurement of about 1/8 of a mile, which would make this winepress 200 miles of "space". The valley of Megiddo is located to the Northwest of the city of Jerusalem. It is roughly 10 miles wide and 20 miles long, which by way of sheer "coincidence" is the space of 200 square miles.

The second sickle in Revelation 14 describes the gathering of the armies of the lost nations to the valley of Megiddo for the final battle of Armageddon. Zephaniah 3:8 prophesies of this event: "Therefore wait ye upon me, saith the LORD, until the day that I rise up to the prey: for my determination is to gather the nations, that I may assemble the kingdoms, to pour upon them mine indignation, even all my fierce anger: for all the earth shall be devoured with the fire of my jealousy." In the Tribulation, the nations of the world will be "United" against Israel to wipe them off the face of the earth once and for all. Satan has been using the lost nations to try to get rid of Israel for 40 centuries and he has failed miserably. He will get one last chance here, but Jesus will be waiting for him. Just when Satan has the armies of the world assembled to the Northwest of Jerusalem, the Lord will stomp them like grapes. Earlier I referenced the parable of the tares in Matthew chapter 13. Verse 30 says that at the time of the harvest (remember that term?) the reapers will gather the tares to be burned. The angel of fire gathers the fruit of a tree that has no value other than as fuel for the fire. Also in Matthew 13:30, the "wheat" is gathered into God's barn. That is the Post-Tribulation rapture just prior to the winepress of Armageddon.

Consider these two passages of scripture in this light (first is Isaiah 63:1-6, then Joel 3:9-17):

Who is this that cometh from Edom, with dyed garments from Bozrah? this that is glorious in his apparel, travelling in the greatness of his strength? I that speak in righteousness, mighty to save. Wherefore art thou red in thine apparel, and thy garments like him that treadeth in the winevat? I have trodden the winepress alone; and of the people there was none with me: for I will tread them in mine anger, and trample them in my fury; and their blood shall be sprinkled upon my garments, and I will stain all my raiment. For the day of vengeance is in mine heart, and the year of my redeemed is come. And I looked, and there was none to help; and I wondered that there was none to uphold: therefore mine own arm brought salvation unto me; and my fury, it upheld me. And I will tread down the people in mine anger, and make them drunk in my fury, and I will bring down their strength to the earth.

Proclaim ye this among the Gentiles; Prepare war, wake up the mighty men, let all the men of war draw near; let them come up: Beat your plowshares into swords, and your pruninghooks into spears: let the weak say, I am strong. Assemble yourselves, and come, all ye heathen, and gather yourselves together round about: thither cause thy mighty ones to come down, O LORD. Let the heathen be wakened, and come up to the valley of Jehoshaphat: for there will I sit to judge all the heathen round about. Put ye in the sickle, for the harvest is ripe: come, get you down; for the press is full, the vats overflow; for their wickedness is great. Multitudes, multitudes in the valley of decision: for the day of the LORD is near in the valley of decision. The sun and the moon shall be darkened, and the stars shall withdraw their shining. The LORD also shall roar out of Zion, and utter his voice from Jerusalem; and the heavens and the earth shall shake: but the LORD will be the hope of his people, and the strength of the children of Israel. So shall ye know that I am the LORD your God dwelling in Zion, my holy mountain: then shall Jerusalem be holy, and there shall no strangers pass through her any more.

This brings us to the conclusion of the third pass through the Tribulation in the book of Revelation. We have laid down a decent three color process so far, but the final account in Revelation chapters 15-19 will finish the picture.

Revelation Chapters 15-19 – The Vials
The Fourth and Final Pass Through the Tribulation

Revelation Chapter 15 – Introduction to the Vials

Revelation chapter 15 is the shortest chapter in the book and has the least amount of actual content on the exact details of the events of the Tribulation. Chapter 15 is essentially just the introduction to the Vials. It is another view into the throne of God as he is preparing to pour out his wrath on the world. On my chart, you will notice that I have placed the Vials toward the end of the Great Tribulation as opposed to the Seals and Trumpets primarily at the beginning. As you look at the descriptions of these judgments, they mirror a lot of the characteristics of the Seals and Trumpets, but they are far more intense. The Vials are essentially "round two" after the first wave of judgments did not result in repentance.

Revelation 15:1-4 – Praise God for His Wrath

VS 1 – John sees "another sign" in heaven, which means the focus has again shifted to the throne and not on earth. Seven angels are "ready to rumble". The wrath of God is filled up. God's grace and mercy is limitless, and so is his wrath against sin and rebellion. Despite his best efforts, mankind by this point has become so hardened that the fate is sealed and the doom is certain.

VS 2-4 – Signs are for the Jews (I Corinthians 1:22), so what John sees is for Israel. This is likely another view of the raptured 144,000 just prior to the return of Jesus. If so, verses 2-4 are a "flash forward" to that time after the Vials are poured out. It could also be the portion of the 144,000 who have already been killed and are waiting for their companions to join them as we saw in Revelation 6:9-11. In either case, this passage clearly describes the Tribulation saints. They will stand on the same sea of glass that John saw in heaven after his rapture in chapter 4. This group has "gotten the victory over the beast", which does not apply to the church since we are gone before his takeover is completed. They sing the song of Moses, which was alluded to in chapter 14, but not named as such then. The song in chapter 14 and this one could be two different songs or the same one. Exodus chapter 15 is also called the song of Moses. It was sung right after Pharaoh (type of the Antichrist) was drowned in the Red Sea. That deliverance is a type of the Tribulation. The plagues of Exodus are repeated; it even says so in verse 1. Only these "last plagues" of the Tribulation are far worse and world-wide instead of just localized in Egypt.

God is praised for his wrath. It is totally contrary to man's ideas that God would be praised for being so incredibly ticked off that he allows most of humanity to be wiped out. But we must always remember how balanced and perfect God is. His perfect love has been rejected. His perfect wrath takes over. "Just and true are thy ways" (verse 3) "for thou only art holy" (verse 4). When his wrath kicks in and his "judgments are made manifest" (verse 4), he will be perfectly justified.

Revelation 15:5-8 – The Vials Announced

Again, this passage simply introduces the Vials, which will not be poured out until the next chapter. The angels are clothed in pure white linen with golden girdles. Gold in the Bible represents the deity of Jesus Christ. As God manifest in the flesh, his judgments are pure and can never be questioned. Well, lots of people DO question the holiness and righteousness of God, but we know how far they get. Verse 8 says no man can stand before God in his wrath. They cry out the same thing when he returns at the Second Advent: "For the great day of his wrath is come; and who shall be able to stand?" (Revelation 6:17).

Revelation Chapter 16 – The Seven Vials

The Vials are placed further down the chronology on my chart than the other disasters of the Tribulation. They are severe, rapid, and much more deadly. Some of the characteristics are the same as the Seals and Trumpets, but in far greater fashion. I will make note of that as we make our way through.

Revelation 16:1-2 – The First Vial

This judgment will be a "noisome and grievous sore" upon those who have taken the mark of the beast. This is the plague of boils from Exodus revisited. We see the word "noisome" and think "noisy" as in loud, but that is not what this word means. The Greek word appears many times in the New Testament and is usually translated "evil". It is related to "noxious" and more offensive to the nose than to the ear. Pardon my gross explanation, but the Bible is not always filled with rainbows and butterflies and roses. The "spot" of the mark of the beast will become leprous. See Leviticus chapter 13 for a discussion of this. It will be a messy oozing lesion with an unfathomable foul odor.

Revelation 16:3 – The Second Vial

The sea will turn to blood as the Nile River did in Egypt. Instead of just a river, this will be the entire sea; at least the Mediterranean if not world-wide. The second Trumpet also turns the water to blood in the sea (Revelation 8:8-9). But the Trumpet only destroys one third of the sea life. This Vial wipes out "every living soul in the sea". That is another reason why I believe these Vials are later in the timeline than the Trumpets and Seals. When Trumpet #2 does not get man's attention, Vial #2 finishes the job.

Revelation 16:4-7 – The Third Vial

This Vial also mirrors the "water to blood" of the Exodus. God always answers man "in kind". In other words, we reap <u>exactly</u> as we sow (Galatians 6:7-9). Catholic cannibals have been drinking the blood of Jesus for centuries, and as I speculated earlier, they will move to human flesh and blood as the Antichrist makes all sacrifices revert to him. False pagan rituals have had "drink offerings of blood" (Psalm 16:4) since the time the Babylonian religion was formulated. Verse 6 says "they have shed the blood of saints and prophets", which is an inference to the bloody drink offerings. Again, God is "true and righteous" to visit this plague on mankind, "for they are worthy" of his judgment.

Revelation 16:8-9 – The Fourth Vial

Al Gore was right. But not in the way he thinks he was. Because of the rejection of the <u>SON</u>, God will crank up the heat of the <u>sun</u>. People will be scorched with great heat. It will be the worst sunburn a man has ever gotten multiplied exponentially. Yet despite the intense suffering, man will refuse to repent and instead blaspheme even further. Job 11:12 says man is born like a wild ass' colt. His blind stubborn will and rejection cannot be tamed. Smart-aleck atheists and skeptics ask, "Can God make a rock so big that he cannot pick it up?" YES. It is called the stubborn rebellious will of the lost skeptic.

Revelation 16:10-11 – The Fifth Vial

This is the plague of darkness revisited from Exodus. God will pour out this darkness on the seat of the beast, which we know to be Rome. Satan's seat (Revelation 2:13) is responsible for so much bloodshed and torture that God will answer it. The text simply says that his kingdom will be full of darkness. It could just be a statement of the spiritual oppression of the prince of darkness, or it could be manifest physically, or both. Back in the plagues of Egypt, Exodus 12:12 says, "For I will pass through the land of Egypt this night, and will smite all the firstborn in the land of Egypt, both man and beast; and against all the gods of Egypt I will execute judgment: I am the LORD." God did not just judge Pharaoh and his people, but he whipped their gods in the spirit world also. Connected with this plague is pain so severe that people "gnaw their tongues". You have probably done that a few times in your life when something was so painful that you tried to find relief by making something else more painful. There has been no rain, the waters are blood, the sun is scorching hot beyond description, and boils cover the entire body. Yet there will be no repentance as man continues to harden himself against God.

Revelation 16:12-16 – The Sixth Vial

VS 12 – This Vial is an overlap of the sixth Trumpet where the oriental armies descend upon Jerusalem in preparation for the battle of Armageddon. In that passage in Revelation 9:13-21, a timeframe is given of just a little over a year. I made the point then that it could be an actual literal time, which means this is the ramp-up to the final battle. It is another reason why I place the Vials toward the end of the 3½ years.

VS 13 – This character called the false prophet is introduced. There is almost as much speculation as to his identity as there is for the Antichrist himself. The problem is that there is very little information about this man in the Bible, and nowhere outside the book of Revelation. One of the cardinal rules of the Bible is to establish doctrine based on multiple witnesses (II Corinthians 13:1). There is a TON of information in the Bible about the Antichrist, both directly and in types. But we are left with a guess at best on this false prophet, and guesses usually create messes in the Bible. So I will give you my opinions (there are more than one) and leave it to others to take their speculations too far.

This is his first mention, and all it says is that he has an unclean spirit coming out of his mouth to work miracles along with the dragon and the beast. Being listed that way makes us believe that he is someone other than the Antichrist himself. Then he is mentioned next in Revelation 19:20, again with the beast. It says, "These BOTH were cast alive into a lake of fire burning with brimstone". Again, the wording leads us to conclude that the beast and the false prophet are two separate characters. Finally, the false prophet is mentioned in Revelation 20:10: "And the devil that deceived them was cast into the lake of fire and brimstone, where the beast and the false prophet are, and shall be tormented day and night for ever and ever." This is at the end of the Millennium. Satan is cast into hell, and the beast and the false prophet are there waiting for him. Again, each passage indicates his separate identity from the beast. That is the sum total of the information we have in the Bible about the false prophet. We know he speaks and can work miracles. We know he will be in hell forever. Since he is such a shadowy character, this man is fodder for the incessant desire of the prophecy gurus to "scoop" the story with their "breaking news" report on his exact identity. If someone claims to have found him, put his book or website down and back away.

So now for my opinions. I have a couple of possibilities, and I am certainly open to more as long as we do not stretch the clear information in the Bible, what little there is. It seems his only activity is to draw people to the worship of the beast. So he could simply be a John the Baptist-type of "advance man" for the Antichrist. If so, his exact identity is unknown and not important. He might just be a world religious leader who champions the cause and helps bring people under the sway of the man of sin. Another idea is that the term "false prophet" could be another title for the Pope who brings about the peace plan. Again, the information is limited, so this is pure speculation. The false prophet is mentioned in the Bible as part of a "trinity" with the beast and the dragon in two of the passages, and with the beast in the other one. So it could be that the dragon is Satan (we know that clearly), the beast is the Antichrist out of the earth after the assassination, and the false prophet is the beast out of the sea in the first half of the Tribulation. That would make the beast Judas and the false prophet the Pope who are the "same thing only different, but the same, but not really… kinda sorta." If that makes no sense and confuses you, you are not alone. Trying to completely grasp the trinity of the Father, Son and Holy Spirit is impossible with our natural intellect. The same is true of the unholy false trinity counterfeited by Satan. So if this possibility raises questions in your mind, join the club and get in line. The line snakes around the building a LONG way.

112

VS 13-14 – The unholy trinity speaks from unclean spirits like frogs. This alludes back to the plague of frogs in Exodus. In fact, that is the only other mention of frogs in the Bible. They are mentioned twice in the Psalms, but both of those verses speak of the plague in Egypt. Since God executed judgment against the gods of Egypt, the frogs are a picture of false gods. This is the plague where Pharaoh gave his first indication of possibly repenting, only to pull it back once he got relief. When Moses asked him when he wanted the frogs gone, Pharaoh said, "Tomorrow". That is one of the strangest things in the Bible, yet it is not so strange once you get a glimpse of the depravity of human nature. Pharaoh wanted "one more night with the frogs". Man wants "one more" sin before he will quit, but he never quits because there is always one more. He will get right with God "tomorrow", but tomorrow never comes. Lost man would rather wallow in his filthy sin when he <u>knows</u> it is sending him to hell. This will be the condition of the heart of man at this point in the Tribulation under the judgment of God. Despite the unbelievable disaster man will refuse to repent because he wants just one more night with the frogs. Frogs are filthy disgusting slimy creatures that eat bugs and pee on you when you pick them up. But they sure are tasty!

VS 15 – This verse is a general truth that applies to all. Specifically, it is addressed to the 144,000 in the Tribulation who can "lose their shirt" (and more) by not staying true to the mission. For a believer in Christ, it speaks of diligence in preparation for the Judgment Seat of Christ. Revelation 19:8 says, "Fine linen is the righteousness of the saints." Ephesians 5:26-27 says the Lord wants to present us to himself as a bride "without spot or wrinkle". Once we get saved, we then embark on a sewing project. We do not work to get saved or even to stay saved, but we work to prepare ourselves for the big day. Sadly, most of God's people will show up for their wedding in ratty cut-offs and a torn, dirty t-shirt, if that.

VS 16 – This verse alludes to the gathering of the armies of the world for judgment that we saw with the sickle in Revelation chapter 14. Here, the gathering is also mentioned in verse 14. The "spirits" doing the gathering in that verse are the "frog men" of the Antichrist. From Satan's view, he is blaming all the world's problems on the Jews and moving his armies into place for the kill. From God's perspective, he is gathering the nations to the valley of Megiddo to stomp them like grapes as we saw earlier. Verse 16 is God gathering the nations for judgment. So, God and Satan are working in the same direction but for two totally different purposes. This is common in the Bible. This is God using his enemy to accomplish his purposes like a martial arts expert will use his opponent against himself. The word Armageddon appears here for the only time in the Bible. It is the place of the final battle.

Revelation 16:17-21 – The Seventh Vial

"It is done." This is God saying, "Stick a fork in it." The sin of mankind and the wrath of God have both reached full measure. We are told that we keep getting better all the time when the Bible says the exact opposite. At this point, man finally hits bottom. The earthquake in the passage has been covered before as one of the registration marks. The "cup of God's wrath" was commented on in Revelation 14:10. The additional plague in this passage is the hail, which also alludes back to the Exodus. The hail at the end of the Tribulation has each stone weighing a talent, a Jewish unit of measurement equaling about 75 pounds. The largest hail stone on record is 4 pounds. Golf ball size hail might be about half a pound, and it does <u>serious</u> damage to anything it hits. Larger baseball and softball size hail is not uncommon. Hail of that size bonking a man on the noggin will kill him. Imagine 75-pound blocks of ice falling from the sky. I am sure the scholars and skeptics will run to the Greek to put those stones on a diet to make them a little lighter than 75 pounds. Let's just pray that they are not here to find out just how much they actually will weigh. Notice again in verse 12 that all this judgment will not get anyone's attention. Mankind in his fallen nature is so completely devoid of understanding that no amount of effort will correct his sin nature. By this time, man has degenerated for 6,000 years. The Holy Spirit was taken out at the rapture, and the preserving "salt" of the church went out with him. The influence of God upon man has been put on hold as the "wind" ceased (Revelation 7:1) and God withdrew his hand from man to let him have what he has always wanted. The utter and complete collapse will be <u>frightening</u>.

Revelation Chapter 17 – The Whore Identified

Revelation chapter 17 is another of the very strategic and vital chapters in the book. It clearly identifies Rome and the Catholic Church as the city and system of the Antichrist. This causes a bunch of scholars and religious people to "run for the hills" (pun intended). The manipulations of this chapter to try to weasel out of Rome are incredible. But if you cannot see Rome in this chapter, you are not looking, and you don't want to look. Perhaps the biggest heresy taught from this chapter has to do with the backdating of the authorship of the book of Revelation. See the introduction for a review of that explanation.

Revelation 17:1-7 – Mystery Babylon

The first Gentile kingdom in history originated from Babylon in Genesis chapter 10 under Nimrod. The oldest religion in history comes from the same kingdom. That area is called "The Cradle of Civilization" because civil societies and religions were born there in their current form after the flood. The religion of ancient Babylon is the "seed" of all false religion. Universities teach a course on "comparative religions" and make the case that they are essentially all the same, with minor twists and variations on major themes. They are right, and dead wrong at the same time. Religion is man's attempt to find his own way to God through laws and rituals. Salvation is God making a way for man to come to God through the sacrifice of his Son (John 14:6). The basic thread of religious similarity is traced to ancient Babylonian paganism.

The theme of Revelation chapter 17 is the link between Babylon of old and spiritual Babylon today. The Roman Catholic religion is Babylonian from its head to its toe and every inch in between. It infuriates me to hear the blithering ignorance of those who try to tell us that Catholic is Christian. They begin with the same letter. That is where the similarities end. Banana and bowling ball begin with the same letter also. Try eating a bowling ball. Then try knocking down pins with a banana. You will have a better chance with either of those than explaining how the Catholic Church is Christian. Don't misunderstand, please. Catholic people are the most wonderful folks on earth. They are just ignorant of their own religion and where it comes from. It is beyond the scope of this book to dive deep into this issue. We will simply see the identity of Rome and its religion as the system of the Antichrist in this chapter. If you want more information on this topic, I will refer you to some sources to get you started. First is a shameless plug for my own book titled *"Church History"* where I walk through the history of Catholicism and identify its core doctrines and perversions of the truth. Just so you do not think I am uninformed and biased, I was raised Catholic, so I know it from the inside as well as from the Bible. Next, get a copy of a little book titled *"Mystery Babylon Religion"* by Ralph Woodrow. It is out of print, but you can still find one online for sale. It is short, sweet, and to the point. The book is about 150 pages and broken into small chapters. It is an easy read without a lot of technical jargon and makes a clear case for the Babylonian Catholicism heritage. If you want the doctoral thesis, get *"The Two Babylons"* by Alexander Hislop. With that rant off my chest, let's go through Revelation chapter 17 and peek under the sheets at the whore of Rome.

VS 1-2 – One of the angels with a vial is dispatched to John to show him this woman. The angel begins with, "Come hither…" It is not "come up hither", but that phrase "come hither" is highly suggestive in a sexual manner, and usually not in a pure marital context. John is about to see the judgment of "the great whore that sitteth upon many waters". The "waters" are defined in the chapter in verse 15 as, "peoples, and multitudes, and nations, and tongues." This woman "sits" as a queen and reigns over nations. The Pope has claimed for centuries to have the universal right of dominion, not just over his church, but over every human being on earth. Many Popes have exercised that dominion with disastrous results. This woman seduces the kings of the earth into her bed. Political leaders for generations have sidled up to this whore to gain favor over her domain. The nations of the earth have diplomatic relations with the Vatican. No other religion on earth has that. It is interesting to note the term "relations". That is what illicit sexual partners partake of, is it not? The "wine of her fornication" is the bloody drink of the Mass that blinds the mind and makes the populace drunk on her "beauty" with the robes and stained glass and all the pomp.

VS 3 – This woman is in the wilderness. Though she sits upon a royal Papal throne in the lap of luxury with the richest splendor known to man, she is dry, lifeless, and destitute of anything that can bring life or sustain life. She sits upon a scarlet colored beast. The blood she has shed over the centuries would fill an ocean. She is full of names of blasphemy. Jesus was accused of blasphemy for claiming he was God. He was right, but this man in Rome takes upon himself the same titles as our Lord and no one ever calls him on it except rabble rousers like me. He is FULL of these names; he takes on many of them and not just one. He is the "Prince of Peace" (no, Jesus is – Isaiah 9:6). He is the "Vicar of Christ", and wore on his mitre the title "Faithful Vicar of God" for generations until people began to point out that the Roman numerals in his title added up to 666. A "vicar" is essentially a representative or an agent. Jesus is my agent and advocate who intercedes for me before the throne (I John 2:1, Hebrews 7:26). Jesus is the only mediator we need (I Timothy 2:5). The Pope is called "Your Holiness" and no one bats an eye when Jesus is the Holy One of Israel, and God alone is holy. He is titled the "Holy Father" when that term is used once and only once in the Bible for the God and Father of our Lord Jesus Christ in John 17:11. That is just a sampling of the names of blasphemy that this man carries around.

Finally, the verse says this woman has seven heads and ten horns. Heads in the Bible represent authority (headship – Colossians 1:18) and dominion. Horns are a symbol of power (Psalm 18:2, Daniel 8:3-10). Revelation 13:2 says the dragon (Satan) will give the beast (Antichrist) upon whom this woman sits his power (horns), his seat (the Papal throne), and great authority (heads). There are seven of these heads, which is the number of perfection or completeness. This beast / woman will exercise complete and total dominion over the earth in the Tribulation, being supported by the god of this world (II Corinthians 4:4). There are ten horns because it is a Gentile kingdom. Here is where a lot of our friends in the prophecy business take off into never-never land trying to specifically identify these heads and horns. I covered in chapter 1 the issue of symbolism in the Bible. The Bible uses symbols, but when it does, the Bible itself will define them so we are not left to wild speculations. Generally, the definitions will be in the same context as the symbol, which is the case in this chapter. The heads and horns are defined in the text.

Let's begin with the seven heads. Revelation 17:9-10 says, "And here is the mind which hath wisdom. The seven heads are seven mountains, on which the woman sitteth. And there are seven kings: five are fallen, and one is, and the other is not yet come; and when he cometh, he must continue a short space." The seven heads actually represent two things: seven mountains and seven kings. That is not my own "interpretation" of the verse, that is exactly what it says. Rome is "the city of seven hills". The woman sits upon seven mountains, and the woman is "that great city which reigneth over the kings of the earth" (Revelation 17:18). The exact location of this woman's kingdom and the beast who rules over it is the city of seven hills. But she also has seven kings connected to her kingdom. Verse 10 says of the seven kings that five are fallen, one is, and another is not yet come. Remember when John wrote historically: 100 AD. By that time, there had been six major Gentile world empires with one more yet to come. History identifies those world-wide empires from the time of the flood of Noah to the Second Coming of Christ as the following. The gap between Egypt (1500 BC) and Assyria (720 BC) covers Israel's kings.

1) Nimrod – Babylon (2300-1800 BC)
2) Pharaoh – Egypt (1800-1500 BC)
3) Sennacerib – Assyria (720-625 BC)
4) Nebuchadnezzar – Babylon (625-536 BC)
5) Cyrus / Darius – Media-Persia (536-330 BC)
6) Alexander the Great – Greece (330-100 BC)
7) Caesar / Popes – Rome (100 BC-Second Advent)

This gets a little "sticky" so stay with me. At the time John wrote (100 AD), one of these world empires was still in control. That would have to be Rome which is number seven on the list. Then John said five are fallen. But that does not match the list and the numbering, until you notice that Babylon is a repeat under Nimrod then later Nebuchadnezzar. So the five fallen are: Babylon, Egypt, Assyria, Media-Persia, and Greece. Rome "is" and another one is yet to come that will "continue a short space." Pay attention to the simple words of the King James Bible. That phrase identifies who is yet to come. Revelation 13:5 says after the false resurrection of the Antichrist, he will continue 42 months. Revelation 12:12 says when Satan is kicked out of heaven he is ticked off because he knows he only has a short time. Now go back to chapter 17 and look at verse 11: "And the beast that was, and is not, even he is the eighth, and is of the seven, and goeth into perdition." The son of perdition (remember him?) is the eighth king / beast who is "of the seven". In other words, the Antichrist is all seven of these kings rolled into one. He will borrow elements from every one of these religious empires because "all religions are the same". So, the seven heads tell us WHERE this woman comes from (Rome) and WHO she draws from to rule: the seven major world empires of Gentile history. Guess which one is first? Guess which one gets repeated just to let you know which empire is behind all this? The other empires descend from this one. They begin from that structure (Babylonian mystical paganism) and then simply add their own little tweaks so that they are "essentially all the same, with minor twists and variations on major themes". All roads lead to Rome, and Rome takes you back to Babylon. That is why she is Mystery Babylon.

Now let's identify the ten horns. Again, you need NO speculation or prophecy guru to find this for you. In the same chapter, God said, "And the ten horns which thou sawest are ten kings, which have received no kingdom as yet; but receive power as kings one hour with the beast" (Revelation 17:12). I am sure you have forgotten this by now, but I mentioned this in the introduction of this commentary. These ten kings are the ten toes of the image of Daniel chapter 2. Since the Antichrist comes out of the area around the Mediterranean, every prophecy teacher for the last several generations has linked these ten kings to a revived "Holy Roman Empire". I agree with all of that so far. In fact, I taught the same thing for a long time that the major prophecy teachers and authors believe: that there would be a federation of ten nations that would form the basis of the rise of the Antichrist from Western Europe, specifically Rome. So here comes the European Union and its expansion in the early 1990's. A bunch of us started doing "rapture practice" jumping up to see how long we could stay in the air. Everyone was dead sure that the European Union would give us the Antichrist as soon as it got to ten nations. Then the EU went past ten. Oh no! Now what? Everyone said that some countries would back out and it would go back to ten. Today the EU stands at 27 nations. This is a classic example of why it is absolutely necessary for the teachers of Revelation to get the BASICS of this book down (its simple structure) and then be very clear in filling in the details that they are subject to change as history unfolds and as we learn more about these events. I can't tell you how many different things were supposed to have been the mark of the beast that proved not to be. So, if the ten horns are NOT a ten-federated bloc of European nations, what are they?

Again, I am not going down the road of the gurus who are proven wrong all the time. So let me give you my opinion about this, remembering that opinions are like armpits. I believe the key to this is found in Revelation 17:12. These kings "have received no kingdom as yet; but receive power as kings one hour with the beast." Let's see if we can unravel this by looking at the time of these kings rather than the area they come from. In 100 AD, these kings had no kingdom yet. But many of the nations of Europe were around at that time. The Bible mentions Greece, Italy and Spain. But let's assume that in 100 AD that there were no kings or nations except Rome, and these ten nations had to arise after that time. The EU still qualifies. But then it says these kings will receive power one hour with the beast. This cannot be a 60-minute time period. The Bible uses units of time to describe things in various ways. An hour in the Bible often stands for "his time". Jesus said in John 12:23, "The hour is come, that the Son of man should be glorified." That was spoken on Palm Sunday. He spoke of his death, burial and resurrection, which took a lot longer than 60 minutes to occur. When Jesus was arrested in Gethsemane, he said to the elders, "When I was daily with you in the temple, ye stretched forth no hands against me: but this is your hour, and the power of darkness" (Luke 22:53). The "hour" these kings receive power is the Tribulation. These kings will receive their power with the beast. I know that the mystery of iniquity doth already work, but the beast is not personally here yet!

My opinion is these ten horns / toes / kings are demonic beings. They will get their kingdom and power once the beast is in place in his "hour" of the Tribulation. They are likely some of Satan's top generals in his army. The spirit world is organized militarily like an earthly army. Ephesians 6:12 says we wrestle against "principalities, powers, rulers of darkness, and spiritual wickedness in high places". Those could just be various terms to describe the same beings, or it could be categories of rankings. Our text says these ten kings receive power one hour with the beast. They are "horns", the symbol of power. Jesus is far above all principality, power, might, dominion and name (Ephesians 1:21). If these kings are spirit beings, these demonic generals will be placed over areas of the earth in the Tribulation to rule with Satan.

That leads us to a very important passage of scripture for a peek into the spirit world. God gave us just a little information in the Bible about devils and spiritual beings by design. We are on a need to know basis with much of this, and with much of it, we do not need to know, nor do we want to. But some of it we do. Daniel chapter 10 shows us spiritual warfare and spiritual wickedness in high places. Read the chapter, I can wait. You will see the prince of Persia in verse 13 and the prince of Greece in verse 20. You will see Michael also in verse 13 as he shows up for a little "border skirmish" with the prince of Persia. Michael is the prince of the Nation of Israel (Daniel 10:21, 12:1). These three spirit beings in this chapter were assigned to specific locations on earth and they exercised spiritual control over them. Various locations on earth have spiritual significance. I dealt with this back in Revelation 9:13-14, which see. Remember the Revealing of the Wicked? Spiritual warfare results in Satan being banished from heaven and cast into the earth, "and his angels were cast out with him" (Revelation 12:9). At the same time, Judas comes out of the bottomless pit with his demon hordes.

When every foul spirit in existence is confined to earth, Satan will likely try to "organize" them into military bands (as best as organized chaos can be). I believe he will pick ten of them to be his "National Security Council". There are ten (the number of the Gentiles) to control the world. If this were simply a ten-federated kingdom in Europe only, what about the rest of the world? Satan deceives the whole world and will likely divide the Gentile world into ten major "blocs" and assign a devil / prince over each one to dominate it spiritually. This is a counterfeit of the Millennial kingdom. Deuteronomy 32:8 says God sets the bounds of the people according to the number of the children of Israel, which is twelve. Jesus promised his apostles they would sit on twelve thrones judging the twelve tribes of Israel, and each tribe will be assigned over a Gentile region just as Satan will try to assign his "rulers" over ten world regions.

That is a long way around one simple statement in Revelation 17:3 to define the heads and horns. But this is a crucial chapter. The heads are fairly easy to identify because it is historical. We have clear data from the past to identify the seven heads. The ten horns are yet future. So we are left to speculate. There is a lot of speculating you can do with the Bible, especially in Revelation, as long as you are clear on a couple of major points. First, NEVER change the words of your King James Bible. Do not add words and do not take words out (Deuteronomy 4:2, Proverbs 30:6, Revelation 22:18-19). Do not fall for the "better translation" ruse of scholars who cannot bring themselves to submit to the word of God because they think they are so much smarter than you. Second, ALWAYS be honest when you offer an opinion or speculation and leave yourself a "trap door" to change your opinion when scripture reveals otherwise. If you keep those two basic principles in place, speculation is a healthy exercise in the word of God.

VS 4 – This woman is decked out in some pretty fancy apparel. Purple and scarlet are the dominant colors of the Vatican Guard. You would think someone there would have read Revelation 17:4 and said, "Hey, guys, maybe we should pick a different uniform color." But you give the whore too much credit. She forbid her people to read the Bible for centuries, do you think she would read it herself? She also has gold, precious stones and pearls. The Catholic Church is the richest institution on earth by far. Imagine the blatant hypocrisy of the Pope lecturing all of us about "economic justice and equality" when he sits on a golden throne in the lap of incredible luxury. This woman has a golden cup in her hand. If you have ever been to Mass, you have seen that cup raised by the priest and filled with the blood of Jesus Christ.

VS 5 – This woman carries a name on her forehead. I mentioned earlier the Pope's mitre and the name of blasphemy he had on it for generations. God writes another name on her forehead. The mother of harlots has in block capital letters 13 words and 65 letters (5 times 13). Five is death and 13 is rebellion. On this throne in Rome sits the death angel in full rebellion against God.

VS 6-7 – When John sees this whore, his mouth drops open. He "wondered with great admiration". It sounds odd that John would "admire" her, but it is not in the same manner we think. The angel responds, "Why do you marvel?" On one hand, we can "give the devil his due" (to a point) in that we understand how "good" he is at his craft. He is pure evil in such a "perfect" fashion that he can pull off all this. But we do not "admire" him in any positive manner. We marvel that he is so good at his evil, and we marvel that so many people are so blinded they cannot see the truth. The angel then tells John he will show him the details, and we have similar promises in the Bible. I Corinthians 2:9-16 tells us that God will reveal the deep things of God by his Spirit. Job 41:12 says God will not conceal the ways of our enemy. Those who have a Bible and love it, learn it, and believe it as it stands can see his footprints and his movements.

Revelation 17:8-18 – The Beast and His Bride Defined

We have already dealt with a lot of this section in laying out Mystery Babylon. But let's walk through and pick up a few things in these verses that have not yet been covered.

VS 8 – This beast is Judas, the son of perdition. We have seen him ascend out of the bottomless pit in chapter 9. He "was and is not", meaning he was alive before John wrote in 100 AD but currently was not. The world shall wonder at him when they "behold the beast that was, and is not, and yet is." This speaks of something different than Judas being dead in 100 AD. Those in "wonder" are viewing something in the Tribulation. They will see a "beast" who was alive, then he is not because he was assassinated, yet he is because he came back from the dead. That is the Revealing of the Wicked.

VS 9-12 – These verses were commented on extensively already.

VS 13-14 – These verses detail some of the activity of the ten kings who will be the "ruling junta" of the spirit world with the Antichrist. For a time, they will have one mind to work with the beast (Antichrist) in his ultimate game of world conquest. Hang on to that however, because we will see it all implode very quickly. This "junta" along with their "fearful" leader will try to take on the Lamb (Jesus). Good luck!

VS 15 – Again, we dealt with this verse in detail earlier.

VS 16-17 – I told you a minute ago to hang on to a thought. The ten horns seem to do a "180" here and turn on their own. Yes, they do, but we need to look carefully at this. First, realize that "there is no honor among thieves". If you are expecting Satan and his crowd to play fair and be at peace with each other, we need to talk. You have seen this played out in the movies dozens of times. A group of guys get together to knock off a Brinks truck, and as soon as they do, the rest of the movie is about them trying to off each other to get the whole pile of loot. Jesus said in Matthew 12:26 that Satan's kingdom is divided. As it gets toward the end, it will be "every demon for himself" just like it will be for people in the Tribulation.

But look carefully at what happens here. Verse 13 says the ten horns have "one mind" with the beast (Antichrist). They DO work together for a great deal of this time, and one of their purposes is not so much to turn on each other, but verse 16 says they turn on the whore. That is the false system and the people who are held in bondage to it. A study of the history of the Catholic Church will find it turning against its own regularly. The Inquisitions ravaged Europe for nearly 500 years. It was a reign of terror that would make the Taliban look like Girl Scouts. They claimed it was a "war against heresy", but over 90% of the victims were Catholic and faithful to the church. It did not matter. The terror was designed to keep everyone in line under the fear of torture and death. In one of the more infamous battles in the Dark Ages, a Catholic army was sent into a town in Southern France to "eliminate the heretics". The leader of the mission asked how he could tell who the heretics were and who were the Catholics. The answer was, "Kill them all and let God sort them out." Roughly 60,000 people were murdered in this campaign, and most of the victims were Catholics. So what? Satan does not care about his own; in fact he will gladly "kill them all" before anyone can get the truth of the gospel to them.

Most people look at the Crusades as "Christian vs Muslim", which is as far from the truth as you can get. Satan raised up the Catholic Church to control and dominate the world and used it for centuries to try to "convert" as many people as possible by military force. Once that institution was fully in place, he raised another religion called Islam for the same purpose. Since "all religions are the same", both Catholicism and Islam have the same basic mission of world conquest by force. By about 1095 AD, the spirits behind both groups "agreed" (Revelation 17:17) with "one mind" (Revelation 17:13) to ignite war against each other called the Crusades. Satan gleefully relished the opportunity to have his two dominant religions wage war against each other to get people into hell as quickly as possible.

That is a couple of historical examples of what will happen toward the end of the Tribulation. The spirits will agree with the help of their mastermind, and operating under the auspices of the beast, they will turn on the members of the whore to kill them off before they can get the truth. I hate to even mention this because it is so disgustingly heinous, but we have all heard of cases where one of the parents in a bitter divorce battle will kill their children to keep the other parent from having them. As the enemy sees the end approaching, rather than give up their children, they will kill them as fast as possible.

VS 18 – This verse was commented on earlier and identifies the whore as the city and religion of Rome.

Revelation Chapter 18 – The Judgment of Rome

The Second Advent of Jesus Christ will result in the complete and total overthrow of civilization as man has built it over the last 6,000 years. There will be no smooth and peaceful transition of power. It will be a one man "revolution" the likes of which has never been seen in even a tiny fraction. Revelation chapter 18 describes the complete destruction of Rome and the system man has built of religion and society.

Revelation 18:1-5 – Babylon the Great Is Fallen, Is Fallen

VS 1-3 – The judgment is announced. Babylon the great "is fallen, is fallen". Doubling of the statement was commented on in Revelation 14:8. We sometimes say to our children, "How many times must I tell you?" When God tells us once he means it and it should be enough, but when he tells us twice it is full confirmation. God confirms his word with multiple witnesses (II Corinthians 13:1, Mark 16:20). When Joseph interpreted Pharaoh's dream, he said this in Genesis 41:32, "And for that the dream was doubled unto Pharaoh twice; it is because the thing is established by God, and God will shortly bring it to pass." The original kingdom of Babylon is the source of this religious perversion, and it will finally be destroyed when its ultimate manifestation in Rome is overthrown by the Lord when he returns. It is the "habitation of devils and the hold of every foul spirit, and a cage of every unclean and hateful bird." Birds in the Bible are a type of unclean spirits. Birds are filthy disease-carrying worm-eating creatures that fly in the air. They say, "Birds of a feather flock together". In this place (Rome), they don't even need to be of a feather. Every devil in existence is drawn to the stinking, putrid, filthy, maggot-infested rot of religion that spawned in Babylon and found its perfect manifestation in the city of seven hills.

VS 4-5 – God gives his people a warning to "come out of her". Since she is the "Mother of Harlots", the language is graphic by design. Notice God's warning is to "my people". That would be Israel physically and the church spiritually. Both groups get drawn in by this "painted lady" way too much and for far too long. Some people take issue with how harsh I am on the Catholic Church. For the umpteenth time, the problem is not the people but the institution and where it comes from. Catholic people are some of the finest folks on earth; I just wish they could pull the blinders off their eyes and see what their religion is doing to them. This warning is to those who name the name of Christ in the New Testament, and Israel in the Old Testament and Tribulation. Get out! NOW! Those who keep fooling around with this whore will get spanked. New Bibles are from the Catholic manuscripts. If you want to keep them around for study and comparison, that is one thing. I have many different versions on my bookshelf for that purpose. I can't explain to people their errors if I don't have a copy to refer to. But to those who make these Bibles their primary source of the word of God, I say, "Drop it like a hot potato!" I will gladly buy you a KJV.

Revelation 18:6-19 – The Judgment of the Whore

VS 6 – This is a rather lengthy section describing the fall of Rome when the Lord Jesus Christ returns and executes judgment upon her. There are several items of note. Verse 6 issues a double judgment against Rome. Led by her "lord" Satan, she has doubled down against God at every turn. At the end of the book of Job, God blesses Job double for the trials he endured. The book of Job is a picture of the Tribulation. It has 42 chapters, one for each month. Job is in the land of Uz which is the same general area where the Jewish remnant will be holed up. He is persecuted by Satan for no reason other than he loves God, just like Israel in the Tribulation. In the first part of the book, Job sits on the ground and mourns his calamity for seven days, one for each of the seven years of the Tribulation. At the end of the book, he gets all his children restored just as the children of Israel will be restored. His double blessing will be the counter to the double judgment levied against the seat of the persecutions against God's people.

VS 7 – This verse shows the arrogance and self-glory of Rome. She claims she is the "church that Jesus founded upon the rock of Peter" in Matthew chapter 16. I don't have time to go into full detail of that passage, but the "rock" in the Bible is always God or Jesus. I could print all the verses and comment on them, but then this book would be too big to carry. The rock is mentioned about 140 times in the Bible. Get out your Strong's Concordance and look them up. You will find almost every one of those references saying that "God is our rock" (Psalm 18:2, 42:9) or "that Rock was Christ" (I Corinthians 10:4). The Catholic Church uses the passage in Matthew 16 as their base text. In that passage, Jesus said he would build his church, "and the gates of hell shall not prevail against it." The Catholic Church claims that all of the opposition and "persecution" it has received proves it is the true church because the gates of hell have not prevailed against it. The absolute audacity of the Roman Catholic Church to claim persecution when she has butchered millions of Bible believers is astounding. Revelation 18:7 says she sits a queen and says in her heart that she shall see no sorrow. Rome's claim of sitting as a "queen" applies to the many centuries she has dominated the world. It is also a reference to her claim of Mary being the "queen of heaven", which is one of Rome's main doctrines. Jeremiah 44:15-19 identifies the queen of heaven as a pagan goddess receiving drink offerings and "cakes" baked in her name which is a direct reference to the pagan Catholic Mass and their eating and drinking the flesh and blood of Jesus.

VS 8-10 – Her judgment will come in one day (verse 8) and one hour (verse 10). I have made the point before that time frames like this are often general in nature in the Bible, and it could be the case here as well. But I tend to take this one a little more literally. The Second Advent of Jesus Christ will not be a "gradual" event. It will be a sudden and cataclysmic overthrow of everything mankind has built for 6,000 years. The Lord could take a little side trip to Rome during his return and lay it waste in an hour without batting an eye. In fact, he could wait for 59 minutes and 59 seconds and still have time for coffee and doughnuts when he is done. The kings of the earth will lament when it happens. Imagine everything you have built in a lifetime being wiped out in a tornado. Then expand that by not just a lifetime but by six millennia, and not just you, but all of civilization. Then put it all on steroids. The weeping and wailing will be heard on other planets. Anyone who is there to watch it will back away so that they do not get caught in the carnage, but it won't matter. Those who rejected Jesus will be judged as well.

VS 11-19 – This passage describes a complete and total collapse of the financial system man has built. Market analysts constantly predict "boom" and "bust" trends, but in this one, the markets will all crash to ZERO. It won't matter. Gold is "dirt" in heaven (Revelation 21:21). Go ahead and do your financial planning now. It is a wise and essential part of life in this age. Do not just sit back and expect everyone else to take care of you. But God has a different plan ultimately. In Leviticus chapter 27, God designed the Jewish economy to "reset" every 50 years in the "year of jubilee". It kept things from getting so far out of inflationary control that causes the massive adjustments we see in our economy. Also, the jubilee in Leviticus is a picture of the Millennial reign. When Jesus returns, everything will reset, not only in the financial world but in every aspect of life. The merchants will weep and mourn when it happens.

The passage lists all the "finer things of life" that man desires. Rome is at the head of this class. The Roman Catholic Church is the richest institution on earth and has their filthy fingers in every conceivable money and business interest known to man. The list of her "delicacies" begins with gold in verse 12 and runs through every high-end commodity through verse 13, ending with "the souls of men". There is a double intent to that. The LAST thing Rome is concerned with is the souls of men, and the ULTIMATE capstone that the mastermind behind Rome wants is the souls of men. The true target of Satan's objective is to damn as many souls as he can. He knows he cannot win. He has read the last page of the book also. His blind rage and complete stubborn arrogance will never allow him to admit defeat. He will go down in flames and he knows it, but he wants to take as many souls with him as possible. Ezekiel 31:17-32 says that the only "comfort" he will have in hell is the billions of souls he took there. He will be tormented with fire and brimstone for eternity, and will look around and say, "At least I am not alone." Watching others suffer with him will give him some "comfort". That is such a sick and twisted mentality that normal people cannot grasp it, even normal sinners who reject Christ. But we see an occasional example of a deviant person who gets a thrill out of torturing others or watching them die. Real human beings with an ounce of common decency cannot wrap their heads around that, but we know it exists. Take that sick perversion and multiply it exponentially and you have a TINY picture of the depravity of Satan. Again, verse 19 says this will happen in one hour.

There is something else in this passage that flies under the radar. Verse 14 ends with, "Thou shalt find them no more at all." That statement appears seven times in the chapter: verse 14, verse 21, verse 22 (three times including "any more in thee"), and verse 23 twice. Seven is God's perfect number. When God is finished with this place, it will remain desolate forever. As we have seen, the earth is going to get pretty messed up during the Tribulation. The eco-system will be devastated beyond our worst nightmare projections. But when Jesus returns, the "desert will blossom as the rose" (Isaiah 35:1). He will clean up the mess, and it won't take him very long to do it. He spoke the whole thing into existence once, he can clean it up pretty easily. We will see more of this in chapter 20 when we discuss the Millennium. But my opinion is (NOTE: opinion) based on this chapter and the seven times "no more" statement, that God will so utterly destroy Rome that it will never be inhabited again. It might not be the entire city, but at least the Vatican, which if you did not know, is a sovereign country. The Vatican is roughly 100 acres and has less than 1,000 residents. It is the smallest country in the world by both land area and population. Yet it holds the most power of any country on earth. When Jesus comes, I suspect he will put a crater in those 100 acres that will never be repaired, and no one will ever live there again. Rome's title is "The Eternal City". God has a different name and a different outcome for it.

VS 20 – The Bible says in Proverbs 24:17-18, "Rejoice not when thine enemy falleth, and let not thine heart be glad when he stumbleth: lest the LORD see it, and it displease him, and he turn away his wrath from him." That is not a contradiction to what God tells us here when he says we are to rejoice when we see the fall of Rome. Proverbs addresses our physical "enemies" during our life here on earth. Notice I put the "enemies" in quotes. Lost people are not our enemies. They are "taken captive" by our only real enemy (II Timothy 2:24-26) and he uses them for his purposes. When they fall, we are supposed to be there to help them up. I was an enemy of God at some point, and Jesus died for me anyway so I could have a home in heaven (Romans 5:10, Colossians 1:21-22). When we gloat over the misfortune of others, even if they are pawns of the devil, God is upset with us more than with them. We are his children, and we are supposed to know better. That is why Jesus could tell us in Matthew 5:43-48 to love our enemies. Our rejoicing in Revelation is for the defeat of the only REAL enemy we have, Satan. But when the time comes of the obliteration of our enemy, God pulls off the restraint and says, "Party down, guys!"

VS 21-23 – The destruction of Rome is likened to casting a huge stone into the sea. It is not gradual. The obliteration of Rome will happen in an instant and be complete. It will happen "with violence". Behind the veneer of the "Prince of Peace" has operated the most violent institution or government in the history of the world. Man reaps as he sows. Some people only understand force, and this Church has employed it for centuries to further its heretical claim on the world. God will answer.

VS 24 – God credits the blood of all slain to Rome. That does not mean that every murder in history was carried out by the Catholic Church. But that mindset is behind most of them. The overwhelmingly vast majority of murders in history have been carried out by repressive governments and institutions trying to force their will on the populace. These people believe that they have the right to play God, and they give themselves the right to kill any dissenters to further their ambition. Millions of people were butchered by the Catholic Church over the last fifteen centuries. World War II claimed over 20 million lives. It was ignited by a Roman Catholic regime in Germany. Joseph Stalin studied for the Catholic priesthood before murdering millions of his own people in Communist Russia. The list is endless.

Revelation Chapter 19 – The Second Advent

This chapter concludes the major section of the book of Revelation detailing the Tribulation. We will see the fourth and final account of the literal coming of the Lord Jesus Christ to earth to defeat his enemies at the battle of Armageddon and to establish his reign upon the earth.

Revelation 19:1-5 – Praise God for His Judgment!

The twenty four elders appear in this passage for the final time. The scene is obviously in heaven as they are leading a "praise team" after the destruction of Rome. Verse 2 says, "He hath judged the great whore, which did corrupt the earth." That is past tense as if it is already done, but it actually does not happen until the events of chapter 19 are concluded. Actually, chapters 18 and 19 are "flipped" in chronological sequence. Jesus will come back to earth first, and as he does he will defeat Rome. Most of what is said in these verses is simply praise to God in terms we have seen many times before.

Revelation 19:6-9 – The Bride and the Marriage Supper

I hate to keep repeating myself, but it is necessary because the price of learning is repetition. How many times in grade school did we hear that 2+2=4? How many hundreds of equations and math homework problems did we have to do until it was finally drilled into our thick skulls? The Bible is not "linear." Things are placed out of chronological order because God is not bound by time. He is the "I AM". That name is eternally existent. No matter when you say it, it is always present tense. Everything happens in the present tense with God even before it happens in the future tense for us. This section in Revelation is a great example of that phenomenon, and it is throughout the Bible in mass quantity. In Revelation 19:11, heaven will open and a white horse rider will come to earth. That is the Lord Jesus Christ in his Second Advent. The destruction of Rome is recorded <u>before</u> that in chapter 18, but it happens in time <u>afterwards</u>. The praise of God that begins this chapter happens <u>after</u> Jesus returns. The marriage of the Lamb and the reception "supper" happens <u>after</u> the Advent, but is recorded in the Bible <u>before</u> it. Just get used to that concept. It will keep you hopping in the Bible because you will be constantly trying to sort things out in our time-chronology, but it will save you a lot of grief and bad doctrine if you will remember it.

Let's talk about the marriage of the Lamb. This is called the day of Christ in the New Testament because it is the day the Lamb gets his bride. If you are married, that was a pretty special day in your life and you commemorate it every year, and appreciate it every day. I absolutely LOVE weddings. They are my favorite part of the ministry. Everyone is so happy. Everything is so regal. The problems of the world go away at a wedding. Many of our wedding traditions are based on the Bible, like everything else in life is. Weddings picture the coming of the Lord to earth. Traditionally, the bride and groom do not see each other that day until the "big reveal" as she walks down the aisle. Right now, we do not see our Lord because we walk by faith and not by sight. June is the traditionally preferred month for a wedding. We covered that when we studied the rapture of the church. The bride is dressed in white, which comes directly from Revelation 19:8. There are attendants at the wedding, which we will cover in a moment. There is a reception after the ceremony which pictures the marriage supper of the Lamb from this text.

The processional at a wedding includes the closest friends of the bride and groom. Jesus will also have a "procession" of attendants at his wedding comprised of his "best friends" from the other ages of history. Ephesians 2:19 and 3:15 calls this the "household" and "family" of God. It is comprised of seven groups or individuals. Any guess why there are seven? The "wedding party" of Jesus is:

1) The Bridegroom – Jesus Christ (Psalm 19:5, John 3:29). Jesus always gets top billing.

2) The Bride – The church (Revelation 19:7, 21:2, Isaiah 61:10, Ephesians 5:25).

3) _The "Best Man"_ – The Old Testament saints under the law (John 3:30, Luke 16:16). John refers to himself in this passage as the "friend of the bridegroom". He stands in representation of a group of people. Luke 16:16 says, "The law and the prophets were until John." So beginning with Moses and the law of Israel until John the Baptist showed up to announce the arrival of the bridegroom, this group encompasses those who came into the family of God from Moses to John the Baptist.

4) _The Virgins_ – The 144,000 (Revelation 14:4, Matthew 25:1-13). These are the "bridesmaids" who are wonderful in their own right, but just not the star of the show like the bride. We have covered this Bible term in detail as those who are saved from the Jewish remnant in the Tribulation.

5) _The Guests_ – The Tribulation Gentiles (Matthew 22:10, Luke 14:15-24). These are the ones that the 144,000 minister to during the Tribulation. As we have noted, some of the Gentiles will respond to the message and take care of "the least of these my brethren". Other Gentiles will somehow manage to "endure to the end" and get into the kingdom and be invited to the wedding. The Lord WILL have guests at his wedding! He promised a kingdom to his people, and there will be subjects for it.

6) _The Queens_ (Song of Solomon 6:8-9)

7) _The Concubines_ (Song of Solomon 6:8-9)

I did not identify these last two groups specifically because I now get to fall back on my three favorite words, "I don't know". But the passage in Song of Solomon chapter 6 is clearly a description of a wedding. The bride is the "dove" in verse 9, and verse 8 lists the queens, concubines and virgins, and we already know who the virgins are. The other groups are easily identified. Then as you scan the people of God from history and line them up with the various "attendants", everyone is covered from Moses through the Tribulation. So the queens and concubines must be Adam to Moses. There really is no clear way to identify them or divide them. You could say Adam to Noah and Noah to Moses. Or you could say Adam to Abraham and Abraham to Moses. Either division would make sense and fit dispensationally. But then which group would be the queens and which would be the concubines? Since queens are listed first, that likely is Adam to whoever with the concubines whoever to Moses.

The exact classification of the various groups is not as significant as making sure that all of the people of God are in attendance at this wedding. No one who is saved will be left out. Satan will try to crash the wedding, but he will be escorted out by the authorities (Matthew 22:11-13). This wedding is also the subject of Psalm 45. In fact, in most Bibles, Psalm 45 is titled "The Wedding Song". No need to detail the entire Psalm, but if you read it for yourself you can see the wedding party fairly clearly. King Jesus is all decked out in his finest. King's daughters are there (verse 9), which are some of the attendants. The daughter of Tyre comes with a gift in verse 12, likely as a "guest". The queen in verse 9 is the bride. She is the queen (singular), not the queens (plural) from Song of Solomon. Verse 13 also describes the bride. She is glorious within. She has been transformed by her Lord from the inside by the operation of spiritual circumcision (Colossians 2:11-12). The bride's clothing is not white in this passage; it is "wrought gold". Gold pictures the deity of Christ in the Bible, and by the time of the wedding, we have been conformed to his image. The virgins "follow" the bride in verse 14 because the Tribulation saints come in to the family of God after the bride. I know this does not match our wedding processionals because the bridesmaids come in before the bride. But after the ceremony, they follow.

Then there is the "reception dinner" called the marriage supper of the Lamb. This will be one of the very first events of the Millennial reign. Jesus will have to finish the battle of Armageddon and deal with the judgment of the nations as we saw from Matthew chapter 25, and possibly clean things up a little which should not take much time, then it is on to the party. It is not 100% clear exactly when this supper takes place. Some have placed it in heaven after the Judgment Seat of Christ and after the wedding service.

I tend to place it on earth after the Second Advent. Matthew chapter 22 and the parable of the marriage gives us perhaps the best information. I spent some significant time on this parable in Revelation chapter 7 and the instructions given to the 144,000 in the Mid-Tribulation appearance of Jesus Christ. You can refer back to that section to review it. The parable ends with guests in attendance. They are the Gentiles of the Tribulation who respond to the message of the 144,000. Stay with me as we inch our way through the time-line of when these guests show up to the wedding.

Matthew 25:31 has the Son of man coming in his glory and being seated upon the throne of his kingdom. THEN the nations are gathered before him to be judged for how they treated Israel during the Tribulation. Some of those Gentiles "pass" this judgment because they harbored a Jew in their persecution. These Gentiles are granted entrance into the kingdom (verse 34). As a guest at the wedding, their invitation is not "stamped" until after the Lord is seated on his throne. So the wedding has to take place on earth after the Second Advent, and the reception dinner called the "marriage supper of the Lamb" will not happen until after the "ceremony". The processional at the wedding is given in Psalm 45, which I just detailed. But notice that this wedding party processional takes place after the King rides his horse to conquer his enemies and is given a throne (verses 3-6). So while it may not be perfectly clear from Revelation 19 when the marriage supper occurs, we can safely conclude from circumstantial evidence that it is one of the first events of the Millennial kingdom.

A couple of final details about the marriage supper can be seen from the words of Jesus himself. In Luke chapter 22, Jesus was talking to his twelve apostles. In verses 29-30, he promised them a special place in his kingdom. They will get to sit on twelve thrones judging the twelve tribes of Israel. We will see more of this when we cover the Millennium in chapter 20. Of course, Judas was among the group at this point. He was replaced by Matthias (Acts 1:15-26). Also in Luke 22:30, Jesus said they would get to "eat and drink at my table in my kingdom". At our weddings, there is traditionally a "head table" at the reception where the entire wedding party gets to sit for the dinner. It is a place of honor with the bride and groom in the center of the table and all their closest friends seated with them. Perhaps at the marriage supper of the Lamb there will be a "head table". Wouldn't it be awesome to see the Lord at that table with his bride seated with him, and the twelve apostles seated at the same table? Then Jesus gives us the "main course" on the menu. Matthew 22:4 says, "Behold, I have prepared my dinner: my oxen and my fatlings are killed, and all things are ready: come unto the marriage." God knew what he was doing when he made cows. A nice thick juicy ribeye with all the trimmings will be on my plate. Since this supper will be on the Millennial earth after it is restored, I can't wait to taste that awesome steak!

Revelation 19:10 – The Testimony of Jesus is the Spirit of Prophecy

This is a simple added detail to let us know that we are dealing with a book that cannot be equaled. What sets the Bible apart from all other literature is its ability to accurately tell the future without ever missing it one time. Our understanding of prophecy certainly lacks, but that does not change the truth of prophetic scripture. It will happen just as the Bible says. We all like to refer to our "testimony" at times, and many of the ones I have heard are quite astounding. The trophies of the grace of God I know of are some of the sweetest testimonies in history. But all of our testimonies pale in comparison to the testimony of Jesus. He is the main character of the book and of all of human history, and he confirmed who he was when he rose from the dead, which by the way, he predicted MANY times. The test of a prophet of God is 100% accuracy (Deuteronomy 18:22), and Jesus is THE Prophet. Many of God's human prophets fulfilled the test of the prophet in their ministries (led by the Holy Spirit – II Peter 1:21). But every other human prophet would have to climb Mount Everest, then get to the top rung of one of those huge fireman ladders, then jump as high as he possibly could just to scratch the instep of the sole of the foot of Jesus. This book begins with "the testimony of Jesus Christ" (Revelation 1:2), and right before we see the final account of his return to the earth, it says his testimony is that he never misses a prophecy.

Here is the fourth account of the Second Advent of Jesus Christ and the final "registration mark" of the record of the Tribulation in the book of Revelation.

VS 11-13 – The white horse rider is Jesus Christ. He carries four names in this passage, and many more names throughout the rest of the Bible. We have a poster on the wall in one of our rooms at church with some of the names of Jesus: Wonderful, Counselor, Prince of Peace, Rose of Sharon, Lily of the Valleys, Immanuel, Son of David… There are 53 on the poster and it does not include all of them in the Bible. A name communicates something about the person, especially in the Bible. Our names are nothing more than a conglomeration of letters that our parents found interesting. The names of Jesus signify who he is, and it is impossible to capture his essence without dozens of them or more. He is Faithful because he is always there and will never let you down. "Old Faithful" geyser in Yellowstone is so accurate you can set your watch to it, but Jesus is more Faithful because he made the geyser. He is True because he does not just speak truth, he exemplifies it in every aspect of his being. True North is anchored by the exact location of the North Pole, but Jesus is the anchor of our soul, sure and stedfast (Hebrews 6:19). He even has a name in verse 12 that no one knows yet. He is so awesome that you can't tag him with everything until he comes back, and we may not even know it then. He is unknowable fully and yet he has 50 names you can know for sure. No one will be able to say, "I never knew" and no one will ever grasp the fullness of Jesus. He is the Word of God because his word is his bond and he gave us the words of God (John 17).

Jesus will mount his trusty white steed to come to make war. One day I was driving through the area of Kansas City known as the Country Club Plaza. It is a famous area of town and those who live here know it well for a number of reasons. One of those reasons is that the Plaza is where a lot of protestors like to congregate. Just after we invaded Iraq in Gulf War I in 1991, a group of protestors was there. I saw a sign that said, "Would Jesus go to war?" I was on my way to an important appointment. I almost called to cancel it. My car swerved briefly on its own to find a parking place. I almost pulled a muscle jerking it back. It took everything I had not to pull over. I would have loved to walk up to the protestors with my Bible open to this verse. I would have another finger in Exodus 15:3: "The LORD is a man of war: the LORD is his name." I wonder if I would have made it out of the crowd in one piece. They would have "gone to war" against me. When Jesus comes to make war, it will be in perfect righteousness since he is Faithful and True. Our wars are never in righteousness and you can feel free to argue the merits of any of them, and you will have a valid point. But YES, Jesus <u>would</u> go to war, and he <u>will</u>, and he <u>WILL</u> <u>WIN</u>!

Verse 12 says when he comes, "his eyes were as a flame of fire". This is the same terminology used for him in Revelation 1:14. It is the look of righteous judgment "with fire in his eyes". You have heard it said, "If looks could kill…" When Jesus returns, looks WILL do just that to his enemies. One of the most chilling verses in the Bible is in Luke chapter 22. Jesus was at his trial, and Peter had followed "afar off". His third denial was barely out of his mouth when the cock crowed. Luke 22:61 says, "And the Lord turned, and <u>looked</u> upon Peter." Jesus was at the front of the room and Peter was out back warming himself by the fire. This probably didn't happen, but it could have. In my mind's eye, I see God freeze the entire room for just a few seconds as Jesus looked at Peter. Those fiery eyes locked in on his trusted friend. Verse 62 says, "And Peter went out, and wept bitterly." Just a simple look from the Lord was all it took for one of his own to bow under the scrutiny of God's judgment; and the judgment for Peter was infinitely mild compared to what it will be when Jesus returns. His eyes of fire will penetrate the hearts of people whom he loved enough to die for, and yet was "despised and rejected" of them (Isaiah 53:3). Those eyes of fire will have seen every single sin every one of his created beings committed, even the ones in their minds they did not have the guts to carry out. The fiery eyes of my Lord and Saviour Jesus Christ will be "in every place, beholding the evil and the good" (Proverbs 15:3). If you have never received him as your Saviour, do not put it off one minute more. You do NOT want to see those eyes.

Verse 13 says he has a vesture dipped in blood. When our Lord went to the cross to shed his blood for my sins, they stripped him of his vesture and gambled for it. When he returns, he will put on another one. It will get stained with the blood of his enemies. Isaiah 63:1-2 says his garments will be dyed red because he will be treading the winevat. We saw this in Revelation 14 in that account of his return. Psalm 68:23 says his foot will be dipped in the blood of his enemies. The Second Advent of the Lord Jesus Christ will not be pretty for those who are here to face it. Skeptics and atheists complain all the time about how the God of the Old Testament was a mean nasty nuclear bomb throwing bully and mad man. They contrast that with a "Jesus" who is the figment of their imagination who was such a mild-mannered wimp that he would never hurt a flea. Wait till he returns. Six thousand years of pent up righteousness and holiness will be unleashed on those who have rejected his every offer of grace.

VS 14 – The armies (plural) of heaven will follow the Lord in his return. There will be many millions divided into two major battalions: Israel and the church. Song of Solomon 6:10-13 shows us the two branches. Verse 13 says, "Return, return, O Shulamite; return, return, that we may look upon thee. What will ye see in the Shulamite? As it were the company of two armies." It says, "return, return" twice to show us that this is the Second Advent in prophetic terms. The "Shulamite" is a woman; the "she" of verse 10 who is "terrible as an army with banners". The Shulamite is the female diminutive form. She is "Mrs. Shulamon" (Solomon). Solomon is a type of Christ on the throne in his kingdom. There has never been a king or kingdom on this earth in 6,000 years that matched the splendor and glory of the kingdom of Solomon. When the anti-type (Jesus) returns, he will have his Father's Old Testament "wife" Israel and his own New Testament bride, the church, in two companies following him. The Lord will come on a white horse, and this verse says his armies will follow him on white horses also. After the Judgment Seat of Christ, the Lord will prepare us for the battle. I suspect we will all get to go to the stables to pick out our own ride. I want a white Mustang. A perfectly restored '65 convertible would be awesome.

The fighting force is described in Joel 2:1-11. It is an invincible army that cannot die or even be injured. One of the problems with fighting a militant Islamic army or the Crusaders of the Dark Ages is that they want to die. Muslims are promised 72 virgins if they die in battle and the Catholic armies were granted eternal life for giving their lives for the Church. Most soldiers do everything they can to survive and go home to their families. Those soldiers keep coming in waves to take out as many of the enemy troops as possible hoping to get taken out in the process. Try taking on an army that CANNOT be killed. The description is so awesome that I am going to print the whole passage then make a few brief comments.

"Blow ye the trumpet in Zion, and sound an alarm in my holy mountain: let all the inhabitants of the land tremble: for the day of the LORD cometh, for it is nigh at hand; A day of darkness and of gloominess, a day of clouds and of thick darkness, as the morning spread upon the mountains: a great people and a strong; there hath not been ever the like, neither shall be any more after it, even to the years of many generations. A fire devoureth before them; and behind them a flame burneth: the land is as the garden of Eden before them, and behind them a desolate wilderness; yea, and nothing shall escape them. The appearance of them is as the appearance of horses; and as horsemen, so shall they run. Like the noise of chariots on the tops of mountains shall they leap, like the noise of a flame of fire that devoureth the stubble, as a strong people set in battle array. Before their face the people shall be much pained: all faces shall gather blackness. They shall run like mighty men; they shall climb the wall like men of war; and they shall march every one on his ways, and they shall not break their ranks: Neither shall one thrust another; they shall walk every one in his path: and when they fall upon the sword, they shall not be wounded. They shall run to and fro in the city; they shall run upon the wall, they shall climb up upon the houses; they shall enter in at the windows like a thief. The earth shall quake before them; the heavens shall tremble: the sun and the moon shall be dark, and the stars shall withdraw their shining: And the LORD shall utter his voice before his army: for his camp is very great: for he is strong that executeth his word: for the day of the LORD is great and very terrible; and who can abide it?" (Joel 2:1-11)

127

No one will have a chance against this army. Israel and the church have been the targets of the armies of the world's persecution for thousands of years, and for most of it, we have been utterly defenseless unless the Lord stepped in, which he often did. The tables will turn. Jesus will come in glory and power and his people will get in on the action with him. In Judges chapter 4, Barak (a type of Christ) defeated Sisera (a type of the Antichrist). Deborah (a woman) was a judge in Israel and part of the winning battle. Sisera was eventually killed by Jael (a woman) when she put him to sleep with some nice warm milk and drove a tent spike through his temples. Two "women" will work with the Lord in his return. Romans 16:20 says the Lord will bruise Satan under <u>our</u> feet shortly. Jesus is the general, but we fight with him.

Verse 2 says this army will be greater than any ever assembled before or since. Verse 3 says nothing (or no one) will escape. The destruction will be so complete that the contrast will be like Eden before and Hiroshima after. Keep in mind that by this point, the earth has been wasted through the disasters of the Tribulation, so it will be quite the "hot mess". Yet the passage says it will look like the Garden of Eden compared to what we will do to it after we are done. Verse 5 says we will hop-skip over the tops of the mountains like fiery chariots, surely faster, louder and fiercer than the greatest fighting jets ever produced. We will be "set in array" and not ever break ranks. There will be no defections and no failures in our mission. Verse 8 tells us that if we take a bullet, it will "tickle". No city, wall, fort or house will be safe (verse 9). The Lord shall utter his voice (verse 11), and with a single command from his everlasting all powerful word and Word, we will mount up and ride in to participate with him in conquering the rebels to establish our Lord and Saviour Jesus Christ as the rightful King of kings and Lord of lords. I was never in the military and it is not really my gig now, but that day will be something to behold!

VS 15 – The King of kings and the Lord of lords cometh. Back in chapter 17 we saw 13 words in block capital letters for the whore of Rome. Here we have seven for our Lord Jesus Christ. In chapter 14 we saw him tread the winepress of the fierceness and wrath of Almighty God. In this passage, Jesus has a couple of instruments with which to rule. The first is the sword of the Spirit that comes out of his mouth. We obviously know that as the word of God, the Bible (Ephesians 6:17, Hebrews 4:12). Jesus will use this instrument to smite the nations in his return. II Thessalonians 2:8 says he will destroy Satan with "the spirit of his mouth". The only thing it will take for Jesus to conquer his enemies is his word. He spoke the Universe into existence with his word (Psalm 33:6), and he will judge it with the same word (John 12:48). When Jesus sends the sword of the Spirit out of his mouth at his coming, people will obey or be destroyed. One of the best examples in the Bible of the power of the words of Jesus Christ is in the Garden of Gethsemane in John 18:6. Judas and a band of men came to arrest him. A band of soldiers in the Roman army was 600 men. Jesus approached them and asked, "Whom seek ye?" They said, "Jesus of Nazareth." Jesus said, "I am *he*." If you are paying close attention, you will see that the word "*he*" is in italics, meaning it was not in the original text but added by the translators because it was implied in the text. Literally, Jesus said, "I AM". As soon as that awesome name of power and deity issued forth from his mouth, "they went backward and fell to the ground." Imagine seeing that! Revelation 6:17 says at his Second Advent, "Who shall be able to stand?" We have our answer: <u>NO ONE</u>!

Then verse 15 gives us the second instrument of his kingdom, the rod of iron. This speaks of his absolute rule during the Millennial reign. It will be a military dictatorship with a righteous benevolent King full of grace <u>AND</u> truth (John 1:14). The kingdom will require both. Sinful humans will be in the kingdom in their natural bodies. Jesus will rule with the rod of iron because he will not put up with rebellion. But he also knows mankind and our weaknesses and grace will be on full display as well. We will see more of this in chapter 20 when we cover the details of the Millennium.

VS 16 – On his vesture (covering him) and on his thigh (the strongest part of the anatomy) is the fifth name he carries in this section: KING OF KINGS, AND LORD OF LORDS. Anyone who thinks he is in charge of something really isn't. He has a King and a Lord over him. Anyone in the kingdom who gets any type of position of authority will only have it under his authority. Colossians 4:1 says, "Masters, give unto your servants that which is just and equal; knowing that ye also have a Master in heaven." Is that verse obeyed today? Really?!?! What planet do you come from? There are small pockets of just and equal treatment implemented by a rare few, but in the kingdom, passages such as this will be carried out in their perfect fulfillment. The King over all kings will see to it.

Revelation 19:17-21 – The Supper of the Great God

This is one of the more gruesome passages anywhere in the Bible. The Bible is an honest book and deals with far more than just "religion". God is not responsible for the carnage that happens here; he made man perfect and gave him every chance and then some to be redeemed even after sin ravaged our race. But laws of nature and laws of the spirit are absolute. We reap what we sow. The downward spiral of sin and filth leads to what we see in this section as we wind down the Tribulation and bring it to a close.

VS 17-18, 21 – An angel stands "in the sun" representative of "The Sun of Righteousness" (Malachi 4:2) to announce to the fowls of heaven that it is time to finish off the battle of Armageddon. This event is prophesied in the Old Testament in Isaiah 18:6, and especially in Ezekiel 39:17-22 which describes it in nearly the same wording. The strategic positioning of Ezekiel 39 also plays in to this. Chapters 38-39 of Ezekiel are commonly linked to Armageddon, and are followed immediately by chapters 40-48 which describe the Millennial city of Jerusalem. Ezekiel calls it a sacrifice. It is the final one before the reign of the Lord begins. The scene is gory. If something is off, we say, "That's for the birds". Jesus also alludes to this in Matthew 24:28: "For wheresoever the carcase is, there will the eagles be gathered together." This yields yet another of the hundreds of common expressions that come directly out of the Bible. We say, "Birds of a feather flock together". They will all gather for this feast of human flesh.

VS 20-21 – As the beast and his armies are "gathered" to wage war on Israel, God is waiting for them. We have seen earlier the intent of God to "gather the nations" (Zephaniah 3:8) to pour out his judgment upon them. I also commented earlier on the false prophet found in these verses. They are cast alive into the lake of fire just as this supper takes place. There is a strong indication that there will be an actual literal lake of fire on earth during the Millennium much like a large volcano. Isaiah 66:23-24 describes people going to this location to look upon the carcasses of men who have sinned as a dire warning to not follow in their footsteps. We spent a little time with this earlier in chapter 9 with the fifth Trumpet, and we will visit this again briefly in the next chapter.

Revelation Chapters 20-22
"The Things Which Shall Be Hereafter"

We now enter the final major section of the book of Revelation. We move past the Tribulation and the Second Advent of Jesus Christ to cover the time period known as the Millennial reign; then we also move beyond that thousand-year period to eternity. If we have trouble grasping the details of the Tribulation, eternity is even more challenging. Some of this can be seen clearly from the scriptures. But a lot of what we find in eternity is speculation that can be inferred by tying together certain passages of the Bible and drawing conclusions based on the consistency of God and his word.

Revelation Chapter 20 – The Millennium, Final Rebellion, and Great White Throne

Revelation 20:1-3 – Satan Bound

In verse 1, an angel comes down from heaven with the key to the bottomless pit to bind Satan. We visited this issue in Revelation chapters 9 and 10. By way of brief review, in Revelation 9:1, an angel falls from heaven, and in 10:1 an angel comes down from heaven. The difference is significant. Satan falls; Jesus comes down. This angel is not described, so we cannot be 100% sure, but I just cannot imagine the Lord delegating this one off to anyone else. After all the conflict of 6,000 years and what Satan has done to him and his people and his creation, I would think he would take this one on himself. He will bind him with a "great chain" and shut him up and set a seal on him. I suspect it will be pretty strong. I get a kick out of some of these Charismatic preachers who run around "binding Satan" all the time. First of all, only Jesus is man enough to do that. Secondly, once Satan is bound, he is BOUND. There will be no need to "bind" him again and again every time someone wants to extort money from gullible Christians.

In verse 3, Satan will be loosed. Hold on to this and I will explain it in verse 7, but it will be a while.

Revelation 20:4-6 – The First Resurrection and the Reign of Jesus Christ

This is the passage in the book of Revelation that defines the 1,000-year reign of Jesus Christ. The phrase "a thousand years" appears six times in the chapter (once each in verses 2-7). The Millennium is the seventh one-thousand-year period of human history. But there is essentially no information here about it. The kingdom of the Messiah of Israel is the main subject of the Bible and can be seen on virtually every page of it. But when we finally get to it in Revelation, God just passes by it without comment. In order to get the details, we have to go the Old Testament to see how the Millennium will function and operate.

Before we do, let's cover the "first resurrection" and "second death" mentioned in these verses. There are thrones for people to reign upon, and they will get to reign for a thousand years. The souls of them which were beheaded are the 144,000 Tribulation saints who refused the mark and were martyred. This group has been discussed many times. They will get a special place in the kingdom as a result of what they had to endure for the Lord in this life. They will obviously be raised to reign with Christ. The term "first resurrection" must be understood in its context. There were others raised before them – obviously Jesus, and yet others like Lazarus as well. But this "first" resurrection is contrasted with a "second" death. The second death is hell, and will be defined in Revelation 20:14 when we cover the Great White Throne Judgment. This first resurrection assures them they will never face the second death. The old expression says it this way, "Born once, die twice; born twice, die once." Then verse 5 says, "The rest of the dead lived not again until the thousand years were finished." When I first read this, it concerned me a little. I thought if I did not get my head cut off that I would just stay dead and not even get to be in the Millennial reign. Then someone pointed out that by this time I will have been raptured and conformed to the image of Christ. I cannot be "dead" at that point or ever again! The "dead" in that verse are those who have rejected Christ and are "dead in their sins" (Ephesians 2:1). But notice it says they will not live again until the thousand years are finished. That means when the Millennium is over, they WILL live again. That is not their "second chance", but a reference to being raised to face God in judgment.

This brings us to the discussion of the details of the Millennial reign of Christ. As we have seen, this subject permeates every facet of the word of God. It will take us some time to go through a lot of the details of these one thousand years, and I will only be scratching the surface of the kingdom. There is more information on this topic than any other subject in the Bible by far. In the next few pages I hope to lay out a simple structure for the Millennium that will get you started on your studies. If I tried to quote every verse, it would bog us down in the study. However, there is a way I can give you a complete and comprehensive list of all the passages that tell us about the reign of Jesus Christ. Get a King James Bible. Read all 31,175 verses from cover to cover. Now you have all the verses that define the kingdom.

The Millennial Reign of Jesus Christ

The PURPOSES of the Millennium – Why?

There are several reasons why Jesus must come to this earth to reign. These are in no particular order and there are probably more, but these are the basic purposes of God for his Son to sit on his throne.

1) To give the glory and honor to the King, Jesus Christ
   Psalm 24, Matthew 25:31

I said these points were in no particular order, but I am going to list this one first anyway. The rest of them can be sorted any way you wish, but this one has to be at the head of the class. Most of the time we talk about the rapture of the church or the Millennium, we touch on things from our perspective. It will be awesome to go out in the rapture because we can just go to heaven immediately without dying. Once we get raptured, there will be no more bills to pay! Whatever we owe on our house or car will be written off. If the bank wants it, they can have it. We have a mansion just over the hilltop anyway (John 14:2). There will be no more cranky abusive bosses or unruly neighbors partying all night. There is no "night" there to party even if they wanted to! The kids will never get sick. In the Millennial kingdom, we get to reign with Jesus and call the shots. We will be in glorified bodies in a perfect paradise. All of that and much more will be awesome with a capital "A" and even all the way to the capital "Z". And all of that is for ME. The majority of our focus about the coming of the Lord is self-centered. That is OK to a point, because God takes care of his children and Jesus wants his bride to be with him to share in his glory.

But the very BEST part of the kingdom is to see Jesus get what he rightfully deserves. For 2,000 years, his name has been used as a cuss word. He was "despised and rejected of men" when he was here the first time (Isaiah 53:3). They hated him "without a cause" (John 15:25). His followers have been hunted and persecuted and tortured for no other reason than they believed in him and wanted to live their lives and raise their children to love and honor God. Finally, he will get the glory due him. Matthew 25:31 calls it "the throne of his glory". The entire world will be his. We throw massive parties and parades for our sports teams when they win the National title or Super Bowl. That is just one city. Imagine the King of glory receiving his parade. I want to see Jesus walk down the streets of Jerusalem and have every eye see him and give him praise. The best part for us is not all the cool "stuff" we get or the things we do not have to put up with anymore. It will be watching our Lord get his glory and sitting back saying, "I know him!" He is the King of the entire earth, and I am a personal friend. Most of us know a famous person at least a little. There is the old game of "six degrees of separation" where most anyone can link themselves to some famous person through no more than five other people. I am a nobody in the middle of nowhere, but I can get to the President of the United States in three. I can get to Jesus without even ONE.

Ezekiel chapters 40-48 is a detailed description of the Millennium and the Millennial city of Jerusalem during those thousand years. It is an awesome passage of scripture. There is a ton of really cool stuff in those nine chapters. The best part is the very last four words: "The Lord is there" (Ezekiel 48:35). It does not really matter about the temple and the streets and the river and the stuff (although it does). It will be amazing beyond anything man has ever seen. What matters the most is "The Lord is there".

There are a few places in the Bible that most everyone is familiar with, even lost people. Some of those places even the lost actually admire and love. The Lord's prayer in Matthew 6 is one of them. Another one is Psalm 23. Everyone loves Psalm 23, but what very few people realize is the strategic placement of this Psalm in the Bible. This is really deep, so hang on to your hats. Psalm 23 is right <u>after</u> Psalm 22 and right <u>before</u> Psalm 24. Before anyone has a right to claim Psalm 23 at any level, they must come through Psalm 22 first. Read it. Psalm 22 is one of the clearest descriptions of Calvary in the Bible. ONLY the people of God can truly say, "The Lord is my shepherd". But we do not stop there. Psalm 23 leads us to Psalm 24 where the gates of the Millennial city swing wide open to welcome in the King of glory. As a believer in Jesus Christ, if your number ONE passion is anything other than seeing your Lord and Saviour get his glory, you are just a "half a bubble off" in your focus.

When Jesus returns, the rightful heir to the throne of the Universe will be crowned. Satan's rebellion was over the issue of a throne. He desires to "exalt his throne above the stars of God" and take God's place as King (Isaiah 14:12-14). For 6,000 years, this struggle over the throne has been played out. It seems like the enemy is in control and winning. We are down 48-7. There are 2 minutes left in the game. The other team has the ball. We are out of timeouts. No worries. I have read the last page. We win. Our King is coming and he will take the throne and have the pre-eminence in all things.

2) To show man how government and society is supposed to function
   Isaiah 9:6-7, Psalm 67:4

Man has tried for 6,000 years to govern himself and has made an absolute miserable mess of it. We have tried every form of government and every "-ism" we can think of without success. Some of the systems have been "better" than others, but that is only relative. We keep comparing systems of government and economics to other failed systems to find the "best" only to fail again. For the record, I am a right-wing conservative fundamental free market capitalist Republican. I do believe it is the "best" system man has ever come up with because it takes into account individual responsibility. But anyone who does not think that capitalism is fraught with a trainload of injustice and abuse and problems "does not have all the paint on his brush" as they say. Jesus is not a Republican. When he comes back, he will torch everything man has built for six millennia, including American capitalism, and then do it right.

Have you ever watched someone struggle with something that you are <u>very</u> proficient at? You want them to learn it, and you know that they can never learn it unless they do it. In patience, you try to advise them without doing it for them. But at some point, you realize they just will NEVER get it. The longer it goes on the worse it gets. Eventually, the only thing you can do is say, "Let me have that." You <u>must</u> do it for them because if you don't it will never get done and someone is bound to die getting there. Magnify that by a trillion-fold or more. God has been patiently sitting in heaven watching his creatures try something that he is really good at, and with each try we get <u>further</u> from the truth. At some point, the Lord Jesus Christ will be required to mount up and come back here and say, "Gimme that".

Man has been <u>TOLD</u> how to function for centuries through the Bible. But he has ignored it (at best) and rebelled against it and burned the copies of it at worst. He must be <u>shown</u> how society is supposed to work. God demonstrates his attributes tangibly. Jesus did not just "send us a text" from heaven and hope we would get it, he came here for 33 years to show us. With no Millennium, man never <u>sees</u> the truth.

132

Let's see just a few brief verses on this. Isaiah 9:6-7 says, "The government shall be on his shoulder". There will be no more Presidents, Senators, Prime Ministers or even city councils. Jesus will run the whole show. There will be no "loyal opposition" or political parties trying to oust the other guys. Jesus will be the King. He will not have to run for re-election every four years. There will be no political ads or rallies and campaigns. Just that much alone ought to make everyone want to get there immediately! Jeremiah 23:5-6 says, "Behold, the days come, saith the LORD, that I will raise unto David a righteous Branch, and a King shall reign and prosper, and shall execute judgment and justice in the earth. In his days Judah shall be saved, and Israel shall dwell safely: and this is his name whereby he shall be called, THE LORD OUR RIGHTEOUSNESS." If you want to see the society be run right, which is what righteousness means, then vote for Jesus. No other man can get anywhere close to it.

King Jesus will execute judgment in the earth. This means when something goes wrong, a righteous King on the throne will get right to the heart of the matter and issue a correct verdict and decision. Trials will not drag on for weeks and months. Crooked sleazebag defense attorneys will not get criminals off on technicalities. No ambulance chasers will extort millions over fake claims. No defendant will be wrongly convicted. No rich or powerful crook will be able to buy his way out of his crime. The truth, the whole truth, and nothing but the truth will be immediately known in every case. Isaiah 11:1-5 describes it:

"And there shall come forth a rod out of the stem of Jesse, and a Branch shall grow out of his roots: And the spirit of the LORD shall rest upon him, the spirit of wisdom and understanding, the spirit of counsel and might, the spirit of knowledge and of the fear of the LORD; And shall make him of quick understanding in the fear of the LORD: and he shall not judge after the sight of his eyes, neither reprove after the hearing of his ears: But with righteousness shall he judge the poor, and reprove with equity for the meek of the earth: and he shall smite the earth with the rod of his mouth, and with the breath of his lips shall he slay the wicked. And righteousness shall be the girdle of his loins, and faithfulness the girdle of his reins."

Everyone wants justice. Our pledge ends, "With liberty and justice for all." How is that working? King Jesus on the throne will make sure that the victims of wrongdoing are immediately made whole. Have you ever had something stolen from you and never recovered? I would guess that every person reading this could say yes. If it happens in the Millennium, the thief will be apprehended as he is leaving your home or business. Your items will be recovered on the spot. Restitution will be made. The aggrieved and abused will no longer suffer the injustices that mark our world. The basic "constitution" will be the Sermon on the Mount from Matthew chapters 5-7. The first word out of Jesus' mouth in that passage is, "Blessed". Blessings will abound, especially to those who obey the law. This is the passage containing the "golden rule" (Matthew 7:12). Righteousness will exceed anything any religion or system man has ever devised (Matthew 5:20). The poor and the least will be lifted up. Even though righteousness will prevail, there will be some who do not like it and rebel. That is why the rod of iron is necessary. When the law is broken, justice will be served immediately, correctly, and in line with the crime. One of the biggest problems in our world today is that justice never really gets served properly and timely. Solomon said in Ecclesiastes 8:11, "Because sentence against an evil work is not executed speedily, therefore the heart of the sons of men is fully set in them to do evil." No consequences for bad behaviour means it will not stop. But with Jesus on the throne, everything will be dealt with swiftly and justly.

Who would not want to live in a world like that? Man has longed for this since the day he got kicked out of Eden. Yet when you tell him that it will someday happen and he can be a part of it if he will trust Jesus as his Saviour, he looks at you like you have three heads and calls you names. "O let the nations be glad and sing for joy: for thou shalt judge the people righteously, and govern the nations upon earth" (Psalm 67:4). "Let the field be joyful, and all that is therein: then shall all the trees of the wood rejoice before the LORD: for he cometh, for he cometh to judge the earth: he shall judge the world with righteousness and the people with his truth" (Psalm 96:12-13). Are you ready?

3) To fulfill the promise of an earthly kingdom for Israel
Matthew 25:34, Matthew 19:28, Genesis 17:1-8

If Jesus does not come to physically reign with his chosen people Israel in charge, then most of the Bible is a lie, including much of what Jesus himself said. A-Millennialists have to spiritualize enough passages in the Old Testament that they might as well not even have a Bible. There is no way I can go through all of those passages. Again, just read the Bible and believe what you read without looking for some deep dark hidden meaning. Acts 1:11 says, "This same Jesus, which is taken up from you into heaven, shall so come in like manner as ye have seen him go into heaven." It is hard to get any clearer. This same Jesus will come. It will not be a different Jesus or a coming in the Spirit only. The same guy, the man they walked with for 3½ years, will come again just like he went up. He stood there bodily in the flesh on that hill outside Jerusalem. He will come back bodily in the flesh. He MUST come because he has promised the Nation of Israel a literal earthly kingdom with him on the throne as their King.

A royal land grant was given to Abraham and his seed. This is actual physical dirt, rocks and trees, not a "spiritual blessing". Genesis 15:18 sets the East / West borders: "From the river of Egypt unto the great river, the river Euphrates." The north boundary is Hamath (Ezekiel 48:1) which is in Northern Syria. The south border is Kadesh (Ezekiel 48:28-29) which is in the wilderness a good bit south of the Dead Sea. That area on the map today encompasses modern day Israel, Syria, Jordan, Iraq, and a small part of Saudi Arabia. Good luck trying to convince anyone today that land belongs to Israel. This land grant is much larger than the Nation of Israel has ever occupied. God promised Abraham that he would get all the land that he saw and walked through. The indication is that the Nation of Israel in the Millennium will stretch from Ur of the Chaldees (Abraham's original home at the tip of the Persian Gulf), to Haran (in modern day Turkey near Mt. Ararat), to Egypt. This is the ground that Abraham traversed in his life, and forms a triangle of immense size covering the heart of today's "Middle East". Deuteronomy 11:22-25 and Joshua 1:3-4 confirm the area of the land grant. David and Solomon conquered this land and subdued it (II Samuel 8:3, I Kings 4:21). But even their kingdoms did not fully acquire the full land grant because foreign nations dwelt in that area. Also, the promise was forever, not just the 80 years of the kingdoms of David and Solomon. When Jesus returns, this entire area will be the land mass of the Nation of Israel. If he does not come back to conquer that land, then the promise to Abraham and his seed cannot be fulfilled. It is certain that Israel will never get that land now.

There are many prophecies of the Nation of Israel being placed in their land safely. Anyone who thinks Israel dwells safely now or ever will under the current world order is not paying attention to the news. Even CNN can get that one right. Ezekiel 34:23-31 and Amos 9:11-15 say Israel will never be removed out of that land. Rome removed them in 70 AD and it took almost 1,900 years to get them back. At some point, Jesus must come to establish his people in their land so that they can never be taken out of it again. Israel is promised to be the "head" of the nations (Deuteronomy 28:13). Instead, they have been the "tail" as the prophecy says for centuries. The King of Israel must return to fulfill this promise.

Israel was established in the Old Testament under the law to be "the lighthouse of the nations". They had a mission to reach the Gentile world for Jehovah God. Their purpose was NOT to put up a wall and keep the "heathen" out, but to draw them to God through their laws and sacrifices. Here is where we need a broader understanding of the purpose of Israel. The vast majority of people read the Old Testament and see God as a nuclear bomb-throwing mad man intent on killing every man, woman and child on earth except the Jews. Nothing could be further from the truth. A mixed multitude went up with Israel out of Egypt. God gave repeated instructions in the law on how to welcome strangers into the fold if they would convert to the God of Israel. They were commanded to love the stranger in Deuteronomy 10:19. They were also told not to pervert the judgment of a stranger in Deuteronomy 24:17. Strangers were allowed to make the same sacrifices as the children of Israel according to Numbers 15:14-16. Strangers were to be treated "as one born among you" as per Leviticus 19:33-34. When Joshua read the book of the law to all

134

Israel at Mount Ebal and Gerizim, he included the "strangers that were conversant among them" (Joshua 8:30-35). Any honest reading of the Old Testament shows that God had a clear intention of establishing Israel as a kingdom with his laws to <u>DRAW</u> the Gentiles to himself. The verses in the New Testament about God drawing the Gentiles do not just apply to the church. They also point to the kingdom.

Most people see it the opposite. They see an angry God telling his people to kill everyone around them. They ignore the contexts of passages like that. God gave the Amorites 400 years before their iniquity reached a full measure (Genesis 15:16). When God told Saul to wipe out the Amalekites in I Samuel 15, it was in judgment for their treatment of his people when Israel came out of Egypt. That was almost 500 years earlier. God was VERY patient and longsuffering with the Gentiles in the Old Testament. When it became abundantly evident that a particular group would not respond to God regardless of his grace, he turned to judgment. That is a common Bible principle. The God of love is the same God of wrath, and whichever of those two attributes a person or a group of people wants to receive is up to them.

Most of the instructions given regarding other people groups were to drive them out of the land, not to eliminate them. The purpose was for God to establish his people in his land to set up his laws and operate his sacrifices so other nations could see it bring it home to their people. The classic case of that is the visit of the queen of Sheba to Jerusalem when Solomon was the king in I Kings 10:1-10. That is the closest Israel ever got to fulfilling their mission under the law. But the law of human collapse set in, and Israel departed from God. Instead of bringing the nations to God, they followed the gods of the nations. God still has a purpose for Israel. He intends for their mission to be carried out. The Millennial kingdom of the Lord Jesus Christ will be that time (Deuteronomy 28:1-14, Isaiah 60:1-7, 62:1-12, 66:18-19).

Jesus told a parable of a fig tree as a picture of the self-righteous Nation of Israel in their national life.

> "He spake also this parable; A certain man had a fig tree planted in his vineyard; and he came and sought fruit thereon, and found none. Then said he unto the dresser of his vineyard, Behold, these three years I come seeking fruit on this fig tree, and find none: cut it down; why cumbereth it the ground? And he answering said unto him, Lord, let it alone this year also, till I shall dig about it, and dung it: And if it bear fruit, well: and if not, then after that thou shalt cut it down. And he was teaching in one of the synagogues on the sabbath." (Luke 13:6-10

God has been seeking fruit from his fig tree Israel for about 4,000 years. Abraham was born in 1996 BC; roughly 4,000 years ago. He will "give it one more year" in the Millennial "sabbath", and they WILL finally produce fruit because their King will be here.

4) To give the "reward of the inheritance" to the servants of Christ in the church age
Colossians 3:23-24, Luke 19:11-27

Throughout the New Testament are admonitions and exhortations to church age saints to remain faithful to the Lord and stay active in service to the King. We beat the drum so loudly about not losing salvation (rightfully so) that many go too far with this and just slide right through their Christian life with no fruit. I could preach sermons on this issue for a couple of years and never come close to exhausting the topic. Just because we cannot lose our salvation does not mean we cannot lose everything else. God promised rewards to his servants. If he does not give them, he is a liar. Do not ever try to convince a true servant of God that it will not be "Worth It All When We See Jesus". God is "just and equal" (Colossians 4:1). That does NOT mean God is "fair". That word is not in the Bible except when it is talking about a fair woman or fair weather or something like that. "Fair" is everyone getting the same thing. Just and equal is God rewarding people justly and equal to their accomplishments. If you have more than one child, and one of them misbehaves, the "fair" thing to do is discipline both of them. The "just and equal" thing to do is to punish and reward each child without respect of persons based on their own individual merit.

Once a person receives Jesus as Saviour, their eternal destiny in heaven is fixed. But then they have the rest of their life to do something with that salvation; not to earn it or keep it, but to serve their Lord who secured it for them on the cross. Some of them give their lives in service to their Lord, a few of them literally. Most believers skate through their Christian life with not much more than church attendance on their resume. Still others don't even bother with that. Do not even try to tell me that God will not take that into account. Rewards at the Judgment Seat of Christ will be manifest in the kingdom by physical positions reigning with the Lord.

The parable of the talents in Matthew chapter 25 is fairly well known by most people who are somewhat familiar with the Bible. Jesus told the story of a man who gave five talents to one person, two to another, and one to a third person. He went away and returned; a picture of the Second Coming. Then he called those servants to find out what they had done with what he had given them. Two of the servants used those talents to gain more and were rewarded. The man with one hid it and did nothing with it. Such is the case with many Christians. Some of the harshest words of the Lord were reserved for this man. In verse 30, this man was ultimately cast into outer darkness, a reference to hell. This parable is in the book of Matthew, the gospel presenting Jesus as the King of the Jews. The loss of salvation is seen because of that doctrinal perspective. But there is a parallel story in Luke 19:11-27 with different details. Luke is the Gentile gospel. Verse 11 mentions the kingdom of God (the church) not the kingdom of heaven for the Jews. There are ten servants, the number of the Gentiles. The monetary unit is pounds, the British "dollar". Each servant gets the same amount to start with. Our physical "talents" (Matthew) vary, but we are all one in Christ Jesus and have the same Spirit (Luke). The bad servant does not get cast into outer darkness, he only loses his pound. The enemies who are slain in verse 27 are his citizens in verse 14 who refused to have him reign over them. That is clearly the Jewish people at the time of Christ who said, "Away with him, crucify him, we have no king but Caesar." This parable is for the church age servants.

But notice the rewards. Those who are faithful with their Lord's resources will get to reign over cities when he returns (verse 17, 19). We cannot do that if we just go to heaven and sit on clouds playing harps. In the Millennium, church age saints who served the Lord faithfully in this life will get positions of honor and authority in his government. Those who waste their opportunity will have their "city" taken away from them (verse 26), but they will still be there in the kingdom. Our service now in this life determines our position in the kingdom. There must be a Millennial reign for this parable to be fulfilled.

Matthew 16:24-27 applies directly to the Jewish remnant in the Tribulation, but the principle applies to us as well. If we take up our cross and "lose" our lives in him, he will reward us (verse 27). No cross, no crown. Jesus set the example himself in his temptation when he refused the crown before he went to the cross. Christians who serve Jesus in this life will be rewarded in the kingdom. Colossians 3:23-24 says, "And whatsoever ye do, do it heartily, as to the Lord, and not unto men; Knowing that of the Lord ye shall receive the reward of the inheritance: for ye serve the Lord Christ." II Timothy 2:12-13 says, "If we suffer, we shall also reign with him: if we deny him, he also will deny us: If we believe not, yet he abideth faithful: he cannot deny himself." This passage is used to make Christians fear losing salvation. They are told that if they deny the Lord he will deny them. But they miss the point. Verse 12 says if we suffer we shall reign, but if we deny, he will deny us [our reign], which is implied. He does not deny us entrance into the kingdom, but position. That is made clear by verse 13 when it says, "He cannot deny himself." A Christian is part of his body, bone of his bone and flesh of his flesh (Ephesians 5:30). Jesus will not deny part of his body, but he will set some of them aside in his kingdom if they do not serve him in this life. They will be ON the team and AT the game, but sitting on the end of the bench in street clothes.

Romans 8:16-17 says, "The Spirit itself beareth witness with our spirit, that we are the children of God: And if children, then heirs; heirs of God, and joint-heirs with Christ; if so be that we suffer with him, that we may be also glorified together." A saved person is a child of God. He is in the family and will go to heaven whether he likes it or not. I Peter 1:4 says we have an inheritance reserved in heaven for us. God does not lose reservations. But there are TWO heirs in the passage in Romans 8. Heirs of God are his children. They are in the family because they have been born again. But a joint-heir with Christ has a condition attached to it: IF we suffer with him. Let me illustrate. All family members are present for the reading of the will, but not everyone always gets the same amount in every case. Sometimes the testator decides to bequeath the estate differently. It is their choice. Jesus is the "testator" of the New Testament (Hebrews 9:15-17). He can decide to divvy up his blessings however it suits him. Those who suffer for him will get a bigger portion in his kingdom. He is just and equal. He will make things right. Suffering is not always physical. You do not have to get tortured for your faith to get a bigger reward. Just "pick up your cross". There are many ways to define that, but here is the best one I have heard. Jesus prayed, "Not my will, but thine be done" then picked up his cross. When your will goes one way, and God's will goes in a different direction, they will "cross". Lay down your will and pick up his. The word "suffer" is often used in the Bible to mean allow. Allow God to be in charge. Let Jesus be your Saviour and your Lord. There will be plenty of occasions for his will to cross yours. Pick up your cross and follow him.

Perhaps the best example in the Bible of the two types of heirs is the famous story of the prodigal son in Luke 15:11-32. Most people are familiar with the story. There were two brothers, and the younger one rebelled. He took his portion of the inheritance and ran off and wasted it. It pictures a believer who takes what God gave him at salvation and wastes his life on himself rather than serving his Father in heaven. After an education in "Pig Pen University", the young man came home. He was welcomed with open arms and a huge party was thrown in his honor. That is a beautiful picture of salvation. It is also a better picture of repentance and restoration of a wayward backslidden Christian. This is not a story of losing salvation then getting it back. At no point in time in the hog trough did the young man cease to be the son of his father. But even more so, it is a picture of rewards. At the party, the older brother got upset that the prodigal got a party and he didn't. The answer of the father is very telling. He said, "Son, all that I have is thine" (verse 31). The younger brother was an heir of his father. When his father died, he was present for the reading of the will. He got nothing because he already got his and wasted it. The older brother was a joint-heir with his father because he received the entire estate.

This concept of rewards for a believer in Jesus Christ is found throughout the New Testament and can be preached from dozens of passages. But none of them make any sense if there is not a venue to pass those rewards on to the children of God. If Jesus does not have a kingdom, there are no cities to reign over and no inheritance for serving the Lord. The greatest motivation a Christian can have is the Judgment Seat of Christ. Service in this life determines rewards when Jesus is on the throne in Jerusalem.

5) To give creation a time of rest
   Isaiah 14:7, Hebrews 4:6-9

God created the physical domain to run on a work / rest cycle. He set the pattern in the first chapter of the Bible when he rested after the six days of creation. God did not need a break. He set an example for his creation that has been ignored and abused. These last 60 centuries have been an endless hornet's nest of sinful activity. God has patiently endured it, but he will soon put his creation in a 1,000 year "time out".

We have a picture of that in the Old Testament with the captivity of the Nation of Israel by Babylon. God sent Nebuchadnezzar to Israel to judge his people, and one of the main reasons is that Israel violated the laws of land sabbath. God commanded Israel to let the land rest every seven years (Leviticus 25:1-7). It was "not good for business" and Israel ignored it. God was patient with them for 490 years, but finally he sent them off into captivity, "To fulfil the word of the LORD by the mouth of Jeremiah, until the land had enjoyed her sabbaths: for as long as she lay desolate she kept sabbath, to fulfil threescore and ten years" (II Chronicles 36:21). One of the purposes of the Millennium is to give the world a thousand year "chill pill" and let his creation rest. Isaiah 14:7 says, "The whole earth is at rest, and is quiet: they break forth into singing." Zechariah 1:11 says, "Behold, all the earth sitteth still, and is at rest."

Hebrews chapter 4 is the "rest" chapter in the New Testament. There are several types of rest mentioned in the chapter, including a rest for the literal physical earth to "slow down and take it easy for a while". Here is how the "rest" of Hebrews 3:17-4:11 breaks down:

The rest of Canaan under Joshua (3:17-19)	Millennial rest (4:6-9)
Salvation rest (4:1-3)	Creation rest picturing salvation rest (4:10)
Creation rest picturing Millennial rest (4:4)	Believer's rest in the promises (4:11)
Canaan rest under Joshua again (4:5)	

Who knows exactly the extent of how the "rest" of the earth will play out, but I suspect the widespread natural disasters that plague our earth today will be put on hold. We will visit this issue later when we cover the details of the Millennium relating to the regeneration of nature.

6) To demonstrate the sin nature of mankind with Satan bound
James 1:14, Psalm 39:5

We have seen many times that there will be natural human beings in physical bodies in this current state who will go alive into the kingdom. They will still have their sin nature contained in their flesh. Right now, we have the added problem of temptation and spiritual attack from Satan. He and all his minions will be chained during the Millennium. There will be no influence of unclean spirits for a thousand years. Yet Jesus will rule with a "rod of iron" which means he will deal with man's sin. Sinful man will have no one to blame but himself. He cannot fall back on, "The devil made me do it." James 1:14 says, "Every man is tempted, when he is drawn away of his own lust, and enticed." We need no help from any outside source to sin. The old joke says, "Lead us not into temptation, for I can find the way myself." During the Millennium, the sin nature of mankind will be on full display.

Psalm 39:5 says, "Every man at his best state is altogether vanity." The kingdom will be man at his best state. He will live in the utopia he has longed for since Adam left the Garden, yet rebellion and sin will be everywhere. We saw earlier that the Sermon on the Mount is the "constitution" for the kingdom. It contains several warnings and penalties for wrongdoing. It will all come directly from the sinful heart of mankind. Man is the only part of God's physical creation that disobeys him. Animals and nature do what God says to do. There is something drastically wrong with man. Sociology tells us that man is basically good and does bad things. The opposite it true. Man is inherently corrupt and occasionally stumbles upon something good. This will become abundantly obvious in the kingdom when Satan is bound and when those who are conformed to the image of Christ reign with him in a perfect society.

John 3:6 says, "That which is born of flesh is flesh." That is obvious, but there is a deeper issue in those words. The flesh nature of man cannot be improved. Once we come out of the womb, we head toward a tomb. The first thing that happens to us is we get spanked on the bottom to get our air moving. We did nothing wrong, yet we get spanked. Man cannot be reformed; he can only be transformed by the new birth and the word of God. We will see it in the Millennium. Unregenerate man will not be happy that he is under the law of God. If a lost person went to heaven, he would not be comfortable there. His own sin would bother him in the perfection. We see a picture of this with our teenagers. They rebel just because they want to. A kid says he is sick and tired of mom and dad telling him what to do, so he joins the army. Now he has a drill sergeant for his mommy. He does that for no other reason than he wants to be his own man. Man will rebel in the kingdom despite perfect conditions simply because it is inbred in his nature.

Romans chapter 7 describes Paul's struggle with his own sin nature. This was the greatest Christian who ever lived, and he could not clean up his own flesh. What makes anyone think they could do better? The perfect kingdom will be such a contrast to sinful man that we will finally be able to see it.

The NATURE of the Millennium – What will it be like?

1) A Theocracy – King Jesus on the throne ruling in absolute power
Revelation 19:16, Jeremiah 23:5-6

Perhaps one of the biggest arguments you can ever get yourself into is the discussion of various forms of government (politics). God will bring it all to a screeching halt instantly when he sets up a theocracy in Jerusalem with his Son as the King. It will be an absolute monarchy with a benevolent dictator on the throne. God's form of government is one man ruling in absolute power according to the laws of God and surrounded by men of like mind and heart toward God ruling with him. They say that power corrupts and absolute power corrupts absolutely, and that is true unless you are Jesus Christ. He is the only one who is man enough to do this the right way. God set kings on the throne of Israel to picture this time, but they were fallible men like the rest of us. Even the ones who did "right in the eyes of the Lord" had plenty of issues. Need I mention David and Bathsheba to remind us? As for Gentile rulers, there have been a tiny handful or two who were "just, ruling in the fear of God" (II Samuel 23:3). But virtually every political ruler in history, no matter the governmental system or their position, is described in Daniel 4:17: "The most High ruleth in the kingdom of men, and giveth it to whomsoever he will, and setteth up over it the <u>basest</u> of men." The vast majority of political rulers over the ages have been men of perverse character. When Jesus returns to reign, he will remove every corrupt politician in history. God has purposed, "Yet have I set my king upon my holy hill of Zion" (Psalm 2:6).

Religion and politics are the two things we are not allowed to talk about because they always cause fights. Every war in history has a religious basis behind it and is a fight to instill whichever political system the combatants think is best: communism, socialism, democracy, Sharia; you name it. But "government of the people, by the people, and for the people" WILL perish from the earth when Jesus returns. In the Millennium there will be no political campaigns. There will be no elections. You will not be inundated with flyers in your mailbox claiming that if you vote for the other guy he will eat your children. Just that alone should make everyone long for Jesus to come back. God will set his King on his throne. His law will be obeyed or else. The word "king" or "kingdom" appears over 3,000 times in the Bible. It is THE subject of the Bible and it is soon to happen. The word "President" appears 5 times; "senate" twice. That tells you what God thinks of our government. In our world, it is necessary to have checks and balances and bodies of civil leaders to keep control of things because we are corrupt. Our system is as good as any and about as good as man can do. But Jesus on the throne is God's desired form of government.

Revelation 19:16 gives his title as King of kings and Lord of lords. Jesus will be the King (capital K) and if anyone wants to reign with him, they will have to be a king (lower case) and reign just the same as he would. You cannot be a "king" if you reign differently than the "King" or a "lord" apart from the "Lord"; they have the same letters. The only way to do that is to be conformed to his image and to rule by his law book. The kingdom will be a righteous perfect King ruling in absolute power with a bunch of kings who are carbon copies of the King running around who can read minds. No crime will go unsolved. In fact, let's say some guy walks into a store all by himself just looking around casing the joint. One of us will show up out of the blue and look him right in the eye and say, "Don't even think about it, pal." Probably all of us have had experience at some level with the robo-call scams that have exploded lately. They have gotten so good at it that it is next to impossible to track them down. The same things happen with identity theft. These slimy scumbags work underground from basements to steal whatever they can. If they put half the effort into a real job, they would make twice the money legally. None of this nonsense will take place in the kingdom. A King who knows all will smoke it out before it happens.

The King will execute judgment and justice as we covered before (Jeremiah 23:5-6). Things will be done RIGHT or not at all. Hebrews 2:2 refers back to the law of Israel in the Old Testament and says, "Every transgression and disobedience received a just recompence of reward." No one got away with anything, and this was with fallible men running the show who could not possibly catch half of what was done. A perfect King who knows all will implement judgment in complete perfection. No dissention will be allowed. In our world, robust dialogue and differing views is healthy as long as it is done in civility. But we have seen that concept be thrown in the dumpster recently. Now, angry riots and mob protests are the preferred method of discourse. That will not be tolerated with a perfect righteous King on the throne. I want to see a protestor scream an F-bomb in the face of Jesus or one of his people in the Millennium.

Isaiah 2:1-5 and Micah 4:1-7 are parallel prophecies of the kingdom. Half of Isaiah 2:4 is carved into the cornerstone of the UN building in New York City: "And they shall beat their swords into plowshares, and their spears into pruninghooks: nation shall not lift up sword against nation, neither shall they learn war any more." Leave it to lost politicians to yank half a verse out of context to further their agenda. The part of the verse they left out says, "And he shall judge among the nations, and shall rebuke many people." The United Nations thinks they can solve the problems of the world by leaving Jesus out of it. No one will beat any swords into plowshares until HE is on the throne in Jerusalem. Don't overlook the next phrase: "And shall rebuke many people." In order for Jesus to rule with the rod of iron, he has to use it regularly. He cannot show mankind how to run a perfect world unless there is some imperfection in it to contrast and demonstrate how it is supposed to operate. Jesus will reign in the midst of his enemies. It will be the golden age of man, but with a "twist" due to the presence of sinful men and women throughout the kingdom. Jesus will rebuke them in righteousness for their sin.

Of course, many would object to even discussing such a rule with the "iron fist". All this sounds like a brutal and oppressive dictatorship where every opposition is silenced and eliminated. But you forget who it is on the throne! You cannot compare the righteousness of Jesus Christ to even the most gracious and benevolent ruler in history. John 1:14 says Jesus is full of "grace AND truth". Yes, he will reign in truth and righteousness with no tolerance for evil. He will ALSO reign in full and perfect grace. God knows human nature and our weaknesses. Psalm 103:14 says, "For he knoweth our frame; he remembereth that we are dust." Romans 5:20 says, "Where sin abounded, grace did much more abound." That applies to Calvary first, but it also applies to the kingdom. Sin will still abound in the Millennium because there will be millions of sinners here. Grace will abound also, and even slightly exceed. James 2:13 says, "Mercy rejoiceth against judgment." God is perfect in BOTH mercy and judgment. He will employ whichever one is necessary to deal with each situation based on the heart of the individual in front of him. Given his choice, he would grant mercy, and in the kingdom, mercy and grace will abound as well.

Every sin will receive a JUST recompense (Hebrews 2:2). It does not say every sin will receive a fierce or brutal recompense. The benevolent dictator on the throne will be BOTH benevolent and in charge. God's matchless grace will be displayed with the same perfection as his judgment. One of the classic examples of this is the famous story of the woman taken in adultery in John 8:1-12. We do not need a long dissertation; most people are familiar with the story. Liberals love to use this story to justify sin. "Jesus forgave the woman in adultery so I can do whatever the H-E-double hockey sticks I want and it is OK and how dare you judge me for it." The woman was set up. If she was "taken in the very act" then a man had to be involved also. Why wasn't he also brought to the Lord? There were TWO sins in this story. The evil wicked heart of the Pharisees tried to entrap Jesus in the law, and a woman gave in to the lust of the flesh. All sin is sin and all sin will be judged in the kingdom. Which sin is worse? Forgiving this woman was just under the larger circumstances when coupled with the grace of our Lord Jesus Christ. The Pharisees received the "greater damnation" (Matthew 23:14) for this and other willful rejection. His condemnation of the Pharisees was also JUST. Jesus did not excuse the sin of the woman and allow her to continue in it. He uttered the famous words, "Go and sin no more." That same type of judgment will be manifest in the Millennial reign. It will be a truly righteous kingdom run by a truly righteous King, and anyone who objects or violates the law will be dealt with. Those who don't like it can go howl at the moon. They might feel better, but it won't get them an ounce of slack.

2) A DUAL Theocracy – The spiritual and physical kingdoms merged
   Revelation 11:15, Obadiah 21

Not only will the Millennium be a righteous kingdom, it will have both physical and spiritual aspects in perfect harmony AND in full view of each other. One of the main problems we have now it that we cannot see what goes on in the "real world" of the spirit. Paul said, "We see through a glass darkly, but then face to face" (I Corinthians 13:12). Revelation 11:15 says, "The kingdoms of this world are become the kingdoms of our Lord, and of his Christ; and he shall reign for ever and ever." I dealt with this earlier in chapter 11. The kingdoms are plural in this verse because the return of Jesus Christ will combine the spiritual kingdom of God and the physical kingdom of heaven so that BOTH of them will be manifest and visible on the earth. They are separated now with rare exceptions. There are cases in the Bible of the "crossover" between the spirit world and the physical world. Jacob wrestled with the angel of the Lord in Genesis 32:24-32. Samson's parents saw the angel of the Lord in Judges 13. Hebrews 13:2 says, "Some have entertained angels unawares." In the kingdom, it won't be "unawares"!

The best picture of this in the Bible is during the 40 day ministry of the Lord after his resurrection. In Luke 24:36-43, Jesus met with the apostles and ate with them. He was in his glorified spiritual form, and they were still in their physical bodies. In John 21, Peter and some of the guys were out fishing when the Lord showed up "out of nowhere". The same thing happened. They sat around a fire and had a fish fry. When the Lord returns, and we come with him, we will have a similar relationship with the people in the kingdom. They will be in natural human bodies, and we will be conformed to the image of the Lord Jesus Christ in glorified bodies (Philippians 3:20-21). Since we will be reigning over cities (Luke 19) we will be relating to each other the same way Jesus did with the disciples after the resurrection.

God stuck an obscure reference to this in one of the Old Testament minor prophets. God loves to "hide" things like this in his Bible right under our noses. The book of Obadiah is a prophecy of Esau the brother of Jacob and his line. It is only one chapter and is a prophecy of the Millennial kingdom. The last verse says, "And saviours shall come up on mount Zion to judge the mount of Esau; and the kingdom shall be the LORD'S" (Obadiah 21). Notice there will be "saviours" (lower case) and it is plural. Jesus is THE Saviour (singular and upper case), but in the kingdom, there will be a bunch of "little Jesus" saviours running around to help him judge the people. A Christian is a "little Christ". In the kingdom the church age saints will reign with him in his physical kingdom.

3) Righteousness and peace
   Isaiah 16:5, Psalm 122:6-9, Psalm 85:7-13

Daniel 9:24 says one of the purposes of Israel is to bring in everlasting righteousness. Until that happens, there can be no peace. Man desperately wants peace. The politicians promise it in every campaign and it only gets worse. John Lennon sang, "All we are saying is give peace a chance." He wanted to implement it through Marxist philosophy which has murdered hundreds of millions of people in its wake. We want peace, but there are too many sinners with free run of the house tearing things up every chance they get. Until Jesus comes to put his foot down (Zechariah 14:4) in righteousness, peace will continue to elude us. Melchizedec is perhaps the most shadowy figure in the Bible. No one can truly identify him for sure. But Hebrews 7:2 says he is first king of righteousness, and after that king of peace. It must be in that order. Psalm 85:10 says, "Righteousness and peace have kissed each other." Again note the order.

The reason the world will be at peace is because a righteous King will be on the throne and he will put up with no nonsense. There is only one prayer in the Bible for "world peace". Psalm 122:6-9 says, "Pray for the peace of Jerusalem: they shall prosper that love thee. Peace be within thy walls, and prosperity within thy palaces. For my brethren and companions' sakes, I will now say, Peace be within thee. Because of the house of the LORD our God I will seek thy good."

The King of peace must be here before that prayer can be realized. Verse 5 right before this prayer says, "For there are set thrones of judgment, the thrones of the house of David." Until that throne is established there will be no peace. Isaiah 16:5 says: "And in mercy shall the throne be established: and he shall sit upon it in truth in the tabernacle of David, judging and seeking judgment and hasting righteousness." We just discussed the United Nations and the twisting of half a verse in Isaiah 2 attempting to bring in world peace. I am looking forward to the time when Jesus puts down all rebellion so it can finally happen.

4) A perfect _Jewish_ society ruled by _Jewish_ societal law
   Isaiah 2:1-5, Psalm 2:6-9, Psalm 110:1-2

We have already covered the "rod of iron" aspect of the kingdom. But we must also understand that it will be Jewish. We get so wrapped up in our own laws and culture that we think the rest of the world lives like us. The Millennial kingdom will NOT be American! When Jesus returns with his rod of iron to smite the nations (Revelation 19:15), one of those nations will be the "good ol' US of A". When Rome was the ruling world Empire, everyone was Roman regardless of their native nationality. Someday soon, a Jewish King will sit on a Jewish throne, and the world will be Jewish. Psalm 110:1-2 says, "The LORD said unto my Lord, Sit thou at my right hand, until I make thine enemies thy footstool. The LORD shall send the rod of thy strength out of Zion: rule thou in the midst of thine enemies." It won't matter what anyone thinks about it. Jesus will rule, and there will be no opposition party.

Psalm 2:6-9 says, "Yet have I set my king upon my holy hill of Zion. I will declare the decree: the LORD hath said unto me, Thou art my Son; this day have I begotten thee. Ask of me, and I shall give thee the heathen for thine inheritance, and the uttermost parts of the earth for thy possession. Thou shalt break them with a rod of iron; thou shalt dash them in pieces like a potter's vessel." This rod of iron is the same one as Revelation 19:15. This King will reign from Zion, not Washington DC or Moscow or Rome. The law will proceed from Zion (Isaiah 2:3), not congress, and there will be no need for continuous sessions to pass more laws. The Bible will be the law book. It is already "settled forever in heaven" (Psalm 119:89), and in the kingdom, it will be settled on earth. There will be no need to "update" it for 1,000 years (and beyond). "The law of the LORD is perfect" (Psalm 19:7). Every case will be judged according to the absolute standard of the word of God.

In order to have a perfect Jewish theocracy and society, their laws will come into affect for all. Please do NOT misunderstand. I think the US Constitution and founding documents are some of the best governing principles ever put to pen by man in 6,000 years of human history. If every nation on earth was governed by those same principles, half the world's problems would be solved overnight. When Jesus returns, he will run those documents through the shredder. His law is much better than ours. We are not just looking for half the world's problems to be solved. Jesus will take care of them ALL.

> "The word that Isaiah the son of Amoz saw concerning Judah and Jerusalem. And it shall come to pass in the last days, that the mountain of the LORD'S house shall be established in the top of the mountains, and shall be exalted above the hills; and all nations shall flow unto it. And many people shall go and say, Come ye, and let us go up to the mountain of the LORD, to the house of the God of Jacob; and he will teach us of his ways, and we will walk in his paths: for out of Zion shall go forth the law, and the word of the LORD from Jerusalem. And he shall judge among the nations, and shall rebuke many people: and they shall beat their swords into plowshares, and their spears into pruninghooks: nation shall not lift up sword against nation, neither shall they learn war any more. O house of Jacob, come ye, and let us walk in the light of the LORD." (Isaiah 2:1-5)

Keep in mind the kingdom will be populated by physical humans in their current natural bodies with a sin nature still very much present. Yet they will "walk in the light of the Lord" (verse 5). Despite our nature, it is possible for people to walk with the Lord. Enoch and Noah did. David did most of his life except for the year he got out of fellowship in the Bathsheba fiasco. The New Testament is filled with admonitions to "walk in the Spirit" (Galatians 5:16) and "walk worthy" (Ephesians 4:1), and dozens more verses like them. Those are written to a believer who is a new creature in Christ, but we all still drag the old man around with us daily. In the kingdom, the law will go forth from Jerusalem and people will be drawn to Jerusalem to learn it so they can walk in it, and a lot of them will succeed. The societal laws of Exodus chapters 21-23 and the book of Deuteronomy will be back in effect. Those laws are foreign to our ears because we are so far removed from a Biblical society that we would not know it if it bit us on the nose.

Again, this will be a Jewish world, so everything will operate by their structure. We have 50 states in the United States; Israel had 12 from the time Joshua conquered the land. Currently there are 193 nations on the earth. In the kingdom, there will be 12 major geo-political Gentile entities governed by the Nation of Israel. Deuteronomy 32:8 says, "When the most High divided to the nations their inheritance, when he separated the sons of Adam, he set the bounds of the people according to the number of the children of Israel." The number of the children of Israel is twelve. Jesus told the apostles that in the kingdom they would "sit upon twelve thrones judging the twelve tribes of Israel" (Matthew 19:28). So each apostle will govern a tribe, who will in turn be linked to one of the Gentile groups. Asher and Zebulon and Gad (etc.) will each be responsible to bring the law of Israel to their assigned Gentile nation under the direction of their assigned apostle. Psalm 2:8 is God the Father speaking to his Son: "Ask of me, and I shall give thee the heathen for thine inheritance, and the uttermost parts of the earth for thy possession." When Jesus comes, he will "inherit" the inhabitants of the earth and he will share that inheritance with his chosen people. Isaiah 42:1-4 says that Jesus will "bring forth judgment to the Gentiles" (verse 1) and "the isles shall wait for his law" (verse 4). Israel's mission will be to take the law of God to the "heathen" Gentiles so they can live like the Jews. That was supposed to be their mission in the Old Testament, but they utterly failed. The Millennium will be their fulfillment.

5) Reinstatement of Jewish feasts and religious observances
Zechariah 14:16-19, II Chronicles chapters 8-9, Ezekiel chapters 40-48

The religious structure of the Nation of Israel in the Old Testament was designed by God to look forward to the time he would be here to reign in their kingdom. Colossians 2:16-17 says the laws and sabbaths are "a shadow of things to come". The Seventh Day Adventists tell us that if we go to church on Sunday we have taken the mark of the beast. They want to drag us back under the law when Jesus took it out of the way on the cross (Colossians 2:14) so we could look forward to its beauty and glory in the kingdom. When Jesus is on the throne in Jerusalem, we will step out of the shadows and into the reality of God's design. The feasts and observances of the Old Testament law are the pictures of the kingdom. If you are "out and about" with your grandkids and want to introduce them to someone, you would not pull out your wallet and show them a picture. Johnny and Susie are right there. The religious celebrations of Israel will finally be fulfilled because the person they "introduce" will be here. They will not just be pictures; they will be the reality of life in a Jewish society.

II Chronicles chapters 8-9 records the beginnings of the reign of Solomon. David was the warrior king who subdued the foreign nations around Israel. He was followed by his son Solomon who ruled over a world in as much total peace as can be accomplished with men running the show. Solomon's reign is the closest thing the world has ever seen to the utopia of the Millennium. Yet it was so far from the true reality of the kingdom of Jesus that Solomon himself will be blown away. These two chapters in Chronicles give one of the clearest Bible pictures of how the kingdom will operate. The entire world will function by these principles. I will briefly detail them here. Watch how this pictures the kingdom.

II Chronicles chapter 8

VS 1-2 – The account begins after Solomon has been the king for 20 years, so it is right in the middle of his reign, at the very zenith. He had finished building the temple and his own house and restored all the cities of Israel regained from Gentile control. The Jews were dwelling safely in their land.

VS 3-6 – Solomon was able to build as he saw fit "throughout all the land of his dominion" (verse 6). We saw earlier the land encompassed a huge area. Verse 3 says he <u>prevailed</u> against the Gentile cities. It does NOT say he warred against them. This is a picture of King Jesus subduing the nations with the rod of iron. Solomon had enemy nations in his domain, but they dared not mess with him.

VS 7-10 – The Gentile nations that were "left" became tributaries and servants. The children of Israel were the rulers over the Gentile nations, just as it will be in the kingdom.

VS 11 – A special place was prepared for the bride of Solomon who was the daughter of Pharaoh, a Gentile. The bride of Christ is a Gentile church with a special place in the kingdom.

VS 12-13 – Sacrifices were offered every day, and special sacrifices were made on the sabbaths and the new moons, which were prescribed under the Mosaic law. In addition, the feasts of the Lord were observed, likely including all of them from Leviticus chapter 23, but more specifically the three main feasts where Israel was to appear before the Lord every year. We covered this in a lot of detail back in Revelation chapter 4 when I laid out the three phases of the harvest. Sacrifices will be reinstated in the Millennial kingdom. Some teachers have had a problem with that. They claim that since the perfect sacrifice was already offered (Jesus) that it would be heresy to go back to the animal sacrifices of the Old Testament again. I understand their issue, and that is a valid point. But there is a detail they are missing in their objection. The Old Testament sacrifices look ahead to the cross, and the Millennial sacrifices look back to the cross and the coming of the Lord in his kingdom. Hold on to this concept for now, and I will get into more detail with it when we cover Ezekiel chapters 40-48 shortly.

VS 14-16 – Before David died he set down an order and structure for the service of the Lord in the kingdom. The priests and the porters and the servants and the singers all had a set "course" in their duties. This order is detailed in I Chronicles chapters 23-29. It is one of those "boring" places in the Bible, yet it is rich with kingdom principles and structure. God is ordered and structured. Solomon set this in order in his kingdom as a picture of the kingdom of Jesus. Then verse 16 says he <u>perfected</u> the house of the Lord. Jesus will make the temple perfect when he arrives and is crowned King.

VS 17-18 – All the glory and riches of the world are for King Jesus.

II Chronicles chapter 9

VS 1-12 – The visit of the Queen of Sheba to Jerusalem is perhaps the greatest picture in the Bible of the Millennium. It is also seen in the parallel passage of I Kings 10:1-13. The most important aspect of the kingdom is for the nations of the world to come to Jerusalem and behold the glory of the King and take his truth back home. Zechariah chapter 8 speaks of this exact same thing in the Millennium. The entire chapter is about the Lord on the throne in his kingdom. It ends in verses 20-23 with the nations coming to Jerusalem to seek the Lord, to learn the law, and to carry it home. Verse 23 tells us the world will become Jewish: "Thus saith the LORD of hosts; In those days it shall come to pass, that ten men shall take hold out of all languages of the nations, even shall take hold of the skirt of him that is a Jew, saying, We will go with you: for we have heard that God is with you."

VS 13-31 – The rest of the chapter of II Chronicles 9 exalts the riches and glory of king Solomon on the throne of Israel, which is the classic type of the glory of Jesus on his throne.

I mentioned a minute ago about the sacrifices in the kingdom and their reinstatement. Ezekiel chapters 40-48 describe the Millennial city in more detail than any other place in the Bible. It would take too long to go through those chapters here. Perhaps another book should be written. But I just want to point out the aspect of those chapters relating to the sacrifices. During the Millennial reign, the animal sacrifices of the law will be back in effect with some minor differences. Those who object to any sacrifices should read these passages: Ezekiel 42:13, 43:18-27, 44:11-16, 44:27-28, 45:14-25, 46:2-8, 46:11-15, 46:20-24. Remember that the entire passage of Ezekiel chapters 40-48 deals with the Millennium. In order to say that there will be NO sacrifices, they will have to edit those verses out of their Bibles. But let me point out one of them to show you the differences in the sacrifices between the law and the kingdom.

The Jewish calendar is lunar, meaning the first day of each month is also the time of the new moon. The initial prescribed sacrifice of the new moon is in Numbers 28:11: "And in the beginnings of your months ye shall offer a burnt offering unto the LORD; two young bullocks, and one ram, seven lambs of the first year without spot." In Ezekiel 46:6, the new moon sacrifice will be one bullock, six lambs and one ram. There were seven lambs in the Old Testament and there will be six in the Millennium. What happened between those two times? Wasn't the Lamb of God offered for our sins? There is your "missing" lamb in Ezekiel. The sacrifices of the kingdom do not go back to the law or replace the cross, they remind the world of the Lamb of God who took away their sins so they could live in this glorious kingdom.

Earlier I covered the seven feasts of Israel from Leviticus chapter 23 when we studied the three raptures. Those feasts will also be back in effect in the Millennium, with a few minor modifications. Any of those differences will be in line with the same concept we just saw with the sacrifices where the true Lamb on the throne will not need to be pictured because he is here physically. The primary feast will be the feast of tabernacles in the fall. This one will commemorate the coming of the Lord to the earth. Zechariah 14:16-19 says every nation must send a delegation to Jerusalem every year to observe the anniversary of the kingdom. Any nation that does not will have the spigot of rain turned off, and if they persist in their rebellion, God will add the plagues to them. Isaiah 60:1-14 gives a blessing to the Gentiles for coming to Jerusalem to see the King. I am sure anyone can come anytime, but there is a special place on God's calendar for the feasts that signify various aspects of God's relationship with man.

There are other times for the world to visit the King in Jerusalem. Isaiah 66:23 says all flesh will come to worship before the Lord in the new moons and sabbaths. The new moon is the first day of the Jewish month and the sabbaths are every week (and a few more), so there will essentially be people coming to see the King just about every day. Then Isaiah 66:24 says, "And they shall go forth, and look upon the carcases of the men that have transgressed against me: for their worm shall not die, neither shall their fire be quenched; and they shall be an abhorring unto all flesh." This is a rather blunt and graphic description of an open crater somewhere on earth of the lake of fire. It will likely be in the area south of the Dead Sea. After a group of people come to Jerusalem to worship the King on the throne, they will take a side trip to this area to get a vivid visual reminder of the consequences of rebellion. "Did you see the glory of the King on the throne, young man?" "Yes, sir, I did." "Now do you see what happens to those who try to rebel against that King?" "Yes, sir, I do." "Now go back home and live as God has designed in his word and remember this." I suspect this will cut down quite a bit on the sin!

Another aspect of Jewish life will be agricultural and financial sabbaths. These are described in Leviticus chapter 25. We think of sabbath as going to church or synagogue on Saturday, but the system of sabbaths extended far beyond just one day a week. God designed the land to rest every seven years. Farmers call it rotating crops. He also designed a financial system that "resets" every 50th year. The Bible clearly supports the concept of work and a fair profit, and sometimes a very large profit. Money is not evil; the love of money is (I Timothy 6:10). God does not condemn people for having money, but for how they use it and their attitudes toward it. Biblical finances are generally merit based. Marxist socialism is as anti-Biblical and evil as anything man has ever devised. College professors shove it down the throats of gullible young unsuspecting idealistic students without telling them how many hundreds of millions of people have been murdered in its implementation. At the same time, God is extremely harsh toward people who abuse and oppress others financially. None of that nonsense will be tolerated in the kingdom.

The reset system of jubilee "levels the playing field" while maintaining the merit-based economy. Psalm 72 is the final song recorded from the library of David's vast musical repertoire. It would be fitting for him to conclude with a Millennial Psalm of glory and praise for his Lord. Verse 4 says, "He shall judge the poor of the people, he shall save the children of the needy, and shall break in pieces the oppressor." Jesus will see to it that there is no economic injustice, and he will do it Biblically. Notice the terms used. Economic equality is NOT economic justice. Psalm 98:9 says, "For he cometh to judge the earth: with righteousness shall he judge the world, and the people with equity." Psalm 99:4 also gives us the same concept, "The king's strength also loveth judgment; thou dost establish equity, thou executest judgment and righteousness in Jacob." Equity is not equality, it is equal justice under the law in line with Biblical principles based on the situation at hand. Besides, there will be no lack and poverty in the kingdom.

6) No preaching – Salvation by obedience to the law
Jeremiah 31:31-34, Zechariah 13:2-3

Hopefully I have been clear about the means of salvation in this commentary. Grace and faith are the key components of salvation in any age including the Millennium. But faith now with just the Bible and faith in the Millennium when Jesus will be visibly and physically manifest cannot be the same. People say, "Seeing is believing!" Not really. I believe Mount Everest exists. I have seen pictures of it. There have been enough other people confirm its existence that it should not really be in doubt. I have a good friend who did missions work in that part of the world, and he has seen it and tells me it is real. I have no reason to doubt his word. But I have never seen Mount Everest personally. I must take what I have been told about it by faith. I do not "believe" that Pike's Peak exists. I KNOW it exists because I have driven to the top of it in my own car. My own eyes have seen Pike's Peak, my own feet have stood on its summit and my own hands have touched the rocks that make up the mountain. Before I did that, I had to believe it was real. I no longer need any "faith" in the existence of a mountain that I have experienced tangibly myself. Seeing is not believing, it is confirming the truth of what has previously been believed.

When Jesus returns to reign, there will be no reason to "preach" about him. I Corinthians 1:21 says, "It pleased God by the foolishness of preaching to save them that believe." When Jesus is here, it will be a different dispensation or "economy". II Corinthians 5:7 says, "For we walk by faith, not by sight." Faith and sight are like stocks and bonds; they move in opposite directions. What has been believed will be seen and confirmed by his presence. Romans 8:24-25 says, "For we are saved by hope: but hope that is seen is not hope: for what a man seeth, why doth he yet hope for? But if we hope for that we see not, then do we with patience wait for it." When Paul said we are saved by hope, it does not mean we "hope we are saved". Hope in the Bible is a sure thing. It is an absolute certainty that we are simply waiting to get at some point. Go back to the Mount Everest example. I have "hope" that it is real, but if I ever get the chance to go Nepal and confirm that "hope" physically and visually, then I will no longer need the "hope" that Mount Everest is real. My faith in Jesus Christ as my Saviour is more real than Mount Everest. Once that faith is confirmed when he is on his throne in Jerusalem, faith will take on a different form.

A great Bible example of this is "Doubting Thomas". You know the story. One of the disciples refused to believe that Jesus had risen from the dead unless he could examine the evidence himself. So Jesus appeared to the group again with Thomas present. He had him physically touch the wounds in his hands and feet. In John 20:27, Jesus said to Thomas, "Be not faithless, but believing." Thomas responded in the next verse with, "My Lord and my God." Until this incident, Thomas was faithless. God's grace was not fully available to him because he had no faith that Jesus was alive. When he SAW it, he moved from faithless to believing. There was some faith after he saw the wounds. Thomas could have seen the risen

146

Lord and touched his scars and walked away saying, "I still do not believe. It is just a hologram. This has been manufactured in a studio as part of a government conspiracy." A crowd gathered at the foot of the cross to ridicule and deride Jesus Christ. Some of them said, "Come down from the cross and we will believe." First, it is a good thing he didn't. We would not be saved if so. But if he had come down from the cross, most if not all of them would have <u>still</u> not believed he was the Son of God. Barabbas looked directly at the Lord Jesus Christ and saw an innocent man take his place in judgment personally. Yet he still did not believe. Thomas physically saw the Lord and exercised some faith. But it was not the same faith we have 2,000 years later. Jesus said that himself in John 20:29, "Thomas, because thou hast seen me, thou hast believed: blessed are they that have not seen, and yet have believed." Both Thomas and church age believers have faith in the risen Saviour. But it is different faith, and the "product" of grace is dispensed differently as a result.

In the Tribulation, the 144,000 Jewish witnesses will <u>see</u> Jesus and believe. They will confirm that belief by going throughout the world preaching the gospel of the kingdom, and if caught, giving their lives for his sake. During the Millennium, the law will go forth from Israel as we have seen, and Jesus and his bride will be here to enforce it. Many will "see" it and believe. Some will see it and rebel out of unbelief and pay the consequences. The grace of salvation will be conferred upon those who by faith see the Lord on the throne and are instructed in his law, then prove that faith by doing what they are told. Obedience to the law will be the evidence that their faith is genuine. It is the difference between my faith that Mount Everest is real and the faith of Sir Edmund Hillary who climbed to its summit.

Jeremiah 31:34 explains why there will be no need for preaching: "And they shall teach no more every man his neighbour, and every man his brother, saying, Know the LORD: for they shall all know me, from the least of them unto the greatest of them, saith the LORD." Prophecy will be "sealed up" at the Second Coming (Daniel 9:24) because the Prophet like unto Moses will be here (Deuteronomy 18:15). Everyone will know him because he will be the world-wide King on the throne. There is no need to preach, "Thus saith the Lord" when the Lord is here to "thus saith" for himself. Jesus will not need a "press secretary". He will communicate directly with everyone personally himself. Zechariah 13:3 prescribes the penalty for preaching in the Millennium. If someone takes it upon himself to try to speak for the Lord, it will be a false prophecy and his parents are charged with carrying out capital punishment against him. That should put the fear of God in both parent and child to let Jesus take care of his own word.

7) Long life spans
Isaiah 65:20, Genesis chapters 5 and 11 (in reverse)

Most skeptics and scholars (generally the same bunch) totally reject the early part of the book of Genesis for a number of reasons, most notably because it "monkeys with" their theory of evolution. If you do not think the pun was intended, you don't know me very well. To them, it is just not possible that people could live to be 900 years old. Surely, primitive man did not know how to count. Yet these would be the same people who would want to try everything we could to get back to that time. Man began in a Garden paradise and is headed toward Armageddon. The course of nature is always DOWN. Things get worse, not better. Are you over 40? Enough said…

In the kingdom, nature will be regenerated. The people of Genesis lived much longer before the flood because they lived in a different world. They had just come out of the perfect environment of Eden. God told Adam he would die "in the day" he ate the forbidden fruit, yet he lived 930 years. That applies two ways. First, Adam died <u>spiritually</u> the very same day he sinned. But there is also the "day system" in the Bible where one day is as a thousand years (II Peter 3:8). Adam did not make it to the end of that "day", but died before it ended. Methuselah is the oldest man in history and he only made it to 969. Sin brought a curse upon the ground (Genesis 3:17). We get sick and die because everything we eat is from the ground that is cursed. You say, "Not everything is grown from the ground. I am on a strict Oreo diet, and there are no Oreo farms." The cookie is made from grains that grow in the ground. The Oreo "stuff" is made from sugar and animal lard, and the animal eats from the ground. Until the flood, the earth was different geologically and the curse and the law of degeneration had just begun. This is not a book on evolution, so we will not delve further. We need to stay with the Millennium study.

The genealogies in Genesis chapter 5 give man about a 900 year life span. In Genesis chapter 11 after the flood, life spans rapidly decreased until we get to the patriarchs of Israel. Abraham died at the age of 175 (Genesis 25:7) "in a good old age and full of years". Based on prior generations, he got shorted about 750 years. Moses made it to 120 (Deuteronomy 34:7), but then he penned the 90th Psalm where he said "the days of our years are threescore and ten". That has held fairly steady since then, with obvious general exceptions based on wars, famines, and conditions of various societies. When Jesus returns and nature is put back to almost like it was in Eden, life spans will revert to that time as well.

Matthew 24:22 says some flesh will be saved for the kingdom. We have seen this verse before. People in natural human bodies will go alive into the Millennium. They will eat from a ground that will be restored to pristine purity. Isaiah 65:20 says, "There shall be no more thence an infant of days, nor an old man that hath not filled his days: for the child shall die an hundred years old; but the sinner being an hundred years old shall be accursed." If someone dies at 100, they will say, "He was just a baby." Even "sinners" will live a long time, even with the curse of sin upon them.

This leads us to another doctrinal picture shown to us by the two witnesses of Revelation 11. Moses died in Deuteronomy 34, and Elijah was taken to heaven in a whirlwind in II Kings 2 without dying. Both will come back in the Tribulation. Moses will die again, and Elijah will die for the first time. Some people will go into the kingdom alive. Others who died in the Tribulation will be raised for the kingdom. No one in a natural body will get a full 1,000 years (Genesis 2:17), so those who begin the Millennium will die at some point during the reign of Christ. Moses pictures the group who die in the Tribulation and in the Millennium both. Elijah pictures the group who only die in the Millennium.

8) Nature regenerated
Isaiah 35:1-2, Ezekiel 36:33-36

When Adam sinned, part of the curse was on the ground. Instead of abundant fruit that grew without any effort, Adam now had to sweat as he tilled the ground to get his food. With the food came "thorns and thistles" (Genesis 3:18). Four thousand years later, they put a crown of thorns on the head of our Saviour. It pictures the payment for the curse on nature. When Jesus returns, the crown of thorns will be replaced by the crown of the King of kings. Isaiah 35:1-2 says, "The wilderness and the solitary place shall be glad for them; and the desert shall rejoice, and blossom as the rose. It shall blossom abundantly, and rejoice even with joy and singing: the glory of Lebanon shall be given unto it, the excellency of Carmel and Sharon, they shall see the glory of the LORD, and the excellency of our God."

Isaiah 51:3 likens this time to the Garden of Eden: "For the LORD shall comfort Zion: he will comfort all her waste places; and he will make her wilderness like Eden, and her desert like the garden of the LORD; joy and gladness shall be found therein, thanksgiving, and the voice of melody." Ezekiel 36:33-36 also says the land in the Millennium will be restored to its pristine beauty like it was in Genesis: "Thus saith the Lord GOD; In the day that I shall have cleansed you from all your iniquities I will also cause you to dwell in the cities, and the wastes shall be builded. And the desolate land shall be tilled, whereas it lay desolate in the sight of all that passed by. And they shall say, This land that was desolate is become like the garden of Eden; and the waste and desolate and ruined cities are become fenced, and are inhabited. Then the heathen that are left round about you shall know that I the LORD build the ruined places, and plant that that was desolate: I the LORD have spoken it, and I will do it."

But it will not be <u>exactly</u> like Eden, because until Adam sinned, the Garden was perfect and there was no sin to contaminate it. During the Millennium, nature will be restored but there will still be sinful men and women here. So it will be close, but not exact. It is quite likely that the weather will be as perfect as it can be. In our part of the country, we get what we call "Indian Summer". It is usually in the fall. If we get an early cold snap and perhaps a freeze in October, it is followed by a few days of simply gorgeous weather. It will be mid to upper 70's, a crystal clear blue sky, a very light breeze and no humidity. You occasionally see days like that in the spring also. I call them "Millennium days". It is absolutely perfect outside. I suspect the weather patterns in the Millennium will be like that all the time. I also suspect that many of the natural disasters that they call "acts of God" like tornadoes, earthquakes and hurricanes will no longer happen. Isaiah 14:7 says the whole earth will be at rest, so why not?

Currently, we deal with constant issues with the weather. It is a never ending battle. We plant a crop a little late because there was too much rain to get out into the field. Then when we need the rain to grow the crop, God shuts heaven and gives us a dust bowl. Then right before harvest there comes a monsoon and ruins the crop. We complain about the weather 350 out of 365 days each year. We try to enjoy our back yard and get eaten alive by mosquitoes. We spray for bugs then get sick from the chemicals.

Have you ever been to Hawaii? It is without a doubt the most beautiful place I have ever been, and God has been good to me to allow me to travel to a lot of places on this globe. Nothing compares to Hawaii. If I lived there, I would be a vegetarian, and not because I don't like meat! The fruits and vegetables in Hawaii are so incredibly good that I would get filled up on them before I could get to the meat. The avocados are the size of softballs and so buttery smooth they melt in your mouth. If you ever get to go, be sure to drive around the island for a while and find one of those farmer's market type places or a roadside stand selling pineapples. They will cut and core it for you on the spot. It is the most incredibly sweet and wonderful thing that will ever grace your taste buds. That is nature under a curse. The produce in the Millennium will make those pineapples taste like dirt. Roses will be as big as basketballs and put out a fragrance unlike anything man has ever experienced. Let's go!!! I get such a kick out of people who give their whole lives to "making this world a better place to live". Don't misunderstand. I am all for doing what you can to brighten the lives of others. I devote my life to that mission through the word of God. But when we have the kingdom in store for us, our passion should be focused on making the NEXT world a better place to live. You get 100 years here at most. You get 1,000 in the kingdom, <u>PLUS</u> eternity!

9) The animal kingdom subdued
Isaiah 11:6-9, Romans 8:19-21

Adam in the Garden had quite the relationship with the animal kingdom. Genesis 2:19 says, "And out of the ground the LORD God formed every beast of the field, and every fowl of the air; and brought them unto Adam to see what he would call them: and whatsoever Adam called every living creature, that was the name thereof." He got to name all the animals. I have often wondered how he came up with names like rhinoceros and aardvark. But look closer at the process. God <u>brought</u> the animals <u>to</u> Adam to name them. It does not say how close they came to him, but it sure looks like he could pet them. If you tried to pet a lion today, what do you suppose might happen? I'm guessing the lion would name you "lunch"!

Adam and Eve were given the trees of the Garden for food (Genesis 2:9, 16-17). Even after they sinned, they still had a plant based diet (Genesis 3:17-18). Nothing more is said of man's diet until Noah. God's instructions to Noah on the ark included the diet in Genesis 6:21: "Take thou unto thee of all food that is eaten, and thou shalt gather it to thee; and it shall be for food for thee, and for them." Noah had the same diet as the animals. Since there were only a few specific animals of each species taken, the animals could not be used for food. All this leads us to the conclusion that both man and animals were vegetarian before the flood. It is not until Genesis 9:3 that any part of God's creation was carnivore: "Every moving thing that liveth shall be meat for you; even as the green herb have I given you all things."

When Jesus returns, the animals will go back to vegetarian. Isaiah 11:6-9 says, "The wolf also shall dwell with the lamb, and the leopard shall lie down with the kid; and the calf and the young lion and the fatling together; and a little child shall lead them. And the cow and the bear shall feed; their young ones shall lie down together: and the lion shall eat straw like the ox. And the sucking child shall play on the hole of the asp, and the weaned child shall put his hand on the cockatrice's den. They shall not hurt nor destroy in all my holy mountain: for the earth shall be full of the knowledge of the LORD, as the waters cover the sea."

Animals eat each other because of the curse of sin. It was not that way in Eden, and the Millennium will revert back to that time. Imagine putting a wolf and a lamb together today. How well would that go for the lamb? It says a child will lead wild animals. I have been asked more times than I can possibly count if there is a "doggie heaven" or if we will have pets. My answer goes back to this passage. No, your deceased pet will not be raised to be reunited with you in heaven. Animals are not a <u>living</u> soul like man (Genesis 2:7). We have all had pets that we have grown very fond of. It's amazing how attached you get to those critters. Growing up, we had dogs all over the place. For years my parents would raise Shelties and sell the pups. They are absolutely the best dogs ever. They are beautiful and smart as a whip, and incredibly loving and gentle around kids. I had my own Sheltie named Lamar. He was my buddy. He got hit by a car and was killed. I was a full grown man in my 30's and I cried like a baby that day. Lamar was just a dog. We took him to the vet and they disposed of the body. He was not a living soul, so I will never see Lamar again but there will be pets in the Millennium. The menagerie will be incredible! Every kind of wild beast will be tamed and available. Animal lovers will be in "hog heaven" to borrow the pun. I have always said that I wanted a white Bengal tiger as a pet in the kingdom. Wouldn't that be awesome! That has to be one of the most majestic and beautiful animals ever created. Imagine walking down the street of one of the cities I hope to reign over (Luke 19:17) with an animal like that by my side. That and a Sheltie on the other side who would not get eaten by the tiger!

Jesus was born in a manger, which is an animal stable. Nativity scenes will usually have several kinds of animals hanging around, which is poetic license since nothing is directly stated in Luke about them. But you know the animal kingdom was at rest when Jesus was around. Just think of Jesus and his disciples out in the wilderness. They would have spent more than one day or night out there. Consider some pride of lions in the area stalking them. Do you suppose they would have any success against the Son of God? Romans 8:19-21 speaks of the animal kingdom during the Millennium: "For the earnest expectation of the creature waiteth for the manifestation of the sons of God. For the creature was made subject to vanity, not willingly, but by reason of him who hath subjected the same in hope, Because the creature itself also shall be delivered from the bondage of corruption into the glorious liberty of the children of God." The animals suffer the results of sin because man brought it on them. That is why they are all afraid of us, and also why some of them would eat you in a New York second if they could. But when Jesus comes back, the "whole earth is at rest" which includes the animals. What a <u>glorious</u> time it will be!

Revelation 20:7-10 – The Final Rebellion of Satan

VS 7 – It has been a while as we made our way through the Millennium, but remember in verse 3 I said I would get into Satan being loosed here in verse 7. Verse 3 says he "<u>must</u> be loosed a little season". For years I would read that and yell, **"<u>NO!!!</u>"** "God, what are you doing?! I know you are always right, but have you lost your mind? DON'T LET HIM OUT!!!" Of course, I didn't really mean it that God had gone crazy, but it always puzzled me why he would let Satan out of the pit, and especially why he would say it <u>must</u> happen. Then it dawned on me. We put our children in "time out" when they do not behave. They tell us to do one minute for each year of their age. So little 4 year old Johnny is acting out his sin nature and we plop his behind in a chair for 4 minutes. His toys are right there ready for him when the time is up. He will cry a little, but he will get over it. After 4 minutes, he gets it at least temporarily and life goes back to its normal dull roar. If that doesn't work, we might use the "board of education" on his backside. It stings a little, but God made a nice soft spot there that can be used to get a child's attention.

150

As they get older, we might take their cell phone or car keys. Rebellion almost seems to be decreed of God for teenagers, but in most cases, they eventually figure out life and at least function as a somewhat responsible adult. But not always. That is when the "long arm of the law" enters the scene and maybe the person will have to be put in "big person's time out" if you follow my drift. We know that many people never get it and either stay there until they die, or go right back in if they are let out. But some finally learn to become at least a little self-responsible after spending some time behind bars. Man is depraved by his nature and can only be truly reformed by faith in Jesus Christ. But most people, even lost people, learn life lessons to some degree by the discipline and punishment they receive. Not Satan. He will be chained for one thousand years (not 4 minutes) in unspeakable torment (not in a prison cell with three squares and cable TV). The instant he is let out, his rebellion goes into warp drive. He is let out to prove that he is unreformable. A Millennium in a lake of fire does NOTHING to get his attention.

VS 8-9 – Another reason Satan is let out is to prove that man is unreformable in his fallen nature also. Mankind is obviously not as bad as Satan, but why even make a comparison like that? This is the law of human collapse that is as absolute as gravity and maybe more so. Man left to himself always falls apart. Given a choice, we will choose wrong most of the time. Let me illustrate. Give a three year old a pair of shoes and tell him to put them on. Statistically, he will get them on the wrong foot 50% of the time. But you KNOW it is actually about 98% in real life. Here is another one. Pick up a two prong plug that has one of the prongs a little bigger than the other for the proper polarization. Without looking, try plugging it in. You are still 98% wrong, aren't you? Man needs no outside help to sin, but by the end of the reign of Jesus Christ, the pent up desire for rebellion is there and Satan taps into it the moment he is let out. Every dispensation ends in apostasy and judgment, and the Millennium is no exception. Even with the Lord on the throne and a perfect utopia for a thousand years, man will still rebel against God.

I just do NOT understand that. I am more puzzled by man's rebellion at the end of the Millennium than I am about Satan being loosed. Everything man has wanted for 6,000 years and has never been able to attain will be given to him on a silver platter. It will be visible in plain sight of all. Society will be as perfect as it can possibly be given man's sin nature still being present. Physical conditions will be almost as perfect as the Garden of Eden. A benevolent King will reign in perfect justice. Every need will be met with no lack. All that will last for 1,000 years, yet there will be millions who will not like it and want to rebel against it. If those people were taken to heaven, they would sit in the corner with a scowl on their face. Someone would ask, "What's wrong?" "It's just TOO perfect here!"

During the Millennium, man's desire for sin will be there but he will be severely restrained from carrying it out. The release of Satan smokes out the rebels and brings sin to a final conclusion just before the Great White Throne Judgment. Let's look at a couple of passages of scripture that cover this. Psalm 66:1-7 is Millennial. ALL lands (verse 1) will sing praise to God and ALL the earth (verse 4) shall worship him. Everyone will be able to "come and see" the works of God (verse 5) because he will be here physically to show us. Twice in the passage it uses the term "terrible" to speak of the works of the Lord on the throne. We see the word and think "bad", but that is not the basic definition of the word. Terrible is "terror-able". God's works are pure and holy and awesome and wonderful (full of wonder) and there is no sin or evil in them. God's works are also able to bring terror to those who rebel against him. That is why enemies will submit themselves to him because of his great power (verse 3). But then there is a warning in verse 7 to the rebellious not to try to exalt themselves. Satan's ultimate goal is to "exalt himself above the stars of God" (Isaiah 14:13). When he is loosed from his prison, he will immediately find that weak spot in man and exploit it for one last attempt to overthrow God. Notice this is at the end of verse 7. At the end of 7,000 years, Satan will be unchained to deceive the nations for one last time.

Look at Psalm 72. This is the final Psalm of David (verse 20), and he wraps up his praise of his Lord with a stirring rendition describing his Millennial reign. Read through the Psalm and note how awesome and glorious that time will be. Yet in the middle of it, he says, "His enemies shall lick the dust" (verse 9).

God told Satan the same thing in Genesis 3:14. After a thousand years of submission to the King, those who "eat dust" because of their rebellion will resent having to do so, and the mastermind behind it will tap into that once he is let out. There are many places in the Old Testament prophets that refer to this. Since the kingdom is the main theme of the Bible, you could find it on almost every page. But let's see one more place just to confirm the mouth of the third witness and move on.

As you continue your studies, you will see this righteous rule of the Lord Jesus Christ and the rebellion of man against it that will ultimately be used by Satan. Isaiah 26:1-11 deals with the Millennium. The Lord is on the throne and righteousness reigns. Verse 10 says that favour will be shown to the wicked, but they will not learn. Again, that is one of the most astounding things in the Bible to me. How can man actually live in this utopia he has longed for, and see it with his eyes and hear it with his ears and STILL not get it? At the end of this passage in verse 11, the fire shall devour them, just as it says in Revelation 20:9.

Verse 8 says the nations will come from the "four quarters of the earth" against Jerusalem. This defines the problem the skeptics have with the "four corners" in Revelation 7:1. It calls these "Gog and Magog". Gog and Magog are the subjects of much prophetic speculation, most of which has a basis in truth. But let's just look at the Bible passages and leave the rest of the speculations to others. Ezekiel 38-39 is the main passage dealing with their judgment and destruction by the Lord. But we need to go back a little to the origins of these groups first, then come back to Ezekiel.

Genesis 10 traces the lineages of the sons of Noah after the flood. Basically, Japheth spread out to the north and west, Ham went south into Africa, and Shem's line went east into the Orient. That was over 4,000 years ago, so obviously by now there has been enough migration and mixing that the three main races are everywhere. But we can still see the general "lay of the land" even to this day. Japheth had seven sons, one of them named Magog. Ezekiel 38:2 defines Gog as "the chief prince of Meshech and Tubal" who are two other sons of Japheth listed in Genesis 10:2. Magog is supposed to come from the Hebrew word which would be transliterated "Rosh". Prophetic teachers have linked "Rosh" to Russia. Meshech is similar to Moscow which is nearly due north of Jerusalem. One of the main cities of Siberia is Tobolsk, which hearkens to Tubal. Other descendants of Japheth have been traced by those who study these things. I will mention a couple lines here, but the genealogical minutia is "above my pay-grade". I spend more time on the practical side of the Bible than these matters, so I will mention here what I have seen in my brief studies and let you take it from here. Gomer is a son of Japheth and has been tied to Germany. Togarmah is one of his grandsons and settled in Turkey. Tarshish is another of Japheth's grandsons. That is the name of the place where Jonah was trying to flee when God called him to preach to Nineveh. If you are going to run away from where God called you, you would run in the opposite direction. Tarshish was a port city in the south of Spain on the other side of Gibraltar. So at least a few of Japheth's descendants can be traced to Europe and Russia. Our passage says Gog and Magog will come against Jerusalem at the end of the Millennium. The speculation is that this will be the base of operations and main area where Satan gathers his rebels for his last ditch kamikaze raid on Jerusalem.

However, we need to "drill down" a little further in the prophecy of Ezekiel chapters 38-39. The passage in Revelation 20 places the destruction of Gog and Magog at the <u>end</u> of the Millennium. Ezekiel places their destruction at Armageddon at the end of the Tribulation a thousand years earlier. The sequence in Ezekiel fits that template. Ezekiel 37 talks about the "dry bones" of Israel and their national restoration in the Tribulation. Then chapters 38-39 deal with the judgment of Gog and Magog. Then chapters 40-48 cover the Millennium. So where does Gog and Magog fit in prophecy? Do they get destroyed <u>before</u> the Millennium at Armageddon, or <u>after</u> the Millennium at the final rebellion? My best answer: YES! I believe there will be a huge army raised from the north against Israel at the end of the Tribulation. They will run into the "buzz saw" of Jesus in the valley of Megiddo northwest of Jerusalem. Then I believe the area will be the seat of the rebellion against the Lord at the end of the Millennium also. Their chances of victory will be even less then. The fire of God will consume them in a nano-second.

So after one thousand years of a perfect righteous kingdom, Satan will be loosed from the bottomless pit to deceive the nations for one last shot at taking the throne. The number will be "as the sand of the sea". With long life spans back in play and a thousand years to work with, man's population will grow by this point rather significantly. They will come from the "breadth of the earth" and encircle Jerusalem. They will likely outnumber the "camp of the saints" by a huge margin. It won't matter. Virtually every battle in the Bible had the same odds. God's people are always in the minority. The judgment will come immediately and completely. "Fire came down from God out of heaven, and devoured them." It will take less time than it took you to read those words.

VS 10 – Satan and all his hordes from the ages, both man and spirit beings, will be cast into a lake of fire for ever and ever. They will go "out of the frying pan into the fire". For ever is a long time. Just in case anyone might think that there will ever be an end, God says, "For ever AND ever". If anyone ever did get to the end of "for ever" (which is not possible) God would add another "ever" to it. They will still know "time" because it says they will be tormented "day and night". People will get completely fed up with the torment and cry out, "Enough, already!" Then they will be reminded that it will never end. How can anyone in their right mind reject the free gift of salvation when that faces them?

Revelation 20:11-15 – The Great White Throne Judgment

Anyone who believes in God realizes that he will someday judge mankind. People get away with things they should not, and others do good things they never get rewarded for. If God is just, he must and he will correct these injustices. The issue of HOW he will do so is the point of contention. Most people have this vision of "St. Peter at the Pearly Gates" as the bouncer of heaven. He has your name and the list of everything you did in life. The good and the bad are weighed against each other. Whichever way he "teeters", you "totter". If you have done "enough good" to offset your bad, you get to go to heaven. If not, then it is off to hell. Catholics add "purgatory" to the list. That is "short time hell" for lack of a better term. It is just like hell, only there will be an end. Once you have sufficiently paid for your own sins, you get paroled and can go to heaven. Never mind that the word or the concept is nowhere to be found in the word of God. God does not grade on the curve. Your judgment is not "You vs You". God is perfect and so is heaven. If he let us in like we are now, it would no longer be perfect. God's standard of judgment is sinless perfection, and that is only found in Jesus Christ. The final judgment is "You vs Jesus". If you can match that standard you get in. If not…

The Great White Throne Judgment is the final judgment of man and angels at the end of the Millennium. It will be the greatest courtroom trial in history. With billions of defendants, it could take a while, but hey, it's not like we have anything else on the schedule. This is the final judgment in a series of seven judgments in the Bible:

1.) The Judgment of Sin at Calvary – II Corinthians 5:21, Galatians 3:13
2.) The Judgment of Believers (chastisement of sons) – I Corinthians 11:31-32
3.) The Judgment Seat of Christ (rewards) – I Corinthians 3:11-15, Romans 14:10-12
4.) The Judgment of Israel in the Tribulation – Ezekiel chapter 5
5.) The Judgment of the Nations – Matthew 25:31-46
6.) The Judgment of Angels – Revelation 20:13, I Corinthians 6:3
7.) The Great White Throne Judgment – Revelation 20:11-15

As a courtroom trial, this judgment will have a very similar "cast of characters" to our courts. God did not copy American jurisprudence; we copied the Bible (as with everything else in life). People have watched law drama shows on television and in the movies for decades, not realizing they are watching their own trial before a holy God.

The Judge: God the Father (Daniel 7:9-14) – Daniel describes a throne with an imposing figure seated on it called "the Ancient of days". Someone "older than days" would have to pre-date Genesis 1:1. The Son of man approaches this person on the throne in verse 13 to receive a kingdom. Revelation 20:12 says the dead will stand before God at this throne, so this has to be God the Father. When the judge enters the courtroom, the bailiff says, "All rise!" The dead, small and great, will <u>stand</u> to be judged.

The Defense Attorney: Jesus Christ (I John 2:1) – Jesus is our "advocate" who pleads our case before the judge. Since the lost have rejected his offer, he cannot defend them. I paid my "retainer" by faith many years ago; what about you? The defense attorney will sit silent in the courtroom unless one of his own is on trial. The lost sinner must defend himself against the charges of sin. In the legal profession they call that "pro-se". There is another expression used in the legal profession: "A man who would choose to defend himself in court has a fool for a client." Don't look for your priest; he has his own sins to worry about. The Pope won't be able to help you; he has more of them than your local priest. Not even Johnny Cochran will be able to get you off. The only attorney who can defend you is the one who died on the cross to pay for your sins. If you have not retained him yet, I would suggest you do so now.

The Bailiff: The Holy Spirit (Romans 1:18-32) – The bailiff has two basic jobs in court: to keep order in case some bozo decides he is above the law, and to read the charges. Everything the Holy Spirit of God does is "decently and in order" (I Corinthians 14:40). The charges are the lists of sins of humanity, and there is an entire book called the Bible which is filled to the brim with a record of them. But the best place to see a summarized and comprehensive list is in Romans 1:18-32. You can read the passage for yourself. There is not ONE item on the list that has the first iota of worth or goodness. Religion and philosophy tell us that man is basically good and does bad things. Read the list again. God begs to differ. Man is inherently evil in every facet of his sinful nature. These "charges" are recorded in the word of God authored by the "bailiff" (II Peter 1:20-21) and will be the basis of judgment against every man.

The Jury: The Church (I Corinthians 6:2-3) – Lost people have quoted the "judge not" verse (Matthew 7:1) against God's people for as long as it has been in print. I think every lost person on earth knows this verse from the womb. The doctor slaps the baby on the rear end, and before he cries he turns around and says, "Judge not, lest ye be judged!" Well, one day we will judge. We do not have the right to sit on the throne and issue the edict of who goes to heaven or hell; that is God's job. That is the true essence of the verse in Matthew. But I Corinthians 6 says we will judge the world AND angels. This will happen at the Great White Throne. As the jury, we will agree with the judge on the verdict because we will have his mind. The same lost people who do not believe the Bible then say, "Oh yeah, who made you judge and jury?" Um, Jesus did. They say, "Who died and left you in charge?" Same answer. Jesus died for my sins and said, "All power is given unto me in heaven and in earth. Go ye therefore…" When we preach his word now, we are not judging. We have been "called for jury duty" but the jury has not yet been fully selected and impaneled until the full body of Christ has been redeemed. Daniel 7:10 alludes to this. It says, "Thousand thousands ministered unto him, and ten thousand times ten thousand stood before him: the judgment was set, and the books were opened." Those who minister to the judge are the jury. Those who stand before him to be judged are the defendants. Notice the ratio is 1 out of 100. Jesus told the parable of the lost sheep in Luke 15:3-7 and used the same ratio. This leads me to surmise that by the time it is "all over" (or just beginning depending on your perspective) that only 1% of humanity will be saved. Jesus said the gate to life is narrow and the gate to hell is wide (Matthew 7:13-14).

The Prosecutor: Satan (Revelation 12:10) – Daniel 7:11 says, "I beheld then because of the voice of the great words which the horn spake." The defense attorney will not speak because he has been rejected. Someone else will "argue" in this court with "great words". Revelation 12:10 says Satan is the "accuser of the brethren". He knows mankind better than we know ourselves. He has all the dirt on every person in history because he was behind all of it. He is the most crooked lawyer ever. His goal is to prosecute as many as possible. So he becomes complicit with every crime and then uses his knowledge of them to ensnare the person that he roped into his crime spree. It is evil genius. In the story of the book of Job, Satan accuses Job before God then inserts himself neck-deep into all his misery. As the sinner attempts his self-defense, Satan will dredge up every foul and evil thing the person did, said, or thought. If Satan is going down, and he is, he is taking as many with him as he can.

The Defendants: Every Lost Person in History (Romans 3:10, 23) – The dead, both small and great, will stand before God to be judged. There is no escape. Job 34:22 says there is no place to hide and our text says "there was found no place for them." All who have ever lived, including the angels who fell, will be lined up for judgment. This could take a while. Grab a seat in the jury and pay attention. If it is allowed, get a Pepsi and some chips. Every shady back room deal in history will be brought into the light of the glory and knowledge of God and be made clear to the assembled Universe. All of the questions of "why did that happen" will be answered. It will be fascinating to watch as the truth will finally be known. Since there is no defense attorney, the sinner will be required to mount his own defense. It will NOT be pretty. Hang on to this and we will walk through the main scenarios and defenses in a moment.

The Gallery (Crowd): The Saved of Other Ages – I Corinthians 6 says the church will judge angels and the world. There are plenty of others who will not be judged like Moses and David and the saints from the Tribulation and Millennium. They are not in the jury but they have already passed one of the previous judgments. Verse 15 in the text says, "Whosoever was <u>not</u> found written in the book of life was cast into the lake of fire." That implies some <u>will</u> be found written in the book of life. The Bible is vague on many of the details of this book of life, but it is clearly the "passport" documentation for salvation or damnation. It has nothing to do with good vs bad. It does not rank people in order of goodness. That is what a lot of people think. We will cover that defense in a moment. It is "in or out" based on <u>LIFE</u>. John 1:4 says, "In him (Jesus) was life." I John 5:12 says, "He that hath the Son hath life; and he that hath not the Son of God hath not life." It is clear. If you have him you are in, if you don't you are out. Look at Isaiah 4:3-4:

> "And it shall come to pass, that he that is left in Zion, and he that remaineth in Jerusalem, shall be called holy, even every one that is written among the living in Jerusalem: When the Lord shall have washed away the filth of the daughters of Zion, and shall have purged the blood of Jerusalem from the midst thereof by the spirit of judgment, and by the spirit of burning."

Those who are written among the living will be welcomed and in attendance for this event. When the roll is called up yonder, I will be there. I received the Son of God as my defense attorney. I have my passport and my papers are in order. Those who cannot produce the "new birth" certificate will be asked to step into another line to prepare their case for judgment.

That is the cast of characters for this trial; now let's go through the likely scenarios of how it will happen. I believe that Romans chapters 1-3 lay out the best information in the Bible for this judgment. Romans was written to explain the doctrines of Christianity, and it begins with getting man "lost" so that he can understand how to be saved. I have already mentioned that Romans 1:18-32 is the section that details the charges against mankind. In the typical courtroom trial, the prosecution presents its case first, then the defense gets their turn. The "defense case" is seen in Romans chapter 2 and the first part of chapter 3. There are five basic defenses given, which are the same five basic excuses people give now for rejecting the offer of salvation. As we walk through these five objections, those of you who have ever tried to tell someone how to be saved will recognize what came back at you from the person you were witnessing to.

The trial will begin with the Judge entering the courtroom. "ALL RISE!" The jury and the gallery will be seated once the Judge has ascended his throne. The Bailiff will read the charges. The Judge will call the defendant sinner to the front and say, "Defend yourself." The prosecutor will bring out a million or more accusations, and the defense attorney will remain silent. The defense will proceed this way.

Defense #1 – I am a good person. I am better than so and so. (Romans 2:1-11) – This is typically the first defense lost people run to. You will hear it said this way, "I never killed anyone..." They use that excuse because it is probably the worst crime a person can commit against another human being. The victim can recover from any other crime (somewhat, to a point) but dead is dead. David murdered Uriah. Moses killed an Egyptian. Paul had Christians arrested and some of them were put to death for their faith. Are those men in heaven? The lost also run to that excuse because they know instinctively deep down inside that it is not true. Your sin caused Jesus to go to the cross. In the movie *The Passion of the Christ*, the only role Mel Gibson had was when Jesus was nailed to the cross. It was Mel's hand holding the nail. He did that by design to demonstrate that his sin was responsible for the death of Jesus Christ. God will remind the sinner of that at this judgment. So even though a lost person never actually pulled the trigger, he still "killed someone". That defense will be denied by the Judge when he looks across the courtroom and sees the scars on the hands and feet of his Son.

The sinner argues, "But I am a good person." God responds with, "There is none righteous, no not one" (Romans 3:10). "But I am better that that guy over there." It doesn't matter. There is no respect of persons with God (Romans 2:11). God does not rank us. He measures us by the perfection of his Son.

Let's just say for sake of argument that God did "grade on the curve". With many hundreds of billions of souls in front of him, suppose God arranged us in order of "goodness" with the godliest of "saints" on his right and Adolph Hitler and Charlie Manson at the end of the line on his left. It would be a big line, but God is big enough to do it. Then God finds the exact point in the "goodness" scale where he draws the line and says to everyone on the right of the line, "Come ye blessed into the kingdom". Then he says to everyone on the left of the dividing point, "Depart from me ye cursed." Can you put that image in your mind? As many as a trillion souls are lined up. The "heaven / hell" mark is drawn somewhere in the middle of it. You are the <u>first</u> guy on the "hell" side of the line. You look at the <u>last</u> guy on the "heaven" side of the line. All secrets are known. You know everything about him. Would there be any difference between you and him with that many people in the line up? Would you not have a perfectly legitimate point to argue? You could honestly say, "Hey, wait a minute, God, I am just as good as him." God then says, "Yeah, you are right, so I will move the heaven / hell line over ONE person." The guy right next to YOU then says, "Hey, wait a minute..." The only JUST thing to do (and God is just) is to move the line to one end or the other. If God judges everyone in history based on the standard of good or bad compared to the guy right next to him, then either everyone goes to heaven or everyone goes to hell.

That is <u>exactly</u> the point of the gospel. "For all have sinned and come short of the glory of God" (Romans 3:23). The line up can be ranked in order of goodness, and to the far extreme "right hand of God" stands his Son, the Lord Jesus Christ. The dividing line between heaven and hell is marked between him and the best human being in history. The gap is HUGE. He that hath the Son hath life. Do you?

Defense #2 – What about the heathen who have never heard? (Romans 2:12-16) – This is one of those theological issues that has been argued for as long as there have been "heathen who have never heard". The rationale goes like this: "If someone in deepest darkest Africa has not heard, God cannot judge him, so therefore God cannot judge me either. Party time!" God can nuke that excuse a hundred ways, but the easiest one is this: Any person who has ever used that excuse <u>has</u> <u>heard</u>!

Truth is truth whether anyone hears it or not. Ignorance of the law is no excuse (Leviticus 5:17). One of those cute little "impossible" questions goes like this: "If a tree falls in the forest and no one hears it, does it make a sound?" The answer to that is so obviously easy that it is almost embarrassing to have to say it. YES, Einstein! The tree created a sound wave when it hit the ground. The sound wave traveled through the forest whether it rattled anyone's ear drums or not. I have had this happen often. I teach something a little different and someone says, "That can't be true! I have never heard that before!" I have heard that exact line dozens of times, and have had people actually leave my church because of it. Question, doctor:

156

Does two plus two equal four? Did two plus two equal four BEFORE you heard it? Since when is the standard of truth measured by the sum total of what YOU have heard? Imagine the first day of class in the first grade. The teacher tells the children that two plus two equals four. In the back of the room, a tiny hand shoots up high in the air. "Yes, Johnny, what is it?" "Teacher, that can't be true. I have never heard that before." "Well, Johnny, that is why you are here in this class!"

Let's run a scenario. There is a tribe in the middle of nowhere. Their ancestors planted a village there hundreds of years ago, and no missionary has been there. They are oblivious to modern life. They have existed for generations with no contact from the outside world. There has never been a page of the Bible in their possession and they have never heard the name of Jesus. Despite our best efforts and modern advancements, there are still places like this on earth. Say there are 500 people in this village. Under the "what about the heathen who have never heard" clause they would be safe (not necessarily saved) because they have never heard. When people die in this tribe, they go to heaven because they never heard. Then a missionary shows up. He brings the gospel to this tribe and they hear about Jesus. Half of them trust the Son of God for their salvation, and half of them do not. BEFORE the missionary got there with the word, 500 souls were destined for heaven. After he arrived, 250 of the souls are now destined for hell. So then why, pray tell, would God ever tell anyone to go preach? Wouldn't the best thing be to keep our mouths shut? Who do you suppose would be more pleased with that "missions strategy", God or Satan?

The Bible answer to this dilemma is in the text. Every human being has the "law written in their hearts". Everyone knows right from wrong to some degree. God will judge people by their own standard. If you went to the "tribe" in our example and stole an item from someone, he would know it was wrong and show that he knew, possibly by cutting off your hand. Romans 2:15 says the "heathen" shows that he knows right from wrong by his thoughts when he sees it happen. When something wrong takes place, you respond in one of two ways. You will accuse or excuse. You will point the finger at the "perp" and say, "That is wrong!" Or you will brush it aside and say, "A little bit won't hurt… boys will be boys… I can stop any time…" or one of the other hundreds of rationalizations you have made all your life. As soon as that thought enters a person's mind (and it WILL), they show that they have the standard of right and wrong embedded in their heart. Based on that standard the person has for himself, God can show him the thousands of times he has violated his own standard. That is enough to declare the person guilty.

Jesus came to "seek and to save that which was lost" (Luke 19:10). The lost are lost. That is why they are lost. That should be elementary, dear Watson. Jesus did not come to leave the lost in their condition so that they would "never hear" and not be accountable. Those who hide behind this excuse will be easily convicted of their rejection of the Lord Jesus Christ at this final judgment.

Defense #3 – I am a Catholic, or Baptist, or some other religion. (Romans 2:17-29) – This is another common objection to the gospel. People want to dump their spiritual relationship off to someone else rather than be personally accountable to God. So they have a priest or a Rabbi or an Imam who is "closer to God" who can act as their agent. The problem with this agent is that he needs one himself and cannot represent you. Religious people are some of the hardest on earth to win to Christ. They are moral and God fearing and have an air of sophistication that makes it very difficult to break through with the plain gospel of Jesus Christ. They say all religions are basically the same and worship the same God and all lead to the same place. That is true. All religions are the same because they are all an attempt by man to gain favor with God by works and ceremonies apart from personal faith in Jesus Christ. All religions do worship the same god (lower case). All religions do lead to the same place: Hell.

In this section, God singles out the Jewish religion, which in case you may not have been paying attention is the only religion that God instituted! This passage tells us that not even God's religion is good enough to get us past our sins. These people "rest in the law" (verse 17) when the law was designed to bring us to the Saviour (Galatians 3:24). But the biggest problem is in verse 20. Religion has a form of knowledge and truth, but not the reality of it. Paul said it later like this, "Having a form of godliness, but denying the power thereof: from such turn away" (II Timothy 3:5). Religion has the outward forms but no substance on the inside. Religion is like cotton candy. It looks pretty and tastes sweet, but as soon as you partake of it, it melts away and leaves you with only a sugar high. God will obliterate this excuse by holding the moral man to his own standard, just like he does with the "heathen" (verses 21-23). He will also find the inner heart that is obscured by all the outward beauty of the pomp and ceremony people hide behind.

Defense #4 – I am an atheist. I don't believe God exists. (Romans 3:1-4a) – This excuse is denied with the shortest answer of any of them. "Let God be true but every man a liar" (Romans 3:3). Right now, the atheist makes his claim because he cannot see God with his physical eyes (although anyone who cannot "see" God is not looking and does not want to look). At the Great White Throne, God will be the Judge seated on the bench. Imagine a person on trial today in the courtroom. He stands in front of the judge and says, "I don't believe you exist." Try that defense the next time you get a speeding ticket. Call me from your jail cell and let me know how it worked out for you.

Defense #5 – It's God's fault. (Romans 3:4b-8) – This is the final defense listed in Romans because it is the "last act of desperation". The language in this passage in Romans is quite "wordy" and it can get your tongue tied and your brain scrambled. The key to the "puzzle" is the end of verse 4 which says, "That thou... mightest overcome when <u>thou</u> art judged." This is a quote from Psalm 51:4. In that passage, David was writing of his repentance for his sin with Bathsheba and the subsequent cover-up and murder of Uriah. The verse says: "Against thee, thee only, have I sinned, and done this evil in thy sight: that thou mightest be justified when thou speakest, and be clear when thou judgest." David acknowledges the right of God to judge and that God is "clear" of any wrongdoing or accusation.

However, many lost people will try to "flip the script" and put God on trial and judge him. They will say, "You could have stopped Adam from sinning, it is your fault." God will answer, "Yes, I could have, but I didn't and instead gave you the provision for it when Jesus died for your sins. Your move."

There are a series of rhetorical questions in these verses from the perspective of the skeptic that can be very confusing. The main reason is that some of these people get "educated beyond their intelligence" and develop philosophical arguments that have no real basis in common sense. I have dealt with a few of these people over the years. They got an educational lobotomy from an institution of higher learning and lost the ability to actually think like normal humans. It is almost impossible to deal with them because as soon as you try to make a valid Biblical point, they wander off into a hypothetical la-la land where there is no reason or rationality.

Verse 5 says, "Our unrighteousness commend(s) the righteousness of God." Verse 7 says, "The truth of God hath more abounded through my lie unto his glory." Then verse 8 says, "Let us do evil that good may come." All those statements have a couple of things in common. First of all, they make no sense whatsoever. If you read those verses and come away confused, that is normal. Secondly, they are all designed to turn the tables on God. Here is essentially what they are saying. "OK, God, I get it. I am a sinner. In fact, I might be one of the worst ones here. But, hey, check this out, God. My sin is so bad that when it is compared to Jesus, it makes him look even better. My lies give more glory to your truth. My unrighteousness makes your righteousness stand out. The more evil I do, the more good you can do to offset it. So in reality, I should be at the head of the class!"

Paul refutes each of these statements with, "God forbid." His basic answer is that if God excuses man because his sin "makes him look better", then God cannot judge the world, and if he does not judge the world, he cannot be just. This final act of desperation turns judgment upside down. It puts the lawgiver on trial and the sinner on the judicial bench.

Those arguments are such twisted perverse thinking that it defies clear logic. But it is the last-ditch effort of the lost to justify themselves. They argue, "God made me this way and being this way makes him look better." In an attempt to worm their way out of their own accountability to God for their own sin, they will try to turn the tables and put God on trial. It won't work. "Whose damnation is just" (Romans 3:8).

While the sinner is making such a futile attempt to defend himself, the prosecutor is hurling all sorts of accusations against him. He has the dirt. Romans 2:16 says God will judge the "secrets of men". All sin and evil will be made manifest (Matthew 10:26, Luke 8:17, Ephesians 5:12-13). One sin is enough to keep a person out of heaven, and the entire trainload for every person will be hauled out by the enemy. Since he knows he is doomed, his only goal is to take down as many others as he can. The sinner does not stand a chance.

But what happens if the prosecutor comes after me? I have just as big a trainload of sins as the next guy, and Satan has the dirt on me as well. So he starts unpacking my baggage. My defense attorney will jump to his feet and yell, "Objection, your honor, I paid for that!" Out comes another accusation. Again my attorney objects. The judgment for all my sins was loaded upon the Lord Jesus Christ at Calvary. I have already passed that judgment when I trusted my defense attorney to pay for my sins, so I cannot be tried again. That is called double jeopardy in our legal system. Should the battle get hot, my attorney could ask to approach the bench. When he gets there, he says, "Hey listen, dad…" I cannot lose!

So concluding the "courtroom trial", we have seen the charges and the prosecution and made it through the defense. Each defense has been utterly destroyed by the Judge. The standard of judgment is the word of God (written) and the Word of God (living). No one comes within light years of the standard. A gavel is now in the hand of the Judge. Romans 3:9-20 declares the verdict. They are all under sin. There is none that doeth good, no not one. No one will pass. Every mouth will be stopped and all the world will be declared guilty before God. The "sea" will give up its dead (Revelation 20:13). This refers to the sea of the Universe which would contain the angelic host of rebels against God. Every man according to his works will be cast into the lake of fire. The final enemy of death will be defeated (I Corinthians 15:26). Sentence will be pronounced: "Depart from me, ye cursed, into everlasting fire, prepared for the devil and his angels" (Matthew 25:41). Hell was not prepared for man. On top of the eternal torment, it will be the loneliest place in the Universe because man will be out of place. Before each lost man departs, he will be forced to confess, "Jesus Christ is Lord, to the glory of God the Father" (Philippians 2:11). Every knee shall bow. Every tongue shall confess. Now or then; it is your choice.

Revelation Chapter 21 – New Jerusalem

Eternity begins in Revelation chapter 21. Most people view heaven as a bunch of winged angels floating around on clouds playing harps. Cartoon images like this are often portrayed, but seldom based on actual truth. In these next two chapters of Revelation, there is a literal tangible physical city with gates and trees and water and other physical things. If all those things are physical, so are the inhabitants of the city.

Revelation 21:1-2 – New Jerusalem Descends From God Out of Heaven

VS 1 – A new heaven and a new earth appear. II Peter chapter 3 describes the Universal purging by fire that will occur at the end of the Millennium. This is likely connected to the fire of God that devours Satan and his enemies in the final rebellion, although there are some differences. The fire of God in Revelation 20:9 devours only the enemies of God, which is followed by the Great White Throne Judgment. Since there is no "time" with God, this event could take as long as he wants. With billions of souls to judge, it could take a while if we view it from the framework of what we know as time. Then we are left to guess about the <u>location</u> of the final judgment. If the heavens and earth are consumed in fire as Peter describes, then <u>where</u> would this occur? That really is not a problem because God is not only transcendent of time but also space. He is outside his creation, so he could have all of us "suspended" in both time and space to conduct this trial. All of this is "sci-fi" (but not fiction). The basic fact is that God will destroy Satan's final army by fire. He will also purge the current physical creation by fire. He will also judge mankind at the final judgment. The <u>order</u> of those three events can be tweaked without doing damage to the text.

The physical purge by fire is described in II Peter 3:10: "But the day of the Lord will come as a thief in the night; in the which the heavens shall pass away with a great noise, and the elements shall melt with fervent heat, the earth also and the works that are therein shall be burned up." Every physical element in existence will be torched and melt. In the next two verses Peter uses the term "dissolved". When we have a fire here, things get reduced to ashes. Elements will undergo a change, but they are not dissolved. The fire purging the Universe is much greater. Evolutionists want us to believe that the Universe began with a "Big Bang". They always have everything exactly 180 degrees opposite of the truth. It will <u>end</u> that way. Then Peter says in verse 13, "Nevertheless we, according to his promise, look for new heavens and a new earth, wherein dwelleth righteousness."

Isaiah 66:22 says God will make a new heavens and a new earth. A side note, but not really: Isaiah has 66 chapters and the Bible has 66 books. There are 39 books in the Old Testament. Isaiah 40:3 introduces John the Baptist, who appears in the 40th book of the Bible and the 3rd chapter. In the 66th chapter of Isaiah and the 22nd verse, an event is mentioned that appears in the 66th book which has 22 chapters. I realize that is only a "coincidence". How did Isaiah know in 700 BC how many books there would be in the Bible and where the main division would be? Back to the point, Isaiah and Peter tell us about the new heavens and new earth and Revelation 21:1 gets us to that point.

The end of verse 1 says, "There was no more sea". This statement is <u>FAR</u> "deeper" (pun intended) than it appears on the surface. This is not referring to a body of water on the earth. There is a river in chapter 22 so there must be a sea for the river to empty into. This is the "deep" we have seen earlier of Genesis 1:2 and Job 38:30. It is the frozen "sea of glass" John saw in Revelation chapter 4. One of the main purposes of this body of water is to separate God from his creation. God is holy and we are sinners. Lucifer led a rebellion and corrupted the angelic host. The "deep" of Genesis 1:2 established a boundary to keep the corruption under the throne of God. Job 26:5-14 describes this. Verse 5 says, "Dead things are formed from <u>under</u> the waters." We are dead in sins (Ephesians 2:1) and Satan is the death angel. Man is <u>under</u> sin (Galatians 3:10) and <u>under</u> a curse (Galatians 3:22). When God gave the law to Moses, he told him to keep the people away from the mount (Exodus 19:10-25). The law separates God from man and keeps man at arm's length because God is holy and we are "dead in sins under the waters".

160

There is another "small" detail (there are no small details in the Bible) that shows this. Genesis 1:1 says, "In the beginning, God created the heaven and the earth." In Revelation 21 when the sea is removed, there is a new heaven and earth. In both places, "heaven" is in the singular. In much of the rest of the Bible, the "heavens" (plural) are mentioned, and we have seen that there are three of them according to Psalm 148. In the original creation, heaven was singular because there was no division. God did not need nor want any separation from his creation because he made it perfect.

Then Lucifer reared his ugly head. The second day of creation is unique. It is the only day of the six where the phrase "God saw that it was good" does not appear. On the second day, God made a firmament (or an expanse of space) with a body of water at the top and waters below. We call that firmament "outer space", and it is the domain of Satan and his demonic hordes. There is a division between the throne of God and the firmament, and it is why that area was not labeled "good". Satan patrols the second heaven and man is confined to earth under it. Psalm 8:5 says man is "a little lower than the angels". This applies to both our location in the cosmos as well as our status as beings. II Peter 2:11 says angels are greater in power and might than humans, and we surely know that. Both man and angels are "under" God in power and might, and also in their general location in God's creation. But when New Jerusalem comes down from God out of heaven, the separation will end. Right now, all things are put under the feet of the Lord Jesus Christ. But in eternity future, God will be "all in all" with no division (I Corinthians 15:27-28).

Let's get one more look at this from a different perspective. Consider the baptism of Jesus Christ. John initially objected, and who wouldn't with what he knew about Jesus and himself. But Jesus said, "Let's do this to fulfil all righteousness." It was an example for us to follow for believer's baptism, but it was more than that. Jesus as our example in baptism is truly valid, but the full scope of what he manifested in his baptism cannot apply to us. We get baptized as a picture of our identification with the death, burial and resurrection of Christ. It signifies that we are a follower of Christ. But Jesus did not get baptized for that same reason. Jesus did not manifest a desire to follow himself in his baptism. His willingness to humble himself and submit to the plan of God is our example, and his manifestation of his own coming death, burial and resurrection is seen in his baptism.

But take a trip with me for a minute to the throne of God. The Father, the Son, and the Spirit are all there, and the plan of God for the Lamb slain from the foundation of the world (Revelation 13:8) has reached its time. Under the throne are dead things to be redeemed. The sinless Son of God is the only one who can do it, so he lays aside his glory and descends through a body of water separating God from his creation. He lives a sinless life, dies on a cross to redeem those who are under sin, and travels back through that body of water to be seated at the right hand of the Father. It is another picture of baptism. Jesus was baptized here to manifest his submission to the will of the Father to redeem his creation. But Jesus was "baptized" from the view at the throne to manifest his deity. That is why when he was baptized here, the heavens opened, a dove appeared (the Holy Spirit), and the voice of the Father confirmed the beloved Son in whom he was well pleased. That part of the baptism of Jesus was unique. No dove or voice happened when I got baptized. When Jesus paid the sin debt, he came through water and went back through water so that someday that water separation could be removed and we could be "all in all" with our God.

VS 2 – New Jerusalem comes down from God out of heaven as a bride. The same description is given in verses 9-10 and it says the city is the bride of Christ. The Lamb's wife is the body of Christ comprised of people. A city is a structure but it is far more a people. Paul went into the city of Antioch of Pisidia on his first mission trip and preached in the synagogue. Acts 13:44 says, "The next sabbath day came almost the whole city together to hear the word of God." The buildings stayed put. The city is the people just as the church is the people. New Jerusalem is the eternal base of operation of the church. It is our home. In that home are "many mansions" (John 14:2) as we will see shortly. The new earth will be for the Jews to fulfil the promise to Abraham. The new heavens will be populated by the Gentiles. New Jerusalem will be the capitol of the Universe and the home of the bride. All three of those are literal physical places.

161

There is an Old Testament picture of this in Genesis chapter 24. It is a lengthy chapter, so let me briefly summarize the story. Abraham (type of the Father) sends his servant Eliezer (type of the Spirit) to find a bride (type of the church) for his son Isaac (type of Christ). In verses 57-58 Rebekah decides to go to be married to Isaac sight unseen, a picture of faith. Then the servant takes her and sets out on a journey to be united to Isaac in marriage. That pictures the Christian life of the believer. In verse 61 it says the servant took Rebekah and went his way. The job of the Christian in this life is to go HIS way, not yours. When they arrived back home, verse 66 says the servant told Isaac all things that HE had done. That is a picture of the Judgment Seat of Christ. The "report" will be what the Holy Spirit has done in your life more than it will be of what you have done. Notice that is in verse 66. I know this is only a "coincidence". The 66 books are the standard of judgment for the lost as well as the saved. The Judgment Seat of Christ will be a record of what the Holy Spirit did through the word of God and how well we allowed those things to work in our lives during our journey "home" to marry our "Isaac". Then when the "66" are completed and the final fulfillment of everything in the "66" is realized, we will move in to a "tent" with Isaac (in verse 67) to become his wife. The weird part of verse 67 is that it was his mother Sarah's tent. Who takes their bride to the "honeymoon suite" at mom's house? But every detail of the Bible is significant. Galatians 4:26 says, "Jerusalem which is above is free, which is the mother of us all." New Jerusalem is our mother's tent where we will live eternally with our Lord and Saviour.

Revelation 21:3-8 – God Wipes Away All Tears

This is the "practical" section of the discussion of New Jerusalem. It deals mostly with our relationship with God during eternity and how sweet it will be. There is obviously plenty of doctrine in this passage, but the main focus is a nice tall cold glass of the sincere milk of the word (I Peter 2:2). Drink heartily!

VS 3 – God will dwell with man. The term "tabernacle" is used by design to tie in to the tabernacle of the Nation of Israel in the wilderness. This simple "box" pictured the presence of God for Israel. Exodus chapters 25-40 give the details of the tabernacle, and it is one of the most "boring" parts of the Bible. But a study of the tabernacle is one of the most incredibly fascinating studies a person can make. There are so many intricate details that picture our relationship with God that entire books have been written about it. I preached a series on it in my church many years ago. It covered 20 messages and there were a lot more things I could have taught about it. The Holy of Holies was the presence of God in the wilderness, and in eternity God will tabernacle with man and we will be with him forever. Ezekiel 37:21-28 is a millennial passage, but it blends into eternity. In verse 27, God promises his tabernacle among men, and several times in the passage he says it will be forever, everlasting, and for evermore. This is what God designed from the beginning. Adam and Eve were in a perfect Garden paradise with no sin, sickness, or death, and God dwelt with them and walked with them every day. Eternity restores that relationship.

VS 4-5 – This is the second time God wipes away tears. In chapter 7, the tears of Israel are wiped away, and here, "All tears forever over in God's eternal day" (to quote one of my favorite hymns). Along with the tears, God will eliminate death, sorrow, crying and pain. We will never hurt again physically or mentally or in any way. The only "death" will be that all the former things will pass away. There was an old TV commercial with a bunch of guys out fishing sitting on the dock drinking beer and the tag line said, "Man, it doesn't get any better than this!" For a lost man, that is true. Things like that are the only "heaven" he will ever see. For us, it doesn't get any worse. This life will be the only "hell" we ever experience, and no matter what the very best day of your life was, eternity with Jesus will exceed it to the nth power. And by the way, "These words are true and faithful." They are not symbolic and figurative. Remember Revelation 19:11 says the names of Jesus include "Faithful and True". These words are as true as the very nature of the one who rose from the dead. They are as real as Jesus is real. These words are just as alive as Jesus is at the right hand of the Father. If you know Jesus as your Saviour, the worst thing that can happen to you is that you can die and go to heaven, and when we all get there, the effects of sin will be known no more.

VS 6 – The Alpha and Omega is mentioned again, which refers us back to Revelation 1:8. We have come full circle. God's original design was perfect, and he intends for it to remain perfect after the issue of sin has been completely dealt with. Those who thirst for the right things (Matthew 5:6) will be filled as they come to the fountain of the water of life FREELY. That is the word Eve left out in Genesis 3 as she fell into sin, and now it is back in all of its glory. Note that this is eternity future where everything is perfect and all sorrow and pain are put away, yet there are still "thirsty" people. Hang on to this concept. We will visit it in Revelation chapter 22 when we cover the tree of life.

VS 7 – An inheritance is mentioned again, and it seems to differ slightly from the millennial inheritance that we have already discussed. There is clearly a "just and equal" inheritance in the kingdom based upon our service to the Lord Jesus Christ in this life. But this verse says we will "inherit all things". I am once again faced with a huge "I don't know" about this inheritance. I cannot fully grasp this concept, but I can at least understand it to some degree. Tears are not all wiped away until the END of the Millennium. In the kingdom, there will still be sorrow and lack to some degree. Christians who served their flesh their whole lives will still be saved, still be in glorified bodies conformed to the image of Jesus Christ, and they will be in a perfect kingdom. Yet they will be "on the sidelines" to a degree. Some will have a greater position than others. Pastors who built their kingdoms and empires here in this life will be relegated to second hand positions in the kingdom. Unfortunately, too many of them are like that. The power of the position makes them develop the "rock star" persona, and they compromise the truth in favor of huge assemblies and the money that goes along with it. Praise God when he grows a congregation, and any pastor should never be satisfied with "us four and no more". But our mission is to build the kingdom of God, not the ministry of our organizations. Then many believers do nothing with their spiritual life other than an occasional church attendance. They think their sole contribution to the work of God is to sit and listen. They do God the "favor" of watching others do the work. Revelation 16:15 alludes to this when it talks about those who walk naked and in shame. So the Millennial inheritance will be quite different than we think. The TRUE servants of God as he sees them will be exalted, and others will be abased.

But then we get to eternity. Those who overcome will inherit ALL things. All saved people are included in this. God will be our God and we will be his sons. Once again we see the full cycle complete. There were sons of God in eternity past who praised God on the day of creation (Job 38:7). One third of them were led astray in the rebellion of Satan (Revelation 12:4). In eternity, sons of God will praise God for his glory. The "cadre" will be complete again. This is one of the basic themes of the Bible. God makes things perfect. His creation steps in and messes it up. Then God restores it to its perfect condition. As it relates to the sons of God, the church will replace the 1/3 of the angels who fell. Jesus alluded to this in Matthew 22:30 when he said we would be "like the angels of God in heaven". This can also be seen by tracing the term "son (or sons) of God" through the Bible. There are only four of them in the Bible. Jesus is obviously the first consideration. Adam is also called "THE son of God" in Luke 3:38. Then there are the angels. They are called sons of God in the Old Testament. In the New Testament, the term "sons of God" refers to born again believers in the church age. Adam and Jesus have a connection to each other, and the sons of God in the New Testament are connected to the sons of God in the Old Testament.

A son bears the image of his father, and Jesus did not just bear the image of the Father, he IS the express image of the Father (Hebrews 1:3). The angels were created to bear the image of God, because when God creates, he uses himself as the pattern. Adam was created in the image of God (Genesis 1:26-28), which must be defined further. Almost everyone uses the terminology that man is made in the image of God, which is technically incorrect. The tense of the verb is vitally important. Man WAS made in the image of God, but that image was marred by sin. Fallen man does NOT reflect the essence of God. Adam had sons in "his own image" after his fall (Genesis 5:3). When a person receives Jesus as his Saviour, he is "renewed in knowledge after the image of him that created him" (Colossians 3:10). Lost man bears the image of his father Adam. At salvation, the Holy Spirit regenerates the inner man to bear the image of God. In eternity, we will not only bear that image spiritually, but physically as well.

Adam lost the image of God when he sinned. Jesus came and defeated sin so that the image of God could be restored in man. That is why Jesus is called the "last Adam" in I Corinthians 15:45, and it is also why Adam and Jesus are compared and contrasted in Romans chapter 5. Stay with me. Do not take this the wrong way. Jesus "replaced" Adam. Jesus did NOT replace Adam because he was eternally existent as God and created Adam. But in the context of time and humanity, Jesus as a man came after Adam. Jesus reversed what Adam did 4,000 years after he did it, so from our time-bound perspective, he is the "last Adam". That is the relationship between Adam and Jesus we need to see relating to the sons of God.

That leaves the angels and the church age saints as the other sons of God in the Bible, and they are related in similar manner. We replace the 1/3 of the angels who fell in the rebellion of Lucifer. Remember, God makes things perfect. His original angelic host was perfect, and when we get to eternity, God will have restored it again to its original form and number. In eternity, those who received Jesus Christ as Saviour will "shine as the brightness of the firmament... and as the stars for ever and ever" (Daniel 12:3). Jesus referred to this verse in the parables when he said, "Then shall the righteous shine forth as the sun in the kingdom of their Father" (Matthew 13:43). If you will recall, stars are a type of angels. In eternity, we will shine as the stars because we will have replaced the "stars" who fell in the rebellion of Lucifer.

With all that support doctrine, let's go back to the original point that led us down this path: the inheritance of the Millennium compared to the inheritance of eternity. Millennial inheritance is based on service to the King during this life and carries a clear inference of lack, loss, tears, and shame for those believers who served themselves instead of Jesus Christ. Eternal inheritance carries none of the negatives. Every believer will inherit ALL things. Yet STILL there will be various levels of inheritance. Paul alluded to this in I Corinthians 15:41 when he said, "One star differeth from another star in glory." In other words, when it is all "over" (or beginning), every person saved in any age and dispensation will have the full glory of God and no lack of any sort, YET, some will have more. I cannot understand that, but the Bible is clear. Some Major League baseball players are better than others, but anyone who has ever donned the uniform is a star. Some stars shine brighter but they are all stars. Our sun is actually one of the smaller stars in the Universe, yet it provides life giving energy and light and heat. It is so intense that if anything got close to it, the power of gravity and the heat of the ball of gas would incinerate it into vapor. Again, I do not know how to explain this. I just know that Paul and Martin Luther and D. L. Moody and William Carey will shine brighter than I will, and I might shine brighter than some others, yet every one of us will shine with the glory of God with no lack in any aspect. When you figure that out, let me know!

VS 8 – The second death is mentioned again in the lake of fire and brimstone "prepared for the devil and his angels" (Matthew 25:41). Man was never designed nor destined for hell, but unfortunately, billions of souls will spend eternity in unimaginable suffering for their rejection of the simple truth of the gospel. The description of the "second death" speaks of eternal separation from God. The basic definition of death is a separation. In the first death, the soul is separated from the body (Genesis 35:18). The second death separates the eternal soul from God. It is "always dying yet never dead". Death does not end the existence of the person because man is a living soul (Genesis 2:7).

In one of the many arguments Jesus had with the religious scholars of his day, he spoke of the God of Abraham, Isaac and Jacob, and said, "God is not the God of the dead, but of the living" (Matthew 22:32). Those men were still very much alive even though their bodies had been dead for centuries. A lost person does not cease to exist at death. He is separated from his body and then separated from God in hell. Jesus confirmed this with the story of the rich man and Lazarus in Luke 16:19-31. The question has often been asked about our loved ones who were not saved. How will we reconcile the knowledge of lost friends and family in hell with all tears being wiped away? As sons of God conformed to the image of Jesus Christ, we will have his mind. We will see things the way God sees them. We will fully understand that every person had many hundreds or thousands of chances to receive Christ and did not. It sounds callous, but it is not. God's grace is unfathomable and his judgment is sure and holy, and we will see it in that light.

164

Revelation 21:9-27 – New Jerusalem

Now we have reached the passage that describes the city of New Jerusalem in all of its glory and detail. This will be the "Capitol of the Universe" for all of eternity where the Lord will sit on his throne and his people will serve him. It is the home of the bride (church), as we have already covered, and the base of operations for the expansion of the kingdom and glory of God forever.

VS 9-11 – New Jerusalem is the city of the Lamb's wife. Of note in these verses is the "great and high mountain" mentioned. John was transported spiritually to this vantage point to see this city descend from God out of heaven, but I believe there is more to it than simply the location of his vision. Mountains play a very significant role in the Bible. Mountains are mentioned in some manner about 600 times, and many of the key events of history occurred on a mountain: Isaac was sacrificed, God appeared to Moses at the burning bush, Israel got the law, Jesus preached his most famous sermon, and Jesus was transfigured, just to name a few. Then there is the reference to Mount Zion as the location of the King and his throne in the Millennial reign. All of this leads me to the conclusion that New Jerusalem itself is a "mountain" that will complete the "mountain" of the Universe when it descends from God out of heaven.

Verse 16 says the length, breadth and height of the city are equal. That could be a description of a cube, or it could also be a pyramid with the "center pole" being 1500 miles high. Either one will fit the text, but I tend to see it as a cube because there is an entry point from earth into New Jerusalem in verses 24-27. I am getting a little ahead of myself, but those verses tell us the nations of the earth will bring their glory into the city through the gates. So allow me to run with this to give you my opinion on the structure of New Jerusalem and its ultimate role in the eternal plan of God.

I mentioned a minute ago about the heaven (singular) and earth of Genesis 1:1 and Revelation 21:1 and how there is no separation between God's creation and his throne in those passages. I also referenced Job chapter 26, which contains more information about the structure of the Universe. Verses 8-10 describe how the waters "holdeth back the face of his throne", which we have already seen as the separation. Then Job 26:7 says, "He stretcheth out the north over the empty place, and hangeth the earth upon nothing." The "north" is True North straight up over our heads, and not the home of Mr. and Mrs. Claus. There is an empty place at the top of the Universe. The earth used to be in that place before the rebellion of Satan, but it was knocked out of its place by the Universal flood of II Peter 3:5-6. When the new heaven and new earth are created, the new earth will be back in its original location. As New Jerusalem comes down from God out of heaven, it will "rest" at the top of the Universe to complete the "mountain" or pyramid. If New Jerusalem is a cube, it will come "point down" to touch at Jerusalem on earth for its entry point. If it is point down, then it will also be "point up" and form the pyramid shape as it comes down and sets in place. If New Jerusalem meets up with a location on earth for entry, then the earth would be toward the "top" of the Universe in the "north" of God's creation.

There are several places in the Bible where this is alluded to. Psalm 75:6-7 says, "For promotion cometh neither from the east, nor from the west, nor from the south. But God is the judge: he putteth down one, and setteth up another." This does not look like anything on the surface until you note the directions given in the passage. East, west and south are mentioned, but not north; in fact, "God is the judge" is in the place where the north would logically appear. It says judgment comes neither from the east, nor the west, nor the south, but from God. That would place God's throne above, which is only logical. In Stephen's message in Acts chapter 7, he quoted Isaiah 66:1: "The heaven is my throne, and the earth is my footstool." This places the earth at the bottom for now. Following that same line of imagery, we can see another clear picture of the heavens through the vesture that Jesus had at his crucifixion. This will take a little while and several passages, so bear with me.

Hebrews 1:10-12 says, "And, Thou, Lord, in the beginning hast laid the foundation of the earth; and the heavens are the works of thine hands: They shall perish; but thou remainest; and they all shall wax old as doth a garment; And as a vesture shalt thou fold them up, and they shall be changed: but thou art the same and thy years shall not fail." This is a quote from Psalm 102 that says the heavens are like a vesture or garment. Jesus wore a vesture, and it is described in John 19:23-24:

> "Then the soldiers, when they had crucified Jesus, took his garments, and made four parts, to every soldier a part; and also his coat: now the coat was without seam, woven from the top throughout. They said therefore among themselves, Let us not rend it, but cast lots for it, whose it shall be: that the scripture might be fulfilled, which saith, They parted my raiment among them, and for my vesture they did cast lots. These things therefore the soldiers did."

It seems very odd that God would stop to take time to give details about this vesture at this point in the story of the crucifixion of his Son. It would be like reporting on a house fire and mentioning the color of the shoes worn by the firemen. That detail would be totally meaningless. But nothing in the Bible is by accident. Since the Universe is likened to the vesture of Jesus, there must be a significant reason for the detail that it was one piece woven from the top down. This garment was like a "poncho". It had a hole in the top for the head to stick out, and draped down covering the body. Ephesians 1:20-23 says, "Which he wrought in Christ, when he raised him from the dead, and set him at his own right hand in the heavenly places, Far above all principality, and power, and might, and dominion, and every name that is named, not only in this world, but also in that which is to come: And hath put all things under his feet, and gave him to be the head over all things to the church, Which is his body, the fulness of him that filleth all in all."

If heaven is the throne of God where the "head" is seated at the right hand of the Father, and the body fills "all in all", and the earth is at the footstool under his feet, we have a description of the Universe in this poncho or vesture of the crucifixion. At some point, God will "fold them up" and make a new heaven and a new earth wherein dwelleth righteousness (II Peter 3:10-13). Then the "head" will come down in the form of a city from God out of heaven to complete the structure. Psalm 118:22 says of Jesus, "The stone which the builders refused is become the head stone of the corner." Jesus quoted this verse more than once to prove his deity. There is only one structure that has a headstone which is also a corner stone, and that is a pyramid. Jesus is the chief corner stone (Ephesians 2:20, I Peter 2:6) which is the top one. The other four corner stones on a pyramid are not unique or "chief". Psalm 48:1-2 says, "Great is the LORD, and greatly to be praised in the city of our God, in the mountain of his holiness. Beautiful for situation, the joy of the whole earth, is mount Zion, on the sides of the north, the city of the great King." This verse speaks of Jerusalem on the earth, and it also refers to New Jerusalem in eternity. Satan desired to gain the "sides of the north" (Isaiah 14:13) and replace God, and that is more than simply reigning in Jerusalem. He wants to take over the entire Universe. If this city only has sides in its north, it is a pyramid shape.

Revelation 21:2 says the city will come down from God and verse 10 says it will descend out of heaven. Obviously implied in that is that it will stop at some point. It will not descend forever; the city comes down to complete the structure. The vesture (poncho) of Jesus had a hole in the top. New Jerusalem will come down from God out of heaven to fill that hole and the Universe will then be complete. Verse 11 says the city will have light emanating from it of the glory of God that is so pure and brilliant that it will be clear even though it is the color of jasper (greenish). Don't ask me to explain that, let's just go see it!

VS 12-14 – The gates and the walls are described. The gates are named for the twelve tribes of Israel. The walls of this city are built upon a foundation of the apostles, and Ephesians 2:20 says the church is built upon that same foundation. This is more evidence of New Jerusalem being the city of the bride. If Peter is at the "Pearly Gates" then he has to be in twelve places at one time, which I suppose would be possible once we are conformed to Christ, but what about the other eleven guys? Besides, verse 12 says there will be an angel posted at each gate, not Peter.

166

VS 15-17 – The dimensions of the city and the walls are given. The walls are 144 cubits (VS 17), and it does not say if that is the height or the thickness, so it could be both. A cubit is roughly a foot and a half, so this wall will be 216 feet high (72 yards). Let's see someone try to scale that or pole-vault himself in without coming through one of the gates. The city itself will be twelve thousand furlongs on each side in all three dimensions (height, width, and length). We have already seen the "cube" shape, now we get the size. A furlong is about 1/8 of a mile, which would make New Jerusalem roughly 1,500 miles cubed. That would be over half the size of the United States in two dimensions, then the same height also. I have always been kind of a "numbers guy", so when I see things like this in the Bible, I like to run the numbers and put it into perspective. New Jerusalem will be roughly 3.5 billion cubic miles. My brother is also a numbers geek. Of course, this is all purely speculative, but he calculated mansions of 1.6 billion square feet each. That is about 8 square miles! He even allowed plenty of space for golf courses and baseball fields, which WILL be in heaven! Regardless of the actual size, the most magnificent palaces on earth today are a guard shack or a storage shed compared to our mansions in New Jerusalem.

Jesus said in John 14:1-2, "In my Father's house are many <u>mansions</u>." The new Bibles are squeamish about that, so they try to help us with other terms. The NIV and ESV both say these are only "rooms". I guess when we get to heaven, Jesus will check us in to the local Motel 6. The New World Translation (JW) calls them "abodes". Yeah, and so is a tent. The NASV says "dwelling places". People in third world countries dwell in a lean-to made out of a few sticks and a piece of tin. The Living Bible says there are many "homes". Get ready to be in a nursing home when you finally arrive in New Jerusalem. I know God has a sense of humor. I suspect that when (if?) some of these Bible revisors get there, God will lead them past all the incredibly glorious mansions on the streets of gold to a corner alley and show them their "room". "But, Lord, what about all those mansions? Is this all I get?" "Well, Dr. Flapjaw, you said they were only rooms, so here you are." A mansion can only mean one thing: a huge sprawling mansion! The old gospel hymn says it best:

> "I've got a mansion just over the hilltop
> In that bright land where we'll never grow old
> And someday yonder we'll never more wander
> But walk on streets that are purest gold!"

VS 18-20 – The construction of the city is given. The dominant material is gold; even the streets are paved with it (verse 21). This gold is so pure that it is transparent. Again I have no concept of that and neither does anyone else. I can only say, "Let's go!" Down here, we count gold as perhaps the most precious metal in existence. But what do we actually DO with gold other than look at it? I am sure there are a few applications for gold, but probably about 99% of the mined gold today either sits in bank vaults or hangs around someone's neck or wraps around their finger. It is valuable to us simply because we say it is, and we do so based on the fact that it is pretty to look at. God paves the streets of New Jerusalem with it. Gold is dirt in heaven, and we fight wars over it here. It illustrates the complete and total lack of understanding of the value of items in God's sight. One soul is worth more than the combined assets of the world (Matthew 16:26). Yet we will ignore a soul to gain a piece of gold, and many millions of lives and souls have been lost fighting over it. The foundations of the wall begin with jasper stone (verse 19) and then build upward through several other very precious stones. We see a house made of stone and think it looks nice, and it does, but imagine one built out of the gem stones you would give to your wife. How expensive would that be? Don't worry; God is not on a budget to build his wife's home.

The stones of the foundation are in twelve layers beginning with jasper through the list to the amethyst. There is another list of twelve precious stones in Exodus chapter 28 in the breastplate of Aaron. The lists do not match, but there is some crossover and similarity. The stones of the breastplate were to represent the people of God. There were twelve of them to match the twelve sons of Israel. Our "birthstones" are a copycat of this breastplate. The high priest wore the names of the children of Israel upon his heart to illustrate the most precious thing to God: the souls of men and women. Precious stones in the Bible are a picture of people. God says of his people in Malachi 3:17, "And they shall be mine, saith the LORD of hosts, in that day when I make up my jewels." Precious stones are costly, and one soul is more valuable than the entire world. Precious stones are multi-faceted. Every person is a unique creation of God, and the various "facets" of our personalities bring out the beauty of God's handiwork. Precious stones have to be "cut" properly in order to bring out their true beauty and value. Until a person has been "cut" by the "circumcision made without hands" (Colossians 2:11), he is only a "diamond in the rough" and is not yet usable for God's service. Once cut, the true beauty of a stone is seen as the light passes through it. Jesus is the light of the world. His light shining through us brings out the true glory of God. The stones of the breastplate of Aaron were all set in gold. Gold is the picture of the deity of Christ. Our lives only find true purpose and meaning when we are "set" in him and Jesus is wrapped around us. When his people are finally secured in his city, God will use precious stones to build her home.

Lucifer also had a covering of precious stones recorded in Ezekiel 28:13. There are only nine in his list. He always comes short of the glory of God. So there are three basic places in the Bible where a list of precious stones is given: Aaron's breastplate, Lucifer's covering, and the foundation of New Jerusalem. Some of the stones match in all three lists and some do not. I do not know why. Someone smarter than me will have to figure that out, and if you find it, please let me know.

VS 21 – This verse is where the common thought of the "Pearly Gates" comes from. Peter supposedly is at those gates granting admission to those who are "good enough". That comes from Matthew 16:19 where Jesus gave the "keys to the kingdom of heaven" to Peter. Once again we see religions and scholars mess up the Bible without the first clue what it actually says. So pardon me while I find it necessary to spend some time here refuting this heresy. I wish I could just forge ahead with the passage in Revelation. If these charlatans would leave the Bible alone, I would not have to spend time running down rabbit holes trying to straighten out their insanity. I will be brief with this explanation.

Entire books can be written about the subject of the kingdom of God and the kingdom of heaven. Peter was NOT given the keys to heaven to unlock the gates to allow "good people" to come in. He was given the keys to the kingdom of heaven. Read the plain words and don't leave any of them out. The kingdom of heaven is the Jewish Millennial reign of the Lord Jesus Christ. It is not the same as the kingdom of God, and the kingdom of heaven is not the same thing as heaven itself. Jesus came to offer himself to his Jewish brethren as their Messiah / King. He said, "The kingdom of heaven is at hand" (Matthew 4:17). He did not say heaven was at hand. That is so fundamentally obvious that it would take a college degree in order to be able to miss it. His first goal was to call his people to repentance so they could get their kingdom. He came unto his own (John 1:11) but they rejected him. His grace and mercy are incredible, so he gave Israel one final chance to get the kingdom of heaven even after they had crucified him.

Peter led the ministry of the apostles and the early church to get this message out to the Jewish people early in the book of Acts. God used him to try to get the Nation to repent to receive their kingdom. Peter had the KEYS in his hand (and mouth) as he proclaimed the message of a risen Saviour to "ye men of Israel" (Acts 2:22). The messages of Acts chapters 1-7 were about Jesus coming back to restore Israel and establish them in their kingdom. Peter led the mission to bring the Jewish people into the kingdom because he had the keys. He concluded his famous Pentecost message with, "Let all the house of Israel know assuredly, that God hath made that same Jesus, whom ye have crucified, both Lord and Christ." When they responded by faith, Peter used the keys to unlock the door for "ye men of Israel" and gave the invitation, "Repent and be baptized" (Acts 2:38). That was a national call to "ye men of Israel" to receive their Messiah whom they had crucified. He gained quite a few entrants until the national leaders made their final rejection in Acts chapter 7 with the stoning of Stephen. At that point, the door was closed on Israel and their kingdom offer was postponed for 2,000 years. God took the keys back.

In Acts chapter 10, Peter was called to the home of a Gentile named Cornelius. He wanted to know how to get saved. Peter's message followed the same line as his earlier messages in Acts. I realize this is very profound and deep, but Acts chapter 10 is after Acts chapter 7. God changed the locks and took the keys back when the leaders of Israel rejected the message of Stephen. Peter did not know that as of yet. Acts 10:43 gives us the final words of Peter's message, and ends with, "...whosoever believeth in him shall receive remission of sins." Peter's next line would have been, "Repent and be baptized" according to the main theme of Acts chapter 2 and the message to "ye men of Israel". But God interrupted the invitation. The keys to the kingdom of heaven were given to Peter to open the door of the Millennial kingdom to the Nation of Israel. But after Acts chapter 7, the keys no longer worked. Cornelius was a Gentile and the offer to Israel had been withdrawn. That is why God stepped in to save Cornelius and his house before Peter could get those words out of his mouth.

Sorry for the brief derailment, but it was necessary so we could get Peter away from the "Pearly Gates". Now we can actually talk about those gates. These gates are the entry points to the city of New Jerusalem and they are never closed (verse 25). The gates are made of pearl because it is the city of the bride. In the parables of Matthew 13, a pearl of great price is mentioned: "Again, the kingdom of heaven is like unto a merchant man, seeking goodly pearls: Who, when he had found one pearl of great price, went and sold all that he had, and bought it" (Matthew 13:45-46). A pearl is a type of the church. It is different than other precious stones because it is made from a living organism. A precious stone can be divided, but a pearl cannot. The church is ONE body because it is ONE pearl of great price. I Corinthians 6:19-20 says we are "bought with a price" and that price is the blood of Jesus Christ. He gave up everything he had to buy that one pearl. He wanted the kingdom of heaven to be set up, but his people rejected it. So he "sold" his people Israel to buy the pearl. A pearl is made because of an irritation. If a grain of sand finds its way into the oyster, it secretes the material to make the pearl to cover the irritation. Sin is an irritation to God. So he sent his Son to sell all that he had to buy the bride, then made the gates of her city out of the by-product of the irritation. Each gate is made out of a single pearl. No dimension is given of the pearl, but remember that the wall of the city is 216 feet high. The gate does not have to be that high, but if it is, imagine the size and beauty of a pearl that big! The streets of gold were commented on in verse 18.

VS 22-23 – The Light of God (John 1:9) powers this city. There will be no need to generate any power because the Lamb is self-generating. There will never be a power outage because the Lamb is eternal. We will never be billed because the Lamb gave his life freely. The sun and moon are no longer necessary because the true "Sun of righteousness" obscures the types. No temple is needed because the one to whom the temple points is the Lamb of the city. There will be no night there (verse 25) because "in him is no darkness at all" (I John 1:5). Night first appears in the Bible in Genesis 1:5. Night is capitalized (along with "Day"), meaning it is Night personified: Satan. By the time we get to New Jerusalem, he has been cast into the lake of fire forever and will never again be manifest.

VS 24-27 – The cube of New Jerusalem has an entry point on earth so people can come in. Where else other than Mount Zion and earthly Jerusalem would this be? This describes a time after the Millennium in eternity, and there is still an earth and kings of that earth, which are humans. God's plan was always to populate the Universe with mankind. He will do it from New Jerusalem. This passage says the nations of them which are saved will enter the city. The glory and honor of the kings (verse 24) and the nations (verse 26) will be brought in to New Jerusalem for a purpose. We will see this in more detail in the next chapter. Anything sinful will be excluded (verse 27). Never again will sin mar God's perfection. Some have wondered if this cycle of sin and restoration could ever be repeated. What if some new "Lucifer" rose up again and tried to usurp God's kingdom? That cannot happen for a number of reasons. Once the issue of sin has been dealt with, it is over. God manifests his glory and attributes, and when his judgment against sin has been fully demonstrated, there will be no need to do it again. Also, Hebrews 10:10-14 says Jesus made ONE offering ONCE for all and for ever. If the cycle of sin is repeated, his sacrifice will have to be repeated also, which would mean the first one was not good enough on its own.

Revelation Chapter 22 – Eternity Future

The Bible is a full circle. Genesis begins with a man and a woman in a Garden paradise with no sin and the tree of life. Revelation ends with man and woman in a Garden paradise with no sin and a tree of life. There are plenty of things in this chapter that are clear and can be taught and understood, but there might be more speculation in Revelation chapter 22 than any other place I know of in the Bible. I will give you the basics and also throw out some strange things at the end of this final chapter of the Bible. Stay tuned!

Revelation 22:1-5 – The Tree of Life

The last time we saw the tree of life for real, it was in the Garden of Eden. Right after Adam sinned, God put a guard on the tree of life so that he would not eat of it. Genesis 3:22-24 says,

> "And the LORD God said, Behold, the man is become as one of us, to know good and evil: and now, lest he put forth his hand, and take also of the tree of life, and eat, and live for ever: Therefore the LORD God sent him forth from the garden of Eden, to till the ground from whence he was taken. So he drove out the man; and he placed at the east of the garden of Eden Cherubims, and a flaming sword which turned every way, to keep the way of the tree of life."

This verse says that if Adam had eaten of this tree, he would have lived forever. It was not God's plan for mankind to gain eternal life by his own efforts, but once the perfect sacrifice of Jesus Christ is made, God intends for man to live forever. He made us a "living soul" (Genesis 2:7) that will never cease to exist. But something has to happen for man to be rid of the curse of sin and death.

VS 1 – A pure river of water flows from the throne of God. The way this is worded seems to indicate the river will flow "out of the Lamb", meaning it would issue forth from his very being. This is possible in the same sense that the "living water" Jesus offered to the woman at the well in John chapter 4 is a type of the Holy Spirit. Jesus said later in John 7:37-38, "If any man thirst, let him come unto me, and drink. He that believeth on me, as the scripture hath said *[Isaiah 58:11]*, out of his belly shall flow rivers of living water." An actual river of "H2O" does not emanate out of our stomachs when we get saved. But the river of Revelation 22:1 is literal. I tend to think it does NOT issue forth directly out of the very body of the Lord. I read the verse this way, "…proceeding out of the throne… *[which is the throne]* of God and of the Lamb." The same term is used in verse 3. Either way, it is water without the first hint of impurity.

VS 2 – The tree of life will be continually fruit-bearing and be all over the city, especially lining the river of verse 1. The strangest part of this verse is the end where it says, "The leaves of the tree were for the healing of the nations". Consider the context. This is New Jerusalem with nothing impure in it and no sin to be found. It is after the Great White Throne Judgment where the lost are banished to hell forever. Then why does anyone need to be healed at this point? The "nations" will enter New Jerusalem in all of their honor and glory (Revelation 21:26) with all tears wiped away and all sin eradicated. But a healing will be necessary to reverse the Adamic nature. Remember that literal human beings in physical bodies will go alive into the Millennial kingdom where they will be ruled with a rod of iron. They will bear children who will inherit a sin nature. "That which is born of flesh is flesh" (John 3:6), and there will be lots of it running around for a thousand years. Some of that flesh will be saved by their submission to the law in the kingdom. The church age saints get their glorified bodies conformed to the image of the Lord Jesus Christ, but these people do not. The tree of life reverses the ultimate effects of sin. Had Adam eaten of it, he would have lived forever. It was not time for that yet. Now it is. In order for the nations to live forever, their Adamic sin nature has to be cleansed.

There is a beautiful picture of this in one of the more "obscure" rituals of Israel in the Old Testament. In Numbers chapter 19, the ashes of a red heifer were used to make what God called "a water of separation" for a specific type of cleansing. If anyone touched the dead body of a man, they were unclean for seven days and had to apply this particular cleansing agent. The red heifer is a type of Jesus Christ because it was without spot or blemish (Numbers 19:2) and slain "without the camp" (Hebrews 13:13). The heifer is female, NOT because Jesus was having a gender identity crisis, but because it also pictures the church which is the bride of Christ. The key to the type is Numbers 19:12: "He shall purify himself with it (the water of separation) on the third day, and on the seventh day he shall be clean: but if he purify not himself the third day, then the seventh day he shall not be clean."

This ritual was for anyone who touched the body of a dead <u>man</u>, not a dead animal. When Adam and Eve ate of the forbidden fruit, they "surely" died (Genesis 2:17). They passed that death on to the rest of us. God considers the flesh of humanity "dead" according to Romans chapter 6 and many other places. We are touching that dead corpse every day of our lives. The saved nations of the Millennium who enter the city of New Jerusalem have been cleansed from their sin, but they still have that dead flesh hanging on to them. In the ritual, the man who touched the dead person had to wash with this specific water on the third day. That always sounded strange to me. Obviously, there was a reason the man died, and the person who tended to this corpse would need to be purified from whatever it was that killed the man. But why wait three days? Was God giving the germs and disease a head start? We always have to view these Old Testament regulations in light of the New Testament truths. What happened "on the third day"? The spotless sacrifice rose from the dead. Those who are purified by the "water of separation" of Calvary have been cut loose (separated) from their dead body by spiritual circumcision (Colossians 2:11). So they are "clean on the seventh day" (Numbers 19:12). Those who have not yet had their dead flesh separated are not clean on the seventh day. One day is as a thousand years with the Lord (II Peter 3:8). Until the seventh "day" of the Millennium is completed, Adam's sin nature is still unclean. The tree of life in New Jerusalem will take care of that when the saved nations enter in Revelation 21-22.

VS 3-5 – The curse of Genesis chapter 3 will be reversed in eternity. The crown of thorns on the head of Jesus pictures the cleansing of the "thorns and thistles" (Genesis 3:18) brought forth by the sin of Adam. There are several items of note about God's people at this time in eternity. They will serve him, which is the main purpose of mankind: to bring glory to our Creator. We will see his face (verse 4). This brings us to the full restoration of man's relationship with God. Adam and Eve had a visible and tangible daily walk with God. The day they sinned, they heard the voice of God as they (and he) were "walking in the garden in the cool of the day" (Genesis 3:8). The cool of the day is the morning. Every day in Eden began with a time with God personally and physically. Adam and Eve saw his face.

After sin, man no longer saw the face of God. Exodus 33:20 says, "Thou canst not see my face: for there shall no man see me, and live." The glory is too great for natural man to behold. I Timothy 6:16 says of God, "Who only hath immortality, dwelling in the light which no man can approach unto; whom no man hath seen, nor can see: to whom be honour and power everlasting. Amen." This says no man hath seen God (past tense) nor can see God (present tense), but by Revelation 22:4 the future tense will be realized and we will see the face of God the Father as he is in all his glory. Verse 5 says we will reign for ever and ever. Jesus is the King of kings, so in order for him to be the King over all kings, there must be kings to reign with him. I do not understand this nor will I ever be able to grasp it until we get to eternity, but for all practical purposes, we will be just like Jesus Christ reigning as a king over a galaxy for ever..

VS 6-7 – Once again, the words are faithful and true because they come from the one who is Faithful and True (Revelation 19:11). These prophecies must shortly be done and he is coming quickly to fulfill them. That was 2,000 years ago. With God, there is no time, and even if there was time, 20 centuries is just a blip on the screen to him. When we've been there ten thousand years, bright shining as the sun, we'll no less days to sing his praise than when we first begun.

VS 8-9 – John gives testimony of his first hand personal knowledge of the prophecy and visions of the book of Revelation. He gave similar testimony of his personal relationship with Jesus Christ in the flesh in I John 1:1-5, and also of his eye-witness account of the crucifixion in John 19:35. John holds a very unique place among the human authors of the Bible. Lots of people saw the death of Christ on the cross. Many wrote about it, even more than just the other three gospel writers. John is the only man in human history to do BOTH. His record should be trusted more than any other because he was the only man to be an eye witness to Calvary AND to write about it. Sadly, John's account is the most questioned and attacked among all the books of the Bible when it should not be. In this passage, John falls at the feet of an angel to worship. That is a natural reaction after what he has witnessed, but he is immediately told not to do so because God alone gets the worship.

VS 10 – The book is unsealed. I will refer you back to our discussion of the seven sealed book in chapter 5 for a full description of this. The book of Revelation "seals up prophecy" by unsealing it.

VS 11-13 – These verses fit into the "sealing" of prophecy. Once we reach this point in the course of human history, what is done is done. Sinners are in hell and unreformable and the saved are in eternity with the Lord and perfected forever. The Lord is surely coming again soon (verse 12). He will "reward" every person based on their faith and their life, either good or bad (II Corinthians 5:10). The Omega will wrap things up and hand it all over to the Alpha who will restart all things like they were in Genesis 1. The parenthesis of time will be completed and the issues of sin, faith and righteousness will be resolved.

VS 14-15 – Again we see the tree of life which is necessary to gain entrance to the city of New Jerusalem. This has been discussed before and I will expand on it in just a few moments as I get into the speculation of the population of the Universe in eternity future. The lost are excluded as we saw in chapter 21.

VS 16 – The "church" reappears in this verse just as we are closing the book. Remember that the church is mentioned 19 times in chapters 1-3, then the word is absent by design from chapters 4-19. The events of those chapters do not include the church, but she is back for the Millennium and eternity. Jesus gives further testimony of his eternal deity in this verse, and the wording is precise. He refers to himself as the "root and offspring" of David, which encompasses both his humanity and his deity. In one of his famous "discussions" with the Pharisees, Jesus got fed up with their mindless rejection and turned the tables on them to ask them a question. He did this quite often. Matthew 22:41-46 says,

> "While the Pharisees were gathered together, Jesus asked them, Saying, What think ye of Christ? whose son is he? They say unto him, The Son of David. He saith unto them, How then doth David in spirit call him Lord, saying, The LORD said unto my Lord, Sit thou on my right hand, till I make thine enemies thy footstool? If David then call him Lord, how is he his son? And no man was able to answer him a word, neither durst any man from that day forth ask him any more questions."

I love it when Jesus sent the Pharisees running out with their tails between their legs. The question is not that hard to answer unless you have a PhD in philosophy or religion. Jesus is the root of David because he is God from everlasting. He is the offspring of David because he came to earth as a man through his lineage. That is why the father (David) calls the son (Jesus) "Lord". Psalm 132:11 states it clearly: "The LORD hath sworn in truth unto David; he will not turn from it; Of the fruit of thy body will I set upon thy throne." Pay close attention to each word. God swore to David that **"I"** (God himself) would set on David's throne, and that he would do so from the fruit of David's body. He is the root and the offspring.

Then he says he is the "bright and morning star". I spent some time with this concept in Revelation 9:1, which you can refer back to. Jesus is the "day star" of II Peter 1:19 and the "Sun of righteousness" in Malachi 4:2. He is the "star" of the Bible and of every show.

172

VS 17 – This is the final "invitation" in the Bible. Three groups or entities issue the call to "come". The Holy Spirit draws men to Jesus Christ and is always active. He uses the bride during the church age to be his mouthpiece to call the lost to salvation. Then the verse says, "And let him that heareth say, Come." Faith cometh by hearing, and hearing by the word of God (Romans 10:17). Those in any age who have exercised their faith and received God's grace in the process will want others to partake of the glories of heaven. It is a natural by-product of genuine faith. Romans 10:9-10 says, "With the mouth confession is made unto salvation." Some have taken this to mean that we must audibly pray "the sinner's prayer" in the presence of others in order to be saved. Let's be precise. The passage says, "With the heart man believeth unto righteousness". Salvation technically occurs when the person's heart turns to the Lord in faith. The prayer is important to seal the decision and give the person a frame of reference in asking for salvation. When it says that with the mouth confession is made UNTO salvation, it generally refers to what happens after the heart belief. Those who "hear" and come to faith as a result will eventually get it out of their mouth in some manner at some time to someone. Jesus said, "Out of the abundance of the heart the mouth speaketh" (Matthew 12:34). If Jesus is in there by his Spirit, he will come out!

I generally do not like to question a person's salvation directly. It almost always leads to arguments, and if the person is not saved, it drives them farther away, and if the person IS saved, it sows needless doubts in their tender hearts. But I do question the salvation of MANY today who say they are saved. Everyone in America is a Christian because they were born here and their parents took them to church when they were young. Then we have all the "closet Christians" who will absolutely refuse to give any witness of their salvation. The tag line is, "My faith is personal and private". What they are really saying is, "Jesus is not in here, so don't ask." Those who have "ears to hear" will eventually SAY something about it.

The invitation is simple. Anyone who is thirsty for the truth can come and take of the water of life – and here is that magic word again – **FREELY**. That is the word Eve left out in Genesis 3:2. Notice also who it is who comes: "whosoever will". Calvinists read it this way, "whosoever of the elect." One of the most famous verses of the Bible says, "For God so loved the world, that he gave his only begotten Son, that whosoever believeth in him should not perish, but have everlasting life" (John 3:16). Man is depraved in his nature, but that does not extend to his will. Anyone can ask. Y'all come – FREELY!

VS 18-19 – I have been asked about this passage of scripture as often as almost any other place in the Bible. It seems to fly in the face of the doctrine of eternal security. It appears as if someone can be taken out of the book of life if he adds to the Bible or takes away from the Bible. The key word in the passage is in verse 19. God will take away his PART, not his NAME. This is not describing the loss of salvation but the loss of rewards. When Jesus washed the feet of the disciples, Peter objected (typical of Peter). Jesus said, "If I wash thee not, thou hast no part with me" (John 13:8). Peter was in no danger of losing his salvation because it is clearly stated in the text that he was "clean" (saved) in verses 10-11.

Don't miss the point. This passage takes dead aim at Bible revisors. Man was plunged into sin as a result of changing the plain words of God. In Genesis 3:1-6, Eve left out freely and added touch and billions of eternal precious souls will spend eternity in a lake of fire as a result. God is quite jealous of his words. He issued several warnings in his book not to change them. Proverbs 30:5-6 and Deuteronomy 4:2 both tell us clearly NOT to add or take away from God's words. Those who have made millions of dollars by altering God's words are in line for a pretty serious whoopin' from the Lord. If they are saved (and there are many who are), they can look forward to a seat on the bench for a thousand years. I played a lot of sports growing up. It is quite frustrating to sit on the bench and watch others play.

VS 20-21 – The Bible ends with what should be the number one overriding prayer request of every single believer: "Even so, come, Lord Jesus." If there is ANYTHING in your life that would make you be upset or disappointed with the return of the Lord Jesus Christ immediately, it is not right. Every problem of man will be solved when those five magic words finally become the literal reality we all long for.

"Boldly Going Where No Man Has Gone"

Now that we have made our way through Revelation, let me toss something out that has always intrigued me that I have not seen anywhere else. Let me go back to one of my most important disclaimer points in this book. When someone says they found something in the Bible that no one else has seen, RUN! And then I am going to give you some of that in this section! So please don't think I am contradicting myself. Every person who has ever commented on any part of the Bible is subject to error, and I am on that list as well. I could be totally wrong with this. We "run" when others find some off the wall speculation in the Bible and start teaching it as doctrine and condemning everyone who might have the audacity to disagree with them. They claim some form of secret knowledge or vision from God which always leads to a cult. Don't lump me in that group. I am simply committing something to writing here that has always puzzled me, with the full understanding that I have little if any support for this from my fellow conservative Bible teachers and commentators. But I see it in the Bible, and I cannot pass by it without comment. I will be the very first one in line to walk this back if clear Bible proof can be shown to the contrary.

New Jerusalem is dominated by the number twelve. God is ordered and structured, and he sets things up to reflect his mathematical perfection. There are twelve different "twelves" connected to the kingdom of Israel and the city of New Jerusalem extending into eternity (in no particular order):

(1) – 12 months
(2) – 12 fruits on the tree of life
(3) – 12 gates to the city
(4) – 12 angels posted at the gates
(5) – 12 tribes of Israel
(6) – 12 thrones
(7) – 12 apostles
(8) – 12 foundations of the wall
(9) – 12 nations or divisions on earth (Deuteronomy 32:8)
(10) – 12 constellations in the heavens (the Zodiac is a counterfeit)
(11) – 12 hours in the "evening" (Genesis 1)
(12) – 12 hours in the "morning" (Genesis 1)

IF (and please note the huge "**IF**") all of these things are in place in eternity, they could form a system whereby man populates the Universe forever. Remember that the Bible is a complete circle. Revelation chapters 21-22 match Genesis chapters 1-2 in their basic structure with a man and a woman in a sinless state with a tree of life. Adam and Eve were given a commission to "be fruitful and multiply" with no sin or death involved. Had they done so, they would still be alive today, and every one of their offspring would also still be alive. Once we get to the "end", it is actually only the beginning. Men and women will reproduce without sin and death just as Adam and Eve could have. We have an overcrowding issue on earth today with only 8 billion of us. Just think what it would be like if no one had ever died in the last 6,000 years. Where would we put all the people? Isaiah 45:18 says, "For thus saith the LORD that created the heavens; God himself that formed the earth and made it; he hath established it, he created it not in vain, he formed it to be inhabited: I am the LORD; and there is none else." The Universe was made to be inhabited. Some might argue that only the earth was made to be inhabited, but the wording of this verse includes both the heavens and the earth. We have only a tiny glimpse of how massive the Universe is. God would not do something of that size and grandeur without a purpose. If Adam and Eve had not sinned, there would be no way for the earth to sustain that population. It would have to expand beyond earth. Hebrews 11:3 says, "Through faith we understand that the worlds were framed by the word of God." That is plural. God created the heavens to be inhabited, and quarantined man on earth for his probationary period in order to settle the issue of sin and faith. Once that has been fully manifest, the original commission will be carried out as God intended. There are lots of "worlds" yet to be inhabited!

This all sounds like sci-fi, but you can remove the "fi" because it is not fiction. For his entire existence, man has peered into the heavens wondering about other intelligent life, and as the old joke goes, we wonder whether there is intelligent life on this planet. Conspiracy theories have abounded from "Area 51" in Roswell, New Mexico to many other paranormal activities and sightings. SETI is a government sponsored effort to find life in outer space (Search for Extra-Terrestrial Intelligence) and has been in operation for decades. One of these days, they will make contact (half way through the Tribulation), and when they do, they will be sorry they did. But no one messes around with anything unless there is a grain of truth in it. Currently, intelligent life in outer space is headed by Satan and his minions, who have the "firmament" of Genesis chapter 1 as their primary domain. But in eternity, a new heaven and a new earth will be in place (II Peter 3:13), wherein dwelleth righteousness. In order for righteousness to <u>dwell</u> in a new heaven, there must be <u>dwellers</u> in it!

But this cannot happen until the sin issue is permanently dealt with. If man conquered outer space in his current form, it would only spread the disease of sin to other planets. That is why we make movies called "Star <u>Wars</u>". There has been no series titled "Star Peace". Once we get to New Jerusalem and eternity, men and women in natural bodies will be reproducing forever. They will enter New Jerusalem to partake of the tree of life and have their Adamic nature cleansed so they can be prepared to reproduce perfect beings in the image of God forever. The system of "twelve twelves" provides a structured way in which this could happen. Let's say Johnny and Susie from Australia come to New Jerusalem in April at 5:00 in the evening and enter gate #7 headed by the apostle Thomas who presides over the tribe of Gad to partake of the fruit "orange" to have their sin nature cleansed. Then they are commissioned like Adam and Eve were to "be fruitful, multiply, and replenish" and are sent into one of the constellations to a planet for that purpose. Twelve to the twelfth power means there are over 9 <u>trillion</u> possible combinations like that.

This is also alluded to in Romans chapter 5. Beginning in verse 12 through the end of the chapter, Paul gives a comparison between Adam and Jesus as he is laying out the doctrine of salvation. It is a very wordy passage and can get your brain a little scrambled if you do not slow down and pay attention to every word. I would suggest you open to the passage and note the two basic keys to unlock what Paul is telling us here. Note the word "NOT" and the phrase "MUCH MORE". For example, verses 15 and 16 both begin with, "<u>Not</u> as the offence...<u>so</u> is the gift..." In other words, this is a contrast more than a comparison. God is telling us that ONE man sinned, but MANY will be made righteous because of the sacrifice of Christ. Then in verses 15, 17 and 20 Paul continues the contrast with the phrase, "much more". Grace will <u>much more</u> abound because of the gift of eternal life through Jesus Christ our Lord. God's plan from the beginning was to manifest his infinite grace through the "Lamb slain from the foundation of the world" (Revelation 13:8). But the end result of that grace provides <u>much more</u> than what Adam had in the Garden of Eden. Again, these are difficult things to grasp. But God put a sinless man and woman in a perfect paradise, then gave them a probationary period for the issue of sin to be dealt with. They could have refused the sin. But they chose to rebel against God, and we see the results of that in our world today. God will ultimately reverse that sin and restore man to his sinless state, but MUCH MORE. If all God does is restore what Adam had in Eden, what would be the point? The whole mess could start over again, and we have already discussed how that cannot happen. Jesus died ONCE for sin (Hebrews 10) and he does not need to have the cycle repeated to do it again. In Eden, Adam had the tree of the knowledge of good and evil and a commandment to stay away from it. We will not have that in eternity because the issue of sin will have been completely resolved. Adam was faced with "NO" every day of his life in the Garden. We will never hear the word again. Adam was confined to earth; man in eternity will inhabit the heavens (Isaiah 45:18). Adam's time in Eden was probationary. There will be no "test" for man in eternity. Adam had something in him that allowed him to sin. In eternity, we will be conformed to the image of Christ (Romans 8:29-30). Satan was present in the Garden. In eternity, "the tempter will be banished, and we will lay our burdens down!" In eternity, God will have restored what Adam lost "much more" and man will have the ability to fulfill his commission to "be fruitful, multiply, and replenish", and not just the earth. Earth will not be able to hold it.

Isaiah 9:6-7 says, "For unto us a child is born, unto us a son is given: and the government shall be upon his shoulder: and his name shall be called Wonderful, Counsellor, The mighty God, The everlasting Father, The Prince of Peace. Of the increase of his government and peace there shall be no end, upon the throne of David, and upon his kingdom to order it, and to establish it with judgment and with justice from henceforth even for ever." These verses encompass the first coming all the way to eternity future. The child / son is obviously his birth. The government on his shoulder is the Millennium. For ever is eternity. But the thing to note is the increase of his kingdom. That speaks of the size of it, not the time duration. That is for ever as already stated. The increase will have no end. The multiplication of humanity will never end. If God did run out of space in the Universe, which is impossible, he could just make more.

Eternity will complete the full circle of the Bible. God commissioned man to be fruitful and multiply for ever with no limit to the size or scope of his expansion. This commission was put on hold due to sin, but once that issue is resolved, it kicks back in. I Corinthians 15:28 says, "And when all things shall be subdued unto him, then shall the Son also himself be subject unto him that put all things under him, that God may be all in all." Again, this is impossible for our finite minds to completely grasp. There has never been a division in the Godhead (except for the three hours on the cross when God forsook his Son to pay for our sins). Yet the Godhead is distinct and separate in its trinity of persons. In eternity, this distinction will no longer exist even though it will. There will still be a Father a Son and a Spirit, but "all in all". Ephesians 1:22-23 uses this same "all in all" terminology for Jesus Christ the Son, who is distinct from the Father but who is the Father in the flesh. "But I just can't understand that!" Get in line. No one else can either. The "all in all" term for Jesus is linked to his body. If you recall an earlier discussion, the vesture of the Lord Jesus Christ at his crucifixion is a type of the Universe and is "pyramid" shaped like a poncho. The body will fill "all in all" as the human race multiplies in the Universe for ever.

The common idea of heaven is a bunch of winged beings in white robes floating around on white clouds playing harps and eating marshmallows. (I like to throw in the marshmallow thing just to keep it all nice and white and fluffy.) I know heaven will be perfect, but quite frankly, that would get old after a few thousand years. I have a different view. Revelation 22:5 says we will reign with Jesus forever. He is the King, we are the kings. I see our role in eternity as being a king over a galaxy. Astronomers tell us if we hold up a dime into the night sky at arm's length that we would be covering up at least a million galaxies. I don't know if that is true, and neither do they, but there is no doubt that the Universe is a hugemongous and ginormous place with plenty of room and lots of galaxies. God told Abraham he would multiply his seed as the sand of the sea and as the stars of heaven. Both are innumerable. There are that many stars in the heavens; each one with "worlds" to be inhabited!

One of the "twelves" of New Jerusalem are angels located at the gates of the city (Revelation 21:12). We have already discussed how the church age saints will replace the one third of the angels who fell in the rebellion of Lucifer. Jesus confirmed this when he said, "For in the resurrection they neither marry, nor are given in marriage, but are as the angels of God in heaven" (Matthew 22:30). From that inference, let me run off into another wild speculation. Go back to Johnny and Susie from Australia coming to New Jerusalem to be commissioned to replenish a planet in some galaxy. You are the king of that galaxy and you are "as the angels of God in heaven". You are posted at their gate ready to take them to their new planet to be fruitful and multiply. As a spirit being, you have the ability to travel the Universe in a nano-second at will. You get to reign over this galaxy as it is populated by perfect beings for ever and ever and the size of it cannot be measured. Sounds a whole lot better than a harp and a marshmallow, doesn't it?

Bottom line, this discussion is "out there", and I hope I have made myself clear how I am on speculative ground that can be easily contested. I just could not end this commentary without putting it on paper. So allow me to finish with the most important statement in the book of Revelation.

"Even so, come, Lord Jesus."

THE BOOK OF REVELATION

The Things Which Thou Hast Seen
Past Tense from the Day of the Lord

False Kingdom of Antichrist
The Beginning of Sorrows - Matt. 24:4-8
A Falling Away - II Thes. 2:3
A World Wide Deception - Rev. 12:9, II Thes. 2:11

Firstfruits
Rapture of the OT Saints
Eph. 4:8, Matt. 27:52-53

Main Harvest
Bride of Christ / Rapture of Church
1 Thes. 4:13-18, 1 Cor. 15:50-52

Judgment Seat of Christ
For Believers / In Heaven
1 Cor. 3:11-15, Rom. 14:10-12, II Cor. 5:9-10

Seals (4-6)

SEAL 1
White Horse (6:2)

The Peace Plan
Jewish Temple Rebuilt in Jerusalem
Dan. 9:24-27

SEAL 7
Opens the Trumpets (8:1-6)

Trumpets (7-11)

CHURCH AGE

Ephesus.............. 33-200 ....Rev. 2:1-7
Smyrna.............. 200-325 ....Rev. 2:8-11
Pergamos...........325-500 ....Rev. 2:12-17
Thyatira............500-1000.....Rev. 2:18-29
Sardis..............1000-1500 ....Rev. 3:1-6
Philadelphia....1500-1900.......Rev. 3:7-13
Laodicea........1900-Rapture...Rev. 3:14-22

Personages (12-14)
1a) The "Beast out of the Sea" - Rev. 13:1
Antichrist / Pope - Architect of the Peace Plan - Dan. 9:27
2) Woman - Israel
3) Man Child - Jesus as a Human
4) Serpent / Dragon - Satan
5) Archangel Warrior - Michael
6) Virgins / Remnant - 144,000
7) Lamb - Jesus as God / King

Vials (15-19)

Kingdom of God
Present on Earth in the Body of Christ

Kingdom of Heaven - Absent
King in Heaven / Subjects Dispersed

Means of Salvation
Grace Through Faith in Jesus Christ
Rom. 10:9-13, Eph. 2:8-9, John3:16

REV. 4:1
Heaven Opens

online chart: lffellowship.com/revelation

The Things Which Are
Present Tense from the Day of the Lord

Daniel's 70th Week

The "Great Tribulation"
Mat. 24:21-28, Dan. 7:25

Gleanings
Post-Tribulation Rapture
Remnant of Israel
Rev. 11:12, Mat. 25:10

The Things Which
Shall Be Hereafter
Future Tense From the Day of the Lord

Marriage Supper of the Lamb
Rev. 19:7-9, Mat. 22:1-10

Final Rebellion
Rev. 20:7-10
Great White Throne Judgment
Rev. 20:11-15

SEAL 2
Red Horse (6:3-4)
SEAL 3
Black Horse (6:5-6)
SEAL 4
Pale Horse (6:7-8)

SEAL 5
A View at the Throne (6:9-11)

SEAL 6
Advent (6:12-17)
Quake (6:12)

MILLENNIAL
REIGN

The Lord Jesus Christ
On the Throne of
David in Jerusalem
Revelation 20:1-6, Ezekiel 40-48

ETERNITY
FUTURE

WOE #1
TRUMPET 1
Environmental Disaster (8:7)
TRUMPET 2
Oceanic Disaster (8:8-9)
TRUMPET 3
Wormwood (8:10-11)
TRUMPET 4
Darkness (8:12)

WOE #2
TRUMPET 6
Armageddon (9:13-21)

WOE #3
TRUMPET 7
Advent (11:15-19)
Quake (11:13)

Revelation Chapters 21-22

Revelation 21
New Jerusalem

TRUMPET 5
Bottomless Pit (9:1-11)

Advent (14:14-20)

Revelation 22
The Dispensation of the Fulness of Times
Eph. 1:10, I Cor. 15:28, Isa. 9:6-7
II Pet. 3:10-13 - New Heavens and a New Earth

The Revealing of the Wicked
II Thes. 2:1-12
Mid-Tribulation Events Which "Pivot" Daniel's 70th Week
1) Head Wound / Assassination
Rev. 13:3, II Thes. 2:7
2) War in Heaven / Satan Cast Out
Rev. 12:7-9
3) Judas Ascend from the Bottomless Pit
Rev. 9:1-11, Rev. 17:8
4) The Abomination of Desolation
Peace Treaty Broken
Mat. 24:15, Dan. 9:27, II Thes. 2:4
5) Israel Flees to the Wilderness
Rev. 12:14, Mat. 24:16-20
6) Mid-Tribulation Appearance of Jesus Christ
The 144,000 Sealed
Rev. 7:1-8, Rev. 14:1-7

1b) The "Beast out of the Earth" - Rev. 13:11
Counterfeit Resurrection / False Trinity of Antichrist
Body - Pope / Soul - Judas / Spirit - Satan

VIAL 1
Boils (16:2)
VIAL 2
Sea to Blood (16:3)
VIAL 3
River to Blood (16:4-7)
VIAL 4
Scorching Sun (16:8-9)
VIAL 5
Darkness (16:10-11)
VIAL 6
Armageddon (16:12-16)

Kingdom of God
The Bride of Christ Conformed to His Image
Rom. 8:29-30, Php. 3:20-21
Ruling on Earth with Jesus Christ Over the Nations
Col. 3:24, Luke 19:17-19, II Tim. 2:12, Rom. 8:17

Kingdom of God - Replenished Sons of God
Reigning as King over Galaxies - Rev. 22:5

Kingdom of Heaven - Restored Sons of Men
Populating the Universe Forever - Isa. 9:6-7

Kingdom of Heaven
The World Wide Rule of Israel
Dan. 2:44, Acts 1:6, Deut. 28:13

<u>Kingdom of God - Absent</u>
King and Subjects in Heaven

<u>Kingdom of Heaven - Absent</u>
False Kingdoms of Antichrist

VIAL 7
Hail (16:17-21)
Advent (19:11-21)
Quake (16:18)

Means of Salvation
1) Endure to the End - Mat. 24:13, Mat. 10:22
2) Refuse the Mark / Martyrdom - Rev. 20:4
3) Harbor a Jewish Witness - Mat. 10:40-42, Mat. 25:31-46

Means of Salvation
Obedience to the Law and Sacrifices
Zech. 14:16-19, Isa. 2:1-5, Jer 31:31-34

REV. 19:11
Heaven Opens

Printed in Great Britain
by Amazon

81713281R10106

GREYSCALE

BIN TRAVELER FORM

Cut By Maria Santamaria 35 Qty Date 01/05

Scanned By _____ Qty_____ Date_____

Scanned Batch IDs

_____ _____ _____

Notes / Exception

_____

_____

_____

_____

_____